EMERGING TECHNOLOGY AND THE LAW OF THE SEA

Autonomous vessels and robotics, artificial intelligence, and cybersecurity are transforming international shipping and naval operations. Likewise, blockchain offers new efficiencies for compliance with international shipping records, while renewable energy from currents and waves and offshore nuclear power stations open opportunities for new sources of power within and from the sea. These and other emerging technologies pose a challenge for the governance framework of the law of the sea, which is adapting to accommodate the accelerating rates of global change. This volume examines how the latest technological advances and marine sciences are reshaping the interpretation and application of the law of the sea. The authors explore the legality of new concepts for military operations on the continental shelf, suggest remote sensing methodologies for delimitation of maritime boundaries, and offer a legal roadmap for ensuring maritime cybersecurity.

JAMES KRASKA is Charles H. Stockton Professor of International Maritime Law and Chair of the Stockton Center for International Law at the U.S. Naval War College, and also Visiting Professor of Law and John Harvey Gregory Lecturer on World Organization at Harvard Law School.

YOUNG KIL PARK is Director of Law of the Sea Research Center at the Korea Maritime Institute and leads the Yeosu Academy of the Law of the Sea. Previously he was a visiting scholar in the Stockton Center for International Law at the U.S. Naval War College and the University of Rhode Island.

T0384610

EMERGING TECHNOLOGY AND THE LAW OF THE SEA

Edited by

JAMES KRASKA

US Naval War College

YOUNG KIL PARK

Korea Maritime Institute

CAMBRIDGE
UNIVERSITY PRESS

Shaftesbury Road, Cambridge CB2 8EA, United Kingdom

One Liberty Plaza, 20th Floor, New York, NY 10006, USA

477 Williamstown Road, Port Melbourne, VIC 3207, Australia

314–321, 3rd Floor, Plot 3, Splendor Forum, Jasola District Centre, New Delhi – 110025, India

103 Penang Road, #05–06/07, Visioncrest Commercial, Singapore 238467

Cambridge University Press is part of Cambridge University Press & Assessment, a department of the University of Cambridge.

We share the University's mission to contribute to society through the pursuit of education, learning and research at the highest international levels of excellence.

www.cambridge.org
Information on this title: www.cambridge.org/9781009045438

DOI: 10.1017/9781009042178

First published 2022
First paperback edition 2023

A catalogue record for this publication is available from the British Library

Library of Congress Cataloging-in-Publication data
Names: Kraska, James, editor. | Park, Young Kil, 1971– editor.
Title: Emerging technology and the law of the sea / edited by James Kraska, United States Naval War College, Newport, Rhode Island; Young Kil Park, Korea Maritime Institute.
Description: Cambridge, United Kingdom ; New York, NY : Cambridge University Press, 2022. | Includes bibliographical references and index.
Identifiers: LCCN 2022008796 (print) | LCCN 2022008797 (ebook) | ISBN 9781316517420 (hardback) | ISBN 9781009045438 (paperback) | ISBN 9781009042178 (epub)
Subjects: LCSH: Law of the sea. | Technological innovations–Law and legislation. | Marine sciences–Research–Law and legislation.
Classification: LCC KZA1145 .E44 2022 (print) | LCC KZA1145 (ebook) | DDC 341.4/5–dc23/eng/20220430
LC record available at https://lccn.loc.gov/2022008796
LC ebook record available at https://lccn.loc.gov/2022008797

ISBN   978-1-316-51742-0   Hardback
ISBN   978-1-009-04543-8   Paperback

CONTENTS

CONTRIBUTORS

JAMES KRASKA, contributing coeditor

Dr. James Kraska is Chair and Charles H. Stockton Professor of International Maritime Law in the Stockton Center for International Law at the US Naval War College and Visiting Professor of Law and John Harvey Gregory Lecturer on World Organization at Harvard Law School. He is also Visiting Professor of International Law at the University of the Philippines College of Law and the University of Reading, and was a distinguished visiting professor at Gujarat National Law University, Mary Derrickson McCurdy Visiting Scholar at Duke University Marine Laboratory in the Nicholas School of the Environment, and Fellow at Woods Hole Oceanographic Institution. Kraska is editor-in-chief of *International Law Studies*, the oldest journal of international law in the United States, and editor-in-chief of the three-volume *Benedict on Admiralty: International Maritime Law*. A former navy commander, he served with operating forces and in the Pentagon, including as Oceans Law and Policy Adviser and then Director of International Negotiations on the Joint Staff.

YOUNG KIL PARK, coeditor

Dr. Young Kil Park is Director of Law of the Sea Research Center at Korea Maritime Institute (KMI), where he directs the Yeosu Academy on the Law of the Sea and other research and capacity-building initiatives. In 2018 he served as a visiting scholar in the Stockton Center for International Law at the US Naval War College and Rhode Island Transportation Research Center at the University of Rhode Island. His scholarly expertise covers the law of the sea, maritime security law, Arctic governance and legal issues concerning North Korea. His publications include the papers "The Complex Legal Status of the Current Fishing Pattern Zone in the East China Sea," published in *Marine Policy* and "Republic of Korea v. Araye: Korean Supreme Court Decision on

Universal Jurisdiction over Somali Pirates," published in the *American Journal of International Law*.

NIELS ANDERSEN

Dr. Niels Andersen is a member of the executive board of the Danish National Space Institute (DTU Space). He has a background as a researcher in geodesy, but soon went into management in public mapping agencies, becoming responsible for transferring the topographical map production of the Kingdom of Denmark into a full digital production line using the newest satellite systems, including transforming the national geodetic reference systems of the Kingdom of Denmark into modern space-derived World Geodetic datum systems. He was one of the founders and drivers for the creation of DTU Space, which is a national institute with strong Earth observation capabilities and was also a part of the group establishing the Danish Continental Shelf Project, which is devoted to the delineation of the outer limits of the Kingdom of Denmark's extended continental shelf (ECS) in accordance with the United Nations Convention on the Law of the Sea. Andersen holds several international positions. He is a bureau member of the International Union of Geodesy and Geophysics (IUGG) and is Denmark's national representative at the International Association of Geodesy (IAG). He is a senior adviser to the Danish Ministry of Foreign Affairs on delimitation and a member of the Danish ECS delegation to the United Nations. He is a member of and has chaired the Advisory Board on the Law of the Sea (ABLOS) and is a member of the International Law Association (ILA) as a technical expert.

ELENA BERNINI

Elena Bernini is the CEO and founder of Oxford Omnia International, editor-in-chief of the *Civil Society Review* and Director of the Centre for International Law and Democracy, all based in Oxford (UK). She also served as a visiting research fellow in the Stockton Center for International Law at the US Naval War College and previously was a visiting researcher at Hanoi University and a Fund for Cooperation and Knowledge Fellow. Bernini has consulted and conducted tabletop exercises and lectured at academic institutions and governmental and non-governmental institutions on security issues, political science, international law, human rights and the law of the sea, including at the

University of Oxford, where she earned an MPhil in Development
Studies. She has also engaged in such efforts with the European Union
and the International Maritime Organization (IMO) International
Maritime Law Institute (IMLI) and served as a high-level delegate at
the United Nations Global Forum on Migration and Development. Her
publications and work have been featured by the Center for Strategic and
International Studies (CSIS), the British Broadcasting Corporation
(BBC), Vietnamese and Italian newspapers, a South China Sea film
documentary and the Oxford University China Centre. She was recognized as a Woman Leader in International Relations by the Italian
Cultural Institute of Brussels, and Oxford University's Enterprising
Oxford awarded her for entrepreneurial achievements.

TAFSIR JOHANSSON

Dr. Tafsir Johansson is an associate research officer at the World
Maritime University (WMU)-Sasakawa Global Ocean Institute (GOI)
in Malmö, Sweden. Johansson holds a PhD in Maritime Affairs from
WMU and an LLM from Lund University on Maritime Law. After
joining WMU in 2013, he has led numerous projects, including seventeen
regulatory development projects covering maritime and ocean research
funded by Transport Canada (Government of Canada). After joining the
GOI in 2018, his research has mainly focused on emerging technologies
and environmental sustainability in the field of ocean governance. He is
currently acting as the Principal Investigator in a Horizon 2020 R&D
project pertaining to regulatory barriers and solutions for autonomous
service robotics based on drone technology. Publications of Johansson
cover a wide array of topics, including corporate social responsibility, oil
spill intervention, marine spatial planning, big data and sustainable
shipping in the Arctic. He delivers guest lectures on environmental
excellence at the Arison Maritime Center Center for Simulator
Maritime Training (CSMART) in the Netherlands.

STEVEN GEOFFREY KEATING

Steven Geoffrey Keating practices international law for the United States
National Geospatial-Intelligence Agency. He has served on numerous
national delegations to the International Hydrographic Organization
(IHO) and currently serves as the United States IHO Observer to the
ABLOS. As a competitively selected national security law fellow at

Georgetown University's Institute for the Study of Diplomacy, he published peer-reviewed articles on maritime domain awareness and the South China Sea arbitration between the Philippines and China. Keating was a US Coast Guard licensed officer with more than a decade of seagoing experience on a variety of operational and research platforms. He also served thirty years in the US Navy Reserve, retiring at the rank of captain. He holds a JD from Campbell University and has earned certificates from the US Army Command and General Staff College and the Harvard University Kennedy School of Government.

RONÁN LONG

Prof. Ronán Long is the Director of the WMU-Sasakawa GOI and holds the Nippon Foundation Chair in Ocean Governance and the Law of the Sea. He is the author/coeditor of twelve books and over fifty scholarly articles on oceans law and policy. He read for his PhD at the School of Law Trinity College Dublin, he has been a senior visiting scholar-in-residence at the University of California, Berkeley, and a visiting scholar at the Center for Oceans Law and Policy at the University of Virginia. Additionally, Long teaches on the Law of the Sea program at Harvard Law School. Prior to his academic career, he was a permanent staff member at the European Commission and undertook over forty missions on behalf of the European institutions to the member states of the European Union, the United States, Canada, Central America and African countries. During his previous career in the Irish Naval Service, he won an academic prize at Britannia Royal Naval College and held a number of appointments ashore and afloat, including membership of the Navy's elite diving unit. As a keen yachtsman, he has represented Ireland at the top competitive level in offshore racing. Long is passionate about the law of the sea, conservation and global sustainability, as well as the implementation of the 2030 Agenda for Sustainable Development.

ALEXANDROS X. M. NTOVAS

Dr. Alexandros X. M. Ntovas is an expert advocate and tenured academic in the areas of international law of the sea, admiralty, navigational freedoms and practice, marine environmental law and shipping regulation, as well as in all issues regarding contemporary safety and security of ships, ports and offshore installations. He is a professor associate (reader) in Maritime Law at the University of Southampton Law School, and the Director of the Institute of Maritime Law (UK).

RAUL (PETE) PEDROZO

Captain Raul (Pete) Pedrozo, US Navy (retired), is the Principal Deputy Staff Judge Advocate of the US Indo-Pacific Command. He previously served as Special Assistant to the Under Secretary of Defense for Policy, Senior Legal Advisor to the Commander of the US Indo-Pacific Command and professor of international law at the US Naval War College. He has lectured extensively at military and civilian academic institutions and participated in numerous multilateral and bilateral negotiations, including the IMO, Transnational Organized Crime Convention, International Civil Aviation Organization and US–People's Republic of China Military Maritime Consultative Agreement. Pedrozo has written extensively on maritime security and South China Sea issues and is the coauthor of *International Maritime Security Law* and *The Free Sea: The American Fight for Freedom of Navigation*. He earned an LLM in International & Comparative Law from Georgetown University Law Center and a JD in Law from the Ohio State University College of Law.

CLIVE SCHOFIELD

Prof. Clive Schofield is Head of Research at the WMU-Sasakawa GOI and is also a professor with the Australian National Centre for Ocean Resources and Security (ANCORS), University of Wollongong (UOW. He holds a PhD in Geography from the University of Durham (UK) and also holds an LLM in International Law from the University of British Columbia. His research interests relate to international boundaries and particularly maritime boundary delimitation and marine jurisdictional issues, on which he has published over 200 scholarly publications. Schofield is an International Hydrographic Office (IHO)-nominated Observer on the ABLOS and is a member of the ILA's Committee on International Law and Sea Level Rise. He has contributed to the peaceful settlement of boundary and territory disputes by providing advice to governments engaged in boundary negotiations and in dispute settlement cases before the International Court of Justice (ICJ). Moreover, he served as an independent expert witness in the international arbitration case between the Philippines and China.

ANDREW TETTENBORN

Prof. Andrew Tettenborn has been attached to the Institute of International Shipping and Trade Law, Swansea University Law School (IISTL) since 2010; he has also taught at the universities of Cambridge,

Exeter and Geneva and held visiting positions in Europe, Australia and the United States. Tettenborn is author or coauthor of books on torts, damages and maritime law, has written extensively on widespread aspects of private, shipping and commercial law, sits on the editorial board of *Lloyd's Maritime and Commercial Law Quarterly* and the *Journal of International Maritime Law*. In addition, he is the general editor of *Clerk & Lindsell on Torts*, and the editor of *Marsden's Collisions at Sea*, together with the leading English student commercial law text, *Sealy and Hooley's Text and Materials on Commercial Law*.

ROBERT VAN DE POLL

Robert van de Poll is Global Director of Law of the Sea for Fugro, one of the world's largest surveying and engineering companies, headquartered in the Netherlands, and he is also the creator of CARIS LOTS, the leading law of the sea and maritime boundary software used by the United Nations and by international courts and tribunals. To date, he has completed more than 1,800 law of the sea projects in 146 of the 162 countries he manages for Fugro (globally). This involved working with and advising governments (minister level), national oil companies and international oil corporations of every jurisdictional aspect of law of the sea (notably on baselines, limits and boundaries, including ECS issues). Van de Poll holds an honorary lecturer position at Dundee University, UK. He is also Geological Director at the DOLFIN (Dundee Ocean and Lake Frontiers Institute and Neutrals) Institute at Dundee. He also holds an honorary fellow position at ANCORS and is a visiting fellow at the IMO IMLI, University of Malta. IMLI was established under the IMO, a specialized agency of the United Nations.

BRIAN WILSON

Captain Brian Wilson, US Navy (retired), is the Deputy Director of the Global Maritime Operational Threat Response Coordination Center, the US government office responsible for coordinating the interagency response to maritime threats involving the United States and US interests; and is a visiting professor at the US Naval Academy and a non-resident fellow at the Stockton Center for International Law at the US Naval War College. Wilson, a retired US Navy judge advocate, has led whole-of-government seminars and tabletop exercises in more than ten countries and has written numerous articles on maritime security law, cyber security and crisis management. He has also served as the academic/legal advisor for several NATO Center of Excellence-sponsored maritime seminars. Wilson has further served as a consultant to the United Nations Office on Drugs and Crime (UNODC) and as a Fulbright Specialist Scholar at Tbilisi State University Law School, where he was a visiting professor for a course on maritime security and the Black Sea.

OLIVIA WOOLLEY

Dr. Olivia Woolley is Associate Professor in Biolaw of Durham Law School at the University of Durham. In her research, she examines how law can be used to support the growth of renewable energy consumption as part of a low carbon energy transition. She has particular interests in offshore wind energy generation and transmission, including legal issues raised by the possibility of developing a North Sea electricity grid. Woolley also specializes in law relating to the preservation of ecosystem functionality. *Ecological Governance*, a monograph setting out her thoughts on how law could be used to arrest and reverse global ecological deterioration, was published by Cambridge University Press in 2014.

PREFACE

This book focuses on the influence of emerging technology on the law of the sea. It was sponsored by the Korea Maritime Institute to develop a better understanding of how marine technologies challenge or shape the application of the international law of the sea. The project also benefited from the generous support of the World Maritime University-Sasakawa Global Ocean Institute at the International Maritime Organization and the Stockton Center for International Law at the US Naval War College. Vishaka Ramesh and Vishesh Bhatia, who serve as research assistants with the Stockton Center, provided diligent assistance and careful copy-editing of the manuscript.

The views of the contributors and editors do not reflect the official policy or position of any of their affiliated institutions.

Emerging Technology and Maritime Boundary Dispute Resolution

CLIVE SCHOFIELD, ROBERT VAN DE POLL AND NIELS ANDERSEN

The authors are indebted to Dr. I Made Andi Arsana of the Department of Geodetic and Geomatic Engineering at Gadjah Mada University, Indonesia Indonesia for his kind assistance in preparing Figures 1.1–1.5. These figures were produced by Dr. Arsana and the first author for inclusion in the International Hydrographic Organization (International Hydrographic Organization *see* IHO; International Hydrographic OrganizationIHO) and International Association of Geodesy *see* IAG; International Association of GeodesyInternational Association of Geodesy (IAG) *Manual on Technical Aspects of the United Nations Convention on the Law of the Sea – 1982* (TALOS Manual). These figures are reproduced with the kind permission of the IHO and IAG subject to the following notice:

Material from IHO-IAG publication C-51, *A Manual on Technical Aspects of the United Nations Convention on the Law of the Sea – 1982* (TALOS), Edition 5.0.0 dated June 2014 is reproduced with the permission of Prof. Clive Schofield and Dr. I Made Andi Arsana,

1.1   Introduction

The advent of broad claims to maritime jurisdiction, most notably the exclusive economic zone (EEZ), has resulted in a proliferation of overlapping maritime claims and thus potential maritime boundaries, only around half of which have been resolved. This chapter explores the state-of-play globally in maritime boundary dispute resolution and outlines the evolution of ocean boundary-making in light of emerging technology. It is recognized that the delimitation of maritime boundaries, in essence the determination of a line on the surface of the Earth, has always had a strong technical dimension, with a view to providing maritime jurisdictional clarity and certainty. It is also apparent that the predominant method of maritime boundary delimitation is the definition of equidistance or median lines between opposite and adjacent coastlines and baselines. Accordingly, the definition of baselines along the coast is a critical consideration as the geodetically robust construction of equidistance lines is ultimately dependent on the location of opposing baselines.

Emerging technologies are transforming the science of both positioning and measuring distances on the surface of the Earth (geodesy), and hydrographic survey techniques essential for determining baselines along the coast and these developments are examined. Concerning advances in geodesy, constellations of satellites have now made a unified global geodetic reference system a reality. Further, progress has been made in terms of realizing a global height level system and concerning the georeferencing of satellite imagery. In particular, this chapter highlights emerging technology that has the potential to lead to global bathymetry from space. The increasing use of novel remote-sensing techniques such as Fugro's SatRecon (4DSSM) satellite sea floor morphology analysis application has the potential to optimize the location of territorial sea baselines compared with the use of charts.

The chapter then demonstrates how these emerging technologies have the potential to influence the definition of baselines along the coast and thus both the delineation of the outer limits to maritime jurisdictional

authors of the animated graphics, and of the Secretariat of the IHO and the Executive Council of the IAG (Permission N° 8/2020) acting for the IHO and the IAG, which do not accept responsibilities responsibility for the correctness of the material as reproduced: in case of doubt, the IHO–IAG's authentic text shall prevail. The incorporation of material sourced from IHO–IAG shall not be construed as constituting an endorsement by IHO (International Hydrographic Organization); IHO (International Hydrographic Organization IHO or IAG (International Association of Geodesy); IAG (International Association of GeodesyIAG of this product.

claims and the resolution of disputes over areas where such claims overlap through the delimitation of maritime boundaries. Consideration will also be given to the use of emerging technologies and technical evidence in the context of differing approaches to maritime boundary dispute resolution, particularly negotiations versus adjudication.

1.1.1 Progress in the Delimitation of Maritime Boundaries

The overarching legal framework governing claims to maritime jurisdiction is provided by the United Nations (UN) Convention on the Law of the Sea (UNCLOS).[1] The Convention has gained widespread international recognition. At the time of writing, there were 168 parties to UNCLOS, comprising 167 states plus the European Union (EU).[2] This is especially impressive since there are only 152 coastal states.

UNCLOS establishes a system of maritime zones adjacent or appurtenant to the coast in keeping with the legal maxim that "the land dominates the sea,"[3] that is, that maritime entitlements arise from sovereignty over coastal land territory. This zonal system comprises the territorial sea, contiguous zone and the EEZ, the outer limits of which are all delineated by reference to distance measurements from baselines along the coast, specifically, to maximum distances of 12 nautical miles (M), 24 M and 200 M (Figure 1.1).[4]

The general international acceptance of these broad maritime claims has had a dramatic impact on the maritime spaces subject to coastal states claims to sovereignty (internal and archipelagic waters and the territorial sea) and sovereign rights (contiguous zone, the EEZ and continental shelf). This is exemplified by the fact that maritime claims out to 200 M EEZ limits cover more than 169 million km^2 (geodetic) globally.

---

[1] United Nations Convention on the Law of the Sea, Dec. 10, 1982, 1833 U.N.T.S. 397 (hereinafter UNCLOS or the Convention).

[2] United Nations DOALOS (United Nations Division for Ocean Affairs and Law of the Sea), chronological lists of ratifications of, accessions and successions to the Convention and the related agreements, Nov. 30, 2020, www.un.org/Depts/los/reference_files/Los104Unclos StatusTableEng.pdf (last visited Mar. 1, 2022) (online).

[3] North Sea Continental Shelf (F.R.G. v. Den., F.R.G. v. Neth.), Judgment, 1969 I.C.J. Rep. 3 (Feb. 20).

[4] UNCLOS, *supra* note 1, arts. 3–4, 33, 57; Christopher M. Carleton & Clive H. Schofield, *Developments in the Technical Determination of Maritime Space: Charts, Datums, Baselines, Maritime Zones and Limits*, 3 MAR. BRIEFINGS 1, 56–58 (2001).

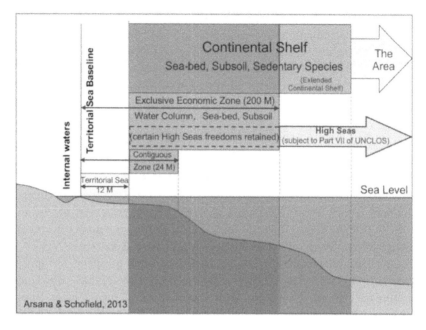

Figure 1.1 Schematic of baselines and maritime claims of a coastal state
Source: Clive Schofield and I Made Andi Arsana[5] (used with permission)

Further, where the continental margin exceeds 200 M EEZ limits, the outer limits of the continental shelf are determined in partnership with a scientific and technical body established through the Convention – the UN Commission on the Limits of the Continental Shelf (CLCS)[6] – in accordance with a complex series of criteria as well as distance measurements from baselines (UNCLOS, Article 76). Indeed, 82 of the aforementioned 152 coastal states have filed 104 submissions with the CLCS, encompassing an additional area of approximately 37 million km[2] (geodetic) of continental shelf areas located seaward of 200 M EEZ limits.

---

[5] International Oceanographic Commission, International Hydrographic Organization & International Association of Geodesy, A Manual on Technical Aspects of the United Nations Convention on the Law of the Sea ch. 5, at 3 (International Hydrographic Bureau ed., 2014) (hereinafter IHO).

[6] UNCLOS, *supra* note 1, art. 76 and annex II, and Commission on the Limits of the Continental Shelf, 2020, www.un.org/Depts/los/clcs_new/clcs_home.htm (last visited Mar. 1, 2022) (online).

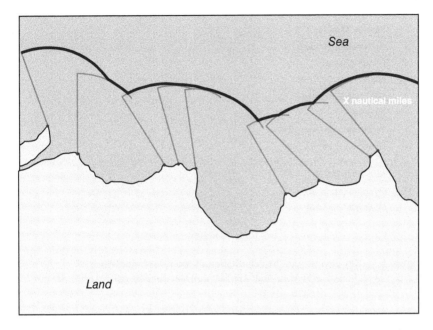

Figure 1.2 Delineating the outer limits of maritime zones through an envelope of arcs
Source: Clive Schofield and I Made Andi Arsana[7] (used with permission)

As a result of the advance of maritime claims seaward, coupled with the proximity of coastal states to one another, overlapping maritime claims and potential maritime boundaries have proliferated. In practice, this means that if there is less than 24 M of opposing coastlines, a potential territorial sea boundary will exist, while if coastal states' coastlines are within 400 M of one another, a potential EEZ boundary will be required (Figure 1.3). Moreover, states with coastlines considerably farther distant from one another may require the delimitation of a maritime boundary relating to their "outer" or "extended" continental shelf rights.

These expansive ocean spaces within national jurisdiction are of vital interest to the coastal states involved in terms of their national sovereignty and security. Additionally, the broad zones under sovereign rights, that is, the EEZ and continental shelf, provide the coastal state with sovereign rights over valuable marine resources. It follows that the delimitation of maritime boundaries to divide areas of overlapping

[7] *Id.*, at 6.

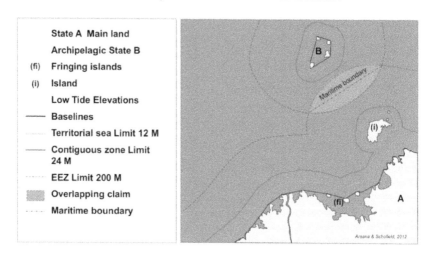

Figure 1.3   Key elements in the delimitation of maritime boundaries
Source: Clive Schofield and I Made Andi Arsana[8] (used with permission)

maritime claims is a significant consideration for coastal states, especially as once established international boundaries are generally considered to be stable and are therefore unlikely to change unless the parties to them agree to alter them, something that occurs only very rarely.

Where each interstate maritime boundary relationship is as one potential maritime boundary, even if it may be composed of multiple distinct segments, the number of potential maritime boundaries within 200 M limits has been calculated to be 454, of which 277 (61 percent) have been at least partially agreed, with 240 of these agreements ratified and in force (52.8 percent of the number of potential maritime boundaries).[9] It should, however, be noted that many of these existing delimitation lines are partial either in terms of their length or because they predate the advent of the EEZ. This means that disputes and overlapping maritime claims may persist even if part of a particular maritime boundary has been delimited or, alternatively, an agreement has been reached regarding only one maritime zone.

---

[8] IHO, *supra* note 5, ch. 6, at 3.
[9] *See* VICTOR PRESCOTT & CLIVE H. SCHOFIELD, MARITIME POLITICAL BOUNDARIES OF THE WORLD 217 (2d ed. 2005); Andreas Østhagen, *Troubled Seas: The Changing Politics of Maritime Boundary Disputes*, OCEAN AND COASTAL MANAGEMENT 205 (2021).

1.1.2 Evolution of Ocean Boundary-Making

In relation to the delimitation of the territorial sea, Article 15 of UNCLOS applies and offers a clear preference for the use of an equidistance or median line. This does not apply, however, if the states concerned agree to the contrary or there exists a "historic title or other special circumstances" in the area to be delimited that justifies a departure from the equidistance line.

Under the 1958 Convention on the Continental Shelf, delimitation was also to be effected by the use of median lines unless, similarly, an agreement to the contrary or "special circumstances" existed that justified an alternative approach.[10] However, the relevant provisions of UNCLOS, Articles 74 and 83, dealing with delimitation of the continental shelf and EEZ, respectively, merely provide, in identical general terms, that agreements should be reached on the basis of international law in order to achieve "an equitable solution" with no preferred method of delimitation indicated. While this provides for substantial flexibility in ocean boundary-making, the lack of guidance offered by the provisions of UNCLOS dealing with EEZ and continental shelf boundary delimitation also affords great scope for conflicting interpretation and dispute. Here it can be observed that the delimitation provisions of UNCLOS were among the last elements of the "package deal" to be agreed on and the general wording used was a means to overcome disagreement on a contentious issue. Indeed, as the arbitral tribunal in the Eritrea–Yemen Arbitration noted in reference to the drafting of Article 83, this was "a last minute endeavour ... to get agreement on a very controversial matter," and therefore, "consciously designed to decide as little as possible."[11]

In order to achieve delimitation of the continental shelf and/or the EEZ in accordance with UNCLOS, a theoretically limitless list of potentially relevant circumstances needs to be taken into consideration in the delimitation equation to reach the goal of an equitable result. Nonetheless, it has become abundantly clear from the practice of coastal states, allied to the rulings of international courts and tribunals, that geography, and particularly coastal geography, has a critical role in the delimitation of maritime boundaries. Aspects of coastal geography

---

[10] Convention of the Continental Shelf, art. 6, Apr. 29, 1958, 15 U.S.T. 471, T.I.A.S. No. 5578, 499 U.N.T.S. 311.

[11] Sovereignty and Maritime Delimitation in the Red Sea (Eri. v. Yemen), Case No. 1996-04, Award in the Second Stage, ¶ 116 (Perm. Ct. Arb. 1999); see UNCLOS, supra note 1, art. 83.

8 SCHOFIELD, VAN DE POLL AND ANDERSEN

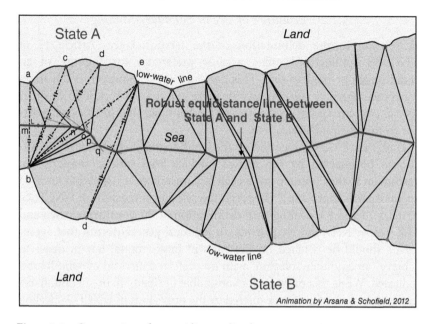

Figure 1.4 Construction of an equidistance line between opposite coasts
Source: Clive Schofield and I Made Andi Arsana[12] (used with permission)

that have proved especially influential include the configuration of the coasts under consideration, the relative coastal length and the potential impact of outstanding geographical features, notably islands, and it is notable that equidistance has found enduring popularity as a method of delimitation in state practice (Figure 1.4).[13]

While, as noted, there has been a shift away from equidistance as a preferred method of delimitation over time in the law of the sea, not least because in certain circumstances the application of strict equidistance can lead to clearly inequitable results, equidistance has nonetheless proved extremely popular as a basis for maritime boundary delimitation in practice. Further, there has been a distinct shift in more recent jurisprudence toward the application of a three-stage approach; the first stage involved the construction of an equidistance line as a provisional delimitation line.

---

[12] IHO, *supra* note 5, ch. 6, at 5.

[13] PRESCOTT & SCHOFIELD, *supra* note 9, at 238–39; *see also* LEONARD LEGAULT & BLAIR HANKEY, *Method, Oppositeness and Adjacency, and Proportionality in Maritime Boundary Delimitation.* 1 INTERNATIONAL MARITIME BOUNDARIES 203, 214, 221–22 (Jonathan I. Charney & Lewis M. Alexander eds., 1993).

This approach was clearly articulated in the 2009 judgment in the Black Sea case[14] between Romania and Ukraine: at the first stage, a provisional delimitation line should be established using geometrically objective methods *"unless there are compelling reasons that make this unfeasible* in the particular case,"[15] at the second stage, assessment is to be made as to "whether there are factors calling for the adjustment or shifting of the provisional equidistance line in order to achieve an equitable result,"[16] and at the third stage, verification of the resulting potential delimitation line is undertaken through what the Court termed a "disproportionality test."[17]

All subsequent international cases involving maritime boundary delimitation have similarly applied this three-stage approach to maritime delimitation. These have included cases before the International Court of Justice (ICJ), the International Tribunal on the Law of the Sea (ITLOS) and international arbitral tribunals.[18] That said, no international court or tribunal has applied a strict equidistance line at the first stage, arguably undermining the objectivity of this approach. Nonetheless, the general reliance on equidistance as a method of maritime boundary delimitation places ever greater emphasis on the definition of baselines along the coast, as such baselines are essential to providing the critical basepoints contributing to the calculation of a geodetically robust equidistance line.

1.1.3 Definition of Baselines

Baselines along the coast provide the international legal representation of the land–sea interface and thus divide land territory and internal waters on their landward side from zones of maritime jurisdiction on their seaward side. As noted earlier, maritime zones are predominantly defined by set distances measured from baselines. Baselines are therefore fundamental to determining the spatial extent of coastal state claims to maritime space. Accordingly, baselines are vital to coastal states as rights and

---

[14] *See* Maritime Delimitation in the Black Sea (Rom. v. Ukr.), Judgment, 2009 I.C.J. Rep. 61 (Feb. 3) (hereinafter Black Sea Case).

[15] *Id.*, ¶ 116 (emphasis added).

[16] *Id.*, ¶ 120. At this point, the Court cited its earlier judgment in the Cameroon/Nigeria Case in support of its ruling. *See,* Land and Maritime Boundary between Cameroon and Nigeria (Cameroon v. Nigeria; Eq. Guinea intervening), Judgment, 2002 I.C.J. Rep. 303 (Oct. 10) at ¶ 288.

[17] *Id.*, ¶ 122 and ¶¶ 210–16.

[18] *See* MALCOLM D. EVANS, *Maritime Boundary Delimitation*. OXFORD HANDBOOK OF THE LAW OF THE SEA 254, 259–61 (Donald R. Rothwell, Alexander Oude Elferink, Karen N. Scott & Timothy Stephens eds., 2015).

jurisdiction over valuable marine resources and activities within these maritime zones are at stake. Additionally, it should be observed that coastal states have important obligations to address within their maritime zones, for instance, to protect and preserve the marine environment within them. Baselines are also frequently critically important in the delimitation of maritime boundaries as a consequence of their direct role in the construction of equidistance or median lines, which are often used in the construction of maritime boundaries.

In the absence of any other baseline claims, the default baselines of a coastal state are "normal" baselines coincident with "the low-water line along the coast as marked on large-scale charts officially recognized by the coastal State," per UNCLOS, Article 5. This article, however, is silent as to which low water line among many options is preferable. These various low water lines are determined by the choice of vertical datum that provides the level of reference for the measurement of depths and elevations.[19] This choice of vertical datum has the potential to influence how far seaward the normal baseline is located, as well as which features will be classified as above high-tide islands or rocks (UNCLOS, Article 121), low-tide elevations (LTEs) that are submerged at high tide but uncovered at low tide, in accordance with Article 13 of UNCLOS, or fully submerged components of the sea floor (Figure 1.5).

The classification of insular features impacts their capacity to generate maritime entitlements and thus their potential to serve as basepoints in the construction of an outer limit to maritime claims or a maritime boundary with a neighboring state. A choice of vertical datum therefore appears to be at the discretion of coastal states, leading to the potential for neighboring states to opt for different vertical datums, resulting in disputes. Such disputes are, however relatively rare, essentially because of the reference in Article 5 of UNCLOS to charts officially recognized by the coastal state. As the primary purpose of nautical charts is to serve as aids to navigation, chart makers tend to apply low or conservative vertical datum levels in the interests of safety of navigation.

UNCLOS also provides specific provisions for the baselines of reefs (Article 6), straight baselines (Article 7), river closing lines (Article 9), bays (Article 10) and ports and permanent harbor works (Article 11), as well as with respect to archipelagos (Article 47). However, it can be noted that the various straight-line alternatives to normal baselines that may be

---

[19] IHO, *supra* note 5.

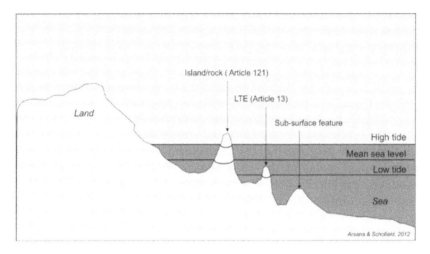

Figure 1.5   Insular features and sea level
Source: Clive Schofield and I Made Andi Arsana[20] (used with permission)

claimed by a coastal state still depend to some extent on the location of
normal baselines, because in order to be valid, they need to at least
broadly reflect the general direction of the coast and be connected back
to points on or above the low-water line, such that each system of
baselines is "closed."[21] Consequently, determining the location of the
normal baseline, coincident with the low-water line along the coast, is a
critical consideration for the delineation of the outer limits of the claims
to maritime jurisdiction of coastal states as well as the delimitation of
maritime boundaries between them.

1.2   Maritime Boundary Delimitation and Changing Technologies

Nautical charts have traditionally served as a primary data source for
determining the normal baselines to be used in the delimitation of

---

[20] *Id.*, ch. 4, at 9.
[21] The United Nations Group of Technical Experts on Baselines indicated that for straight
baselines, for example, this meant that "whether the baselines are drawn along the coast
of an island or of the mainland, the system must start and finish on or above the low
water line" and that where straight baselines were drawn connecting a fringe of islands,
"all the intermediate basepoints must be located on or above the low water line." *See*
UNITED NATIONS, BASELINES: AN EXAMINATION OF THE RELEVANT PROVISIONS OF THE
UNITED NATIONS CONVENTION ON THE LAW OF THE SEA 23 (1989).

maritime boundaries. Indeed, prior to the widespread use of computed equidistance lines, the majority of maritime boundaries were delimited relying on the low-water lines shown on charts, with boundary lines being constructed graphically, leading to plotting errors. This is well illustrated by the discrepancy in position of the terminal points of the continental shelf boundaries between Norway and the UK agreed in 1965 and 1978, respectively. Although these points were calculated from the same basepoints on either side and should therefore be identical, the northernmost point of the 1965 agreement is 331 meters east of the southernmost point of the 1978 agreement because the former was produced graphically while the latter line was computed. As the 1965 treaty was considered to be stable and absolute in law, rather than amend it, the two positions were instead connected by a parallel of latitude 331 meters in length.[22]

Other problematic uses of charts in maritime boundary delimitation have involved the drawing of apparently straight lines on nautical charts, due to the fact that most nautical charts are on the Mercator projection. For example, in the Anglo-French Arbitration case the Court ruled that the final section of the maritime boundary, that extended broadly south-westwards into the approaches to the Channel, should be an equidistance line giving half effect to the Scilly Islands. This outcome was achieved by constructing an equidistance line giving full effect to the Scilly Isles together with one giving them nil effect and splitting the difference between the two. This was apparently effectuated by means a long straight line was drawn on a Mercator chart. However, this really meant that the line in question did not represent a straight line on the surface of the Earth. Instead, the line drawn was a loxodrome or rhumb line that at its south-western terminus lay around four miles farther north, to the advantage of France, than a true half-effect line would have been.[23]

Further, nautical charts of unsuitable scale or lacking a geodetic datum have been used to construct maritime boundary agreements. For example, the Thai–Malaysian Memorandum of Understanding (MoU) on establishing a joint development area of 1979 and the Malaysia–Vietnam MoU on establishing a joint zone in a "Defined Area" of the Gulf of 1992 relate the coordinates contained therein to British Admiralty Chart 2414 at a scale of 1:1,500,000, which lacks a horizontal

[22] 2 INTERNATIONAL MARITIME BOUNDARIES 1, 879–1890 (Jonathan I. Charney & Lewis M. Alexander eds., 1993); Carleton & Schofield, *supra* note 4, at 12–13.

[23] 2 INTERNATIONAL MARITIME BOUNDARIES, *supra* note 22, at 1735–54.

datum.[24] Similarly, the ICJ in its 2002 ruling in the case concerning the land and maritime boundary between Cameroon and Nigeria, opted to upheld the validity of two previous agreements between them, namely the Yaoundé II Declaration of April 4, 1971 and the Maroua Declaration of June 1, 1975. Unfortunately, these agreements also refer to a nautical chart, British Admiralty Chart 3433, which also lacks datum information. Consequently, the Court in effect perpetuated uncertainty, potentially of the order of hundreds of meters, concerning the absolute positioning of the coordinates defining the maritime boundary lines in question.[25]

The introduction of global navigation satellite systems (GNSS), notably the global positioning system (GPS) of the United States, Russia's global navigation satellite system (GLONASS) and the EU's GALILEO system, marked a major breakthrough for the definition of a unified global geodetic reference system. The geodetically robust construction of equidistance lines coupled with referencing geographic coordinates to the global geodetic reference systems has largely addressed the errors earlier outlined in modern ocean boundary-making. Significant technological advances are also emerging in respect of the more fundamental issue of detecting the location of baselines along the coast.

1.2.1 Emerging Technologies for Detecting the Edge of the Land (Baselines)

1.2.1.1 Charts and Changing Coasts

According to the International Hydrographic Organization's (IHO's) International Hydrographic Dictionary, nautical charts are "specifically designed to meet the requirements of marine navigation showing depths of water, nature of bottom, elevations, configuration and characteristics of coast, dangers and aids to navigation."[26] In keeping with this objective, they comprise bathymetric information regarding depths of water, the

---

[24] 1 INTERNATIONAL MARITIME BOUNDARIES 1099–124 (Jonathan I. Charney & Lewis M. Alexander eds., 1993).

[25] CLIVE H. SCHOFIELD & CHRISTOPHER M. CARLETON, *Technical Considerations in Law of the Sea Dispute Resolution*. OCEAN MANAGEMENT IN THE 21ST CENTURY: INSTITUTIONAL FRAMEWORKS AND RESPONSES UNDER THE LAW OF THE SEA CONVENTION 231, 242–43 (Alexander Oude Elferink & Donald R. Rothwell eds., 2004). *See also* Land and Maritime Boundary between Cameroon and Nigeria (Cameroon v. Nigeria; Eq. Guinea intervening), Judgment, 2002 I.C.J. Rep. 303 (Oct. 10).

[26] IHO, "nautical chart," International Hydrographic Dictionary, IHO Publication S-32, at 70, http://iho-ohi.net/S32/engView.php?page=170 (last visited Mar. 1, 2022) (online).

characteristics and elevation of, particularly, the sea floor in shallow waters, and the configuration of the coast and/or any shallow water hazards to ensure safe vessel transit. As technology has improved, surveys are continuously updating the nautical chart, with subsequent chart revision issued. However, because hydrographic surveying has traditionally been a slow, time-consuming and expensive task, such surveys are generally not undertaken for the whole area covered by a particular chart simultaneously but rather are conducted in a piecemeal fashion, sometimes over many years.[27] Consequently, hydrographic data for some parts of a given chart may not meet modern standards.[28] Unfortunately, this is especially so with respect to the shallowest areas of the ocean, that is, at the coast, which is generally the most problematic and expensive to survey using traditional methods and is also prone to rapid and potentially radical positional change such that the coastline as depicted on the chart can easily be off by thousands of meters.

Thus, the information concerning the location of the coastline depicted on most nautical charts currently produced or maintained by national hydrographic offices or publicly and readily available from global charting agencies (such as those of the United States, the UK, France and Russia) are commonly positionally inaccurate. This is because such coastal information was collected and interpreted long before high-resolution seabed mapping was possible. Large sections of the coast are therefore yet to be surveyed to modern standards, especially in remote locations and close to the coast in shallow waters. As the delineation of the outer limits of maritime claims and often the delimitation of maritime boundaries is dependent on measurements from baselines along the coast, if the depiction of these baselines is inaccurate, the outer limits and maritime boundaries calculated from them will inevitably also be inaccurate. The application of technologies such as vessel-based multibeam echo-sounders, airborne light detection and ranging (LIDAR), and bathymetry surveys from aircraft have helped improve data accuracy at localized levels but these technologies cannot efficiently address the broader and immediate need for truly global regional coastal data sets. Accordingly, comprehensive mapping of the world's coastlines to a consistently high level of accuracy has remained out of reach until the advent of recent technological advances.

Here it is also important to observe that it has long been understood that many if not most coastlines are dynamic features of the land and

[27] IHO, *supra* note 5, ch. 3, at 3.
[28] IHO, *supra* note 26.

seascape. Changes in the location of the coast and thus normal baselines coincident with the low-water line can occur as a result of a range of processes, for example, natural depositional and alluvial processes that serve to advance coastlines such as those of deltas around the world. Coastlines may also incrementally advance thanks to deformations of the Earth's crust as a result of isostatic (or postglacial) readjustment whereby parts of the continental crust is gradually rising following the removal of the enormous weight of major icesheets, some several kilometers thick, after the end of the last ice age. Although rates of uplift because of such isostatic or postglacial rebound are minimal (commonly of the order of 1 centimeter per annum or less), even this seemingly slight rise *can have significant consequences in the context of low-lying, shallow gradient coastlines*. Similarly, vertical displacements associated with volcanic or tectonic activity can also lead to the emergence of additional land, and therefore coasts, above the surface of the sea.[29] Moreover, in addition to human influences on the fundamentally coupled climate–ocean system through excess heat and greenhouse gas emissions leading to climate change, anthropogenic activities can also substantially influence sea level rise directly, both positively and negatively. For example, deforestation and the loss of wetlands will tend to contribute to increased runoff and thus sea level rise, while the trapping of waters behind dams will have the opposite effect.[30]

The counterpoint is that just as coasts can advance, so they can retreat. For example, coasts and offshore features formed as a delta advances can be trimmed back and disappear because of erosion. Thus, coastal erosional and depositional processes can occur cyclically such that parts of the coastline are continually being reshaped, with the fringing islands forming and then being eroded away, and consequently shifting in location as well as changing shape and elevation over time. Such changes

---

[29] For example, the Boxing Day earthquake of 2004 and subsequent earthquakes in 2005 resulted in vertical deformations ranging from +3 meters to subsidence of −1 meter. POH POH WONG et al., *Coastal Systems and Low-lying Areas*. CLIMATE CHANGE 2014: IMPACTS, ADAPTATION, AND VULNERABILITY, PART A: GLOBAL AND SECTORAL ASPECTS. CONTRIBUTION OF WORKING GROUP II TO THE FIFTH ASSESSMENT REPORT OF THE INTERGOVERNMENTAL PANEL ON CLIMATE CHANGE 361, 369 (Christopher B. Field and Vincente R. Barros eds., 2014).

[30] It has been estimated that such direct anthropogenic impacts may account for as much as one-third of observed sea level rise. *See* VIVIEN GORNITZ, *Monitoring Sea Level Changes*. LONG-TERM CLIMATE MONITORING BY THE GLOBAL CLIMATE OBSERVING SYSTEM 515, 521 (Thomas R. Karl ed., 1995).

are, moreover, likely to be increasingly impacted by significant and accelerating sea level rise. The Intergovernmental Panel on Climate Change (IPCC) has been explicit in stating that sea level rise currently being experienced is "unprecedented over the last century" and rising at about 2.5 times the previous rate.[31]

It is anticipated that complex interactions between sea level and the shape and elevation of the land as well as those between sea level and coastal ecosystems, such as corals and mangroves that may be capable of autonomous *in situ* adaption to changing sea levels, will have major impacts on the position of the coast and thus normal baselines. In particular, sea level rise has the potential to inundate parts of the coast and/or exacerbate erosion of the coast, leading to a retreat landward in the location of the coast. This inevitably imperils critical basepoints from which maritime zones and boundaries are measured and thus the extent of national maritime jurisdictional claims of states, especially those possessing low-elevation and easily eroded coasts composed of soft, depositional materials.

An important distinction can be made here between the outer limits to maritime jurisdictional claims that are generally delineated by coastal states by means of distance measurements from baselines along the coast and maritime boundaries delimited between neighboring states where their maritime claims overlap with one another. The former are commonly viewed as being susceptible to change, while the latter are considered to be stable and permanent unless the parties to a maritime boundary agreement mutually agree to alter its course.

This difference arises from the traditional view that just as the coastline, and thus normal baselines consistent with low-water lines along the coast, are dynamic and can change their location over time, so normal baselines are susceptible to change or can "ambulate" and fluctuate in position.[32] The consequence of this is that as normal baselines alter in location and as a result of sea level rise retreat landward, the outer limits of maritime claims may also shift and contract.[33] In contrast,

---

[31] UN Intergovernmental Panel on Climate Change, Special Report on the Ocean and Cryosphere in a Changing Climate 6 (2019).

[32] 3 Michael W. Reed, Shore and Sea Boundaries: The Development of International Maritime Boundary Principles through United States Practice 185 (2000).

[33] That said, there is emerging state practice, especially among the Pacific small island developing states, toward declaring and fixing their maritime baselines, limits and

international boundaries have tended to be viewed as not being susceptible to change, even where a "fundamental change of circumstances" has
occurred.[34] It can also be noted that in the only international judicial case
that has been directly faced with arguments concerning the permanence
of a maritime boundary in the face of climate change–induced instability
in the location of coastlines and thus baselines, that is, the arbitration
between Bangladesh and India concerning their maritime boundary in
the Bay of Bengal, the Tribunal was explicit in the view that "maritime
delimitations, like land boundaries, must be stable and definitive to
ensure a peaceful relationship between the States concerned in the long
term and that in its view . . . neither the prospect of climate change nor its
possible effects can jeopardize the large number of settled maritime
boundaries agreed between states and to those established through international arbitration."[35]

1.2.1.2   Advances in Geodesy for the Determination
of Baselines, Limits and Boundaries

Geodesy is, essentially, the science to determine the size and shape of the
Earth, and exact positioning of points at its surface, including variations
of the gravity field to yield precise positions in all three dimensions.[36]
The introduction and growth of space geodesy in general with emerging
GNSSs and the global high-precision mapping of the Earth's gravity field
(GRACE and GOCE) has today offered routine positioning at the
millimeter-level for long-term measurements.[37] Further, these developments enable detection of Earth surface point movements in high time
resolution. The launch of advanced radar and gravity satellites with
improved satellite orbit determination has enabled mapping of the

---

boundaries. *See, e.g.,* David Freestone & Clive H. Schofield, *Islands Awash amidst
Rising Seas: Sea Level Rise and Insular Status under the Law of the Sea,* 34 INT'L
J. MARINE & COASTAL L. 391 (2019); David Freestone & Clive H. Schofield, *Securing
Ocean Spaces for the Future? The Initiative of Pacific SIDS to Develop Regional
Practice Concerning Baselines and Maritime Zone Limits,* 33 OCEAN Y.B. ONLINE
58 (2019).
[34] Vienna Convention on the Law of Treaties, art. 62(2), May 23, 1969, 1155 U.N.T.S. 331.
[35] Bay of Bengal Maritime Boundary (Bangl. v. India), Permanent Court of Arbitration
(PCA) Case Repository, ¶¶ 216–17 (Perm. Ct. Arb. 2014).
[36] WOLFGANG TORGE & JÜRGEN MÜLLER, Geodesy 91–108 (4th ed. 2012).
[37] US Air Force, *GPS Accuracy,* www.gps.gov (last visited Feb. 27, 2021) (online).

ocean floor as variation in the sea floor morphology affects the corresponding gravity and consequently the sea level measured from the radar satellite.[38]

Maritime boundary dispute resolutions require consistent technical frameworks to determine their location robustly. Modern space infrastructures now deliver coherent satellite observing systems where optical and radar satellites are georeferenced using GNNS realizations with international adopted parameters at a given epoch.[39] With respect to determining and updating baselines, the coherent space infrastructure is of utmost importance to provide opportunities both in situ in the field and/or using optical satellites to deliver high-precision baselines with coordinates in an adopted international geodetic reference system.

The last century was characterized by physical geodesy that led to a progressively enhanced understanding of the dynamic geophysical surface of the Earth due to continental drifting. To keep track of continental drift and to secure high-quality topographical mapping, all continents were covered with large relative geodetic triangulations, levelling and gravity networks anchored with absolute or core geodetic basepoints. Such core basepoints are measured and referenced to interstellar objects like quasars through the use of very long baseline interferometry (VLBI).[40] However, this was a very costly and time-consuming process, requiring long time series of geodetic measurements to achieve enough accuracy in the calculations to be able to realize and determine a geodetic datum for a given region, for example, North America or Europe. Further, this still only yielded a regional datum as opposed to a coherent global datum! Significant advances were realized at the end of the twentieth century through the launch of GPS.[41] The introduction of space geodesy made possible a coherent global geodetic reference system. Thus, the defining terrestrial geodetic basepoints were literally moved to space through high-precision satellite orbits from which coordinates of the terrestrial geodetic networks could be determined by using the GPS receivers.

[38] SATELLITE ALTIMETRY OVER OCEANS AND LAND SURFACES (Detlef Stammer & Anny Cazenave eds., 1st ed. 2018).

[39] See, e.g., European Global Navigation Satellite Systems Agency, What Is GNSS?, www .euspa.europa.eu/european-space/eu-space-programme/what-gnss (last visited Feb. 27, 2021) (online).

[40] See, e.g., NASA Jet Propulsion Laboratory, Space Very Long Baseline Interferometry, www.jpl.nasa.gov (last visited Feb. 27, 2021) (online).

[41] See US Air Force, GPS: The Global Positioning System, www.gps.gov (last visited Feb. 27, 2021) (online).

The first realized global geodetic reference system was the World Geodetic System (WGS84), which is an Earth-centered, Earth-fixed terrestrial reference system and geodetic datum comparable to the North American Datum of 1983 (NAD83).[42] Since then and with the rapid development of GNSS, the International Terrestrial Reference System (ITRS) has been further developed to have the geocenter of the ITRS at the center of mass of the whole Earth, including the oceans and atmosphere.[43] As a result of these developments, it is not only possible to define precise horizontal coordinates, but also to determine the elevation of a point on a global scale relative to mean sea level. The reference surface needed here is the geoid, which is a model of the mean sea level extended through the land mass and determined by dense gravimetric measurements from space and in situ at the surface of the Earth.[44]

The geoid model of the gravimetric undulations due to changing mass distributions in the Earth define the plumb line, and thereby the correct horizontal level can be determined.[45] To realize a global vertical datum, and by this to create a global unified height system, the regional high-density gravity and levelling networks, including tide gauges, have to be added with satellite gravity measurements from missions like GRACE, GRACE FO and GOCE.[46] Having very dense gravity coverage, such as in the Scandinavian area, it is possible to achieve a mean error of the geoid down to 1 centimeter and consequently approach the order of size of global sea level changes, which again is important for maintaining the baselines from which zones of maritime jurisdiction are measured, especially in low-lying, shallow gradient coastal areas.

The emerging satellite infrastructure thus provides the possibility of uniting existing regional or continental height systems into a global vertical height system that can gradually be improved to match and verify global sea level changes. The high-precision gravity satellite missions combined with radar altimeter satellites measuring the sea surface topography also provide information or mapping of the deep sea floor morphology as the change of the sea floor relief gives rise to a change of

---

[42] US National Oceanic and Atmospheric Administration, National Geodetic Survey: Datums and Reference Frames, www.noaa.gov (last visited Feb. 27, 2021) (online).

[43] International Earth Rotation and Reference Systems Service, The International Terrestrial Reference System, www.iers.org (last visited Feb. 27, 2021) (online).

[44] IHO, *supra* note 5, ch. 2, at 5–8.

[45] *Id.*

[46] *See, e.g.,* ROGER HAAGMANS et al., ESA's Next-Generation Gravity Mission Concepts, 31 Rendiconti Lincei: Scienze Fisiche e Naturali 15 (2020).

gravity and consequently the geoid equivalent to the mean sea level. These data are an important supplement to the general mapping of the world ocean floor led by GEBCO (General Bathymetric Charts of the Oceans).[47] As the altimeter data supply information on the general sea floor morphology, the newest multispectral satellite imagery may be used for detailed mapping of the coastal areas, including the nearshore morphology if the water conditions in the given area are optimal for the satellite optics to look through the water column.

1.2.1.3   SatRecon (4DSSM) Four-Dimensional Satellite-Derived Seafloor Morphology

SatRecon (4DSSM Image) Analysis is an example of an emerging technology that is being applied to yield present-day accurate coastline mapping.[48] This novel approach allows for the identification of smaller shallow water and nearshore-foreshore coastal features including islands, islets, sandbars, sand-spits, drying reefs, shoals and/or isolated rocks. This can result in substantial enhancements in the calculation of outer limit measurements from coastal states' baselines.

The resulting SatRecon (4DSSM Image) do not actually define specific water depths (bathymetry), but rather define a morphological seabed continuous surface, that is, the skin of the Earth. Of particular note is the fact that there are archives of readily available images (over 5,000 terabytes, Landsat-8/Sentinel-2) of global-coverage satellite data (as high-resolution satellite imagesry) available, featuring hundreds of scenes, for almost any area of interest along the coasts of for most coastal states.[49] Moreover, the availability of high-resolution commercial satellite imagery,

---

[47] General Bathymetric Charts of the Oceans, www.gebco.net (last visited Feb. 27, 2021) (online).

[48] Robert van de Poll (2019). Fugro SatRecon 4DSSM Image (4 = time / D = three-dimensional / S = satellite / S = sea floor / M = morphology) is a new and evolving technique, developed by the second author of this chapter in the software CARIS LOTS (itself developed and created by Mr. van de Poll while at CARIS, 1991–2006), and with new modern development algorithms and techniques has provided new results (while at Fugro) to create these SatRecon (4DSSM) images. At Fugro, these support all projects that require a preliminary shallow water site investigation tool (4DSSM) for nearshore-foreshore mapping. To date, this new technique has successfully been used on +2,000 mapping project in 146 countries.

[49] In 2018, the second author of the chapter used SatRecon (4DSSM Image) technology to review the straight baselines of sixty-six states on behalf of the International Law Association (ILA) Committee on Baselines under the International Law of the Sea. *See* COALTER G. LATHROP, J. ASHLEY ROACH & DONALD R. ROTHWELL, *Baselines under the International Law of the Sea: Reports of the International Law Association Committee on Baselines under the International Law of the Sea.* 2 BRILL RESEARCH PERSPECTIVES IN THE LAW OF THE SEA 1, 126–62 (Davor Vidas & Donald R. Rothwell eds., 2019).

coupled with the time-component application utilized in this technology, allows for a unique "feature identification procedure," to rule out any false positives.[50] This new mapping application offers a very accurate, rapid procedure to fully remap vast coastal sections, involving the use of optical image analysis to manipulate medium- and/or high-resolution satellite images to yield detailed understanding of nearcoast seabed morphology. This promising new technique, incorporating a series of proprietary mathematical routines, developed by Fugro's Law of the Sea Global Mapping Team, can "see" through the water column to the seabed, allowing for rapid nearshore-foreshore mapping of coastal states' critical intertidal zones, with the ability to accurately map and identify smaller features. This approach also allows coastal states to efficiently identify where their existing nautical charts could or should be updated.

This technology is on the cusp of being proven as a new and viable methodology that utilizes the latest in technology with the potential to allow for rapid regional mapping of remote regions and coastlines. A particular advantage is that this evolving technology no longer requires the use of costly and time-consuming traditional on-site in the field survey vessels to actually and physically put "boots on the ground" at the sites needing to be surveyed. It also can be a rapid tool to quickly rule out sections of coastal frontiers not needing precision mapping and will define only the coastal sections that can be of maximum benefit to a coastal states' law of the sea measurements that could still require field survey vessels on site.

Termed four-dimensional satellite-derived seabed morphology (4DSSM Imagery), this emerging technology means that once the raw original sources of satellite images are processed, up-to-date imagery in shallow waters (<20–25 meters water depth) in the vicinity of the coast can be delivered.[51] The new technique uses the unprocessed satellite imagery, either at high resolution (Landsat-8 @ 15m or Sentinel-2 @ 10m) and/or extreme high resolution (submeter) (Maxar, Airbus or Kompsat) as an optical imagery data source.[52] A series of proprietary

---

[50] *See* Robert van de Poll, Using Satellite Seafloor Morphology for Coastline Delineation and Coastal Change Analysis (unpublished presentation), International Hydrographic Remote Sensing Workshop (2018) (on file with the authors).

[51] As noted earlier, this technique was used to evaluate straight baseline claims on behalf of the ILA Committee on Baselines under the International Law of the Sea. See, LATHROP ET AL., *supra* note 49.

[52] Internal Fugro advanced development techniques can utilize commercially available high-resolution satellite images (submeter ground resolution) from any of these three commercial satellite vendors to create Fugro SatRecon Extreme high resolution (4DSSM Images).

and customized tools (methodology and technique developed by Fugro) are then applied. This can provide outputs (as medium- or high-resolution) images for any area of interest over near-global coverage of 85°N to 85°S and 180°W to 180°E. With available archival satellite imagery covering the past fifteen years, these 4DSSM results for shallow water seabed morphology can produce near-real time results, which are mapped as visually intuitive data sets for understanding changes over time in dynamic shallow water environments.

Extensive research and ground-truthing featuring testing of over 2,000 sites in over 125 coastal states have produced results that are robust and reveal near–present-day seabed morphology useful for preliminary project site planning and mapping almost anywhere with global coverage. As satellites are and have been continually collecting data covering almost the entirety of the planet, going back now for up to fifteen years, we have an immense global archive to draw upon for comparative analysis. Consequently, it is possible to, as it were, "step back in time" to see with confidence changes in shallow water seabed (morphological) conditions. For example, when specifically considering medium-resolution raw satellite data sources such as the Landsat-8 scenes, these cover nearly any area of interest on the planet for coastal zones and coastal regions, with on average two new scenes being collected monthly. At the time of writing there were over ~1,045 terabytes (for Landsat-8 @15-meter) and ~4,033 terabytes (for Sentinel-2 @ 10-meter) of available images that have been continually collected at a global level at 15-meter ground resolution for almost eight years. These images allow for time comparisons – that is, the "4D" component – for a particular part of the coast.[53] This new technique makes it possible to evaluate, modify, update and identify where additional mapping should take place for coastlines or nearshore foreshore coastal waters that were observed long ago.

Thus, using these recent SatRecon (4DSSM) images, locating critical coastal areas that show that excessive change has taken place and then processing several individual 4DSSM images (over a period of time, starting with the most recent and going back in time) with consistent reproducible results would allow for initial interpreted confidence that these older mapped coastlines and or offshore fringing (barrier) islands

---

[53] *Supra* note 48. At Fugro, this approach provides a preliminary shallow water site investigation tool for nearshore-foreshore mapping, where multiple (time-separated) satellite images can be stacked to offer dynamic seabed analysis over time, ruling out false positives while also mapping seabed mobile structures such as shifting sediments in the shallow seabed morphology.

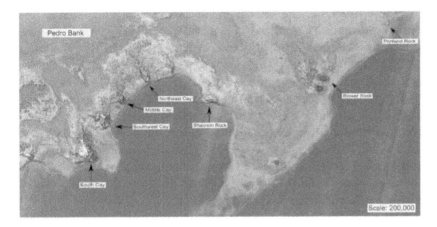

Figure 1.6 Pedro Bank
Source: Robert van de Poll[54]

can be seen to have shifted, and in some more extreme situations, named islands and features (from long ago) are no longer even existing in the present day. This dynamic is illustrated in Figure 1.6, which depicts part of Pedro Bank, Jamaica. This SatRecon (4DSSM Image) shows all shoaling areas and shallow water information, including smaller drying rocks, drying reefs, sand bars, sand spits, smaller islets and larger cays.

This methodology provides for the evaluation of both natural and man-made modifications to the seabed that may present hazards, thus helping ensure proper risk identification and mitigation for any shallow water project. Further, from a law of the sea perspective, the technology facilitates relatively low-cost, rapid turnaround detailed mapping of

---

[54] This particular image was collected on Jan. 5, 2020, and details 10-meter ground resolution imagery that can show seabed morphology to a maximum of 25 meters depth. Although individual scenes appear similar to a bathymetric digital terrain model (DTM) or a digital elevation model (DEM), Fugro SatRecon (4DSSM Images) are not a bathymetric product. This Fugro SatRecon (4DSSM Image results were produced from raw 2D satellite Images coming from the European Space Agency (ESA) Copernicus Sentinel-2 satellite (at 10-meter native ground resolution). This image is part of a proprietary Fugro Global Law of the Sea Database, containing law of the sea relevant digital data sets, with global coverage (containing in excess of 95 terabytes of digital data) and more than 10,000 legal law of the sea documents (most of which are not in public circulation) that were acquired by working on more than 2,000 law of the sea studies in 146 countries. *See also* David Freestone & Clive Schofield, Sea Level Rise and Archipelagic States: A Preliminary Risk Assessment, 35 Ocean Y.B. Online 340 (2021).

nearshore-foreshore waters, including updated, accurate mapping for the normal baselines of mainland coasts and/or smaller relevant offshore insular features such as small islands or rocks and LTEs. The SatRecon (4DSSM Image) technology provides images that not only allow for quick reviews of coastlines and new smaller uncharted offshore features critical to many law of the sea applications required by all coastal states but can also act as a quality control check on existing data, allowing for the identification of areas where additional detailed shallow water data is lacking and required as an aid to rapidly updating hazards for coastlines and offshore coastal features, and identifying new shallow water features for nautical charts, all the while keeping the costs for more detailed hydrographic surveys to a minimum.

1.2.1.4   Enhanced Baselines Models, Extended Maritime Jurisdiction

This emerging technology produces processed images used specifically in CARIS LOTS (Law of the Sea), a law of the sea–specific geographical information system (GIS) software package.[55] Specific tools in this software allow for the preprocessing of the original satellite images result in a three-dimensional digital elevation model, and the production of sun-illuminated seabed shaded relief georeferenced images with a fourth (time-capable) dimension.

The elevation of the seabed is not determined nor absolutely established but all shallow water hazards (sea floor trends and seabed isolated features) for seabed morphology are displayed, providing a valuable tool for shallow water mapping applications. The morphological "seabed feature detection" has a maximum depth limit of 25 meters (which is 100 percent dependent upon aerosol/water conditions for the marine conditions to be analyzed).[56] Such imagery ensures that the coastal state is armed with the most current knowledge of shallow water morphology proximate to the coast. The coastal state can produce a significantly more sophisticated and detailed rendering of their official territorial sea baseline model (TSBM). Any coastal state's TSBM can include complex combinations of normal and or straight line type baselines that, in turn, can be used to delineate the outer limits of claimed maritime zones and utilized in the construction of robust equidistance-based lines in the

[55] Teledyne CARIS, CARIS LOTS (Law of the Sea) Software Package, www.teledynecaris .com (last visited Feb. 27, 2021) (online).
[56] *See* van de Poll, *supra* note 50.

context of the delimitation of maritime boundaries. This direct link between understanding of the location of the coast and the extent of maritime jurisdiction has prompted a dramatic increase in interest from coastal states as to how best to update their TSBM. In practice, the TSMB is derived from analysis of coastlines and relevant features in the nearshore-foreshore coastal shallow waters. It follows that a coastal state that has poorly mapped, poorly interpreted and poorly defined coastlines will face limitations when assembling its TSBM. These issues necessarily lead to poor results in terms of the delineation of the outer limits to maritime claims and the delimitation of maritime boundaries.

The counterpoint then is offered by this type of emerging technology that has the potential to shift outermost basepoints significantly seaward compared with more conservative or antiquated nautical charting. Indeed, enhanced coastal mapping can dramatically add to the offshore mathematically computed outer limit lines for maritime jurisdictional zones, as is thus key to achieving the most seaward position for the outer limits of maritime jurisdictional claims. For example, by correcting mis-mapped islands (different by several thousands of meters), missed smaller islets, sandbars and sand spits, shallow reefs (that fall dry) and/ or isolated rocks (that become exposed as changes in tidal sequences occur), substantial shifts in territorial sea, contiguous zone, EEZ and even extended continental shelf limits can be achieved. At the more extreme end of the scale of coastal areas tested to date (in over 125 coastal states by Fugro), updates and redefinitions of older, poorly mapped and pos-itionally inaccurate representations of coastlines or nearshore-foreshore relevant coastal features have delivered precision improvements of up to 16 kilometers.[57] The potential impact of this technology is illustrated at Figure 1.7 in the context of the definition of straight baselines – specific-ally a comparison between a SatRecon (4DSSM Image) of Vietnam's coastline and its claimed straight baselines, showing a potential gain in basclinc location of approximately 1.1 kilometers.

1.2.1.5   Limitations

This technology does have its limitations, but under ideal conditions, and with extensive global testing, the results have consistently shown an

---

[57] Robert van de Poll & Neils Anderson, New Modern-Day 3D SSM Satellite Imagery Analysis to Aid in Baseline Quality Controls (unpublished presentation) at Advisory Board on the Law of the Sea (ABLOS) 9th Conference: Pushing the Limits of UNCLOS (2011) (on file with the authors).

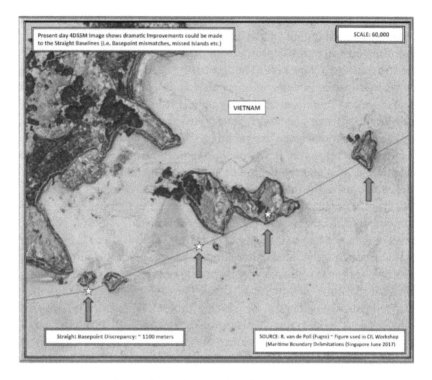

Figure 1.7   Vietnam's straight baselines overlayed on a SatRecon (4DSSM Image)
Source: Robert van de Poll[58]

ability to "see" through the water column up to 25 meters.[59] The resulting data (for this technology) depict seabed morphology only, not bathymetry, as actual water depth corrections are neither possible nor being considered.

Penetration of data is based upon turbidity levels and/or aerosol at time of imaging and is limited to approximately 20–25 meter morphological imaging for the purposes of determining changes in ground gradients to aid in highlighting possible navigational obstructions and hazards. As this is still optical technology, aerosol (air) conditions and/or marine (water) conditions can greatly affect the results.

[59] Pieter Bekker & Robert van de Poll, Unlocking the Arctic's Resources Equitably: Using a Law-and-Science Approach to Fix the Beaufort Sea Boundary, 34 INT'L J. MARINE & COASTAL L. 163, 191 n. 81 (2019).

[58] *Id.*

The main concept of the "4D" is a time-based (4th "D") seabed analysis technique, where three-dimensional identified seabed morphological features on one satellite scene can be identified and when cross-referenced across multiple other satellite scenes covering the same area of interest from other dates, can consistently show these features do exist over time, verifying that these are "real" mappable features. This technique is well-defined and consistently rules out false positives.

These false positives can be classified as being "image artifacts" that can impact what the final results for the SatRecon (4DSSM Images) will look like. This still uses satellite imagery as a source of information and features present in the various satellite scene sources will impact the final results; therefore, considerations must be made for image artifacts, as these could lead to false 4DSSM feature identification. These would include, but are not be limited to, the following features: (1) water depth; (2) water clarity; (3) wind; (4) waves; (5) currents; (6) cloud cover; (7) haze; (8) fog; (9) rain; (10) sedimentation (turbidity); (11) algae; (12) smoke; (13) ice; (14) vessels; (15) man-made infrastructure; and (16) ports and harbors (dredging).[60]

1.2.2 Emerging Technology in Maritime Boundary Dispute Resolution

Coastal states, in common with other members of the international community, are bound to settle disputes, including those with respect to competing maritime claims, through peaceful means as provided for by the UN Charter. This requires that all member states "shall settle their international disputes by peaceful means in such a manner that international peace and security, and justice, are not endangered."[61] This is reaffirmed in the dispute settlement provisions of UNCLOS contained in Part XV of the Convention, with Article 279 providing that parties to the Convention "shall settle any dispute between them" concerning its interpretation or application "by peaceful means" in accordance with the UN Charter. Further, Article 283(1) of UNCLOS underscores this by indicating that where a dispute arises between parties to the Convention regarding its interpretation or application, they "shall

---

[60] Robert van de Poll (2020), Address at the University of Southern Mississippi: New Developments in Mapping Sub-section (May 26–27, 2020) (unpublished presentation) (on file with the authors).

[61] UN Charter, art. 2, ¶ 3.

proceed expeditiously to an exchange of views regarding its settlement by negotiation or other peaceful means." As far as the means of peaceful dispute settlement, Article 33(1) of the UN Charter refers to dispute resolution through "negotiation, enquiry, mediation, conciliation, arbitration, judicial settlement, resort to regional agencies or arrangements," but makes it clear that this is a nonexhaustive list through the phrase "or other peaceful means of their own choice."

With respect of maritime boundary dispute resolution specifically, the vast majority of settlements have been achieved through bilateral negotiations, with some trilateral negotiations also occurring with respect, for example, to establishing tripoint agreements where bilateral maritime boundaries converge and meet. Negotiations can also be considered as an essential precursor to the application of any other form of peaceful dispute resolution. As the ICJ observed in its ruling in the North Sea Continental Shelf cases, the parties are "under an obligation to enter into negotiations with a view to arriving at an agreement, and not merely to go through a formal process of negotiation as a sort of prior condition for the automatic application of a certain method of delimitation in the absence of agreement."[62] Such negotiations must therefore be meaningful, something that cannot occur if the parties concerned merely insist on their own positions "without contemplating any modification of it."[63]

Conciliation, a formalized version of mediation or a facilitated negotiation has to date only been used to achieve two maritime boundary agreements. Nonbinding conciliation was used to resolve a maritime delimitation dispute between Iceland and Norway in the early 1980s. The unanimous recommendations of the Conciliation Commission delivered in June 1980 were essential to the parties agreeing on both a continental shelf boundary between Iceland and the Norwegian island of Jan Mayen and a joint zone straddling that line but in an uneven manner, with 39 percent on the Icelandic side and 61 percent on the Norwegian side.

More recently, Timor-Leste invoked compulsory conciliation under UNCLOS to help resolve its disputes with Australia over maritime delimitation in the Timor Sea.[64] While Australia initially challenged the

---

[62] North Sea Continental Shelf (F.R.G. v. Den., F.R.G. v. Neth.), Judgment, 1969 I.C.J. Rep. 3 (Feb. 20), ¶ 85, p.47.

[63] Id.

[64] Timor Sea Conciliation (Timor-Leste v. Austl.), PCA Case Repository (Perm. Ct. Arb. 2018); see also Press Release, Conciliation between the Democratic Republic of Timor-Leste and the Commonwealth of Australia (July 29, 2016).

competence of the Conciliation Commission, once the objections were dismissed and the Commission concluded that it had competence,[65] the conciliation process proceeded in good faith. Although the conciliation process was compulsory under the dispute resolution provisions of UNCLOS, the Conciliation Commission could only facilitate negotiations and provide nonbinding recommendations. The Commission was, however, successful in positively engaging the parties and facilitating an integrated package of confidence-building mechanisms.[66] Ultimately, the conciliation led to Australia and Timor-Leste signing a treaty that established their maritime boundaries in the Timor Sea on March 6, 2018.[67]

Additionally, the international jurisprudence in maritime boundary delimitation is rich, featuring over two dozen cases. As noted earlier, since the 2009 Black Sea case, international courts and tribunals have adopted a three-stage process to maritime delimitation. Maritime boundary dispute resolution has long had a technical dimension alongside legal and, crucially, political ones. Unsurprisingly, coastal states have tended to be keen adopters of emerging technologies where they can deliver a better outcome. In the context of negotiated solutions to maritime boundary delimitation disputes, the uptake and acceptance of new technologies is generally achieved by mutual consent and so is arguably less problematic. In the boundary negotiations context, the technical experts from either negotiation team will likely meet at an early stage in discussions. Alternatively, a technical subcommittee to the negotiations may be formed. The objective of such discussions is to reconcile technical approaches, for example, to confirm the geodetic datum to which the coordinates of the turning points will be referred. A further and potentially key consideration is often to exchange information on the parties' respective baselines and ideally verify each other's territorial sea basepoints. Once this is achieved, calculation of a geodetically robust strict equidistance line can be jointly determined by the technical teams involved, which can serve as an important starting point for negotiations.[68]

---

[65] *Id.*

[66] These included termination of the 2006 Australia–Timor-Leste Treaty on Certain Maritime Arrangements in the Timor Sea (CMATS) and withdrawal of two cases Timor-Leste had initiated against Australia before the PCA concerning alleged espionage.

[67] Treaty Establishing Maritime Boundaries in the Timor Sea (Austl.–Timor-Leste), Mar. 6, 2018, as Annex 28 of the Report and Recommendations of the Compulsory Conciliation Commission between Timor-Leste and Australia on the Timor Sea, May 9, 2018.

[68] CHRIS CARLETON & CLIVE H. SCHOFIELD, DEVELOPMENTS IN THE TECHNICAL DETERMINATION OF MARITIME SPACE: DELIMITATION, DISPUTE RESOLUTION,

A pertinent example of this approach is provided by the recent negotiation of the maritime boundary agreement between Denmark and Poland concerning the maritime area in the Baltic Sea between the Danish Island of Bornholm and Poland's mainland coast. At the very outset of the negotiation process, the parties reached accord on an agreed geodetic and digital framework, including the datum, coordinate systems and charts to be used, as well as the methods and software to be used in the discussions. This agreement on these issues ensured transparency and reproducibility of the calculations of the proposed maritime boundary delimitation lines and associated distance, relevant coastal lengths and area calculations such that the two sides had confidence in a level technical playing field on which to negotiate within their respective legal and diplomatic mandates (Figure 1.8).

As explored with respect to SatRecon (4DSSM Images), the technologies for collecting information on the location of the coast and/or relevant nearshore-foreshore coastal features and thus normal baselines, especially through novel remote-sensing techniques, are advancing rapidly. Technically oriented exchanges at the early stage of negotiations as to the appropriate and agreed method of collecting, in particular, baselines information. This can thus provide an important foundation for negotiations. Additionally, such exchanges can help to build trust, especially where capacity may be lacking or where asymmetry between negotiating partners exists.

Regional capacity-building initiatives can assist in helping to overcome technical deficiencies and imbalances. For example, among the Pacific island States and territories, initial technical work supported by the Pacific Islands Forum Fisheries Agency (FFA) focused on defining baselines with the objective of defining indicative equidistance lines to divide income arising from fishing license fees. More recently, the Pacific Boundaries Project, a partnership involving the South Pacific Community (SPC) and Australia, with the support of the FFA, Global Resource Information Data Network (GRID-Arendal) and the Commonwealth Secretariat, has made remarkable progress, enabling the Pacific Island States to clarify the extent of their maritime jurisdictions. The project has provided support for Pacific Island States in the preparation of their extended continental shelf submissions for the CLCS, which inevitably included technical support on baselines definition. Moreover, the project offered technical and diplomatic capacity-building, support and, importantly, a forum including annual

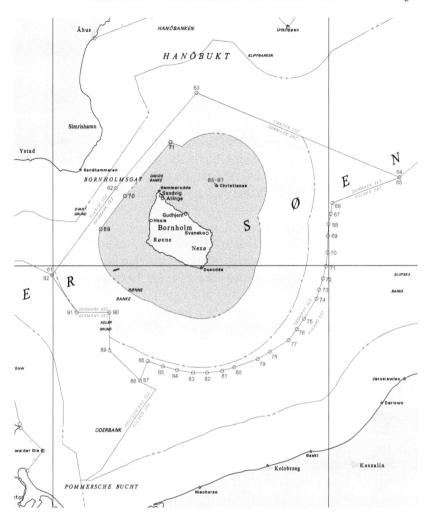

Figure 1.8   Maritime boundary delimitation between Denmark (Bornholm) and Poland
Source: Danish Geodata Agency, Map D, 2021

meetings in Australia to assist in furthering negotiations toward the delimitation of maritime boundaries between them, resulting in a doubling in maritime boundary agreements in the region over the past decade.[69] There are also technical and technological dimensions to visualizing and

---

[69] *See* Robyn Frost et al., *Redrawing the Map of the Pacific*, 95 MARINE POL'Y 302 (2018).

presenting negotiating positions, formulating fallback positions, and, ultimately, ensuring that the technical content of any final agreed boundary treaty is robust and free of error.

1.2.2.1   International Cases

Technical errors have occurred in the context of maritime boundary disputes that were resolved by resorting to international courts and tribunals to render binding decisions. Fundamental technical considerations have been largely addressed in more recent decisions. For example, international judgments and awards now routinely include specifications as to the geodetic datum to which the coordinates of delimited maritime boundary lines refer, as well as indications as to what type of straight line joins the coordinates. These improvements are to be welcomed and arguably represent an important response to criticism of past decisions on technical grounds.

It is also clear from the sketch maps supporting these rulings that international courts and tribunals increasingly have access to cartographic and some degree of technical support. Despite such decisions commonly including long lists of the members of the court or tribunal as well as of the opposing legal teams, technical experts and support staff, in some cases, it is unclear precisely who provides cartographic and technical support. This lack of transparency over the source of technical support for international courts and tribunals is troubling.

As is the case in the context of negotiations, there is a technical or cartographic role in the presentation of each party's case and the presentations of the parties have, over time, become ever more sophisticated. This trend can be expected to continue. There is also some evidence of a greater openness of at least some courts and tribunals to taking into account in their deliberations emerging technologies and scientific and technical expertise. For example, in the South China Sea case, in which China refused to participate, the arbitral tribunal nonetheless went to considerable lengths to take China's views into consideration and not to simply rely on evidence presented by the Philippines and its experts alone. On the scientific and technical side, the Tribunal appointed its own independent hydrographic expert. Grant Boyes of Geoscience Australia was appointed as the Tribunal's independent expert hydrographer.[70] Additionally, expert reports were commissioned on navigational safety and coral reef issues.[71]

---

[70] China Sea (Phil. v. China), PCA Case Repository, ¶ 85 (Perm. Ct. Arb. 2016).
[71] Id., ¶ 133.

Yet, while the Tribunal viewed the satellite imagery evidence presented by the Philippines to be "helpful," it was unconvinced concerning its value with respect to the determination of the low-water line on the basis that the time of image capture did not align with high or low tide.[72] This is an issue that the four-dimensional nature of the SatRecon (4DSSM Image) techniques addresses through evaluation of multiple satellite images over time. Instead, the tribunal relied on historical surveys dating back over 150 years.[73] This example demonstrates there is a degree of caution and lack of comfort of some international judges with emerging technologies of this character. Overcoming such reluctance likely will take some time.

1.3 Conclusion

Space-based technology is evolving swiftly. A unified global geodetic reference system has already been realized, which has helped achieve submeter positioning. This progress has proved a significant step forward in terms of enhanced positioning in ocean boundary-making and has assisted in eliminating technical errors. Advances have also been reached with respect to the development of a global height reference system and in the georeferencing of satellite imagery.

Emerging technology also has the potential to yield major advances in determining the location of the coast and thus normal baselines along it. This chapter highlighted the example of SatRecon (4DSSM Image) techniques for examining the land/sea interface at medium and/or high-resolution satellite images. These images have the potential to be a step change in interrogating and visualizing seaward most coastal and thus baseline positions. Rather than providing a substitute for hydrographic surveys, such images have the potential to indicate to coastal states priority areas for verification, with a view to

---

[72] *Id.*, ¶ 323. *See also* Steven Keating, *Rock or Island? It Was an UNCLOS Call: The Legal Consequence of Geospatial Intelligence to the 2016 South China Sea Arbitration and the Law of the Sea*, 9 J. Nat'l Sec. L. & Pol'y 509, 534–37 (2018).

[73] Despite this, global mean sea level rise over the period was conservatively suggested to be "at least 20 cm." *See* Youna Lyons, Lou Quang Hung & Pavel Tkalich, *Determining High-Tide Features (or Islands) in the South China Sea under Article 121(1): A Legal and Oceanography Perspective.* The South China Sea Arbitration: The Legal Dimension 128, 133 (S. Jayakumar et al. eds., 2018).

advancing the limits of maritime claims seaward and assisting in the delimitation of maritime boundaries.

Ultimately, these emerging technologies and technical advances in maritime boundary dispute resolution have significant potential to assist in the delivery of more stable and enduring maritime delimitation lines in the interests of good ocean governance, the rule of law at sea, and international peace and security.

2

Renewable Energy and the Law of the Sea

OLIVIA WOOLLEY

2.1   Introduction

Over the past few decades, several different technologies have been developed for generating electricity offshore.[1] Offshore wind energy produced by turbines fixed to the seabed is well-established, and turbine generating capacities continue to increase.[2] Tidal barrage energy is also well-established.[3] Wave and tidal current energy technologies are moving gradually from prototype stages toward potential future commercialization.[4] Ocean thermal energy conversion has been discussed as a means of producing power with enormous potential for decades, but high capital costs, a lack of practical experience and environmental concerns

---

[1] INTERNATIONAL RENEWABLE ENERGY AGENCY, OFFSHORE INNOVATION WIDENS RENEWABLE ENERGY OPTIONS: OPPORTUNITIES, CHALLENGES, AND THE VITAL ROLE OF INTERNATIONAL CO-OPERATION TO SPUR THE GLOBAL ENERGY TRANSFORMATION 1 (2018) (hereinafter IRENA OFFSHORE INNOVATION BRIEF).
[2] *Id.*, at 2.
[3] INTERNATIONAL RENEWABLE ENERGY AGENCY, INNOVATION OUTLOOK: OCEAN ENERGY TECHNOLOGIES 12, 26–35 (2020) (hereinafter IRENA OCEAN ENERGY TECHNOLOGIES).
[4] IRENA OFFSHORE INNOVATION BRIEF, *supra* note 1, at 8–9.

have prevented progress beyond small-scale prototypes.[5] Possibilities for using well-established onshore technologies for solar and geothermal power generation offshore are being explored. Finally, the introduction of floating wind turbines makes it possible to produce electricity from wind in marine areas that have previously been off limits because shallow water depths were needed to situate turbine foundations on the seabed.[6]

The emergence of these technologies has coincided with major advances in direct current cable technologies for transmitting electricity from where it is produced to consumers. High-voltage direct current (HVDC) cables now offer a preferable alternative to alternative current (AC) cables for the transmission of electricity from wind farms situated far out to sea.[7] Emerging HVDC voltage source converter (VSC) technologies offer more scope than was previously available for linking separate offshore transmission cables to create a meshed grid that is capable of conveying power from offshore wind farms to several potential destinations.[8] In this regard, Denmark has announced plans to create two "energy islands," one (Bornholm) on a Baltic Sea island, and the other as an artificial structure in the North Sea. The islands will serve as hubs for electricity generated by surrounding offshore wind farms, and will be connected and distribute power between Denmark and neighbouring countries.[9] It is envisaged that the hubs will also accommodate other technologies including for storage and hydrogen production from electricity supply when this is not required to meet consumer demand.[10]

The United Nations (UN) Convention on the Law of the Sea (UNCLOS) presciently anticipates offshore power production as an activity states may wish to undertake in their exclusive economic zones (EEZs).[11] Even so, the rapid rollout of marine power generation and transmission, coupled with possibilities opened up by floating wind

---

[5] IRENA Ocean Energy Technologies, *supra* note 3, at 13, 46–49.

[6] International Renewable Energy Agency, Floating Foundations: A Game Changer for Offshore Wind Power 1 (2016) (hereinafter IRENA Floating Foundations); IRENA Offshore Innovation Brief, *supra* note 1, at 10–11.

[7] Asimenia Korompili, Qiuwei Wu & Haoran Zhao, *Review of VSC HVDC Connection for Offshore Wind Power Integration*, 59 Renew. & Sustain. Ener. Rev. 1405 (2016).

[8] *Id.*

[9] Danish Energy Agency, About Energy Islands, www.ens.dk (last visited Mar. 31, 2021) (online); BBC, Denmark to Build "First Energy Island" in North Sea, www.bbc.co.uk/news/world-europe-55931873 (Jan. 27, 2022; last visited Mar. 6, 2022) (online).

[10] Danish Energy Agency, *supra* note 9.

[11] United Nations Convention on the Law of the Sea, Dec. 10, 1982, art. 56(1)(a), 1833 U.N.T.S. 397 (hereinafter UNCLOS).

turbines for their conduct without constructing fixed turbine foundations and in areas lying beyond the 200 nautical miles (M) maximum extent of coastal states' EEZs, raises questions of the legal framework that UNCLOS establishes. Fundamental considerations arise over whether and, if so, how offshore power technologies, particularly floating turbines, fit with the treaty's conceptualization of "installations," "structures" and "artificial islands." Possibilities for establishing an offshore grid that serves multiple states test the treaty's provision on the exercise by states of jurisdiction over sea uses. The anticipated massive growth of offshore power necessitates the fleshing out of its provisions on managing conflict between the rights and duties of states offshore. In addition, detailing of high-level duties for marine environmental protection is needed both to address the effects of offshore energy development on an industrial scale, and to manage them whilst addressing the combined existential threats posed for marine ecosystem functioning by climate change, ocean acidification, biodiversity loss and other consequences of already excessive pressures from human activities.

The chapter categorizes ways in which marine energy technologies are challenging the legal framework established by UNCLOS. It focuses on offshore wind energy, as it far exceeds other such technologies in its current development and future potential, but similar issues are raised by wave and tidal current electricity technologies as their commercialization progresses. Section 2.2 examines the allocation of rights to exploit offshore resources for electricity production, to undertake related activities and to apply national laws to their conduct amongst states. Section 2.3 looks at guidance on states' rights to apply their laws to the transmission of electricity from offshore turbines to onshore grids and at related potential for concurrent and conflicting jurisdictional claims. Particular consideration is given to rights to govern the development and operation of a multistate offshore wind electricity grid. Section 2.4 considers direction on situations where states' exercise of rights may affect other states in the exercise of their rights under the law of the sea, including of navigation. Do "due regard" and other requirements for reciprocal respect by states for each other's rights and duties under UNCLOS need further detailing to address problems that offshore renewables are likely to cause due to the immense areas of the seabed occupied by relevant projects?[12] Sections 2.5 and 2.6 examine the environmental aspect. Much

---

[12] For example, the Hornsea One development, located off the UK's east coast in the part of the North Sea under UK jurisdiction and currently the world's highest capacity

additional detailing of existing laws has already been provided under relevant treaty organizations to tackle the impacts of offshore power technologies. What more needs to be done to address the unprecedented scale of development at a time of environmental threat? How can the environmental benefits driving massive expansion of noncarbon-emitting means of energy generation be reconciled with the effects that these will have on already vulnerable marine environments?

The chapter concentrates on UNCLOS, which has been ratified by 167 of the 193 UN member states as well as the European Union (EU) and signed by fourteen more.[13] Some states, notably including Turkey and the United States, are either party only to one or more of the treaties agreed in 1958 at the first UN Conference on the Law of the Sea or to no law of the sea treaties.[14] Their relations with other states offshore are therefore governed either by the 1958 treaties when states concerned have ratified them or by customary international law. Space does not allow for examination of positions that differ to those under UNCLOS, and even the United States accepts that the balance of interests and regimes in the treaty reflect customary international law. Nearly all UN member states are parties to UNCLOS and it is the normative point of departure for any analysis in the field of oceans law and policy. Many of UNCLOS's key provisions are part of the law of the sea in customary international law or a strong case can be made for this because such a high proportion of UN member states, some 93 percent, have either ratified or signed UNCLOS.[15]

2.2   Rights to Exploit Resources

2.2.1   Electricity Generation

Coastal states have sovereignty over the territorial sea zone extending up to 12 M from their coastlines, and therefore have exclusive rights to conduct activities in them, including the generation and transmission of electricity and the construction and regulation of associated installations

---

operational offshore wind farm, covers an area of 407 km^2. *See* About the Project, Ørsted, https://hornseaprojectone.co.uk/about-the-project#project-timeline-2020   (last   visited Mar. 25, 2021) (online).

[13] UNCLOS, *supra* note 11.

[14] ROBIN CHURCHILL, *The 1982 UN Convention on the Law of the Sea.* THE OXFORD HANDBOOK ON THE LAW OF THE SEA 24, 35 (Donald Rothwell et al. eds., 2015).

[15] *Id.,* at 37–38, 45.

and infrastructure.[16] The position with regard to electricity generation in the EEZ is also clear. Article 56 of UNCLOS includes "the production of energy from the water, currents and winds" amongst "other activities for the economic exploitation and exploration of the zone," which the relevant coastal state has sovereign rights to conduct.[17] Coastal states also have the exclusive right in their EEZs to authorize and regulate the construction, operation and use of artificial islands and of installations and structures for the purposes provided for in Article 56.[18] The position is less clear where the continental shelf subject to the jurisdiction of a coastal state extends beyond its EEZ as Part VI of UNCLOS does not expressly confer permission for energy production from the waters, currents and winds. This determination is not surprising as the continental shelf regime laid down in Part VI is concerned with exploitation of the seabed and subsoil, and waters lying above it where it extends beyond a coastal state's EEZ belong to the high seas.

It has been suggested that Article 80 of UNCLOS may create de facto exclusive rights for states to produce electricity from turbines placed on their continental shelves by advising that "Article 60 applies *mutatis mutandis* to artificial islands, installations and structures on the continental shelf."[19] Article 60 refers back to the sovereign rights conferred by Article 56. Yet there are grounds for questioning an interpretation of this provision that would turn it into a backdoor route for conferring a right to conduct activities not involving the exploitation and exploration of the natural resources of the seabed and its subsoil in the continental shelf zone.[20]

All states have the freedom to construct artificial islands and erect installations for any purpose, including power generation, in waters forming part of the high seas.[21] The high seas include waters overlying

---

[16] UNCLOS, *supra* note 11, art. 2.

[17] *Id.*, art. 56(1)(a).

[18] *Id.*, arts. 60(1)(a)–(b).

[19] Sarah McDonald & David L. VanderZwaag, *Renewable Ocean Energy and the International Law and Policy Seascape: Global Currents, Regional Surges*, 29 OCEAN Y.B. ONLINE 299, 302–3 (2015).

[20] Karen N. Scott, *Tilting at Offshore Windmills: Regulating Wind Farm Development within the Renewable Energy Zone*, 18 J. ENV'T L. 89, 96 (2006);

Paul Elsner & Suzette Suarez, Renewable Energy from the High Seas: Geo-spatial Modelling of Resource Potential and Legal Implications for Developing Offshore Wind Projects Beyond the National Jurisdiction of Coastal States, 128 ENERGY POL'Y 919, 925 (2019).

[21] UNCLOS, *supra* note 11, art. 87(1)(d).

the seabed in areas where the seabed subject to a coastal state's jurisdiction extends beyond its EEZ – that is, an "extended" or "outer" continental shelf. States other than the coastal state would be entitled to generate power in these waters if the exclusivity argument previously discussed is not made out.[22] The exercise of this freedom would be subject in practice to the coastal state's exclusive right to authorize, construct and regulate artificial islands and also installations and structures that may interfere with the exercise of its continental shelf rights.[23]

Questions arise over whether the legal status of floating offshore wind turbines would differ from that of fixed turbines under UNCLOS because of differences in how they are fixed to the seabed. Floating turbines sit on top of foundations that are anchored or moored to the seabed.[24] They are therefore easier to move than fixed turbines whose foundations are pile-driven into the seabed or held to it by their weight.[25] In view of their greater mobility, could floating turbines be viewed as "ships" under UNCLOS rather than as "installations"? If so, they would be required to register with a flag state and would be partially subject to that state's jurisdiction even where being used to produce electricity in the EEZ of a different coastal state.[26] In addition, rights and responsibilities of coastal states in respect of installations in EEZs, including the establishment of safety zones, would not apply.[27] Some treaties concerned with shipping include floating devices within their definition of "ship" even where they are not able to move independently, although others do not, using the ability to navigate and to transport people or goods as essential characteristics in their definitions.[28]

Unfortunately, the terms "ship" and "installation" are not defined under UNCLOS.[29] That lack of fidelity necessarily allows coastal states

---

[22] Id., arts. 78, 87(1)(d).

[23] Id., art. 80.

[24] IRENA Floating Foundations, supra note 6, at 5.

[25] Alexander Severance & Martin Sandgren, Flagging the Floating Turbine Unit: Navigating towards a Registerable, First-Ranking Security Interest in Floating Wind Turbines, 39 Tul. Mar. L.J. 1, 7–13 (2014).

[26] UNCLOS, supra note 11, art. 92.

[27] Id., art. 60.

[28] Rainer Lagoni, Merchant Ships. Max Planck Encyclopedia of Public International Law, ¶¶ 1–2 (Anne Peters ed., 2011); Robert Veal, Michael Tsimplis & Andrew Serdy, The Legal Status and Operation of Unmanned Maritime Vehicles, 50 Ocean Dev. & Int'l L. 23, 25–26 (2019).

[29] Id.; Alex G. Oude Elferink, Artificial Islands, Installations and Structures. Max Planck Encyclopedia of Public International Law, ¶ 1 (Anne Peters ed., 2011).

some discretion in defining what should be regarded as a ship or installation in national legislation but does not give them unbridled freedom to
do so. To reach that conclusion would be to ignore that the intended
scopes of these two terms are implied by their use to allocate certain
rights, duties and powers to specified states.[30] The current stage of
technological development for floating turbines would make it difficult
to argue credibly that it would be inappropriate to view them when in
situ as falling under "installation" as the term is used in UNCLOS. The
fact that means are used to hold them to a particular location, albeit
without the permanence of turbines with fixed foundations, fits within an
ordinary understanding of "installation."[31] UNCLOS, whilst not defining
installations, clearly views them alongside artificial islands and structures
as entities that shipping should be protected from and vice versa, including by the establishment of safety zones because of their occupation of
marine space and their more than momentary immobility.[32] In addition,
turbines installed to date and planned developments have been or are to
be towed by ships to their destination.[33]

As with other resources that all states have equal rights to exploit in
principle, concerns arise that a resource for low carbon energy supplies
from which all could benefit if it is used appropriately for this purpose is
currently open for exploitation by any state possessing the capacity to do
so. The fear with such resources is that their "commons" nature allows
capture and use of the resource by the wealthiest most technically
advanced states in ways that only they benefit from, or that is suboptimal
for states collectively in other respects.[34] Alternatively, the potential value
for decarbonization could be squandered by use of the high seas for
activities that prevent their use for renewable energy production.
Concerns of this nature were of academic interest only until recently
due to the limitations of offshore renewable energy technologies (e.g.,

---

[30] Veal et al., *supra* note 28, at 26–27.
[31] Oxford English Dictionary Online, Installation (defining *installation* as "a mechanical
apparatus set up or put in position for use") https://shib.dur.ac.uk/idp/profile/SAML2/
POST/SSO?execution=e1s1 (last visited Mar. 31, 2021) (online).
[32] UNCLOS, *supra* note 11, arts. 60(3)–(7), 147, 258–62.
[33] Zhiyu Jiang, *Installation of Offshore Wind Turbines: A Technical Review*, 139 RENEW. &
SUSTAIN. ENER. REV. 110, 576 (2021).
[34] PHILIPPE CULLET, DIFFERENTIAL TREATMENT IN INTERNATIONAL ENVIRONMENTAL
LAW 23 (2003); Elisa Morgera, *The Need for an International Legal Concept of Fair and
Equitable Benefit Sharing*, 27 EUR. J. INT'L L. 353, 358 (2016).

offshore wind energy could only be exploited in areas with a maximum seabed depth of around 50 m because of their fixed foundations), but have been made more tangible by the development of floating wind turbine technology.[35] The early stage of the technology's development, the currently very high capital costs of floating turbine power plants, and questions over the feasibility and financial viability of transmitting electricity from areas lying much farther out to sea than the most distant wind farms under current contemplation mean that related problems are not imminent.[36] Even so, advance consideration of them would be desirable in view of potential benefits from the resource for humankind. It should also be borne in mind that the rate at which offshore power technologies have improved and that costs for producing electricity from them have declined have far exceeded expectations.[37]

The development of floating turbine technology has prompted questions on the legal basis for electricity generation in the high seas. The high seas freedoms set out at Article 87(1) of UNCLOS do not include the production of energy from water, currents and winds, but states are free to "construct artificial islands and other installations permitted under international law."[38] The list of freedoms is also not exclusive.[39] UNCLOS is silent on which state has the right to exercise jurisdiction over an installation established on this basis.[40] However, references in the treaty to installations having a "state of registry" in connection with the prosecution of unauthorized broadcasting, the adoption of pollution controls for activities in the area and identification markings for scientific research installations envisage that jurisdiction for applying and enforcing relevant laws will lie with whichever state an installation is registered.[41] It would therefore fall to the registry state to comply with its duty under UNCLOS to reduce, control and prevent pollution from installations including by "preventing accidents," "dealing with emergencies" and "ensuring the safety of operations at sea."[42] UNCLOS does not establish an equivalent regime for installations to that of the flag state

---

[35] *See* IRENA FLOATING FOUNDATIONS, *supra* note 6, at 1, 4.

[36] *Id.*

[37] *See* IRENA OFFSHORE INNOVATION BRIEF, *supra* note 1, at 3–5.

[38] UNCLOS, *supra* note 11, art. 87(1)(d).

[39] Elsner & Suarez, *supra* note 20, at 924–25.

[40] *Id.*, at 925; CHATHAM PARTNERS, OFFSHORE WIND IN HIGH SEAS: UNLIMITED POTENTIAL BEYOND NATIONAL CONTROL? 13–14 (2019).

[41] UNCLOS, *supra* note 11, arts. 109(3)(b), 209(2), 262.

[42] *Id.*, art. 194(3)(d).

under which parties must set conditions for conferring their nationality on a ship whilst ships must register with a state and take on its nationality.[43] This suggests that, under UNCLOS, the nationality of a high seas installation is that of the state exercising its freedom to construct an installation in or to produce power from the winds of the high seas. However, UNCLOS is silent on this.

Express permission is lacking for states to establish safety zones around installations in the high seas save where they are used for carrying out activities in the area or for marine scientific research.[44] Compliance with national laws that establish such zones would therefore depend on whether other states regard themselves as bound by their "due regard" duty to respect constraints on their enjoyment of freedoms, such as in the vicinity of a wind farm. Section 2.4 examines the scope for interstate disputes over whether blocking off high seas areas by constructing large offshore wind farms with safety zones around them is compatible with the sponsoring state's duty to show due regard to the enjoyment of freedoms by other states.

In addition, legal scholars have asked questions about how power production from floating wind turbines would fit with certain UNCLOS provisions governing activities offshore. First, will rules concerning uses of the seabed apply to this technology, given that the turbines are not fixed to the seabed by permanent foundations?[45] As with fixed turbines, the answer will turn on whether Chapter VI of UNCLOS on the continental shelf is applicable to development that does not involve exploitation of the seabed and its resources. Second, would floating wind turbine developments be subject to the regime established for the area, and, if so, how would the regime affect such development?[46] Impacts are likely to be limited to rules governing relationships between area activities and other sea uses. Attachment of floating turbines to the seabed does not fall under UNCLOS's definition of the "activities of exploration for and exploitation of resources of the area" to which the Part XI regime applies.[47]

[43] *Id.*, arts. 91–92.
[44] *Id.*, arts. 147(2)(c), 194(3)(d).
[45] McDonald & VanderZwaag, *supra* note 19, at 303; Richard Barnes, *Energy Sovereignty in Marine Spaces*, 29 INT'L J. MARINE & COASTAL L. 573, 591 (2019).
[46] Barnes, *supra* note 45, at 591.
[47] UNCLOS, *supra* note 11, arts. 1(3), 133(a), 134(2).

2.2.2   Electricity Transmission

UNCLOS is silent on the laying of cables for transmitting electricity from generating stations that it gives coastal states the exclusive right to establish in their EEZs. It has been suggested that this was not seen as necessary as the exclusive right to produce energy in the EEZ must carry with it a right to lay cables from generating stations to the coastal state's onshore transmission system if it is to be given effect.[48] The later confirmation that rules at Article 79 on laying cables on the seabed where this is subject to the jurisdiction of a coastal state do not interfere with the coastal state's "jurisdiction over cables constructed or used in connection with the ... operations of artificial islands, installations and structures under its jurisdiction" appears to confirm this assumption.[49] In any event, Article 79 advises that "[a]ll States are entitled to lay submarine cables ... on the continental shelf," subject to coastal state regulation and other considerations that the article mentions.[50] This provision means that power from generating stations situated in one state's EEZ could be transmitted through another state's EEZ if that was more convenient than exclusive direct connection to the onshore grid of the state in whose EEZ the generating station is situated. This right would be of little value without agreement of the coastal state concerned for cable laying and electricity transmission in the territorial sea over which it has full sovereignty and for connection to its onshore electricity system. This is a first instance of the need for collaboration between states if best use is to be made of the offshore renewable electricity resource.

All states enjoy the freedom to lay submarine cables in the high seas. This freedom is subject to Part VI of UNCLOS where cables are laid on parts of the continental shelf under the jurisdiction of a coastal state.[51] It has again been argued, although it is not stated in UNCLOS, that the freedom must include the right to use cables laid to transmit electricity if it is to be given effect.[52] As with the right to lay cables to transmit electricity produced in one state's EEZ across another state's EEZ, the freedom would be of limited value without ultimate agreement from terminus states for cables to be laid in their territorial seas and connected

---

[48] HANNAH KATHARINA MÜLLER, A LEGAL FRAMEWORK FOR A TRANSNATIONAL OFFSHORE GRID IN THE NORTH SEA 34–38 (2015).

[49] UNCLOS, *supra* note 11, art. 79(4); MÜLLER, *supra* note 48, at 36.

[50] UNCLOS, *supra* note 11, art. 79(1).

[51] *Id.*, art. 87(1)(c).

[52] MÜLLER, *supra* note 48, at 42.

to their onshore electricity systems for onward transmission to consumers. Again, collaboration is needed for states to derive full benefit from the freedom.

2.2.3 Collaboration on Offshore Renewable Electricity Generation and Transmission

Interstate collaboration on developing offshore generation and transmission capacities could be more advantageous for states individually than exploiting offshore renewables resources alone. This is particularly the case where exploitation takes place in semienclosed seas such as the North Sea. It can enable greater economic efficiency and reduced environmental effects in exploiting the resource.[53] Grids combining connections to the electricity systems of other regional states with network connections for offshore renewables assist both with addressing renewable energy intermittency by giving access to electricity from more controllable renewables (e.g., hydropower) and with reducing regional costs of a low carbon electricity system by enabling flows from areas in which windy or sunny conditions are leading to electricity overproduction to those experiencing weather-related shortfalls. Such benefits may be lost if states do not collaborate from the outset on exploiting shared offshore renewable resources.

Adoption of interstate framework treaties under which relevant development takes place would assist with taking advantage of the benefits that collaboration may offer, including by preventing states from following pathways individually that would prevent a network able to yield those benefits from being constructed.[54] The North Sea states have recognized this in part through their work together under the North Seas Countries Offshore Grid Initiative and the North Seas Energy forum, founded respectively through a memorandum of understanding in

---

[53] OLIVIA WOOLLEY, PETER J. SCHAUMBERG & GRAHAM ST. MICHEL, *Establishing an Offshore Electricity Grid: A Legal Analysis of Grid Developments in the North Sea and in US Waters*. ENERGY NETWORKS AND THE LAW: INNOVATIVE SOLUTIONS IN CHANGING MARKETS 180, 181–82 (Martha M. Roggenkamp et al. eds., 2012); Olivia Woolley, *Overcoming Legal Challenges for Offshore Electricity Grid Development: A Case Study of the Cobra and Kriegers Flak Projects*. EUROPEAN ENERGY LAW REPORT IX 169, 169 (Martha M. Roggenkamp & Olivia Woolley eds., 2012).

[54] Olivia Woolley, *Governing a North Sea Grid Development: The Need for a Framework Treaty*, 14 COMPETITION & REGUL. IN NETWORK INDUS. 73, 91–94 (2013).

2010 and a political declaration on energy cooperation in 2016.[55] The Baltic Sea states have also made a joint declaration of intent to "work together to achieve sustainable, cost-efficient and environmentally friendly deployment of offshore wind in the Baltic Sea," including by coordinating relevant planning regimes.[56] In addition, Belgium, Germany and the Netherlands have each concluded political agreements with Denmark to assess options for cooperating on the latter's energy island projects and related offshore renewable generation and transmission developments.[57] The instruments, although they do not create binding legal obligations, illustrate how the advantages of collaboration on exploiting offshore renewable resources can lead to more formal arrangements with a soft law character, which may harden in time as the advantages of collaboration become more apparent. Economic and environmental efficiency considerations also inform arguments for collaboration within US waters between New England states on establishing a shared offshore grid to support their ambitions for substantial and rapid growth of offshore wind energy during the next fifteen years.[58]

2.3   Rights to Regulate

Clarity over which states' laws will apply to offshore energy development is essential for accessing the substantial investment needed for its construction and operation. Investors need knowledge of this to assess a project's financial viability and risks associated with its conduct. It is also vital for the gradual development of multistate electricity grids.[59] For example, which state's or states' law would govern decision-making on a request to connect a new offshore wind farm to existing infrastructure? To what extent can coastal states obstruct the development of such a grid in waters under their jurisdiction? In addition, legal control over wind farms connected to such a grid and over flows of electricity through them

---

[55] *See* NORTH SEAS ENERGY COOPERATION, THE NORTH SEAS COUNTRIES' OFFSHORE GRID INITIATIVE MEMORANDUM OF UNDERSTANDING (2010); *see also* NORTH SEAS ENERGY COOPERATION, POLITICAL DECLARATION ON ENERGY COOPERATION BETWEEN THE NORTH SEAS COUNTRIES (2016).

[56] EUROPEAN COMMISSION, JOINT DECLARATION OF INTENT: BALTIC SEA OFFSHORE WIND 3 (2020).

[57] Danish Energy Agency, *supra* note 9; *see also* § 1 herein.

[58] JOHANNES PFEIFENBERGER, SAM NEWELL & WALTER GRAF, OFFSHORE TRANSMISSION IN NEW ENGLAND: THE BENEFITS OF A BETTER PLANNED GRID 14–25 (2020).

[59] WOOLLEY ET AL., *supra* note 53, at 189–90.

are vital for electricity system security. Electricity systems must keep inputs and consumption of electricity in balance, and therefore cannot countenance legal uncertainty over responsibility for controlling access for electricity to networks and input from wind farms wherever they are located.

UNCLOS provides this clarity where electricity produced by wind farms constructed in a coastal state's EEZ is transported through cables connected to the state's onshore electricity transmission system. UNCLOS confers jurisdiction on coastal states over activities that it permits them to undertake in its EEZ, including the erection of installations.[60] Jurisdiction over cables from wind farms in a state's EEZ is not mentioned specifically, but it has been argued that this necessarily follows from the right to lay such cables.[61] That coastal states have control over their laying and operation is confirmed in Article 79.[62]

The ability to transport electricity directly from a power plant in a state's maritime areas to the onshore electricity system of other states is a core benefit of multistate offshore electricity grid projects such as the North Sea grid concept. It enables a pooling of renewable energy reserves among participating states so that they can be channelled to states to meet demand when renewable electricity produced in their own territories and maritime areas falls short. Offshore interconnectors linking the electricity systems of two states are already common in EU waters, and possibilities for hybrid developments combining interconnectors with offshore wind farm hubs as early contributions to the larger grid concept are being explored.[63]

As noted, states have the right or freedom to lay such cables on other states' continental shelves and in the high seas. States with exclusive rights over the continental shelf on which cables are being laid have rights to exercise jurisdiction over them for specified reasons, including protection of the marine environment, of national plans for seabed exploitation, and of existing cables and pipelines.[64] Where UNCLOS is less clear is on which states have the right to exercise jurisdiction over the development and operation of cables transmitting electricity through the continental shelf and EEZ areas attributable to coastal states (other than

---

[60] UNCLOS, *supra* note 11, arts. 56(1), 60(1)–(2).

[61] MÜLLER, *supra* note 48, at 33–36.

[62] UNCLOS, *supra* note 11, art. 79(4).

[63] NORTH SEAS ENERGY COOPERATION, Work Programme 2020–2023, 1–2 (2019).

[64] UNCLOS, *supra* note 11, art. 79.

the electricity-producing state) or on the high seas seabed in other respects. Rights and freedoms to lay cables on the seabed in these areas are not accompanied by direction on jurisdiction. There is no equivalent to the flag state concept for cable laying.[65] Indeed, it is hard to see how this would work with cables, such as interconnectors that have a physical connection to two different states' territories and electricity systems.

Principles of jurisdiction under public international law would support applying law to different facets of grid development and operation, such as initial construction, operation, further development, control over power production from offshore generating stations to maintain onshore electricity system balance of inputs/outputs, and prevention of harmful voltage fluctuation. Space does not allow for the full consideration of the principles and their application to scenarios that such an analysis would require. However, it is possible to conclude that it would reveal much scope for concurrent and potentially conflicting claims. This conclusion is based on the fact that offshore cables and generating stations are always in a relationship with the onshore electricity systems of states to which power is being transmitted at a point in time through physical interconnections that are only made possible by those states' consent. For example, this approach may support jurisdictional claims over:

- the development of cables by the states from which and to which electricity is to be transmitted
- operation of an interconnector by the two states whose onshore electricity systems are connected. Legal control over electricity flows is necessary to ensure that the connected systems can be kept in balance and for market functioning
- cables transmitting offshore electricity by the state in whose waters it was generated and by the state to whose territorial system the offshore generating plant is ultimately connected

The potential for concurrency and conflict grows with an offshore grid concept in which multiple states' electricity systems are connected via interlinked cables to offshore generating stations in several states'

---

[65] Douglas R. Burnett & Lionel Carter, International Submarine Cables and Biodiversity of Areas beyond National Jurisdiction: The Cloud Beneath the Sea 1, 45 (2017); Tara Davenport, *The High Seas Freedom to Lay Submarine Cables and the Protection of the Marine Environment: Challenges in High Seas Governance*, 112 Am. J. Int'l L. Unbound 139, 141–42 (2018).

maritime areas.[66] For example, multiple consumer states could have claims to exercise jurisdiction over the operation of an offshore network simultaneously where links between cables create a connection between their onshore electricity systems and wind farms producing electricity in other states' waters. The resulting uncertainty is not compatible with transnational projects for which a common position on design, development and operation is needed if they are to happen in the first place and function thereafter. In view of this, new international agreements may well be needed that capture the terms of such interstate agreements and particularly where institutions are required to oversee ongoing relations between them concerning offshore energy and grid development.[67] A framework treaty of the type adopted by the UK and Norway to govern collaboration on pipeline projects linking their territories with offshore oil production under their jurisdiction exemplifies a use of law to provide clarity over rights to regulate a category of infrastructure development.[68]

2.4 Conflict between Sea Uses

The introduction of offshore power production on an industrial scale to marine environments significantly increases potential for conflict between uses of the sea. The very large offshore wind farms now being constructed in farther out UK waters will occupy over 500 km^2 of the seabed.[69] Coastal states are permitted by UNCLOS to establish safety zones of up to 500 m radius around each turbine lying in their EEZs that vessels are not permitted to enter in the interests of safe navigation.[70] This rule can render the affected areas off-limits to other sea uses, including navigation and fishing in practice. It also creates potential for offshore renewable energy development to breach states' rights to undertake activities offshore in international law. Clarity is therefore desirable on where conflict in practice and in law may arise as well as thought on how this could be managed.

---

[66] MÜLLER, supra note 48, at 58–62; WOOLLEY ET AL., supra note 53, at 185–89.
[67] WOOLLEY ET AL., supra note 53, at 192–93.
[68] Framework Agreement Concerning Cross-Border Boundary Petroleum Cooperation, Nor.–UK, Apr. 4, 2005, Treaty Series No. 20 (2007) (UK); WOOLLEY ET AL., supra note 53, at 192–93.
[69] See, e.g., Dogger Bank Wind Farm, About the Project, www.doggerbank.com (last visited Mar. 31, 2021) (online).
[70] UNCLOS, supra note 11, arts. 60(4)–(5).

All states and their nationals are free in marine areas under the high seas regime (including waters lying above continental shelves extending beyond a coastal state's EEZ) to undertake activities including navigation, overflight, laying submarine cables and pipelines, the construction of artificial islands and installations, fishing and marine scientific research.[71] Exercise of the freedoms is constrained by the duty to show due regard both "for the interests of other States in their exercise of the freedom of the high seas" and for other states' rights "with respect to activities in the Area."[72] Article 58 preserves these entitlements to an extent in EEZs by allowing continued enjoyment in them for all states of freedom of navigation and overflight, and of laying cables and pipelines as well as "other internationally lawful uses of the seas related to these freedoms."[73] The coastal state and other states must have due regard to each other's rights and duties as well as respectively acting "in a manner compatible with" the Convention's provisions and in compliance with laws and regulations adopted by the coastal state in accordance with the Convention's provisions and other rules of international law "in so far as they are not incompatible with" Part V of UNCLOS. Article 78(2) states that the exercise of rights held by coastal states in their continental shelves "must not infringe or result in any unjustifiable interference" with navigation and other rights and freedoms of other states as provided for in UNCLOS.

In addition to these general duties, other provisions of UNCLOS require coastal states and other states to avoid obstruction of particular sea uses to a specified extent. Coastal states must respect the rights of ships under other states' flags to enjoy "innocent passage" through their territorial seas.[74] Article 60(7) of UNCLOS advises that coastal states may not erect artificial islands, structures and installations or adopt safety zones around them "where interference may be caused to the use of recognized sea lanes essential to international navigation."[75] Article 79(5) obliges all states when laying cables to have due regard to cables and pipelines already in place, including by not prejudicing possibilities for their repair.[76]

---

[71] *Id.*, arts. 78(2), 87(1).
[72] *Id.*, art. 87(2).
[73] *Id.*, art. 58(1)
[74] *Id.*, art. 17.
[75] *Id.*, art. 60(7).
[76] *Id.*, art. 79(5).

A number of questions are left unanswered by UNCLOS as to how conflicts between sea uses should be addressed. These concern the extent to which the exercise of coastal state rights in the EEZ and on continental shelves should be constrained because they would unlawfully impede navigation and the requirements to show due regard for and avoid undue interference over other states' rights and freedoms. How may offshore energy production and transmission be affected by such constraints? To what extent must other sea uses be preserved where threatened by offshore energy development?

On navigation, vessels of all states have a right to transit in innocent passage through the territorial seas of coastal states.[77] Given that the territorial sea is 12 M in breadth and that offshore wind farms can occupy large areas, commentators have questioned the extent renewable energy development could impede innocent passage without this becoming unlawful.[78] UNCLOS does not offer complete clarity on the position, but ships conducting innocent passage must adhere to coastal state regulations.[79] These may include requirements such as the use of sea lanes and traffic separation schemes for reasons including the safety of shipping in the vicinity of offshore installations.[80] Commentators conclude from this that states conducting innocent passage should accept a certain amount of interference by coastal states in order to exploit energy production possibilities in sovereign waters, although not to the extent that this would preclude innocent passage completely or otherwise interfere with it unreasonably.[81]

In the EEZs and waters overlying the continental shelves of coastal states, UNCLOS advises that installations and structures may not interfere with recognized sea lanes essential for international navigation but does not give guidance on compliance with the constraint.[82] There is no definition of the sea lanes concerned, and no international body is

---

[77] *Id.*, art. 17.

[78] HOSSEIN ESMAEILI, THE LEGAL REGIME OF OFFSHORE OIL RIGS IN INTERNATIONAL LAW 73 (2001); David Leary & Miguel Esteban, *Climate Change and Renewable Energy from the Oceans and Tides: Calming the Sea of Regulatory Uncertainty*, 24 INT'L J. MARINE & COASTAL L. 617, 632–33 (2009).

[79] UNCLOS, *supra* note 11, art. 21.

[80] McDonald & VanderZwaag, *supra* note 19, at 304–06; Yen-Chiang Chang, *Marine Renewable Energy: The Essential Legal Considerations*, 8 J. WORLD ENERGY L. & BUS. 26, 28–29 (2015).

[81] *Id.*; Leary & Esteban, *supra* note 78, at 632–33; Scott, *supra* note 20, at 102–03.

[82] UNCLOS, *supra* note 11, art. 60(7).

recognized as the authority for designating them.[83] Some educated guesses can be made as to the extent of the constraint this may impose. Sea lanes for which the International Maritime Organization (IMO) has adopted routeing schemes and traffic separation schemes are likely to fall among those that should not be interfered with.[84] Guidelines of the IMO advise states that structures must not be erected within them or near their terminations or seriously obstruct sea approaches to and from them.[85] It is a reasonable assumption therefore that noninterference with IMO-approved schemes is likely to represent a minimum requirement for respecting Article 60(7). Even so, further clarity on the provision's ramifications would be desirable in view of likely significant expansion of potential for conflict between offshore renewables and well-established sea routes.

The general due regard requirements aimed at achieving a balance of interests between states in pursuing their interests are necessarily non-prescriptive. What may amount to showing due regard depends on the particulars of cases under consideration.[86] There is an implicit expectation underlying this desire for balance that states will collaborate in order to prevent sea uses from precluding the exercise of rights and freedoms by other states.[87] Arbitral interpretation of the "due regard" duty under Part V of UNCLOS found that its discharge "will necessarily involve at least some consultation with the rights-holding State" in the "majority of cases."[88]

Growing potential for conflict between sea uses add to the desirability of transboundary environmental impact assessment (EIA) and transboundary involvement with and cooperation on marine spatial planning exercises as ways by states of observing their due regard requirements to their mutual satisfaction.[89] For example, commentators advocate the replacement of sectoral regulation of activities in areas beyond national jurisdiction (ABNJ) with a framework for coordinated spatial management in view of growth in the use of ABNJ and related risks of conflict

---

[83] Scott, *supra* note 20, at 100–01.

[84] *Id.*

[85] IMO Res. A.572(14) (Nov. 20, 1985); IMO Res. A.671(16) (Oct. 19, 1989); *see* Chang, *supra* note 80, at 34–35; Scott, *supra* note 20, at 100–02.

[86] BURNETT & CARTER, *supra* note 65, at 19.

[87] Barnes, *supra* note 45, at 590–92.

[88] Chagos Marine Protected Area (Mauritius v. UK), 31 R.I.A.A. 359, 571–72, para. 519 (Perm Ct. Arb. 2015); *see* BURNETT & CARTER, *supra* note 65, at 19.

[89] WOOLLEY ET AL., *supra* note 53, 192–93.

between incompatible activities and of harm to fragile marine ecosystems.[90] The prospect of offshore wind energy development in ABNJ lends further support for this argument.[91]

It also promotes exploration by relevant international organizations of how sea uses within their remit and offshore renewable energy development could be accommodated. The IMO's role in achieving such an accommodation regarding navigation is already noted. As an example of its work, the IMO agreed to a request for an extension to its traffic separation scheme operating in waters surrounding the UK's Land's End and Scilly Isles to accommodate the Wave Hub generating project.[92] The International Civil Aviation Organization (ICAO) has used powers under the Chicago Convention to lay down rules on marking and lighting for wind turbines if they are determined to be obstacles.[93] The ICAO also advised with regard to the potential for wind turbines to affect communications between air traffic controllers and flights, and whether that initial screening should be used to determine whether reference to an engineering authority for fuller analysis is required.[94] A conclusion that a wind farm development would affect aviation communications could lead to relocation of the proposed project. Alternatively, the ICAO has a reserved right under the Chicago Convention to restrict or prohibit flights over delineated areas for reasons of public safety.[95] There is no equivalent international authority to the IMO and ICAO for cable laying and operation. The International Cable Protection Committee (ICPC), a body representing the great majority of companies operating in the offshore telecommunications and power cables sector, has sought to fill this gap.[96] It recommends that those laying new power cables should observe a default 500 m exclusion zone for existing cables.[97] It has also explored

---

[90] Susanne Altvater, Ruth Fletcher & Cristian Passarello, *The Need for Marine Spatial Planning in Areas beyond National Jurisdiction*. MARITIME SPATIAL PLANNING: PAST, PRESENT, FUTURE 397, 398 (Jacek Zaucha & Kira Gee eds., 2019); Glen Wright et al., *Marine Spatial Planning in Areas beyond National Jurisdiction*, 132 MARINE POL'Y 103384 (2021).

[91] Elsner & Suarez, *supra* note 20, at 925.

[92] Leary & Esteban, *supra* note 78, at 64–65; Glen William Wright et al., *Establishing a Legal Research Agenda for Ocean Energy*, 63 MARINE POL'Y 126, 128 (2016).

[93] McDonald & VanderZwaag, *supra* note 19, at 312–14.

[94] *Id.*

[95] *Id.*

[96] International Cable Protection Committee, www.iscpc.org/ (last visited Mar. 28, 2021) (online).

[97] International Cable Protection Committee Res. 13 (Nov. 2013).

ways of observing reasonable regard for existing cables and new cable laying in relation to seabed minerals exploitation in the area and vice versa with the International Seabed Authority.[98] Whether the ICPC's recommendations have any legal influence will depend on whether states follow them in their practices on power cable laying. A recent European Commission study records that some EU states recommend protection zones for cables, but for varying reasons and with varying extents and degrees of impact on other activities.[99]

To conclude, initial growth in offshore renewable energy is already driving thought and action on how vague international law requirements on relations between different sea uses can be given effect. Need for further steps will only increase as demand for offshore power production grows. The ramifications for this prospect are likely to be twofold. First, we may expect further refinement and detailing of initial statements by sectoral authorities on how due regard toward activities for which they are responsible should be shown and of circumstances that would not be viewed as showing due regard and/or that would be prohibited by specific provisions of UNCLOS, such as Article 60(7). Second, we may expect growth in the conduct of state practice supporting the case for viewing conduct of marine spatial planning for all sea uses in areas covered and of strategic environmental assessment and EIA as essential components of showing "due regard" or avoiding "undue interference" under UNCLOS.

2.5   Marine Environmental Protection

Massive new development of offshore renewable energy generation and transmission would have potentially significant environmental effects, including by introducing energy and noise to the marine environment.[100] How may international law on protecting the marine environment affect such development?[101] Is further development of marine environmental

---

[98] INTERNATIONAL SEABED AUTHORITY, SUBMARINE CABLES AND DEEP SEABED MINING: ADVANCING COMMON INTERESTS AND ADDRESSING UNCLOS "DUE REGARD" OBLIGATIONS 5 (2015).

[99] MARTA PASCUAL, SECTOR FICHE: CABLES AND PIPELINES 198 (2018).

[100] Andrew B. Gill, *Offshore Renewable Energy: Ecological Implications of Generating Electricity in the Coastal Zone*, 42 J. APPLIED ECOLOGY 605 (2005); George W. Boehlert & Andrew B. Gill, *Environmental and Ecological Effects of Ocean Renewable Energy Development: A Current Synthesis*, 23 OCEANOGRAPHY 68 (2010).

[101] For an overview of international law on protecting the marine environment from the effects of offshore wind energy development, *see* Carlos Soria-Rodriguez, *The*

law required to accommodate rapid and ongoing growth of this sea use? A very broad duty on all states is conferred in UNCLOS to "protect and preserve the marine environment."[102] It also places more specific requirements on them for preventing, reducing and controlling pollution of the marine environment.[103] Pollution of the marine environment is defined in Article 1 of UNCLOS as

> the introduction by man, directly or indirectly, of substances or energy into the marine environment, including estuaries, which results or is likely to result in such deleterious effects as harm to living resources and marine life, hazards to human health, hindrance to marine activities, including fishing and other legitimate uses of the sea, impairment of quality for use of sea water and reduction of amenities.

Noise is not mentioned in the definition, but Scott makes a convincing argument that "energy" should be understood as covering not only heat but also sound waves "as a flow of acoustic energy."[104] The same argument could be applied to electromagnetic fields (EMFs) from cables,[105] although scientific studies have not established conclusively whether or not cable-derived EMFs are likely to harm marine species.[106]

The impacts of offshore energy may fall within UNCLOS's regime for environmental protection, but this offers little detailed guidance on what should be done. It leaves the development of regimes for addressing particular effects of sea uses to states to determine individually and in collaboration, including through regimes established to regulate uses of regional seas and to address specific sources of environmental concern.[107] To the extent that there is detailed guidance, this concerns polluting activities.

Some of the most significant effects of offshore renewable energy development, such as bird strikes and presenting barriers to wide-ranging

---

International Regulation for the Protection of the Environment in the Development of Marine Renewable Energy in the EU, 29 REV. EUR. COMPAR. & INT'L ENV'T L. 95 (2020).

[102] UNCLOS, *supra* note 11, art. 192.
[103] *Id.*, arts. 194, 207–12.
[104] Karen N. Scott, *International Regulation of Undersea Noise*, 53 INT'L & COMPAR. L.Q. 287, 292–94 (2004); *see also* JAMES HARRISON, SAVING THE OCEANS THROUGH LAW: THE INTERNATIONAL LEGAL FRAMEWORK FOR THE PROTECTION OF THE MARINE ENVIRONMENT 26–27 (2017).
[105] World Health Organization, Radiation: Electromagnetic Fields, www.who.int/newsroom/questions-and-answers/item/radiation-electromagnetic-fields (Aug. 4, 2016) (online).
[106] BURNETT & CARTER, *supra* note 65, at 41–42.
[107] McDonald & VanderZwaag, *supra* note 19, at 303–04.

marine mammals, are not due to pollution but to the conduct of the authorized activity itself.[108] It is unsurprising therefore that treaty regimes concerned with the birds, bats and migratory species for which offshore renewables specifically can pose environmental threats if incautiously sited have been proactive in developing guidance for state parties on how relevant development should be conducted and operated thereafter.[109] Resolutions concerned with planning and licensing for renewable energy development onshore and offshore have been adopted by parties to the Convention on Migratory Species of Wild Animals, to the Agreement on the Conservation of Populations of European Bats (EUROBATS), to the Agreement on the Conservation of African–Eurasian Migratory Waterbirds (AEWA), to the Convention on the Conservation of European Wildlife and Natural Habitats (the Bern Convention), to the Convention for the Protection of the Marine Environment of the North-East Atlantic (the OSPAR Convention) and to the Ramsar Convention on Wetlands of International Importance.[110] Resolutions that are not concerned with offshore renewables specifically but are likely to impact them have been adopted under these regimes as well as the Convention on Biological Diversity, Agreement on the Conservation of Cetaceans of the Black Sea, Mediterranean Sea and Contiguous Atlantic Area (ACCOBAMS), Agreement on the Conservation of Small Cetaceans of the Baltic, North East Atlantic, Irish and North Seas (ASCOBANS) and the International Whaling Commission.[111] Several of these resolutions concern the cumulative effects of noise on marine species, particularly cetaceans and other species whose hearing is important for migration and feeding.[112]

Some common themes emerge from these resolutions. First, several of them advocate precaution in offshore development.[113] In doing so, they

---

[108] Scott, *supra* note 20, at 104.

[109] Soria-Rodriguez, *supra* note 101, at 102–06.

[110] McDonald & VanderZwaag, *supra* note 19, at 306–12, 321–24; Scott, *supra* note 20, at 107–08; Soria-Rodriguez, *supra* note 101, at 101–05.

[111] McDonald & VanderZwaag, *supra* note 19, at 306–08, 311–12, 319–21; Scott, *supra* note 20, at 107–08; Soria-Rodriguez, *supra* note 101, at 99–104.

[112] Soria-Rodriguez, *supra* note 101, at 101–04.

[113] *See, e.g.,* Parties to the Agreement on the Conservation of Populations of European Bats Res. 8.4, ¶ 4 (Oct. 10, 2018) (hereinafter EUROBATS); OSPAR COMMISSION, OSPAR GUIDELINES ON ENVIRONMENTAL CONSIDERATIONS FOR OFFSHORE WIND FARM DEVELOPMENT 11 (2008); Conference of the Parties to the Convention on the Conservation of Migratory Species of Wild Animals Res. 7.5, ¶ 1 (Oct. 2017) (hereinafter Convention on Migratory Species Resolution 7.5); Parties to the Convention on the

recognize that much is unknown about how offshore development, including for energy production, may affect marine species. There is profound uncertainty over the impacts of noise to which offshore renewables will add significantly, and about how offshore wind development such as that envisaged by North Sea coastal states will affect the marine environment cumulatively.[114] In view of this, approaches to planning and conducting development are recommended that aim to reduce risks of negative impacts by avoiding environmentally sensitive areas.[115] Areas providing suitable habitats for species and for their key life stages such as mating, breeding, migrating and molting should be identified and development that could impact on them negatively avoided where possible. This is particularly the case where the species and habitat types concerned are endangered or rare. The identification of zones in which offshore energy development would not be problematic is also encouraged.[116] States should conduct strategic environmental assessments (SEAs) of plans for offshore development and EIAs for individual developments to help avoid environmentally harmful development. These provide transparency about environments and the predicted effects of development on them.[117] This information should be made available when a plan or project is put forward for adoption so that it can be taken into account by decision-makers. The process also enables the review of and comment on proposals by members of the public and civil society, including persons in other states, with comments received forming part of the information package that decision-makers may take into account. Assessment at the strategic stage assists with steering development away from locations where it would be harmful, hopefully reducing weight placed on EIAs at a later stage when major departure from schemes is made more difficult by time, money and political capital

Conservation of Migratory Species of Wild Animals Res. 12–14, ¶ 16 (Oct. 28, 2017) (hereinafter Convention on Migratory Species Resolution 12–14); Scott, *supra* note 20, at 107–08.

[114] Gill, *supra* note 100, at 612; Boehlert & Gill, *supra* note 100, at 77–78.

[115] *See, e.g.*, EUROBATS, *supra* note 113, ¶¶ 2–3; Parties to the Agreement on the Conservation of African–Eurasian Migratory Waterbirds Res. 5–16, ¶¶ 1.1–1.2 (May 18, 2012) (hereinafter AEWA); OSPAR COMMISSION, *supra* note 113, at 4; Convention on Migratory Species Resolution 7.5, *supra* note 113, ¶ 1.

[116] OSPAR COMMISSION, *supra* note 113, at 4–5.

[117] *See, e.g.*, EUROBATS, supra note 113, ¶ 6; AEWA, *supra* note 115, ¶ 1.1; OSPAR COMMISSION, *supra* note 113, at 3–5, 9–12; Parties to the Convention on the Conservation of Migratory Species of Wild Animals Res. 11.27, ¶ 2(a) (Dec. 3, 2014); Convention on Migratory Species Resolution 12–14, *supra* note 113, ¶ 7.

having been expended in the pursuit of strategic plans. In the same vein, marine spatial planning supports rational sea uses including the implementation of policy on offshore renewables by steering them away from areas and practices that could conflict with environmental obligations and with other valued marine activities.[118]

Assessment and planning at the national level will assist with reducing risks of environmental harm. However, uncoordinated action at the national level is by itself insufficient. It is not meaningful when thinking about the effects of development to separate marine ecosystems into separate national spaces and to focus only on particular types of development.[119] Collaboration among all coastal states bordering regional seas for planning and on the assessment of plans and project proposals can address the cumulative effects of offshore energy developments in combination with other anthropogenic effects in waters subject to the jurisdiction of coastal states bordering a marine area.[120] A review of cumulative effects should include the significant effects climate change is expected to have on the functioning of marine ecosystems.

Concerns over increasing anthropogenic pressures on marine ecosystems and their biodiversity offer further justification for introducing marine spatial planning in ABNJ alongside the growing risks of conflict between sea uses referred to earlier in this chapter.[121] Legal bases for interstate planning in remote areas already exist under UNCLOS. Article 118 places a duty on states to "cooperate with each other in the conservation and management of living resources in the areas of the high seas." The duty to cooperate on marine environmental protection under Article 197 interacts with an obligation when taking measures under Part XII of UNCLOS "to protect and preserve rare or fragile ecosystems as well as the habitat of depleted, threatened or endangered species and other forms of marine life."[122] The main legal challenge with introducing marine

---

[118] See, e.g., AEWA, supra note 115, ¶ 2.3; OSPAR COMMISSION, supra note 113, at 4–5; Conference of the Parties to the Convention on Biological Diversity Decision X/29, U.N. Doc. UNEP/CBD/COP/ DEC/X/29, ¶¶ 15, 37, 78 (Oct. 29, 2010); Soria-Rodriguez, supra note 101, at 100–01.

[119] Olivia Woolley, Ecological Governance for Offshore Wind Energy in United Kingdom Waters: Has an Effective Legal Framework Been Established for Preventing Ecologically Harmful Development?, 30 INT'L J. MARINE & COASTAL L. 765, 792 (2015) (hereinafter Ecological Governance).

[120] Id.

[121] See supra § 2.4.

[122] UNCLOS, supra note 11, art. 194(5).

spatial planning for ABNJ is that states lack the jurisdiction needed to create a holistic framework for regulating sea uses.[123] They would need to negotiate and adopt a treaty for this purpose that establishes an authority to oversee marine activities in areas subject to spatial planning regimes.[124] The ongoing negotiations for an international legally binding instrument under UNCLOS on the conservation and sustainable use of marine biological diversity of ABNJ focus on how area-based management tools such as marine spatial planning could assist with addressing global cooperation and coordination challenges in ABNJ.[125]

In summary, marine spatial planning, SEAs and EIAs are increasingly recognized in resolutions of treaty regimes as useful tools for advancing their environmental protection goals. Growing recognition supports arguments that rules of customary international law are emerging or have become established that require that they be used to aid adherence to common duties such as the prevention of harm to the marine environment and due diligence by states in the regulation of activities subject to their jurisdiction and the pursuit of sustainable development as an aspiration held in common. The rollout of offshore energy production on an industrial scale is a major reason for using these tools. In addition, the interest of multiple states in exploiting offshore renewable energy potential promotes their use by states collaboratively in order to counter cumulative environmental effects.

2.5.1   Climate Change, Offshore Renewables and Marine Environmental Protection

Marine ecosystems are suffering doubly due to climate change. Global warming is already causing negative changes due in part to oceans acting as heat sinks.[126] Absorption by oceans of much of the carbon dioxide that humans have added to the atmosphere is simultaneously causing acidification of sea water.[127] Both phenomena impact significantly on

---

[123] Altvater et al., *supra* note 90, at 405; Wright et al., *supra* note 90, at 8.

[124] Altvater et al., *supra* note 90, at 405.

[125] *See* G. A. Res. 72/249, U.N. Doc. A/RES/72/249 (Jan. 19, 2018); *see also* G. A. Res. 69/292, U.N. Doc. A/RES/69/292 (July 6, 2015).

[126] Andrew S. Brierley & Michael J. Kingsford, *Impacts of Climate Change on Marine Organisms and Ecosystems*, 19 CURRENT BIOLOGY R602, R608–11 (2009).

[127] Andreas J. Andersson et al., *Understanding Ocean Acidification Impacts on Organismal to Ecological Scales*, 28 OCEANOGRAPHY 16, 17–18 (2015).

marine species adapted to conditions that have remained relatively stable for millennia.[128] From this perspective, offshore renewable development is to be encouraged as a replacement for greenhouse gas–emitting energy sources. However, policy and law on marine environmental protection may discourage such development because of the negative impacts on ecosystems that are already deteriorating.[129] In addition, bolstering ecosystem resilience is a key aspect of climate change adaptation as conceptualized under the Paris Agreement on Climate Change.[130] How can the push for climate change mitigation and the pull of ecosystem protection, including from climate change adaptation, be reconciled? To further complicate matters, there are significant gaps in knowledge and understanding over how offshore renewable projects may affect marine ecosystems and their component species individually (e.g., noise, benthic disturbance), cumulatively and in combination with other stressors.[131] A precautionary approach is therefore required to regulate such development.

Answering the question of how development with both positive and negative ecological impacts should be regulated in circumstances where the functioning of marine ecosystems and the combined impacts of human activities on them are poorly understood would provide a foundation for developing legal frameworks that can support socioeconomic transition toward ecological sustainability. At present, legal approaches remain rooted in minimizing potential for developments to have negative impacts by using legal tools such as marine spatial planning and SEAs to identify and avoid areas of particular environmental significance. However, there are limits to their usefulness for preventing harm to dynamic, complex, adaptive ecosystems about which so much is unknown and during a period of accelerated ecological change driven

[128] Brierley & Kingsford, *supra* note 126, at R605–08; Andersson et al., *supra* note 127, at 21.
[129] Roger Hildingsson & Bengt Johansson, *Governing Low-Carbon Energy Transitions in Sustainable Ways: Potential Synergies and Conflicts between Climate and Environmental Policy Objectives*, 88 ENERGY POL'Y 245, 249–51 (2016); OLIVIA WOOLLEY, *Climate Law and Environmental Law: Is Conflict between Them Inevitable?* DEBATING CLIMATE LAW 398 (Benoit Mayer & Alexander Zahar eds., 2021) (hereinafter *Climate Law and Environmental Law*).
[130] Paris Agreement to the United Nations Framework Convention on Climate Change, Dec. 12, 2015, 27 U.N.T.S. 7, arts. 2(1)(b), 7(2); Olivia A. Woolley, *What Would Ecological Climate Law Look Like? Developing a Method for Analysing the International Climate Change Regime from an Ecological Perspective*, 29 REV. EUR. COMPAR. & INT'L ENVIRONMENTAL L. 76, 83–84 (2020) (hereinafter *What Would Ecological Climate Law Look Like?*).
[131] Woolley, *Ecological Governance*, *supra* note 119, at 766–67.

by human alteration of the planetary climate system that affects all ecosystems. The problems posed by ecosystem preservation are complex and multilayered. Our understanding of the combined impacts of human activities are not well known and solutions are tentative.[132] Analyses in these works point to offshore renewable energy development within a context of interstate collaboration on restoring Earth's ecological capacity to support life as the necessary direction of travel.

2.6 Conclusion

Fixed offshore wind energy technology has moved in the short space of twenty years from a promising precommercialization technology to a means of producing affordable low carbon electricity at scales equivalent to output from fossil fuel generating stations. Floating offshore wind and other technologies for offshore power production are at early stages of commercialization and have the potential to contribute significantly to decarbonization in their own right. Offshore renewable energy technologies are seen as highly desirable from the perspective of combating climate change, but their use creates practical and legal difficulties. As we have seen in this chapter, practical difficulties include transmitting electricity produced far from load centers to consumers, significant potential for conflict with other sea uses created by the very large areas that offshore wind energy can render off-limits to them, the negative impacts that renewable energy developments can have individually and cumulatively on already vulnerable marine environments, and the extreme difficulty verging on impossibility of accurate predictions of those impacts that would be required to craft effective regulations to prevent ecological harm on an informed basis.

Offshore wind's rapid rollout, together with prospects for much expanded use of other marine renewable energy technologies, makes it necessary to further detail UNCLOS's high-level rules on allocating jurisdiction over sea uses for states and particularly for transboundary electricity transmission, on balancing interests of different states in

---

[132] *See generally* OLIVIA WOOLLEY, ECOLOGICAL GOVERNANCE: REAPPRAISING LAW'S ROLE IN PRESERVING ECOSYSTEM FUNCTIONALITY (2014); OLIVIA WOOLLEY, *Ecological Law in the Anthropocene.* FROM ENVIRONMENTAL TO ECOLOGICAL LAW (Kirsten Anker, Peter D. Burdon, Geoffrey Garver, Michelle Maloney & Carla Sbert eds., 2021); WOOLLEY, *Climate Law and Environmental Law, supra* note 129; Woolley, *What Would Ecological Climate Law Look Like?, supra* note 130.

enjoying rights and freedoms to use the seas, and on marine environmental protection. They also add to pressures from other technologies considered in this volume for a reappraisal of the legal framework established by UNCLOS nearly forty years ago.

Does the treaty provide an adequate legal framework for enabling and regulating sea use technologies that could not have been anticipated at all or at the scale that they are now employed at when the treaty was adopted? Are duties of showing due regard and undue interference suited to managing offshore renewable energy's interaction with other sea uses in view of the very significant constraints this can place on their conduct? Is the concept of the high seas as an area in which all states are free to undertake activities compatible with their possible use for activities such as power generation that occupy large areas to the exclusion of others (including other renewable power producers) and that are accessible only to the most technologically advanced and wealthiest states and their corporations? In connection with this, should the high seas' resources for power production be designated in law as the common heritage of mankind, alongside those of the seabed, so that benefits from exploiting them can be shared more equitably? Finally, is the existing legal framework suited to address the serious threats presented to the functioning of marine ecosystems and the survival of their species by climate change and ocean acidification? These and other questions that this chapter identifies provide an agenda for further scholarship on the law of the sea.

3

Striking an Equitable Balance under the Biodiversity Agreement

The Elusive Case of New Technologies, Marine Genetic Resources and the Global South

RONÁN LONG*

* The first draft of this paper was presented at the workshop in December 2020. The author wishes to acknowledge comments on the second draft from Professor Marcel Jaspars (University of Aberdeen) and Kahlil Hassanali in February 2021. The Research is supported by The Nippon Foundation and undertaken at the WMU-Sasakawa Global Ocean Institute.

3.1   Introduction

The technical and scientific capability to explore the ocean is intrinsically linked with human endeavor in the marine environment. In ancient times, the ineffectiveness of rudimentary salvage technologies in recovering lost cargo from the deep influenced the codification and application of the law of obligations and the rules on jettison under Roman law.[1] Today, state-of-the-art technologies are opening up new frontiers in marine science and improving the pathways for states and intergovernmental organizations to undertake evidenced-based decision-making in ocean affairs.[2] As a result, intergovernmental cooperation and ocean science diplomacy underpin many aspects of the international regulation of industries that are science and technology dependent such as fisheries, shipping and seabed mining.[3] The technological revolution has gathered pace with the advent of the information era, the increased coverage and resolution of satellite remote-sensing technologies, and artificial intelligence and robotics, as well as with the launch of autonomous submersibles that are capable of exploring and mapping the seafloor in distant ocean regions.[4]

The social and economic consequences of these advancements are manifold but mostly benign, with the Organisation for Economic Co-operation and Development (OECD) forecasting that every sector of the ocean economy will be affected by technological innovation by 2030.[5] However, there are growing international awareness and concerns about a handful of powerful transnational corporations and their subsidiaries in highly industrialized countries asserting market dominance in offshore industries, especially in sectors with high entry costs, such as marine

[1] Reinhard Zimmermann, The Law of Obligations: Roman Foundations of the Civilian Tradition 407 (1996).
[2] Oscar Pizarro & Leonard Pace, *Editorial: Emerging Technologies with High Impact for Ocean Sciences, Ecosystem Management, and Environmental Conservation*, 8 Frontiers in Marine Sci. (2021).
[3] Harriet Harden-Davies, *The Next Wave of Science Diplomacy: Marine Biodiversity beyond National Jurisdiction*, 75 ICES J. Marine Sci. 426, 428 (2018).
[4] Mark Anderson, *Bon Voyage for the Autonomous Ship Mayflower*, ieee Spectrum, Jan. 3, 2020. On the use of new technologies for sample collection and collection by industry, also *see* Alex Rogers et al., Marine Genetic Resources in Areas *beyond* National Jurisdiction: Promoting Marine Scientific Research and Enabling Equitable Benefit Sharing, 8 Frontiers in Marine Sci. (2021).
[5] Organisation for Economic Co-operation and Development, The Ocean Economy in 2030 14 (2016) (hereinafter OECD).

biotechnology.[6] The oligopoly risks are obvious and in many ways run counter to international commitments to transfer marine technology to developing countries and to build their research capacity in marine science.[7]

In light of these developments, the discussion in this chapter is predicated on the view that new technologies are transforming the world of ocean exploration but at the same time that they have the potential to exacerbate existing inequalities under the United Nations (UN) Convention on the Law of the Sea (UNCLOS).[8] In doing so, they are also exposing fundamental weaknesses in the rules on marine scientific research and technology transfer set forth in Parts XIII and XIV of UNCLOS.[9] As seen elsewhere in this volume, a major cause for concern is that emerging technologies are easily outpacing the codification of new normative rules in the law of the sea.[10]

A case in point arises with respect to the application of new technologies in the search for novel genetic material belonging to organisms that live in the deep ocean. The areas of interest were first discovered in the 1990s and are primarily hydrothermal vent sites associated with tectonic and volcanic activity in the Atlantic, Pacific, Indian and Arctic Oceans.[11] Research at such sites holds great promise for scientists to gain a better understanding of biological and chemical processes such as chemosynthesis, as well as the origins and functioning of life in extreme environments.[12] The exploration of marine genetic features of plants, animals and microorganisms can also lead to innovative discoveries of biotechnological and biopharma importance of commercial value.[13] These features may include chemical compounds, genes and their products, or, in

---

[6] John Virdin et al., *The Ocean 100: Transnational Corporations in the Ocean Economy*, 7 SCI. ADVANCES 1, 9 (2021).

[7] G. A. Res. A/RES/70/1, ¶ 14.a (Sept. 25, 2015).

[8] United Nations Convention on the Law of the Sea, Dec. 10, 1982, 1833 U.N.T.S. 397 (hereinafter UNCLOS).

[9] See discussion on unfinished business and inherent biases *infra*.

[10] *See e.g.*, Chapters 8 and 10.

[11] Evan Lubofsky, The Discovery of Hydrothermal Vents: Scientists Celebrate 40th Anniversary and Chart Future Research, Oceanus, June 11, 2018.

[12] Jesús M. Arrieta, Sophie Arnaud-Haond & Carlos M. Duarte, *What Lies Underneath: Conserving the Oceans' Genetic Resources*, 107 PROC. NAT'L ACAD. SCI. U.S. AM. 18318, 18319 (2010).

[13] ROBERT BLASIAK ET AL., THE OCEAN GENOME: CONSERVATION AND THE FAIR, EQUITABLE AND SUSTAINABLE USE OF MARINE GENETIC RESOURCES 14–17 (2020); *see also* Fernando de la Calle, *Marine Genetic Resources: A Source of New Drugs, the Experience of the Biotechnology Sector*, 24 INT'L J. MARINE & COASTAL L. 209–20 (2009).

some cases, the physical properties of the material in question.[14] One
other consequence of the rapid progress in deep ocean exploration and
monitoring technologies at such sites is that there is greater international
awareness that most of the work related to marine genetic resources is
carried out by a small number of companies and countries in the Global
North and that much of the field work is a high seas freedom from a law
of the sea perspective.[15]

In response to these and related concerns regarding the regulatory
gaps appertaining to the deep ocean environment under the law of the
sea, the topic of the conservation and sustainable use of Marine
Biodiversity of Areas beyond National Jurisdiction has come to the fore
of intergovernmental treaty-making efforts under the auspices of the UN
General Assembly over the past two decades.[16] Since 2018, these deliberations have come to a hiatus at an intergovernmental conference tasked
with elaborating the text of an international legally binding instrument
under UNCLOS.[17] They in turn brought into sharp relief some daunting
legislative challenges that need to be overcome if the law of the sea is to
provide a sophisticated and equitable framework that balances the interests
and needs of both developed and developing countries in the conservation
and use of biodiversity for the benefit of present and future generations.

3.2   Significant and Substantial Legal Issues

The prospect of new scientific discoveries is exciting on many levels but it
also raises significant issues about how emerging technologies have the
potential to influence the progressive development and codification of
the law of the sea. With this in mind, the following discussion highlights

[14] BLASIAK ET AL., *supra* note 13, at 21–22.
[15] UNITED NATIONS, DIVISION FOR OCEAN AFFAIRS AND THE LAW OF THE SEA, THE
SECOND GLOBAL INTEGRATED MARINE ASSESSMENT: WORLD OCEAN ASSESSMENT 21,
506 (2021).
[16] For developments in the treaty-making process, *see, e.g.*, David Freestone, *The UN Process
to Develop an International Legally Binding Instrument under the 1982 Law of the Sea
Convention: Issues and Challenges.* CONSERVING BIODIVERSITY IN AREAS BEYOND
NATIONAL JURISDICTION 3–46 (David Freestone ed., 2019); David Leary, *Agreeing to
Disagree on What We Have or Have Not Agreed On: The Current State of Play of the BBNJ
Negotiations on the Status of Marine Genetic Resources in Areas beyond National
Jurisdiction*, 99 MARINE POL'Y 21–29 (2019); J. Ashley Roach, *BBNJ Treaty
Negotiations 2019.* MARINE BIODIVERSITY BEYOND NATIONAL JURISDICTION 25–89
(Myron H. Nordquist & Ronán Long eds., 2021).
[17] G. A. Res. 72/249, ¶ 1 (Jan. 19, 2018).

global inequalities to explore and benefit from the ocean and argues that this stems in several important respects from fundamental lacunae in the provisions on marine scientific research and technology transfer in UNCLOS.[18] The discussion traces intergovernmental efforts to negotiate a new marine biodiversity treaty at the UN and showcases how existing and emerging technologies are central to designing functional and reasonable solutions that will attract consensus support from the plenipotentiaries on key strands of the treaty-making deliberations that are still open prior to final sessions of the intergovernmental conference. Through the lens of emerging technologies, the chapter reviews several aspects of the draft treaty, namely: the use and meaning of terms and objectives; normative principles and approaches; monitoring and the sharing of benefits from marine genetic resources; along with the establishment of new institutions and a clearing-house mechanism for technology transfer and capacity-building purposes.[19]

In doing so, the discussion draws attention to the positions adopted by several delegations on some of the most contentious issues concerning technology under negotiation at the intergovernmental conference, especially as they pertain to the interests and needs of the small island developing states and least developed countries in the Global South.

[18] The shortcoming in UNCLOS are well documented in the specialist literature on marine scientific research and the law of the sea, *see, e.g.,* ALFRED H. A. SOONS, MARINE SCIENTIFIC RESEARCH AND THE LAW OF THE SEA (1982); UNITED NATIONS, DIVISION FOR OCEAN AFFAIRS AND THE LAW OF THE SEA, MARINE SCIENTIFIC RESEARCH: A REVISED GUIDE TO THE IMPLEMENTATION OF THE RELEVANT PROVISIONS OF THE UNITED NATIONS CONVENTION ON THE LAW OF THE SEA (1991); MONTSERRAT GORINA-YSERN, AN INTERNATIONAL REGIME FOR MARINE SCIENTIFIC RESEARCH (2004); FLORIAN H. TH. WEGELEIN, MARINE SCIENTIFIC RESEARCH: THE OPERATION AND STATUS OF RESEARCH VESSELS AND OTHER PLATFORMS IN INTERNATIONAL LAW (2005); KRISTIN BARTENSTEIN & SHOTARO HAMAMOTO, *Part XIV, Development and Transfer of Marine Technology.* UNITED NATIONS CONVENTION ON THE LAW OF THE SEA: A COMMENTARY 1605–1807 (Alexander Proelss ed., 2017); NELE MATZ LUCK ET AL., Part XIII, Marine Scientific Research. UNITED NATIONS CONVENTION ON THE LAW OF THE SEA: A COMMENTARY 1605–1807 1605–1763 (Alexander Proelss ed., 2017).

[19] U.N. Doc. A/CONF.232/2020/3, Intergovernmental Conference on an International Legally Binding Instrument under the United Nations Convention on the Law of the Sea on the Conservation and Sustainable Use of Marine Biological Diversity of Areas beyond National Jurisdiction, Revised Draft Text of an Agreement under the United Nations Convention on the Law of the Sea on the Conservation and Sustainable Use of Marine Biological Diversity of Areas beyond National Jurisdiction (2019), annex (hereinafter REVISED DRAFT TEXT).

The chapter also flags a number of potential amendments to the draft treaty text with a view to advancing a more even-handed approach to marine genetic research and the transfer of technology under the law of the sea, as well as to future-proof the agreement in light of technological, environmental and legal developments over time. As will be seen, the chapter advocates that the final sessions of the intergovernmental conference presents a once-in-a-generation opportunity to effect real change and to ensure a more equitable balance of interests in the law of the sea that advances peace, stability, prosperity and genuine international cooperation in the conservation and sustainable use of marine biodiversity.

Before turning to these issues, it is first necessary to set the scene by making a few general observations from historical, geographical and scientific perspectives about global disparities in technical capabilities to explore the deep ocean and to benefit from research on marine genetic resources in areas beyond national jurisdiction.

3.3   North–South Capabilities and Disparities

One may start with the term "capabilities," which, when used in this chapter, is a sweeping and poorly defined reference to the differences between developed and developing states. In practice, what counts in any specific situation is the level of scientific knowledge and technical capability available to a given state or research entity in the relevant scientific and technical fields.[20] That said, technical and scientific capability has long since been a dynamic feature and driver of ocean exploration. One can point to the extraordinary skill and knowledge of Polynesian navigators who explored the South Pacific in one of the earliest of human migrations across the ocean.[21] Indeed, the draft text of the agreement provides for the utilization of the traditional knowledge of indigenous peoples in decision-making processes, the first such reference in a law of the sea instrument, which ought to make future decision-making more

---

[20] A similar point is made by the International Tribunal for the Law of the Sea (ITLOS) Seabed Dispute Settlement Chamber in related to seabed mining. Responsibilities and Obligations of States with Respect to Activities in the Area, Case No. 17, Advisory Opinion of Feb. 1, 2011, ITLOS Rep. 10, ¶ 162 (hereinafter Advisory Opinion of Feb. 1, 2011).

[21] Geoffrey Irwin, The Prehistoric Exploration and Colonisation of the Pacific 5–6 (1992).

inclusive and reflective of the links between nature and community values.[22]

In Europe, innovations such as the magnetic compass, the astrolabe and developments in nautical cartography went hand-in-hand with the projection of naval imperial power overseas along with the search for new navigational routes during the Age of Exploration.[23] These early navigational instruments also facilitated the setting down of demarcation lines in ocean space including the division of the world into two spheres of influence by Portugal and Spain under the Treaties of Tordesillas and Saragossa in 1494 and 1529, respectively.[24] Technical innovation influenced the cannon-shot rule for determining the seaward limit of the territorial sea and the emphasis on what states do in practice, which shaped the rise of positivism in the law of the sea and in international relations pertaining to ocean affairs since the Treaty of Westphalia in 1648.[25] In the late nineteenth century, astounding scientific discoveries were made through the use of relatively simple mechanical devices to collect sediment and biological samples from the deep sea during the course of the *H. M. S. Challenger* expedition, technologies that are still used today.[26] International collaboration in the development of new tools in fisheries science took a major step forward with the establishment of the International Council for the Exploration of the Sea in Copenhagen in 1902.[27]

After World War II, the United States took the lead in developing ocean technologies and the rapid pace of technological change continued to have a notable bearing on developments in the law of the sea pertaining to seabed resources, including the proclamation by President Truman in 1945 claiming that the resources on the continental shelf contiguous to the United States belonged to the United States.[28] Indeed, technological

---

[22] REVISED DRAFT TEXT, *supra* note 19, arts. 5(i), 10, 46(b), 49(2); *see* Clement Yow Mulalap et al., *Traditional Knowledge and the BBNJ Instrument*, 122 MARINE POL'Y (2020).

[23] DAVID WOODWARD, *Cartography and the Renaissance: Continuity and Change.* THE HISTORY OF NAVIGATION 3, 15, 17 (2007).

[24] Lawrence A. Coben *The Events That Led to the Treaty of Tordesillas*, 47 TERRAE INCOGNITAE 142–62 (2015),

[25] YOSHIFUMI TANAKA, THE INTERNATIONAL LAW OF THE SEA 27 (2019).

[26] MARGARET DEACON, TONY RICE & COLIN SUMMERHAYES, UNDERSTANDING THE OCEANS: A CENTURY OF OCEAN EXPLORATION 25–69 (2001).

[27] Convention for the International Council for the Exploration of the Sea, Sept. 12, 1964, 24 U.S.T. 1080, 652 U.N.T.S. 237.

[28] U.S. Presidential Proclamation 2667, Policy of the United States with Respect to the Natural Resources of the Subsoil and Sea Bed of the Continental Shelf, 10 Fed. Reg. 12,305 (1945).

capability and the exploitability test in accessing such resources was codified subsequently as one of criteria to define the seaward limit of the continental shelf under the 1958 Convention on the Continental Shelf.[29] In the late 1960s, the United States ably demonstrated its ocean technology capabilities by using salvage and sonar technologies to recover parts of a lost Soviet submarine in the Pacific Ocean.[30] There were also spin-off technologies from the NASA space program and from the deep-water oil and gas drilling programs in the Gulf of Mexico and elsewhere. In parallel with the on-going development of deep-water extraction technologies for hydrocarbons and minerals, the adoption of unliteral seabed mining measures by the United States and other industrialized countries influenced the revision of multilateral arrangements on seabed mining under UNCLOS and the 1994 Implementation Agreement.[31] The mining industry tested deep-water technologies in the Clarion Clipperton Fracture Zone in the 1970s with mixed success.[32] Many other aspects of international law pertaining to deep ocean science remained unresolved, including the rules on collecting oceanographic data.[33] The first discovery of hydrothermal sites near the Galapagos Islands by a team from Woods Hole Oceanographic Institute in 1977 heralded a new era in the study of marine organisms for their unique molecular properties including the commercial benefits that may be derived from marine genetic resources.[34] This period was also the beginning of international scientific concerns about the impact of technologies on deep-water habitats and the need for responsible research practices at sites that were often new to science and poorly understood.[35]

---

[29] Convention of the Continental Shelf, art. 1(i), Apr. 29, 1958, 15 U.S.T. 471, T.I.A.S. No. 5578, 499 U.N.T.S. 311.

[30] Frederic A. Eustis, *The Glomar Explorer Incident: Implications for the Law of Salvage*, 16 VA. J. INT'L L. 177 (1975).

[31] G. A. Res. 48/263, ¶ 5 (Aug. 17, 1994).

[32] Dennis Arrow, *The Proposed Regime for the Unilateral Exploitation of Deep Seabed Mineral Resources by the United States*, 21 HARV. INT'L. L.J. 337 (1980).

[33] UNESCO, SAFETY PROVISIONS OF OCEAN DATA ACQUISITION SYSTEMS: AIDS AND DEVICES, NOT IN FORCE (1972); *see* Nikos Papadakis, *Some Legal Problems Associated with the Ocean Data Acquisition Systems, Aids and Devices*, 5 INT'L RELATIONS 825–37 (1975).

[34] On existing and other potential benefits, BLASIAK ET AL., *supra* note 13, at 12–20.

[35] *See, e.g.*, INTERRIDGE, STATEMENT OF COMMITMENT TO RESPONSIBLE RESEARCH PRACTICES AT DEEP-SEA HYDROTHERMAL VENTS (2006).

In the 1980s and 1990s, there were several important transnational initiatives to improve global cooperation in marine science including the Census of Marine Life, a major baseline study on marine biodiversity undertaken by scientists from eighty countries, which saw the development of new internet tools for taxonomy and metadata analysis.[36] Improvements in North–South and triangular cooperation were facilitated by the implementation of ocean mapping programs including tools to map the seafloor, which brought their own challenges in relation to interpretation and implementation of UNCLOS.[37] In recent years, further progress was made in technological innovation under the seabed mining regime including the training of scientist from developing countries in environmental monitoring and other deep-water technologies.[38] The availability of new technologies also boosted the scope for greater participation by women scientists in ocean science.[39] With the arrival of the digital era, different maritime sectors continue to develop technical and science-driven solutions to the many challenges encountered in the law of the sea and ocean affairs.

Despite this progress, disparities in technical capabilities remain pronounced worldwide, especially in scientific disciplines that are skill-intensive and dependent upon access to research vessels and expensive technologies to undertake research at sea. This is also true in relation to the access to remote-sensing technologies and autonomous platforms, as well as shipborne technologies and submersibles for many of the tasks in deep ocean exploration.[40] The latter can collect water, geological,

---

[36] Paul V. R. Snelgrove, Discoveries of the Census of Marine Life: Making Ocean Life Count 49–52, 75 (2010).

[37] Larry Mayer & J. Ashley Roach, *The Quest to Completely Map the World's Oceans in Support of Understanding Marine Biodiversity and the Regulatory Barriers We Have Created.* Marine Biodiversity Beyond National Jurisdiction 149, 153–54, 163–66 (Myron Nordquist & Ronán Long eds., 2021).

[38] Ronán Long, Zhen Sun & Maraimalia Rodríguez-Chaves, *Gender Leadership and the United Nations Decade of Ocean Science: Pioneering Role of the International Seabed Authority.* The United Nations Convention on the Law of the Sea, Part XI Regime and the International Seabed Authority: A Twenty-five Year Journey 109–36 (Alfonso Ascencio-Herrera & Myron Nordquist eds., 2022).

[39] See discussion on these structures *infra. See also*, Ronán Long, *Beholding the Emerging Biodiversity Agreement through a Looking Glass: What Capacity-Building and Gender Equality Norms Should Be Found There?* Marine Biodiversity Beyond National Jurisdiction 241, 269–70 (Myron H. Nordquist & Ronán Long eds., 2021).

[40] Remote-sensing technologies have their limitations in so far as they can only be used in the photic zone, that is to say down to the 100-meter isobath. *See* Ved Chirayath & Alan Li, *Next-Generation Optical Sensing Technologies for Exploring Ocean Worlds: NASA*

biological and chemical samples in the deepest and remotest parts of the ocean including for commercial purposes.[41] The vessels are also capable of deploying coring systems to sample seabed substrata in water depths greater than the 6,000-meter isobath. Onboard, they are kitted out with specialist laboratories and instrumentation that facilitates in situ sampling and monitoring of biodiversity, along with equipment to commence the scientific processes of DNA and environmental DNA analyses of genetic material, biomolecule characterization and metabarcoding, as well as manipulating genomic information through the use of advanced genome-editing tools.[42] Many modern research vessels are fitted out with teleworking facilities, which allow scientists to work from land-based hubs or from home with direct access to video and data transmitted in real-time from submersibles as they explore the deep. A further phenomenon is that modern research vessels and autonomous platforms are increasingly owned and operated by private individuals and philanthropic foundations and thus not subject to the same oversight mechanisms of government-funded or international science programs.[43] These vessels can deploy in all ocean regions, along with undertaking a limited range of capacity development activities.[44]

The global disparities and the North–South divide in marine scientific research programs has not gone unnoticed and there is disquiet about scientists from higher-income countries conducting field studies, particular on inshore marine ecosystems, without undertaking capacity development activities or sharing their knowledge and resources with local scientists in low-income countries.[45] This in turn is influencing the

---

FluidCam, MiDAR, and NeMO-Net, 6 Frontiers in Marine Sci. (2019); Mayer & Roach, *supra* note 37, at 149–66.

[41] Rogers et al., *supra* note 4. Examples of vent bacteria that have been commercialized are cited by Blasiak et al., *supra* note 13, at 18.

[42] *Id.*

[43] For instance, the private company REV Ocean is currently building a research vessel in Norway. *See* The Vessel, www.revocean.org/vessel (last visited Mar. 9, 2021) (online). Also, ocean sampling programs have been undertaken by the J. Craig Venter Institute in the United States and the Tara Ocean Expedition in France. In relation to the latter, cheap technology enables the sequencing of entire genomes at sea without bringing samples ashore, see Rogers et al. *supra* note 4.

[44] *Id.*

[45] *See, e.g.*, Asha de Vos, *Opinion, The Problem of "Colonial Science,"* Sci. Am., July 1, 2020; Paris V. Stefanoudis et al., *Turning the Tide of Parachute Science*, 31 Current Biology Mag. R184–85 (2021). Aleke Stöfen-O'Brien et al., *Parachute Science through a Regional Lens: Marine Litter Research in the Caribbean Small Island Developing States and the Challenge of Extra-regional Research*, 174 Marine Pollution Bull. 113291 (2021).

positions adopted by delegations from developing countries at the intergovernmental conference on a new biodiversity treaty, especially with respect to the provisions on benefit sharing and capacity-building.[46] They are aware that the prohibitive costs associated with research on the ocean genome means that the opportunities to commercialize scientific findings rests almost exclusively in the hands of public and private laboratories in developed countries.[47] The global disparities in technology is also reflected in corporate holdings and ownership of gene patents associated with the deep-sea and hydrothermal vent systems, which are almost exclusively the preserve of corporate entities in the Global North.[48]

Indeed, a brief perusal of the number and nationality of vessels in the global fleet of research ships and vessels of opportunity that are capable of undertaking deep ocean science tells its own story,[49] with the majority of vessels flagged and operated by public and private entities in developed countries.[50] In addition, China has major ocean science capability and a large fleet of research vessels that deploy across the entire Indo-Pacific ocean region and as far afield as the Arctic Ocean.[51] Only a handful of developing countries, namely Brazil, Chile, Argentina, India, Iran, Turkey, Morocco and South Africa, have research vessels that can undertake prolonged research cruises on the high seas. The fifty-eight countries that constitute small island developing states have almost no research ship capacity beyond inshore vessels with limited range and equipment.[52] Apart from South Africa, African countries bordering the Western Indian Ocean have little capacity in molecular biotechnology and few opportunities to participate in transnational marine scientific research

---

[46] See discussion in sections 10 and 11, as well as notes 106 and 191, *infra*.

[47] *Id.*

[48] Robert Blasiak, Jean-Baptiste Jouffray, Colette C. Wabnitz, Emma Sundström and Henrik Österblom, *Corporate Control and Global Governance of Marine Genetic Resources*, 4 SCI. ADVANCES (2018).

[49] UNESCO, GLOBAL OCEAN SCIENCE REPORT 2020: CHARTING CAPACITY FOR OCEAN SUSTAINABILITY 110–12 (2020).

[50] *Id.* The United States leads the field in research ship resources with 441 vessels, followed by Japan (50), Sweden (42), Canada (40), the Republic of Korea (26), the UK (26) and Germany (25).

[51] Haili Wang, Marine Operations, Xiamen University, Address at the at the International Research Ship Operators' Meeting: Recent New Builds in China and the Operation of RV *Tan Kah Kee* (Oct. 8, 2019).

[52] UNESCO, *supra* note 49, at 112.

projects.[53] As a result, one expert report concluded that the "costs of research and technologies remains prohibitively high; scientific capacity is low; and there are significant gaps in taxonomic and ecological knowledge."[54] Efforts are made by public and private science bodies to provide participation and training opportunities to scientists from developing countries in scientific work programs at sea under bilateral science projects and other arrangements, as well as under the auspices of programs administered by international bodies such as the International Seabed Authority.[55] Overall, however, the North–South disparities in infrastructure and technical capabilities in marine scientific research are extensive and further compounded by significant shortcomings in the provisions on marine scientific research and technology transfer in UNCLOS, as will be seen next.

3.4   Unfinished Business and Inherent Biases

Although science and modern technologies are vital catalysts for the implementation and development of the law of the sea, the architects of UNCLOS left a range of significant issues open to interpretation and devoid of substance with respect to the scientific, educational and technical needs of developing countries.[56] In this regard, four general points can be made about UNCLOS that appear to tilt the regulatory balance in favor of the interests of the holders of infrastructure and technology in conducting research on marine genetic resources of areas beyond national jurisdiction.

First, UNCLOS provides a solid legal basis for all states and competent international organizations to conduct research as a high seas freedom subject to the rights and duties of other states.[57] Accordingly, the deployment of technologies for marine genetic research in international waters must comply with the general obligations on marine scientific research set down by UNCLOS.[58] Although clearly drafted in treaty language, these provisions are largely declarative in ambit and place few constraints

---

[53] RACHEL WYNBERG, *Marine Genetic Resources and Bioprospecting in the Western Indian Ocean*. REGIONAL STATE OF THE COAST REPORT 407, 412 (José Paula ed., 2015).

[54] Id., at 414.

[55] BILIANA CICIN-SAIN ET AL., POLICY BRIEF ON CAPACITY DEVELOPMENT AS A KEY ASPECT OF A NEW INTERNATIONAL AGREEMENT ON MARINE BIODIVERSITY BEYOND NATIONAL JURISDICTION 17–21 (2018).

[56] Bartenstein & Hamamoto, *supra* note 18, at 1605–761.

[57] UNCLOS, *supra* note 8, arts. 87(1)(f), 238.

[58] Id., art. 258.

on the holders of technology, apart from the requirement that the deployment must be for peaceful purposes, undertaken with appropriate scientific methods, not unjustifiably interfere with other legitimate uses of the sea, and comply with other regulations such as the rules adopted for the protection and preservation of the marine environment.[59] The Convention provides scope for international organizations to regulate the use of technologies for environmental and other purposes but this in practice has left many matters unresolved about the conduct of science by the holders of new and emerging technologies. As a result, tensions arise when states and international organizations seek to regulate new research activities. For example, UNCLOS provided little in detail regarding the practical matters and ethical considerations that need to be overcome in the international regulation of emerging technologies, as became evident in regulatory efforts by the International Maritime Organization (IMO) to legislate environmental technologies that manipulate ocean processes in order to mitigate human induced climate change.[60] Another example on the horizon with the advent of new molecular tools relates to the use of Clustered Regularly Interspaced Short Palindromic Repeats (Crispr) technology for marine genetic research, where the scientific risks are considerable but not directly addressed by UNCLOS or related law of the sea instruments.[61]

Second, a relatively longstanding conundrum in the law of the sea is that UNCLOS does not define the meaning of the term marine scientific research.[62] Nevertheless, UNCLOS provides for the deployment and use of "scientific research installation" and "equipment" for the conduct of scientific research in the marine environment,[63] as well as setting forth rules on their legal status, safety zones, noninterference with shipping

---

[59] *Id.*, art. 248.

[60] KAREN N. SCOTT, *Not an Intractable Challenge: Geoengineering MSR in ABNJ.* MARINE BIODIVERSITY BEYOND NATIONAL JURISDICTION 189–210 (Myron H. Nordquist & Ronán Long eds., 2011); *see also* Ronán Long, *A European Law Perspective: Science, Technology, and New Challenges to Ocean Law.* SCIENCE, TECHNOLOGY, AND NEW CHALLENGES TO OCEAN LAW 63, 78 (Harry N. Scheiber, James Kraska & Moon-Sang Kwon eds., 2015).

[61] *See* discussion *infra* on the institutional arrangements and a clearing-house mechanism in the draft text.

[62] *See, e.g.*, RONÁN LONG, *Regulating Marine Scientific Research in the European Union: It Takes More Than Two to Tango.* THE LAW OF THE SEA CONVENTION: U.S. ACCESSION AND GLOBALISATION 428, 435, 440 (Myron H. Nordquist et al. eds., 2012); J. ASHLEY ROACH & ROBERT W. SMITH, EXCESSIVE MARITIME CLAIMS 414 (3d ed. 2012).

[63] UNCLOS, *supra* note 8, art. 258.

routes, identification and warning signals.[64] In the context of legislating access and the sharing of benefits derived from marine genetic resources, UNCLOS offers little in the way of regulatory guidance on the use of installations and equipment in specialist fields of inquiry such as marine biotechnology or the deployment of scientific tools to undertake marine genetic research.[65] Indeed, other than the research vessel itself, the two terms "scientific research installation" and "equipment" as used in UNCLOS appear to cover all technologies and devices deployable in the ocean for genetic investigations in the marine environment.[66] This latitude is exacerbated by the absence of clarity in the rules that apply to the deployment of devices that operate autonomously without the support of a research vessel.[67] As alluded to previously, the regulatory gaps in the law of the sea became apparent with respect to the deployment of International Oceanographic Commission (IOC)–UN Educational, Scientific and Cultural Organization (UNESCO) Argo floats within and beyond national jurisdiction, which opened its own Pandora's box of challenges regarding the practical implementation of a transnational scientific program as part of the Global Ocean Observing System and the Global Climate Observing System.[68] Likewise, the law is unsettled regarding the liability rules that apply to environmental damage caused by the deployment of new technologies for genetic research in areas beyond national jurisdiction.[69] There is however considerable scope to resolve this issue at the biodiversity treaty negotiations, discussed later, should the plenipotentiaries choose to do so.[70]

Third, UNCLOS regulates the use and deployment of technologies for marine scientific research according to the jurisdictional framework that applies to maritime space. Again, there appears to be a strong bias in favor of technology holders in so far as all states are free to deploy technologies for marine scientific research purposes in areas beyond national jurisdiction, even though this freedom is qualified by

---

[64] Id., arts. 259–62.

[65] Bartenstein & Hamamoto, *supra* note 18, at 1733–35.

[66] *Id.*, at 1734.

[67] Robert Veal, Michael Tsimplis & Andrew Serdy, *The Legal Status and Operation of Unmanned Maritime Vehicles*, 50 OCEAN DEV. & INT'L L. 23–48 (2020).

[68] MAYER & ROACH, *supra* note 37, at 149–66.

[69] Ronán Long, *Restoring Marine Environmental Damage: Can the* Costa Rica v Nicaragua *Compensation Case Influence the BBNJ Negotiations?*, 28 REV. EUR. COMPAR. & INT'L ENV'T L. 244–57 (2019).

[70] *Id.*, at 254–56.

UNCLOS. Thus, for example, in relation to the International Seabed Area, the technologies must be deployed exclusively for peaceful purposes and for the benefit of humankind as a whole, as well as in conformity with Part XI of UNCLOS, the 1994 Implementation Agreement and the seabed mining code as promulgated by the International Seabed Authority.[71] Particularly problematic from a law of the sea perspective is that UNCLOS does not provide a comprehensive regulatory framework to ensure the conservation and sustainable use of biodiversity beyond national jurisdiction including its genetic components, an oversight that provides the raison d'être underpinning the negotiation of a new international agreement to address this and other lacunae in the law of the sea.[72] As a consequence, the holders of technology are free to sample biodiversity for genetic properties on the high seas, as well as in the subjacent water column beyond the 200 nautical mile (M) exclusive economic zone (EEZ) limits and above the seafloor and subsoil of the continental margin of the coastal state without its consent.[73] As will be seen, the freedom to sample biodiversity has given rise to a vexed and central question in the biodiversity treaty-making process at the UN, which is how to share the benefits derived from research on marine genetic resources.[74] Some of the technologies discussed in this volume are essential to making an accurate determination of the precise geographical location of research activities on biodiversity and to ensuring that they are conducted without prejudice to the sovereign rights of the coastal state.[75] This determination is not always clear-cut and in practice may often be very difficult to monitor in deep-

---

[71] UNCLOS, *supra* note 8, arts. 143, 147.

[72] Considerable efforts have nonetheless been made at the intergovernmental conference to ensure that the draft Marine Biodiversity of Areas beyond National Jurisdiction (BBNJ) Agreement is consistent with UNCLOS and does not to undermine relevant legal instruments and frameworks and relevant global, regional and sectoral bodies, *see* Roach, *supra* note 16, at 26–29.

[73] This is a contentious issue in relation to the agreement and is discussed further in the section on monitoring and benefit sharing, as well as in relation to the sedentary species of the continental shelf, *infra. See also* UNCLOS, *supra* note 8, art. 246(6).

[74] Marcel Jaspars & Abbe E. L. Brown, *Benefit Sharing: Combining Intellectual Property, Trade Secrets, Science and an Ecosystem-Focused Approach*. Marine Biodiversity Beyond National Jurisdiction 97–130 (Myron H. Nordquist & Ronán Long, eds., 2021).

[75] Clive Schofield & Joanna Mossop, *Biodiversity beyond National Jurisdiction and the Limits of the Commons: Spatial and Functional Complexities*. Marine Biodiversity Beyond National Jurisdiction 285, 285–305 (Myron H. Nordquist & Ronán Long, eds., 2021).

water ecosystems such as cold-water corals that straddle the jurisdictional divide between the legal regimes that apply to the seabed and water column under UNCLOS as it pertains to the continental margin.[76] The latter difficulty is especially true for small island developing states and least-developed countries that do not have access to the relevant technologies in most instances, thus curtailing their capacity to implement UNCLOS and to avail of their rights and discharge their duties in ocean development.

Fourth, UNCLOS falls well short on the delivery of one its primary objectives, which is to "contribute to the realization of a just and equitable international economic order which takes into account the interests and needs of mankind as a whole and, in particular, the special interests and needs of developing countries, whether coastal or landlocked."[77] The obligations to provide technical assistance to developing states parties to realize this objective are grouped in four sets of provisions in UNCLOS concerning: seabed mining;[78] the protection and preservation of the marine environment;[79] marine scientific research;[80] and the development and transfer of marine technology.[81] Apart from the obligations pertaining to seabed mining,[82] UNCLOS is silent on the resources to be applied to the tasks of capacity development and technical training and this shortcoming works to the detriment of developing states, particularly in the technology and infrastructure intensive fields of marine biodiscovery.[83] This weakness is compounded further by the absence of any legally binding obligation to transfer marine technology

---

[76] Ronan Joseph Long & Anthony J. Grehan, *Marine Habitat Protection in a Coastal Member State of the European Union: The Case of Deep-Water Coral Conservation in Ireland*, 17 INT'L J. MARINE & COASTAL L. 235, 243 (2002).

[77] UNCLOS, *supra* note 8, preamble.

[78] *Id.*, arts. 144, 274.

[79] *Id.*, arts. 202, 203.

[80] *Id.*, art. 266.

[81] *Id.*, art. 266.

[82] *Id.*, art. 15, annex III; G. A. Res. 48/263, Seabed Mining Agreement, art. 5 (Aug. 17, 1994); U.N. Doc. ISBA/16/C/WP.2, International Seabed Authority Council, Draft Regulations on Prospecting and Exploration of Cobalt-Rich Ferromanganese Crusts in the Area, regulations 3.i(a), 29 (2012); Responsibilities and Obligations of States Sponsoring Persons and Entities with Respect to Activities in the Area, Advisory Opinion of Feb. 1, 2011, ITLOS Rep 10, ¶ 163.

[83] *See, e.g.*, CICIN-SAIN ET AL., *supra* note 55; U.N. Doc. A/65/69, UN Secretary-General, Oceans and the Law of the Sea (Mar. 29, 2010), especially conclusions ¶ 323–25 at 88; *see also* discussion of new institutional setting and clearing-house mechanism *infra*.

to developing countries.[84] The hortatory nature of such obligations are particularly evident in Part XIV of UNCLOS, which sets out the ways and means for international cooperation and coordination in the voluntary transfer of technology on an equitable basis and the protection of the legitimate interests of technology holders, as well as on the establishment of national and regional marine scientific and technological research centers.[85] The Convention places emphasis on the voluntary transfer of technologies that can be used for deep seabed mining activities and the conservation of marine living resources,[86] along with the protection and preservation of the marine environment.[87] The inherent weakness of these provisions were well understood by the delegations representing developing countries attending the Third Law of the Sea Conference (1973–82) and their concerns were reflected in and informed the Resolution on Development of National Marine Science, Technology and Ocean Service Infrastructures, appended to the Final Act of the Conference.[88] The latter foresees a growing technological gap between developed and developing countries,[89] thereby undermining the effectiveness of UNCLOS.[90] For this reason, it urges industrialized countries to assist developing countries with respect to their scientific, technological and infrastructural needs.[91] Such assistance was further undermined by the 1994 Implementation Agreement, which effectively eliminated mandatory technology transfer in relation to seabed mining, as well as struck out the definition of technology in UNCLOS for this purpose.[92]

Despite these shortcomings, there have been a number of intergovernmental efforts since the coming into force of UNCLOS to operationalize

---

[84] The United States is a longstanding and well-versed opponent to the transfer of technology provisions in Parts XIII and XIV of the Law of the Seas Convention. *See* Jon M. van Dyke & David L. Teichmann, *Transfer of Seabed Mining Technology: A Stumbling Block to U.S. Ratification of the Law of the Sea Convention?*, 13 OCEAN DEV. & INT'L L. 427–55 (2009).

[85] UNCLOS, *supra* note 8, arts. 266–77.

[86] *Id.*, arts. 62(4)(j), 144(1).

[87] *Id.*, art. 202.

[88] Annex VI of the Final Act of UNCLOS III was firmly based on the contribution that UNCLOS was to make to the realization of a just and equitable international economic order through the establishment of a new régime for the seas and oceans, and the study, protection and preservation of the marine environment.

[89] Annex VI, Final Act, UNCLOS III.

[90] *Id.*, ¶ 3.

[91] *Id.*

[92] Agreement Relating to the Implementation of Part XI of the United Nations Convention on the Law of the Sea of Dec. 10, 1982, Sec. 5(2), July 28, 1994, 1836 U.N.T.S. 41.

the technology transfer provisions therein, especially in response to the requirement to develop "guidelines, criteria and standards for the transfer of marine technology on a bilateral basis or within the framework of international organizations and other fora."[93] Most notably, IOC–UNESCO adopted the Criteria and Guidelines for the Transfer of Marine Technology in 2003, which applies to "instruments, equipment, vessels, processes and methodologies required to produce and use knowledge to improve the study and understanding of the nature and resources of the ocean and coastal areas."[94] The Guidelines are predicated on the transfer of technology free of charge or at a reduced rate with a view to stimulating social and economic growth of developing states.[95] They also provide for the establishment of a clearing-house mechanism to coordinate the transfer of technology.[96] In practice, however, little has happened in the intervening period of twenty years since the adoption of the Guidelines and few requests have been received from developing countries in the absence of such a mechanism, a matter to which we will return.[97]

In summary, there are considerable shortcomings in UNCLOS and related instruments that lead directly and indirectly to the preferential treatment of the holders of ocean science infrastructure and related technologies in the practical aspects of implementing law of the sea obligations in relation to marine scientific research and technology transfer. More generally, the cumulative effect of these shortcomings is that they do little of substance to assist developing countries in implementing their law of the sea obligations or indeed in establishing a just

---

[93] UNCLOS, *supra* note 8, art. 271.

[94] International Oceanographic Commission Res. XXII-12, § A, ¶ 2 (July 2, 2003) (hereinafter IOC Guidelines); *see also* ARIEL W. GONZÁLEZ, *Cutting a Gordian Knot? Towards a Practical and Realistic Scheme for the Transfer of Marine Technology.* LAW, SCIENCE AND OCEAN MANAGEMENT 345–80 (Myron Nordquist et al. eds., 2007); U.N. Doc. A/66/70/Add.2, UN Secretary-General, Oceans and the Law of the Sea (Aug. 29, 2011); UNESCO & INTERGOVERNMENTAL OCEANOGRAPHIC COMMISSION, TRANSFER OF MARINE TECHNOLOGY: KNOWLEDGE SHARING AND CAPACITY DEVELOPMENT FOR SUSTAINABLE OCEAN AND COASTAL MANAGEMENT, U.N. Doc. IOC/BRO/2014/3 (2015); INTERGOVERNMENTAL OCEANOGRAPHIC COMMISSION, NON-PAPER ON EXISTING AND POTENTIAL CONTRIBUTIONS OF IOC-UNESCO TO THE BBNJ PROCESS 9–17 (2020).

[95] IOC Guidelines, *supra* note 94, § A, ¶ 2.

[96] *Id.*, § C, ¶ 1.

[97] See discussion of new institutional setting and clearing-house mechanism *infra*; *see also* Stephen Minas, *Marine Technology Transfer under a BBNJ Treaty: A Case for Transnational Network Cooperation*, 112 AM. J. INT'L L. UNBOUND 144–49 (2018).

and equitable international economic order in relation to the ocean.[98] As noted in one economic assessment, UNCLOS "responds in a confusing and occasionally unwise fashion to poor nations' legitimate interests in equitable treatment. In some respects, it completely ignores issues of fairness."[99] The absence of fairness appears to be most acute in relation to developing countries deriving benefits under UNCLOS from biological discoveries, technological innovation, deep ocean exploration and advances in biotechnology research on marine genetic resources of areas beyond national jurisdiction.[100] However, as will be seen next, there has been considerable efforts to resolve these shortcomings through protracted intergovernmental law of the sea negotiation processes that have been underway under the auspices of the UN for two decades and more.

3.5   Slow Road to Damascus via the UN

The rapid pace of technology developments in ocean science can be contrasted with the slow pedantic nature of international law-making to protect the marine environment. In this respect, international efforts to plug the regulatory gaps relating to marine biodiversity have been undertaken under various processes, which can be traced back to the deliberations of the UN Open-ended Informal Consultative Process on Oceans and the Law of the Sea in 2003 and 2004.[101] The subsequent UN General Assembly decision to establish an Ad hoc Open-ended Informal Working Group to study issues relating to the conservation and sustainable use of marine biological diversity beyond areas of national jurisdiction, which convened on nine occasions between 2006 and 2015,

---

[98] See *supra* note 88.

[99] Eric Posner & Alan Sykes, *Economic Foundation of the Law of the Sea*, 104 Am. J. Int'l L. 569, 569 (2010).

[100] *See, e.g.*, Lyle Glowka, *The Deepest of Ironies: Genetic Resources, Marine Scientific Research, and the Area*, 12 Ocean Y.B. 154–78 (1996); Craig Allen, *Protecting the Oceanic Gardens of Eden: International Law Issues in Deep-Sea Vent Resource Conservation and Management*, 13 Geo. Int'l Env't L. Rev. 563, 563 (2001); Doris König, *Genetic Resources of the Deep Sea: How Can They Be Preserved?* International Law Today: New Challenges and the Need for Reform? 141, 148 (Doris König et al., eds., 2008).

[101] Kristina Gjerde, *Perspectives on a Developing Regime for Marine Biodiversity Conservation and Sustainable Use beyond National Jurisdiction.* Ocean Law Debates: The 50-Year Legacy and Emerging Issues for the Years Ahead 354–80 (Harry N. Schreiber, Nilufer Oral & Moon-Sang Kwon eds., 2018).

moved the subject forward in the contorted labyrinth of treaty-making processes at the UN. A major milestone was achieved in the latter process when the Ad hoc Working Group agreed in 2011 to focus the negotiations on a package of measures concerning: marine genetic resources, including questions on the sharing of benefits; measures such as area-based management tools, including marine protected areas; environmental impact assessments; and capacity-building and the transfer of marine technology.[102] Again at the behest of the UN General Assembly, a preparatory committee to prepare the treaty-making process met on four occasions between 2016 and 2018 and made recommendations on the elements for inclusion in a new treaty under UNCLOS, specifically focused on the conservation and sustainable use of biodiversity beyond national jurisdiction.[103] Thereafter, the recommendations of the preparatory committee were carried forward to an intergovernmental conference with the task of developing a legally binding instrument on the basis of the package of measures previously agreed in 2011.[104]

Throughout these processes, the discussion on the legal status afforded to marine genetic resources rekindled to a degree the great ideological debates and diplomatic tensions that permeated the Third UN Conference between the proponents of the freedom of the high seas and the common heritage of mankind, including the relationship between the latter and the benefit sharing arrangements that will apply under the new agreement.[105] Moreover, it was evident from the early days of the negotiations that disparities in infrastructure and technical capability influenced the positions adopted by developing countries on many of the main issues tabled for negotiation.[106] At the same time, new

---

[102] G. A. Res. 72/249, *supra* note 17, para. 2.

[103] Ronán Long & Mariamalia Rodríguez-Chaves, *Anatomy of a New International Instrument for Biodiversity Beyond National Jurisdiction: First Impressions of the Preparatory Process*, 6 ENV'T LIAB. 213–29 (2015).

[104] G. A. Res. 72/249, *supra* note 17.

[105] *See, e.g.*, DIRE TLADI, *The Common Heritage of Mankind in the Proposed Implementing Agreement*. LEGAL ORDER IN THE WORLD'S OCEAN: UN CONVENTION ON THE LAW OF THE SEA 72–90 (Myron H. Nordquist, John Norton Moore & Ronán Long eds., 2018).

[106] *See, e.g.*, Rena Lee, President, Intergovernmental Conference on an International Legally Binding Instrument under the United Nations Convention on the Law of the Sea on the Conservation and Sustainable Use of Marine Biological Diversity of Areas beyond National Jurisdiction, Address at the Closing of the Third Session (Sept. 13, 2019); International Institute for Sustainable Development (IISD), *Summary of the Third Session of the Intergovernmental Conference (IGC) on the Conservation and Sustainable Use of Marine Biodiversity of Areas beyond National Jurisdiction: 19–30*

technologies may be part of the solution to resolve some of the most contentious matters that need to be resolved, including: the sharing of benefits from marine genetic resources; the building of scientific and technical capacity of developing countries; and the development and transfer of marine technology.[107] Much of the detail on how this is to be achieved remains unsettled after the fourth and a further session of the intergovernmental conference.[108] Nonetheless, at the time of writing, the lion's share of the deliberations at the UN appear to be complete and the broad contours of what is possible in terms of options is already sketched out in considerable detail in the draft text for the purpose of taking the negotiations forward to a successful conclusion. Accordingly, at the time of writing, it is easy to surmise that the outcome of the negotiations may well mark a new era in the regulation of marine technologies and a turning point in providing technical assistance to developing states. A number of facets of the draft text of the agreement therefore calls for further comment.[109]

3.6 Questions of Terms and Objectives

The Convention and law of the sea instruments in general are in the main part silent on the meaning of marine science- and technology-related terms.[110] In contrast, several scientific and technical terms are the subject of negotiation at the intergovernmental conference.[111] Most notably, one of the options canvassed by the draft text of the agreement relates to the meaning of "marine technology," which reads as follows:

August 2019, 25 EARTH NEGOTIATIONS BULL. (Sept. 2, 2019) (hereinafter IISD); *see also* Roach, *supra* note 16, at 25–89.

[107] *Id.*

[108] The fourth session was held on Mar. 7–18, 2022. The United Nations General Assembly may decide to convene an additional session in August 2022 as required to bring the process to a conclusion.

[109] The text referred to is the REVISED DRAFT TEXT, *supra* note 19.

[110] For a definition of technology that no longer applies, see art. 5(8), Annex III, UNCLOS. In the law of the sea, undefined terms more generally remain particularly problematic *see, e.g.*, GEORGE WALKER, DEFINITIONS FOR THE LAW OF THE SEA: TERMS NOT DEFINED BY THE 1982 CONVENTION *passim* (2012); *see also* J. ASHLEY ROACH & ROBERT W. SMITH, EXCESSIVE MARITIME CLAIMS 486–500 (4th ed. 2020).

[111] *See* REVISED DRAFT TEXT, *supra* note 19, art. 1; *see also* SIVA THAMBISETTY, *Biodiversity beyond National Jurisdiction: (Intellectual) Property Heuristics.* MARINE BIODIVERSITY BEYOND NATIONAL JURISDICTION 131, 132–35 (Myron H. Nordquist & Ronán Long, eds., 2021).

information and data, provided in a user-friendly format, on marine
sciences and related marine operations and services; manuals,
guidelines, criteria, standards, reference materials; sampling and methodology equipment; observation facilities and equipment (e.g., remote
sensing equipment, buoys, tide gauges, shipboard and other means of
ocean observation); equipment for in situ and laboratory observations,
analysis and experimentation; computer and computer software, including models and modelling techniques; and expertise, knowledge, skills,
technical, scientific and legal know-how and analytical methods related to
marine scientific research and observation.[112]

There is also a proposal to define the transfer of marine technology to
mean "the transfer of the instruments, equipment, vessels, processes and
methodologies required to produce and use knowledge to improve the
study and understanding of the nature and resources of the ocean."[113]

These two relatively open-ended definitions are informed by the
scheme for the transfer of technology set out in the 2003 IOC–
UNESCO Criteria and Guidelines on the Transfer of Marine
Technology, discussed previously.[114] If adopted, these broad definitions
have the potential to tip the scales toward serving the needs of developing
states in so far as they will bring both physical and intangible assets
within the scope of the capacity-building and technology transfer provisions of the agreement including information and computer software, as
well as expertise and skills in technology, science and law. The definitions
also appear wide enough to bring many if not all emerging technologies
and nonmarine-related technologies within the scope of the substantive
provisions on capacity-building and technology transfer set out in the
agreement. Unsurprisingly perhaps, the wide scope and need for expansive definitions were questioned at the third session of the intergovernmental conference by developed countries including those represented by
the European Union (EU) and its member states, Japan, the United
States, the Republic of Korea, Canada, Australia and Switzerland.[115] In
marked contrast and perhaps in recognition of the well-founded belief

[112] REVISED DRAFT TEXT, *supra* note 19, art. 1(11). This is a more expansive definition than
that found in art. 5(8), Annex III, UNCLOS, which states that technology "means the
specialized equipment and technical know-how, including manuals, designs, operating
instructions, training and technical advice and assistance, necessary to assemble, maintain and operate a viable system and the legal right to use these items for that purpose on
a non-exclusive basis."
[113] REVISED DRAFT TEXT, *supra* note 19, art. 1(14).
[114] *See* IOC Guidelines, *supra* note 94.
[115] *See* IISD, *supra* note 106, at 3–4.

that emerging technologies are primary drivers of sustainable economic growth, developing states including most especially Pacific Small Island Developing States supported strongly their inclusion in the draft text.[116]

In relation to the meaning of other terms that are closely related to the provisions on technology transfer, the draft text is notably reticent in several respects. For instance, it does not define the meaning of the term "capacity-building."[117] Instructively and perhaps indicative of the difficulties that need to be overcome, three options were canvassed at the first three sessions of the intergovernmental conference on how best to address this aspect of the agreement, namely: the inclusion of an indicative list of capacity-building activities in the agreement, or in an annex thereto; or mandating a future Conference of the Parties or a Scientific and Technical Body to develop such a list in due course.[118]

Another remarkable aspect of the deliberations is that there has been a dearth of discussion about the meaning of core terms such as "conservation" and "sustainable use,"[119] or to link such terms with the attainment of specific conservation or sustainable use targets on marine biodiversity.[120] This omission is surprising as the meanings of the aforementioned terms go to the very heart of the objectives of the new instrument and will have a major bearing on the material scope, as well as the rights and responsibilities of states parties. In the longer-term, there is a danger that the absence of clarity on the precise meaning of these terms will lead to a relatively shallow instrument in terms of

---

[116] *Id.,* at 4.

[117] During the intersessional period after the third session of the intergovernmental conference, the core Latin American states proposed defining the term as "any activity intended to enable or improve academic, professional and technical training; the exchange of knowledge and skills; access to physical infrastructure; institutional strengthening; communication between relevant actors; the exchange of scientific information, technological development and innovation; and raising awareness through public information and basic knowledge about marine biodiversity in areas outside of national jurisdiction." This proposed definition draws from the concepts included in the IOC's capacity development strategy. *See* UNESCO & INTERGOVERNMENTAL OCEANOGRAPHIC COMMISSION, IOC CAPACITY DEVELOPMENT STRATEGY: 2015–2021 15–18 (2016).

[118] REVISED DRAFT TEXT, *supra* note 19, art. 46; *see also* Lee, *supra* note 106, at 17–21.

[119] Roach, *supra* note 16, *passim.* On the many unresolved issues on how conservation and sustainable use objectives are to be realized going into the fourth session of the IGC, *see also* Fran Humphries & Harriet Harden-Davies, *Practical Policy Solutions for the Final Stage of BBNJ Treaty Negotiations,* 22 MARINE POL'Y 103, 910, 1–7 (2020).

[120] *See, e.g.,* Paris Agreement to the United Nations Framework Convention on Climate Change, art. 2(a), Dec. 12, 2015, 27 U.N.T.S. 7 (hereinafter Paris Agreement); *see also* discussion on technology mechanism, *infra.*

substance.[121] In order to rectify this shortcoming, it is still open to the plenipotentiaries at the final session of the conference to flesh-out the meaning of these terms by embedding specific conservation targets in the preamble or operative parts of the agreement. With this in mind, they could for instance set down a minimum threshold of spatial coverage of the ocean in relation to the designation of marine protected areas and the application of area-based management tools, such as a 30 percent target of marine protected areas by 2030.[122] Apart from adding substance to the meaning of the term conservation under the agreement, an added advantage of doing so is that the attainment and implementation of spatial coverage targets are easily monitored using remote-sensing technologies such as the systems described elsewhere in this book.

Perhaps wisely, there appeared to be little appetite throughout the negotiations to define technical terms pertaining to genetic research such as "biotechnology," "derivative" or "digital sequence information."[123] Likewise, it is doubtful that the agreement when adopted will provide a definition of marine genetic research or indeed marine scientific research.[124] The latter lacuna is unlikely to compromise the effectiveness

---

[121] This is a relatively common weakness in international treaties. *See* Andrew T. Guzman, *The Design of International Agreements*, 16 Eur. J. Int'l L. 579, 602 (2005).

[122] There have been a number of political initiatives including the démarche taken by the UK and forty-one other countries to designate 30 percent of the ocean as marine protected areas by 2030, as one of the goals for the post 2020 biodiversity framework under the Convention on Biological Diversity. *See* U.N. Doc. CBD/WG2020/2/4, Open-Ended Working Group on the Post-2020 Global Biodiversity Framework, Report of the Open-Ended Working Group on the Post-2020 Global Biodiversity Framework on Its Second Meeting, at 11–13 (2020); U.N. Doc. CBD/WG2020/REC/2/1, Open-Ended Working Group on the Post-2020 Global Biodiversity Framework, Recommendation Adopted by the Open-Ended Working Group on the Post-2020 Global Biodiversity Framework, at 10–12 (2020).

[123] There is little international consensus on what many of the technical terms mean *see e.g.*, U.N. Doc. CBD/DSI/AHTEG/2020/1/3, Ad hoc Technical Expert Group on Digital Sequence Information on Genetic Resources, Digital Sequence Information on Genetic Resources: Concept, Scope and Current Use, at 2 (2020); *see also* Charles Lawson & Michelle Rourke, *Digital Sequence Information as a Marine Genetic Resource Under the Proposed UNCLOS Legally Binding Instrument*, 120 Marine Pol'y 103878 (2020). On the importance of digital sequence information and new technologies and the implications of the agreement, see Rogers et al., *supra* note 4.

[124] There has been some discussion of the meaning of marine scientific research in the context of access or activities in relation to marine genetic resources, see statement of the president at the closing of the third session and the oral reports of the facilitators of the informal working groups to the plenary on August 30, 2019. *See* Lee, *supra* note 106, at 6, 23; *see also* Roach, *supra* note 16, at 33.

of the agreement, particularly when one considers that the International Court of Justice did not find it necessary to define scientific research in order to render its judgement in the Antarctic Whaling case.[125]

Overall, the approach of the negotiators and their reluctance to insert definitions of technical terms into the text appears prudent. Similar to other law of the sea treaties, the agreement cannot be expected to define technical standards or to prescribe in detail the regulatory requirements that will apply to new technologies. Indeed, such a task would be almost impossible, and, in all likelihood, such terms run the risk of becoming outdated rather quickly. Nonetheless, the agreement needs to be responsive to the dynamic nature of technological innovation in marine science as well as to the adoption of complementary instruments of binding character by other international organizations such as the IMO. Instructively in this regard, the parent Convention to the agreement uses a variety of terms and expressions to incorporate generally accepted international rules, standards, regulations or procedures into its provisions and states parties are obliged to implement and conform to such requirements, whether or not they are party to the legal instrument establishing them.[126] In some instances, UNCLOS uses peremptory language to indicate the standard of national laws to enforce international minimum requirements in so far as they must have "at least the same effect as," "no less effective than" or "taking into account rules and standards" established by competent international organizations.[127]

---

[125] Whaling in the Antarctic (Austl. v. Japan), Judgement, 2014 I.C.J. 226, ¶ 86 (Mar. 31).

[126] UNCLOS, supra note 8, art. 211(2). There are several different formulations of these requirements in the provisions in the Convention on the international rules and national legislation to prevent, reduce and control pollution of the marine environment, see, arts. 207(1), 209(2), 210(6), 212(1), 213, 214, 216(1) and 222; on the duties of flag states on the high seas, arts. 94(3)(4) and (5); on the conservation and management of the living resources of the high seas, art. 119(1)(a). Also, art. 10(c), Fish Stocks Agreement. The instruments corresponding to "generally accepted international rules and standards" are set out in IMO Circ. Ltr. No. 2456, Implication of UNCLOS for the Organization, Annex II (Feb. 17, 2003). For commentary on rules of reference, see, inter alia: UNITED NATIONS, OBLIGATIONS OF STATES PARTIES UNDER THE UNITED NATIONS CONVENTION ON THE LAW OF THE SEA AND COMPLEMENTARY INSTRUMENTS (2004); JAMES HARRISON, SAVING THE OCEANS THROUGH LAW 176–77, 214–17, 282 (2017). On the role of other instruments in developing the law of the sea, see CATHERINE REDGWELL, Mind the Gap in the GAIRS: The Role of Other Instruments. CONVENTION REGIME IMPLEMENTATION IN THE OFFSHORE ENERGY SECTOR 600, 617 (Nigel Banks & Seline Trevisanut eds., 2015).

[127] In relation to the need to "take into account" rules and standards established by competent international organizations on the markings of scientific and research

One can therefore argue that there is a compelling case for the inclusion of a clause in the draft text that requires states parties to comply with "generally accepted rules and standards established or adopted by a competent international organization or diplomatic conference," in relation to future technologies that may be applied to attain the objectives of the agreement.[128] This legal drafting technique, commonly referred to as rules of reference is used by UNCLOS and international environmental treaties to maintain uniformity in the international regulation of offshore activities.[129] Such a reference will update obligations arising under the agreement with legislative developments in other sectors in response to technological, environmental and legal considerations that change over time. States parties will thus be required to conform to generally accepted international rules and standards as they apply to new and emerging technologies, thereby establishing a coordination and compliance mechanism linked to international minimum standards without having to amend the agreement. The inclusion of a clause on rules of reference will also facilitate an evolutionary approach to treaty interpretation by international dispute settlement bodies should the need arise in the future.[130] Crucially, the proposed approach will ensure that the agreement will be read and interpreted by international courts and tribunals in light of other international treaty regimes.

3.7   Future-Proofing the Agreement through a Process of Normative Accretion

The draft text sets out a number of normative principles and approaches to guide states parties in attaining conservation and sustainable use objectives of the agreement.[131] To a greater or lesser degree, all of the principles and approaches may well entail the application of scientific

---

installations to ensure safety at sea and air navigation, for example, see UNCLOS, supra note 8, art. 262.

[128] See REDGWELL, *supra note* 126, at 40–61.

[129] See, e.g., UNCLOS, *supra note* 8, arts. 210(6), 211(2); U.N. Conference on Straddling Fish Stocks and Highly Migratory Fish Stocks Res. 164/37, art. 10(c) (Sept. 8, 1995); *see also* HARRISON, *supra* note 126, at 176–77, 214–17, 282.

[130] A violation of the Convention on the International Regulations for Preventing Collisions at Sea, as "generally accepted international regulations" concerning measures necessary to ensure maritime safety, was deemed to constitute a violation of UNCLOS itself in the South China Sea Arbitration (Philippines v. China) (Award) (July 12, 2016) (PCA Case No 2013-19) ICGJ 495, para. 1803.

[131] REVISED DRAFT TEXT, *supra* note 19, art. 5.

technologies, including: the principle of nonregression; the polluter-pays principle; the precautionary principle/approach; the ecosystem approach; an approach that builds ecosystem resilience to the adverse effects of climate change and ocean acidification and restores ecosystem integrity; and the use of best available science, as well as the traditional knowledge of indigenous peoples and local communities.[132] If adopted, these principles and approaches, as direct obligations under international law, will be particularly important in the context of interpreting, applying and developing the rights and responsibilities of future states parties. At an organizational level, they will also inform the work and decision-making of the proposed new institutions including the proposed Scientific and Technical Body, discussed further later on.[133]

In light of the dynamic and rapid pace of technological developments in ocean science, one can again make a strong argument in favor of setting down additional normative requirements that obliges states parties to use "best available techniques (technologies)" and "best environmental practices" in the attainment of the objectives of the agreement.[134] These normative constructs, as evaluative standards, feature in several global and regional treaties pertaining to the marine environment and are especially useful in instances where there is a need to adopt precautionary measures to mitigate environmental risk or in response to climate change.[135] As such, they establish one of the most formidable benchmarks governing the use of new and emerging technologies in the protection of the marine environment.[136] If included in the agreement, these normative requirements will create direct obligations that are dynamic and that will evolve over time in line with technology developments and scientific knowledge. Furthermore, their precise normative content and weight can be determined by

---

[132] *Id.*

[133] REVISED DRAFT TEXT, *supra* note 19, art. 49.

[134] *See* Advisory Opinion of Feb. 1, 2011, *supra* note 20, ¶¶ 136–37; *see also* HARRISON, *supra* note 126, at 78–80, 224–25.

[135] Convention for the Protection of the Marine Environment of the North-East Atlantic app. ¶¶ 2, 6, Sept. 22, 1992, 2354 U.N.T.S. 67; Convention on the Protection of the Marine Environment of the Baltic Sea Area, art. 6(21), Mar. 22, 1974, 1507 U.N.T.S. 166; *see also* Convention on the Prevention of Marine Pollution by Dumping of Wastes and Other Matter ¶ 8, 1046 U.N.T.S. 120 (as amended).

[136] André Nollkaemper, *Legal Implications of the Obligation to Apply the Best Available Technology*, 26 MARINE POLLUTION BULL. 236–38 (1993).

international courts and tribunals by means of their contentious and advisory jurisprudence.[137]

There are several broad formulations of obligations that states parties must ensure under the draft text including taking the necessary measures to ensure implementation and compliance with its provisions.[138] The agreement will thus create obligations of conduct and due diligence for states parties in taking reasonable measures to ensure that public and private operators under their jurisdiction or control adhere to the general obligation to conserve and sustainably use biodiversity. Instructively, international courts and tribunals have held that due diligence to protect and preserve the marine environment can be measured against the technical and scientific standards commonly accepted by states.[139] Moreover, in instances of dispute settlement concerning environmental harm, due diligence is a flexible and evolving standard of responsibility.[140] Due diligence also requires vigilance on the part of states parties in the enforcement and the exercise of administrative control over public and private operators,[141] including one must assume on the use of new technologies to undertake research on marine genetic resources of areas beyond national jurisdiction. The due diligence obligations that will flow from the agreement are a vital long-term consideration that will go to the effectiveness of the instrument in many ocean regions, where there are few means to ensure compliance with international obligations.

A noteworthy and related question concerns the level of developing country capability to deploy new technologies and if this is a factor that ought to be taken into consideration in determining the standard of due diligence that applies in the conservation and sustainable use of biodiversity. There is jurisprudential guidance to be derived on this issue from the International Tribunal for the Law of the Sea (ITLOS) Seabed Mining Opinion, which held that UNCLOS did not accord preferential treatment

---

[137] *See, e.g.*, Pulp Mills on the River Uruguay (Arg. v. Uru.), Judgment, 2010 I.C.J. 14; Advisory Opinion of Feb. 1, 2011, *supra* note 20, ¶ 117; Request for Advisory Opinion submitted by the Sub-regional Fisheries Commission, Advisory Opinion of Apr. 2, 2015, ITLOS Rep. 4 (hereinafter Advisory Opinion of Apr. 2, 2015); South China Sea Arbitration (Philippines v. China), 33 R.I.A.A. 153, ¶¶ 743, 754, 944, 956, 959, 964, 971, 974 (Perm Ct. Arb. 2016).

[138] Revised Draft Text, *supra* note 19, art. 53(1).

[139] *Id.*; *see also* Duncan French & Tim Stephens, ILA Study Group on Due Diligence in International Law, First Report 29–30 (2014).

[140] Advisory Opinion of Feb. 1, 2011, *supra* note 20, ¶ 117.

[141] Advisory Opinion of Apr. 2, 2015, *supra* note 137, ¶ 131, *quoting* Pulp Mills on the River Uruguay, *supra* note 137, ¶ 197.

to sponsoring states that are developing states in the context of seabed mining activities.[142] With a view to establishing a level playing field in relation to international obligations, the ITLOS Seabed Disputes Chamber advised that the responsibilities and liability of the sponsoring state apply equally to all sponsoring states, whether developing or developed.[143] Accordingly, one can expect that disparities in accessing and deploying technologies will not detract disproportionately from the due diligence obligations that arise under the agreement. Furthermore, the due diligence obligations imposed on developing states parties are all the more reason to have adequate and meaningful capacity-building and technology transfer provisions embedded in the agreement.

3.8   Role of Technology in Monitoring and Benefit Sharing

Maritime boundary and ocean observation technologies are germane to monitoring and ensuring compliance with the geographical and material scope of the agreement.[144] In this context, the agreement will apply to areas beyond national jurisdiction, defined as the high seas and the area.[145] As seen elsewhere in this volume, the precise geographical limits of these maritime jurisdictional spaces can be determined using the seabed survey tools to survey the outer limits of the continental margin in accordance with UNCLOS,[146] as well as to measure and chart EEZ and territorial sea limits in other geographical regions such as the Mediterranean Sea, which remains predominantly high seas with some exceptions.[147] Similarly, video and positional data can be used to identify the precise geographical locus of genetic research activities in the supra-jacent waters of the continental margin beyond 200 M, as well as to ensure compliance with the sovereign rights and responsibilities of the coastal state over continental shelf resources, including with respect to living organisms belonging to sedentary species on the outer continental margin.[148]

Since the treaty-making negotiations commenced at the UN, it is evident that modern tracking technologies have the potential to play a

---

[142] Advisory Opinion of Feb. 1, 2011, *supra* note 20, ¶ 158.
[143] *Id.*
[144] REVISED DRAFT TEXT, *supra* note 19, art. 4(2).
[145] *Id.*, art. 1(4).
[146] UNCLOS, *supra* note 8, art. 76.
[147] REVISED DRAFT TEXT, *supra* note 19, art. 15(4).
[148] UNCLOS, *supra* note 8, art. 77(4); *see* SCHOFIELD & MOSSOP, *supra* note 75, at 297–99.

vital role in resolving many of the intractable issues associated with access and the use of marine genetic resources, especially with respect to the sharing of benefits under the agreement.[149] This aspect of the draft text has been the source of an intense debate, particularly about the realization of a just and equitable international economic order in relations to the law of the sea.[150] As mentioned previously, a principal challenge relates to balancing the principle of the common heritage of humankind and the freedom to undertake marine scientific research on the high seas.[151] Significantly, at the third session of the intergovernmental conference, the plenipotentiaries expressed divergent views about the establishment of a track-and-trace mechanism under the agreement for the purpose of benefit sharing, or establishing a role for a clearing-house mechanism (reviewed later), or indeed assigning a role to the Scientific and Technical Body to this end.[152] One of the most sensitive issues concerns the establishment of an obligatory notification system under the agreement in relation to the sampling and use of marine genetic resources.[153]

In line with their longstanding positions on such issues, the United States and the Russian Federation in particular have opposed the setting down of prescriptive requirements in relation to marine genetic resources, especially measures that will impede the freedom to conduct marine scientific research or indeed inhibit the generation of scientific data and information.[154] Moreover, diverging views were expressed by the plenipotentiaries on the types of activities subject to monitoring or whether it should be a voluntary or mandatory benefit sharing scheme that is established by the agreement.[155] Nonetheless, it is clearly apparent that modern technologies can be applied to ensure the orderly functioning of a fair and effective scheme. For instance, should the plenipotentiaries agree, information and communication technologies can be applied to facilitate the notification, permitting or licensing arrangements for access to marine genetic samples in situ, along with

[149] UNCLOS, *supra* note 8, arts. 7–13.
[150] *See* JASPARS & BROWN, *supra* note 74, at 98–130; THAMBISETTY, *supra* note 111, at 134.
[151] This has been a fundamental challenge since the commencement of the negotiation processes and most particularly at the intergovernmental conference, see TLADI, *supra* note 105, at 72–90.
[152] Lee, *supra* note 106, at 5-22–7-22; IISD, *supra* note 106, at 6–8.
[153] *Id.*
[154] IISD, *supra* note 106, at 6–8.
[155] *See* Lee, *supra* note 106, at 5-22–7-22.

any requirements concerning the bioinformatic recording of marine genetic resource data, marker identity and gene sequence data.[156] Information technologies can also be used to protect the intellectual property entitlements of those involved in research and development of genetic resources.[157] There is also considerable scope to use blockchain and distributed ledgers to facilitate the sharing of information and the tracing of samples for benefit sharing purposes including in silico information and digital sequence data.[158]

All of these issues remain on the table going into the final session(s) of the conference but remain highly contentious. Most notably, throughout the treaty-making processes at the UN, doubts have been expressed about the merit the establishment of an expensive track-and-trace system, or the alternative of a more workable traceability system, primarily because of the relatively remote possibility of generating scientific discoveries with commercial potential.[159] Moreover, diverging views have been expressed about the substantial costs, the administrative burden and the informatic requirements, as well as feasibility and desirability of a proposed identification and notification system.[160] Technology solutions nonetheless appear to provide the key to balancing the respective interests and needs of states parties in sample collection and data access,[161] as well as in the establishment of transparent and effective modalities for the sharing and monitoring of benefits derived from marine genetic resources.[162] Although not yet agreed, this may include monitoring compliance with the rules and standards adopted under the auspices of the World Intellectual Property Organization and the World Trade Organization.[163] Irrespective of the outcome of the negotiations on these matters, one study points out that "developments in technologies for discovering, collecting, using, storing and sharing genetic resources and associated information will continue to push the boundaries" of

---

[156] See JASPARS & BROWN, *supra* note 74, at 98–130; *see also* FRAN HUMPHRIES, MURIEL RABONE & MARCEL JASPARS, Traceability Approaches for Marine Genetic Resources Under the Proposed Ocean (BBNJ) Treaty, 8 FRONTIERS IN MARINE SCI. (2021). Also see the discussion on unique identifier postcollection that ties the sample to a specific sampling event by Rogers et al., *supra* note 4.

[157] REVISED DRAFT TEXT, *supra* note 19, art. 12.

[158] JASPARS & BROWN, *supra* note 74, at 124.

[159] See Long & Rodríguez-Chaves, *supra* note 99, at 221–23.

[160] See Lee, *supra* note 106, at 7; IISD, *supra* note 106, at 8.

[161] REVISED DRAFT TEXT, *supra* note 19, art. 10.

[162] *Id.*, arts. 11, 13.

[163] *Id.*, art. 12.

regulatory systems.[164] In anticipation of these developments, a fundamental and closely related aspect of the agreement concerns the structure
and mandate of the institutions that sit at the heart of the proposed
governance arrangements for biodiversity beyond national jurisdiction.

3.9   New Institutional Architecture

The draft text proposes the establishment of three institutions, namely: a
Conference of the Parties, supported by a Scientific and Technical Body;
and a Secretariat.[165]

The precise form and functions of the proposed institutions are contingent upon the outcome of the negotiations on the substantive parts of
the agreement. By the end of the third session of the intergovernmental
conference, the outline of the institutional architecture was nonetheless
evident from the draft text and includes the establishment and role of a
Conference of the Parties as the decision-making body responsible for
the implementation of the agreement.[166] The work of the latter will be
supported by a subsidiary Scientific and Technical Body with consultative, advisory, monitoring and reporting functions.[167] The name of this
body alone is a good reason for optimism and its powers may extend to
providing advice on a wide range of technical and other matters concerning the four substantive strands of the agreement.[168] Much of the
detail has yet to be agreed but it may include: the identification of state-
of-the-art technology and expertise related to the conservation and
sustainable use of marine biological diversity;[169] the establishment of
working relationships with bodies with similar mandates under other
regulatory frameworks;[170] and with respect to the use of the knowledge of
indigenous peoples and local communities.[171]

Notably, at the third session of the intergovernmental conference,
there was a divergence of views expressed by the plenipotentiaries on
the precise role of the Scientific and Technical Body. The Pacific Small
Island Developing States have advocated that the body should be called

---

[164] *See* Humphries & Harden-Davies, *supra* note 119, at 13.
[165] REVISED DRAFT TEXT, *supra* note 19, arts. 48–50.
[166] *Id.*, art. 48(4).
[167] *Id.*, art. 49(4).
[168] *Id.*
[169] *Id.*, art. 49(4)(g).
[170] *Id.*, art. 49(3).
[171] *See* Humphries & Harden-Davies, *supra* note 119, at 12.

the Scientific, Technology and Technical Body. In this regard, delegations from the Global South and small island developing states have called for the body to be granted an express technological mandate,[172] a proposal that attracted support from a range of developing countries including the EU, Switzerland and Japan.[173] The Russian Federation opposed this proposal, China and Iceland erred on the side of caution, and the United States advocating a role for nonparty states in the work of such a body.[174] There was no discussion of how, or if, the advisory body will have a mandate to make recommendations on ethical matters pertaining to the use of molecular engineering technologies in marine genetic research, such as the one mentioned previously concerning the use of Crispr-Cas for gene editing.[175] The delegation representing the Holy See was the only one to propose that research on marine genetic resources must not be undertaken "to the detriment of the human race for unethical or unapproved purposes as recognized by national or international law."[176] Remarkably, the whole issue of biosafety was not discussed in any detail at the first three sessions of the intergovernmental conference.[177] Overall, however, it is foreseeable that the new institutions will end up with significant powers and responsibilities to respond to technical innovation and new scientific discoveries, which may extend to the use of artificial intelligence to enable quicker and more advanced drug discovery.[178] They will thus be well placed to drive future regulatory developments with respect to new technologies. That may even include a role concerning the development and application of blue/green technologies to further understand and mitigate the impacts of environmental and climate change pressures on biodiversity,[179] a topic that we will return to later.[180]

---

[172] See Lee, *supra* note 106, at 22; IISD, *supra* note 106, at 17–18.

[173] IISD, *supra* note 106, at 17.

[174] *Id.*

[175] See BASIAK ET AL., *supra* note 13, at 43.

[176] IISD, *supra* note 106, at 7.

[177] See Humphries & Harden-Davies, *supra* note 119, at 12.

[178] See Ewen Callaway, "*It Will Change Everything*": DeepMind's AI Makes Gigantic Leap in Solving Protein Structures, NATURE, Nov. 30, 2020.

[179] For example, the project underway at Woods Hole Oceanographic Institute and Harvard University on fuelling ocean robots. See Evan Lubofsky, *Opinion: Microbial Methane: New Fuel for Ocean Robots?* OCEANUS, Mar. 8, 2021.

[180] See discussion in Section 3.10 on how the agreement can strike a more equitable balance in the law of the sea in relation to benefit sharing.

3.10   Empowering a One-Stop Information Sharing Platform

Part and parcel of the new institutional setting is the proposal to establish a clearing-house mechanism to facilitate the implementation of the agreement.[181] This proposal draws from similar mechanisms operating under other environmental and climate change treaties.[182] If it comes to fruition, the clearing-house mechanism will be a very welcome and long overdue development in the law of the sea that will draw together the scientific and technical dimensions, along with the engagement of public and private actors, to ensure the conservation and sustainable use of biodiversity.[183] At an operational level, the clearing-house mechanism will operate as a centralized web-based platform that facilitates the collective implementation of the agreement in a transparent and effective manner. As such, it will have to serve the interests and needs of states parties and the new institutions, as well as delivering on the many practical aspects of operationalizing the provisions on marine genetic resources, environmental impact assessment, area-based management tools, and capacity-building and the transfer of marine technology.[184] As seen previously, this may extend to the benefit sharing arrangements with respect to marine genetic resources, as well as information on access and the use of samples and data, intellectual property rights and patents, and scientific reports, along with opportunities for transnational collaboration in research and the development of new technologies.[185]

---

[181] REVISED DRAFT TEXT, *supra* note 19, art. 51; *see also* Humphries & Harden-Davies, *supra* note 119, at 13.

[182] *See* Convention on Biological Diversity, June 5, 1992, 1760 U.N.T.S. 79; Basel Convention on the Control of Transboundary Movements of Hazardous Wastes and Their Disposal, Mar. 22, 1989, 1673 U.N.T.S. 57 (as amended); Rotterdam Convention on the Prior Informed Consent Procedure for Certain Hazardous Chemicals and Pesticides in International Trade, Sept. 10, 1998, 2244 U.N.T.S. 337; Stockholm Convention on Persistent Organic Pollutants, May 22, 2001, 2256 U.N.T.S. 119; Intergovernmental Science-Policy Platform on Biodiversity and Ecosystem Services, IPBES Capacity-Building Rolling Plan (2017); *see also* HARRIET HARDEN-DAVIES, *Towards a Capacity-Building Toolkit for Marine Biodiversity beyond National Jurisdiction*. MARINE BIODIVERSITY BEYOND NATIONAL JURISDICTION 231–40 (Myron H. Nordquist & Ronán Long, eds., 2021); Minas, *supra* note 97, at 144–49; Marjo Vierros & Harriet Harden-Davies, *Capacity Building and Technology Transfer for Improving Governance of Marine Areas Both Beyond and Within National Jurisdiction*, 122 MARINE POL'Y 104158 (2020).

[183] UNITED NATIONS, THE FIRST GLOBAL INTEGRATED MARINE ASSESSMENT 923–33 (2016).

[184] REVISED DRAFT TEXT, *supra* note 19, arts. 51(2)–(7).

[185] *Id.*, arts. 51(3)–(4).

One possibility is that the clearing-house mechanism will be operated by IOC–UNESCO, acting in concert with the International Seabed Authority, the IMO and other relevant organizations.[186] Again, the draft text draws from the 2003 IOC–UNESCO Criteria and Guidelines on the Transfer of Marine Technology, which, as mentioned earlier, provides for such a mechanism.[187] One of the core and essential functions of the latter is to provide scientists in developing countries with technical expertise and practical experience in technology transfer.[188] As such, the IOC–UNESCO clearing-house mechanism for the Latin America and Caribbean region, within the framework of the Caribbean Atlas project, may prove to be a useful prototype in so far as it shares information at a regional level on education and training opportunities, laboratories, institutions and research vessels, along with geospatial data and the findings of marine environmental research.[189] Furthermore, the IOC is developing a clearing-house mechanism in the form of the "Ocean InfoHub" aimed at integrating data, information and knowledge resources services, which can also be adapted to service the agreement.[190]

At the third session of the intergovernmental conference, delegations representing both developed and developing states stressed the importance of the proposed clearing-house mechanism as a "vital information exchange platform."[191] Moreover, the EU, CARICOM (Caribbean Community), Australia, the United States, the Russian Federation, China and Switzerland envisage that its future development could entail a role for the planned Conference of the Parties.[192] Another novel proposal is that the clearing-house mechanism will be used to share information on the legislative, administrative and policy measures to ensure compliance with the agreement.[193] Clearly, the precise modalities on how such a mechanism will operate in practice and facilitate the collecting of scientific information, as well as matching the capacity-building needs of developing states, will be closely linked to the mandate and work of the proposed Scientific and Technical Body, as well as the

---

[186] *Id.*, art. 51(6).
[187] *See* IOC Guidelines, *supra* note 94, at 11–12.
[188] *Id.*
[189] *See* UNESCO, *supra* note 49, at 116–17.
[190] *See* IOC Guidelines, *supra* note 94, at 15–16; *see also* OCEAN INFOHUB PROJECT, https://oceaninfohub.org/ (last visited Mar. 24, 2021) (online).
[191] *See* Lee, *supra* note 106, at 19; IISD, *supra* note 106, at 22.
[192] IISD, *supra* note 106, at 18.
[193] *Id.*

financial resources underpinning the agreement. If resourced properly, the web-based platform has the potential to be a vital operational mechanism linked to the day-to-day implementation of the four substantive parts of the agreement, including the provisions on marine genetic resources.[194] Again, concerns have been raised at the third conference session about some quintessential technical matters, with Israel pointing out for instance that the mechanism should not undermine intellectual property rights, or compromise any information that would normally be subject to protection under the national law of states parties, a view supported by the United States and the Russian Federation.[195]

3.11   Match-making and Establishing a Technology Mechanism

In view of the dynamic nature of ocean science and related technologies, it is difficult to see how the prospective regulatory arrangements for the conservation and sustainable use of biodiversity will deliver on its goals unless it provides access to science, technology, expertise and other resources to states parties based on their specific needs. Therefore, one of the important options set out in the draft text relates to the match-making functions of the clearing mechanism with a view to aligning capacity-building needs with donor support from governmental, nongovernmental or private entities.[196]

   The IOC–UNESCO anticipates that the Ocean InfoHub clearing-house mechanism under development can discharge important match-making functions under the agreement.[197] Fortuitously in this regard, there are several examples of successful technology mechanisms in other areas of international environmental law that lessons can be drawn from and applied under the agreement.[198] In view of their proven success, perhaps there is still scope at the final session of the intergovernmental

---

[194] *Id.*

[195] *Id.*

[196] Revised Draft Text, *supra* note 19, art. 51(4). On the importance of capacity-building and technology transfer under the agreement, see Harriet Harden-Davies & Paul Snelgrove, *Science Collaboration for Capacity Building: Advancing Technology Transfer through a Treaty for Biodiversity beyond National Jurisdiction*, 7 Frontiers in Marine Sci. (2020).

[197] *See* IOC Guidelines, *supra* note 94, at 15–16.

[198] They include the technology facilitation mechanism, the technology bank for least developed countries, and the technology transfer work of the IMO. *See* Minas, *supra* note 97, at 144–49.

conference to expand the mandates of the Scientific and Technical Body and the role of the clearing-house mechanism to align them more clearly with the establishment and development of a technology mechanism for the conservation and sustainable use of biodiversity.[199]

Should the negotiators seize the opportunity to do so, important lessons can be drawn from the technology mechanism established under the UN Framework Convention on Climate Change (UNFCCC), which supports the implementation of the Paris Agreement on technology-related matters, including the implementation of nationally determined contributions (NDCs).[200] This has proved to one of the great strengths of the climate change legal regime. Instructively, almost 50 percent of all developing countries specifically referred in their initial NDCs under the Paris Agreement to the importance of technological innovation or research and development for achieving their climate objectives.[201] The mechanism is guided by a technology framework adopted by parties to the Paris Agreement and consists of two bodies: the Technology Executive Committee and the Climate Technology Centre and Network, who are answerable to the Conference of the Parties.[202] The principles of inclusiveness, results-oriented approach, transformational

[199] U.N. Doc. FCCC/CP/2010/7/Add.1, U.N. Ad hoc Working Group on Long-Term Cooperative Action under the Convention on Climate Change Dec. 1/CP.16, Cancun Agreements, ¶¶ 113–29 (Mar. 15, 2001); *see also* Minas, *supra* note 97, at 144–49; JASPARS & BROWN, *supra* note 74, at 128–29.

[200] Paris Agreement, *supra* note 120, art. 10; *see also* Stephen Minas, Matt Kenned & Karsten Krause, *Navigating a Just Transition through the Climate Emergency: What Role for Finance and Technology*, 31 IRISH STUD. INT'L AFFAIRS 131–52 (2020); Stephen Minas, *The Paris Agreement's Technology Framework and the Need for "Transformational Change,"* 4 CARBON & CLIMATE L. REV. 213, 241–54 (2020).

[201] TECH. EXEC. COMM., U.N. FRAMEWORK CONVENTION ON CLIMATE CHANGE, TECHNOLOGICAL INNOVATION FOR THE PARIS AGREEMENT: IMPLEMENTING NATIONALLY DETERMINED CONTRIBUTIONS, NATIONAL ADAPTATION PLANS AND MID-CENTURY STRATEGIES passim (2017). The UNFCCC Secretariat synthesis report on forty-eight new NDCs found that 88 percent contained information on technology. U.N. Doc. FCCC/PA/CMA/2021/2, The Nationally Determined Contributions under the Paris Agreement (Feb. 26, 2021), at 31.

[202] Article 10, paragraph 4, of the Paris Agreement provides a legal basis for the technology framework and the precise modalities were negotiated over the course of 2016–2018 and finalized at the 2018 Katowice Conference of the Parties. *See* Paris Agreement, *supra* note 120, art. 10, ¶ 4; U.N. Ad hoc Working Group on Long-Term Cooperative Action under the Convention on Climate Change Dec. 4/CP.7, annex, ¶ 14 (Nov. 10, 2001); U.N. Ad hoc Working Group on Long-Term Cooperative Action under the Convention on Climate Change Dec. 15/CMA.1, annex, ¶ 4 (Dec. 15, 2018) (hereinafter Ad hoc Working Group Dec. 15/CMA.1).

approach and transparency underpin the framework, which is focused on advancing the thematic areas of innovation, implementation, enabling environment and capacity-building, and collaboration and stakeholder engagement, as well as support.[203] The Technology Executive Committee engages in "iterative regulatory dialogue" on technology matters with the Conference of the Parties, who are empowered to further develop the climate change regulatory regime in light of this advice.[204] The Climate Technology Centre and Network are well-versed in providing practical technical assistance to developing countries and ensuring greater access to information and knowledge on new technologies through networks of stakeholders and external experts, including partner institutions.[205] The mandate of the Climate Technology Centre and Network is broad and extends to the identification of climate-friendly technologies for mitigation and adaptation, the preparation of project proposals, research and development, the enhancement of capacity to manage the technology cycle and the facilitation of financial support.[206]

Undoubtedly, considerable guidance on successful regulatory design can be derived from the functioning of the technology mechanism to support the implementation of the UN climate change regime. Again, many of the latter regulatory approaches are salutary and could inform the marine biodiversity negotiations at the final session of the intergovernmental conference with a view to strengthening the agreement so that states can benefit from new technologies. Most notably, since its inception, the sophisticated approach to collaboration and partnerships under the climate change regime has allowed the Climate Technology Centre and Network to marshal the support of more than 600 participants in 160 countries and to draw upon the expertise of public and private research and technology bodies, and finance and civil society organizations, along with nationally designated entities.[207] Despite the modest nature of the legal obligations, the scale of practical outcomes is nothing

---

[203] *Id.* U.N. Ad hoc Working Group Dec. 15/CMA.1, annex.

[204] *See* Minas, *supra* note 200, at 242.

[205] U.N. Doc. FCCC/SB/2020/4, Subsidiary Body for Sci. & Tech. Advice & Subsidiary Body for Implementation, U.N. Framework Convention on Climate Change, United Nations, Joint Annual Report of the Technology Executive Committee and the Climate Technology Centre and Network for 2020 5–27 (2021) (hereinafter JOINT ANNUAL REPORT).

[206] U.N. Doc. FCCC/CP/2011/9/Add.1, U.N. Conference of the Parties to the Framework Convention on Climate Change Dec. 2/CP.17, ¶ 135 (Dec. 11, 2011).

[207] *See* JOINT ANNUAL REPORT, *supra* note 205, at 22–23.

short of impressive over the first seven years of operation, with the mechanism facilitating technology development and transfer assistance to 102 countries and received 216 requests for technical assistance, including 15 multicountry requests.[208] Crucially, the mechanism operates very successfully without any mandatory transfer of intellectual property rights to developing countries.[209] Indeed, it ought to be noted that a technical assistance project may lead to a subsequent technology transfer agreement in which the technology transfer is entirely voluntary. Another formidable strength of the climate change technology framework is that it derives assistance from a broad suite of donors and financial sources including the Climate Change Financial Mechanism and private philanthropy, as well as in-kind contributions from participants.[210] Furthermore, apart from impacting upon the future development of the regulatory framework for climate change, it influences states, intergovernmental organizations, international financial institutions, the private sector and the research community. Somewhat ironically, the success of the climate change technology mechanism can be contrasted with the inertia of the approach adopted under the law of the sea previously, including the absence of resources and international commitment to operationalize the 2003 IOC–UNESCO Criteria and Guidelines on the Transfer of Marine Technology.[211]

Hence it is easy to conclude that the establishment of a similar technology mechanism for biodiversity beyond national jurisdiction will greatly facilitate the implementation of the agreement. As such, it can be used to regularly update the agreement and influence the work of the institutional bodies and states parties on the practical aspects of technology support, development and transfer in practice during all aspects of the technology cycle. In this context, it will mark a shift away from the binary choices between developed and developing countries and top-down approaches to technology transfer that are a feature of the law of the sea. Accordingly, a case can be made for the inclusion of a treaty basis for such a mechanism in the agreement and to embed it in the provisions

[208] *Id.*, at 15–16.
[209] Minas, *supra* note 97, at 144–49.
[210] In the period 2013–2020, it received donor support of US$74 million from various public and private sources, as well as financial and in-kind and pro bono contributions from partners and participants. The principal donor countries were the EU, Japan, Norway, Denmark, the United States, Canada, Switzerland, Germany, Korea, Italy, Sweden, Finland, Ireland and Spain. *See* JOIN ANNUAL REPORT, *supra* note 205, at 24.
[211] *See* IOC Guidelines, *supra* note 94.

on the institutional bodies, clearing-house mechanism and financial resources.[212]

In the latter respect, the establishment of a sustainable funding stream for the agreement, including its capacity-building and technology transfer components, cannot be overemphasized and will ultimately have a major bearing on the success of the regulatory arrangements governing marine biodiversity of areas beyond national jurisdiction. In this regard, developing countries have argued that there is a requirement for ring-fence funding to support the work of the institutions and the clearing-house mechanism, as well as financial support for capacity-building and technology transfer. At the end of the third session of the intergovernmental conference, the draft text provides for both voluntary and mandatory funding options from a range of public and private sources to support the work of the institutions and also to assist developing states in the implementation of the agreement.[213] There was however strong divergence of views evident on this crucial element of the agreement, with developing countries calling for mandatory sources, which were opposed by developed countries, including the EU.[214] In designing and agreeing the financial resource provisions, it is again open to the plenipotentiaries to draw from successful approaches adopted under the Global Environment Facility, the Minamata Convention and the Convention on Biological Diversity, as well as the scheme that operates for seabed mining.[215] Ultimately, it is easy to anticipate that the financial architecture will define the success of the agreement and its ability to forge more equitable regulatory arrangements on this crucial aspect of the law of the sea. Interestingly, most of the decisions concerning the development of the technology transfer mechanism for climate change was achieved through decisions of the parties, rather than by a highly prescriptive treaty obligations, which as mentioned previously only provides overarching guidance on the matter.[216]

---

[212] REVISED DRAFT TEXT, *supra* note 19, arts. 48–49, 51–52.

[213] See discussion UNCLOS, *supra* note 8, art. 52(2).

[214] *See* Lee, *supra* note 106, at 22–23; IISD, *supra* note 106, at 22.

[215] Minamata Convention on Mercury, Oct. 10, 2013, T.I.A.S. No. 17-816, 2256 U.N.T.S. 119; *see also* RONÁN LONG, *Beholding the Emerging Biodiversity Agreement through a Looking Glass: What Capacity-Building and Gender Equality Norms Should Be Found There?* MARINE BIODIVERSITY BEYOND NATIONAL JURISDICTION 241, 269–70 (Myron H. Nordquist & Ronán Long, eds., 2021).

[216] DANIEL BODANSKY, JUTTA BRUNNÉE, & LAVANYA RAJAMANI, INTERNATIONAL CLIMATE CHANGE LAW 140–41 (2017).

3.12 Can the Agreement Strike a More Equitable Balance in the Law of the Sea?

Advances in science, automation and technologies are continuously influencing ocean affairs. Yet the provisions in UNCLOS that promote transnational cooperation in marine scientific research and technology transfer were agreed forty years ago. They provide a strong conceptual basis for capacity development and technology transfer but do little else to support the implementation of UNCLOS.[217] With the benefit of hindsight, it is easy to see that the international community has promised much but has undertaken little beyond lightweight efforts to ensure greater access to infrastructure and technologies in order to meet the interests and needs of developing countries with respect to deep ocean biodiversity, or to strengthen engagement with public and private technology stakeholders and other networks.[218] In view of these shortcomings, the discussion in this chapter was premised upon two arguments. First, the special interests and needs of developed and developing countries are distinguishable on the basis that the latter do not have the infrastructure and technology to undertake scientific research on marine genetic resources in international waters. Following on from this, second, the final session(s) of the biodiversity negotiations represent a unique opportunity to redress the scientific and technological inequalities between developed and developing countries with a view to facilitating a more equitable balance of interests in the law of the sea.

The ultimate success of the treaty-making process at the UN will therefore be judged on how fine a balance it strikes in resolving the many issues that are still subject to negotiation. As seen, developing countries have been very active on the strands of the negotiations addressing marine genetic resources and benefit sharing, as well as the provisions on capacity-building and technology transfer. Furthermore, they have forged alliances with the EU, Monaco and other developed countries such as New Zealand with a view to advancing their common interests on

---

[217] Ronán Long, *Marine Science Capacity Building and Technology Transfer: Rights and Duties Go Hand in Hand Under the 1982 UNCLOS.* Law, Science and Ocean Management 297, 308 (Myron Nordquist et al. eds., 2007).

[218] See Cicin-Sain et al., *supra* note 55, *passim.* Also see the conclusion that regional networks are underdeveloped apart from Europe, Petro Tolochko & Alice Vadrot, *The Usual Suspects? Distribution of Collaboration Capital in Marine Biodiversity Research,* 124 Marine Pol'y 10431 (2021).

these issues.[219] Somewhat surprisingly, the anticipated ideological battle between developing and developed countries concerning the freedom of the high seas and the common heritage of mankind as they apply to marine genetic resources has not impeded the search for innovative treaty-based solutions at the intergovernmental conference. If anything, the deliberations have demonstrated that new technologies continue to inform the progressive development of international rules on the conservation and sustainable use of biological diversity. Furthermore, the examples cited in this chapter show how considerable diplomatic efforts are being made by all delegations to ensure that technological considerations underpin several aspects of the agreement, including the institutional arrangements. Technologies thus offer a route to the middle ground between the principles of freedom of the high seas and the common heritage of humankind, as well as a means to avoid encroaching on the sovereign rights and jurisdictional interests of coastal states in maritime spaces adjacent to areas beyond national jurisdiction.

Despite this progress, many questions remain open and at play as the multilateral treaty-making process draws to a close. Most notably, questions arise about how profound a role technology can play in providing an equitable framework for the exploitation of genetic resources under the new regulatory arrangements, or indeed can technology be applied to mitigate the existential risks associated with the loss of biodiversity in the absence of adopting binding conservation targets.[220] What is more, although many delegations have noted the importance of technology to the implementation of the agreement, it is not clear that they share a common vision on what technology measures should be set down therein or what matters ought to be left to future meetings of the Conference of the Parties to act upon. In reflecting on the answers to these questions, one should bear in mind that new technologies for marine genetic research and ocean observation will inevitably develop over time, especially in combination with advances in artificial intelligence, drones, submersibles, robotics for mapping, imaging and sampling, as well as for data acquisition and use. In parallel, the challenges encountered in

[219] RONÁN LONG & JOHN BRINCAT, *Negotiating a New Marine Biodiversity Instrument: Reflections on the Preparatory Phase from the Perspective of the European Union.* COOPERATION AND ENGAGEMENT IN THE ASIA-PACIFIC REGION 443–68 (Myron H. Nordquist, John Norton Moore & Ronán Long eds., 2019).

[220] *See* discussion *supra* on a question of terms.

managing activities in the marine environment will also change over time.

In order to meet these challenges and with a weather eye to future-proofing the agreement, the chapter argues that the plenipotentiaries attending the final session of the intergovernmental conference have the opportunity to make fundamental and very positive changes to the regulatory environment by amending the draft text in three respects. First, by inserting "rules of reference" provisions into the agreement in order to ensure that the technical standards applying to technologies used in the conservation and sustainable use of biodiversity shall be no less effective than "generally accepted international rules and standards."[221] Second, by setting down express requirements in the normative principles and approaches provisions regarding states parties use of "best available technologies or techniques" and "best environmental practices" to attain the objectives of the agreement.[222] Third, by codifying obligations of conduct and due diligence for states parties under the agreement, especially in relation to the adoption national rules and standards to ensure that public and private operators under their jurisdiction or control adhere to conservation and sustainable use objectives. As pointed out previously, these amendments will build into the agreement a process of normative accretion that is inherently evolutionary in ambit and capable of responding to environmental, technological and regulatory developments in the fullness of time.[223] The crucial point is that the agreement should not stand still in devising functional and reasonable solutions to meet the needs of both developing and developed countries in light of scientific and technological advancements.[224]

Looking to the future, it appears that the international community is at the cusp of a golden era for scientific investigation of the ocean with the advent of the UN Decade of Ocean Science for Sustainable Development (2021–30), which will see the rapid development of an ocean data-sharing mechanism through a global online open-access data-sharing platform and data clearing-house mechanism; the collection of new baseline data on living resources, as well as on the pressures and risks

[221] UNCLOS, *supra* note 8, art. 211(2).

[222] REVISED DRAFT TEXT, *supra* note 21, art. 5.

[223] For similar arguments in relation to the process as it applies to the offshore energy sector, see REDGWELL, *supra* note 126, at 40–61.

[224] Louis B. Sohn, *The Impact of Technological Changes on International Law*, 30 WASH. & LEE L. REV. 18 (1973).

to the marine environment; and the enhanced transnational coordination of ocean observation efforts.[225] In parallel, there is a global ocean mapping campaign under the auspices of a private nonprofit organization based in Japan, the Nippon Foundation, which will provide a high-resolution map of the seabed.[226] When fully implemented, these non-regulatory approaches to ocean science will bring about transformational change in human knowledge of the ocean. They may also shift the focus of capacity development and technology transfer to the creation of viable business opportunities in partnership with developing countries to tackle the sustainability challenges such countries face. Indeed, one should not overstate the importance of law in promoting capacity development and technology transfer in so far as the OECD has pointed out in the context of fostering sustainable blue economic growth worldwide: "what is increasingly required, however, is also a better understanding of how knowledge markets and networks can facilitate access to the globalizing knowledge market, supporting knowledge flows and transfers of intellectual property through such institutions as technology transfer offices, business incubators and multi-sector service provision centers."[227] In light of the latter finding, the fourth point made in the previous discussion is that consideration should also be given by the plenipotentiaries attending the final session of the intergovernmental conference to expanding the mandates of the Scientific and Technical Body and the role of the clearing-house mechanism to align them more clearly with development of a technology mechanism, similar to the approach adopted under the climate change regime. Indeed, it is easy to conclude this chapter by pointing out that the future success of the agreement is largely contingent on the establishment of a sophisticated clearing-house mechanism and the financial resources that are committed to support its effective functioning in due course.

Taken all together, the proposed amendment to the draft agreement set out in this chapter presents a unique opportunity to reform an outdated, ineffective and unfair system of capacity-building in relation to marine scientific research and technology transfer under UNCLOS. Finally, it needs to be borne in mind that the global health emergency associated with the COVID-19 pandemic has demonstrated the extraordinary power of modern communication and information technologies.

---

[225] G. A. Res. 72/73, ¶ paras. 292–95 (Jan. 4, 2018).
[226] See MAYER & ROACH, *supra* note 37, at 156–61.
[227] See OECD, *supra* note 5, at 38.

The pandemic has also highlighted the vulnerability of people living in developing countries. Strikingly, the relatively rapid development of vaccines to combat COVID-19 shows the astounding potential of the pharmaceutical industry to produce and license new pharma products through the use of new screening and other biotechnology tools. There is good cause to believe that great scientific discoveries that benefit humankind will also come about through the application of similar nano-technologies and innovative tools in ocean science in the fullness of time. A note of caution has however to be sounded regarding the inequalities encountered in delivering a global vaccination program, which provides salutary evidence that we continue to live in a bifurcated world in relation to access to the life-saving benefits derived from new science including new drugs in particular. Thus, it is entirely understandable why developing countries are seeking a more equitable balance in relation to regulatory arrangements under the draft agreement pertaining to the conservation and sustainable use of biodiversity, which truly considers the interests and needs of humankind as a whole. To that end, the outcome of the BBNJ negotiations will attest to the dynamic nature of treaty-making at the UN, as well as the importance of the rule of law in maintaining peace and public order as it applies to the ocean.

4

Small Modular Reactors and Transportable Nuclear
Power Plants

ELENA BERNINI

4.1 Introduction

The paradigm of large, land-based nuclear reactors is shifting due to technological advancements in miniaturization and portability. Small modular reactors (SMRs) are the next generation of nuclear reactors. Placed on board transportable nuclear power plants (TNPPs), SMRs are being developed to power offshore oil and gas rigs, artificial islands and other remote strategic areas. Small modular reactors and TTNPs will be one of the defining emerging technologies and investment areas of the coming years and the backbone of surface and subsurface naval operations on the peripheries of superpower military and commercial operations. Small modular reactors may power a panoply of applications on land, at sea and in outer space, where remote operations benefit from reliable energy. This chapter focuses on three types of TNPPs: floating (e.g., nuclear reactors on barges); submerged and fixed (within capsules and cylinders); and submerged and capable of navigation (e.g., as unmanned vehicles). Transportable nuclear power plants are power plants built to be moved and used in conjunction with SMRs, and include ground mobile land-based nuclear power plants, such as the Pele Project in the United States, floating nuclear power plants (FNPPs), currently developed by Russia and China, submerged unmanned and artificial intelligence (AI)-driven nuclear power plants, including the Poseidon developed by Russia, and submerged nuclear power plants, including those that are fixed, such as Flexblue developed by France, and SHELF and ATGU developed by Russia. Small reactors such as these may play a pivotal role for states' ability to gain competitive economic and military advantages at their peripheries.

This chapter starts with the foundation of the law of the sea in determining the legal status of TNPPs: whether they can be considered "ships" or "installations," and their navigational rights. Then, it presents hypothetical scenarios that highlight legal questions that TNPPs face in the international law of the sea and rules governing nuclear liability. Potential damage caused by TNPPs may be included in the civil liability nuclear regime. The nuclear liability conventions do not exclude military nuclear reactors. Furthermore, "ships" may be considered within the geographical scope of application for purposes of liability even if they are affected by nuclear damage on the high seas. In conclusion, the chapter suggests some legal avenues by which an injured state may seek remedies and attach liability to a state that has caused nuclear damage, even in cases where the latter is not party to any of the nuclear liability conventions.

4.1.1   Use of SMRs at Sea

Traditional nuclear reactors have been used at sea since the 1950s for propulsion of surface ships and submarines. Nuclear reactors also have provided the propulsion for cruise missiles (such as Russia's SSC-X-9 Skyfall), ballistic missile submarines, aircraft carriers and icebreakers.[1] Reactors at sea are mainly for military use of major naval powers because of their reliability and longevity, without the need for replenishment. Today, there are over 200 nuclear reactors propelling over 160 ships, most of which are submarines.[2]

Traditional nuclear reactors in aircraft carriers, submarines or icebreakers are based on engineering premises like SMRs. Yet SMRs are an emerging technology because nuclear reactors on board ships have never been part of a global production effort at economies of scale, built in a short time in prefabricated modules, or transportable for commercialization and sale to third states. Small modular reactors, therefore, are not only an emerging technology compared to land-based reactors but also compared to reactors that power ships.

The United States, Argentina, China, Russia, Korea, France, Canada and the UK are developing SMRs, with different designs and at different levels of progress. Small modular reactors are defined by the CORDEL (Cooperation in Reactor Design Evaluation and Licensing) Working Group of the World Nuclear Association to mean, "nuclear reactors generally 300MWe equivalent or less, designed with modular technology using module factory fabrication, pursuing economies of series production and short construction times."[3] This definition raises two points. First, the power generated from a single SMR is much smaller than a traditional nuclear power plant, but multiple SMRs together can generate the power equivalent to a large nuclear power plant. Second, an SMR is a miniature version of a traditional nuclear reactor, produced offsite for fitting to inaccessible facilities, including those at great distances from developed ports and industrial centers. Small modular reactors have or will have multiple applications, which include offshore electrical power

---

[1] Only the United States and France operate nuclear-powered aircraft carriers. Russia dominates the field of nuclear-powered icebreakers.

[2] World Nuclear Association, Nuclear-Powered Ships, https://world-nuclear.org/information-library/non-power-nuclear-applications/transport/nuclear-powered-ships.aspx (last visited Mar. 13, 2021) (online).

[3] WORLD NUCLEAR ASSOCIATION, FACILITATING INTERNATIONAL LICENSING OF SMALL MODULAR REACTORS 4 (2015).

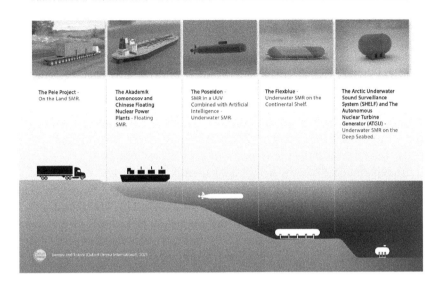

Figure 4.1   SMRs and TNPPs, and where they may be deployed.[4]
Source: Elena Bernini and Marco Tosoni (Oxford Omnia International), 2021 (used with permission)

supply to ships (including submerged submarines at great depth, which is a new salient feature); installations; onshore grid; offshore oil and gas platforms; underwater surveillance sound systems; and machines and autonomous underwater vehicles, such as those for deep seabed mining (Figure 4.1). Small modular reactors can supplement the conventional electrical supply to aid in shoreside water desalination and environmental controls (heating). The SMRs fitted to TNPPs at sea optimize the ocean for the necessary water coolant.

---

[4] While in Figure 4.1 the TNPP has been positioned in the exclusive economic zone (EEZ), it is possible to have the FNPPs deployed farther than the EEZ – for instance, to power other assets and craft. However, the Chinese FNPPs will probably be deployed either in the territorial sea of China's occupied artificial "islands" of the South China Sea or in foreign territorial sea and foreign EEZs of coastal states, as the farther they are from the coast, the higher the costs of energy output. In fact, for practical and possibly security reasons, the Russian FNPP is located in the internal waters of Pevek, a Russia Arctic town. Moreover, while the Poseidon has been portrayed in this image to be deployed in the EEZ, it is able to navigate in further and deeper zones like the deep seabed.

4.2   Emerging TNPPs at Sea: Strategic Usage and Description

4.2.1   Akademik Lomonosov Floating SMR

The Akademik Lomonosov consists of two SMRs that have been fitted into a floating nonself-propelled barge that is 144 meters in length, 30 meters wide and has 21,000 tonnes displacement and 5.6 meters draught. It has a crew of approximately seventy people.[5] These units will produce either 70 MW of electrical or 300 MW of heat power, sufficient for a city of 200,000 people.[6] Rosatom, the Russian state-owned company, built and installed it at a cost of US$480 million.[7]S

In September 2019, the finished Akademik Lomonosov was towed on its sole voyage, from St. Petersburg through part of the Northern Sea Route (NSR), to the Russian Arctic port of Pevek. The TNPP had to be towed by Russian icebreakers and tugs because it lacked self-propulsion. Satellite imagery reveals that the TNPP has since remained in port.[8] Like offshore wind turbines, the Akademik Lomonosov provides energy to the shore through cables.

Russia claims that the Akademik Lomonosov is the first floating power plant that uses SMR technology. Power production is about 100 times less than land-based Russian nuclear power plants.[9] Despite the smaller power output, however, the SMR promotes Russian military and economic power in distant Arctic locations, such as along the NSR. President Putin has prioritized NSR development to facilitate trade between Asia and Europe.[10]

Officially, Moscow's narrative is that the Akademik Lomonosov will have a commercial purpose by providing electric energy to the town of

---

[5]   BBC, Russia Floating Nuclear Power Station Sets Sail across Arctic, www.bbc.co.uk/news/world-europe-49446235 (last visited Aug. 23, 2019) (online).

[6]   Rosatom Atomic Power Agency 70MW FNPS, www.power-technology.com/projects/fnpsnuclear/ (last visited Aug. 15, 2020) (online) (hereinafter POWER TECH.).

[7]   Atomic Power Stations *out* at Sea May Be Better *than* Inland Ones, The Economist, Aug. 12, 2017.

[8]   Elena Bernini, Imagery and GPS Satellite Analysis of Transportable Nuclear Power Plants (Nov. 28, 2020) (unpublished manuscript) (on file with author).

[9]   Refuelling will be required every three to four years, and the operating life of the FNPP is expected to be forty years. E-mail from Aleksander V. Bychkov, Representative of Russian State Atomic Corp. "Rosatom" to the Int'l Atomic Energy Agency (May 30, 2020) (on file with author); *see also* POWER TECH., *supra* note 6.

[10]   Alec Luhn, Russia's "Slow-Motion Chernobyl" at Sea, www.bbc.com/future/article/20200901-the-radioactive-risk-of-sunken-nuclear-soviet-submarines (last visited Sep. 2, 2020) (online).

Pevek. Pevek is an important outpost on the NSR, and is connected to the mining industry in the peninsula.[11] The FNPP will also ostensibly provide power for oil and gas projects in the Arctic Ocean. While gas and oil exports are an important component of the Russian economy, the steep costs of FNPPs can only be justified by their role in hard power projection. As Russia has increasingly militarized its Arctic areas with construction and upgrade of seven military bases and extensive anti–air defense infrastructure, the demands on electrical power risk outstrips supply.[12] TNPPs can fill this gap.

The Akademik Lomonosov will not be the only FNPP that Russia is planning. While unreported, an official presentation by Rosatom[13] mentions five other TNPP deployment sites across the NSR that feature highly militarized and strategic bases: the Kola Peninsula;[14] the Yamal Peninsula; the Taymiyr Peninsula; the Yakutia Region; and the Kamchatka Peninsula. The FNPP would be an effective solution to supplying power to such remote military bases in the Arctic by acting as auxiliary ships in a similar remote expeditionary role analogous to that played by replenishment oilers of the US Navy Military Sealift Command (MSC).

Russia plans to export and lease the TNPPs abroad, in a similar fashion to what it does already with its land-based nuclear power plants around the world. Rosatom claims to have thirty-six overseas reactor construction projects in progress, including working agreements with Uganda, Rwanda, Ethiopia and the Republic of Congo.[15] To extend Russia's economic and political influence in Africa, Russia likely will sell the energy produced by these reactors while retaining ownership and

---

[11] HENRIK FALCK, *Arctic Shipping Perspective in the Context of Global Shipping*. THE ARCTIC IN WORLD AFFAIRS: A NORTH PACIFIC DIALOGUE ON ARCTIC 2030 AND BEYOND – PATHWAYS TO THE FUTURE 237, 245 (Robert W. Corell et al., eds., 2018).

[12] Nastassia Astrasheuskaya & Henry Foy, *Polar Powers: Russia's Bid for Supremacy in the Arctic Ocean*, FIN. TIMES, Apr. 28, 2019.

[13] E-mail from Aleksander V. Bychkov, Representative of Russian State Atomic Corp. "Rosatom" to the International Atomic Energy Agency, to author (May 29, 2020) (on file with author).

[14] For instance, the Kola Peninsula is the home of the Russian Northern Fleet and provides critical training areas for new Russian weapons like nuclear-powered cruise missiles and underwater drones. *See* Jackie Northam, In a Remote Arctic Outpost, Norway Keeps Watch on Russia's Military Buildup, NPR radio broadcast (Nov. 3, 2019).

[15] Darrell Proctor, Russia, China Drive Africa's Plan for Nuclear Expansion, Power Mag., July 1, 2020.

operational control of them.[16] This approach makes host coastal states reliant on Russian TNPPs.[17]

4.2.2   Chinese FNPPs

The second application of TNPP comes from China General Nuclear Group (CGN) and China National Nuclear Corporation (CNNC). These two state-owned companies are in the final stage of building around twenty FNPPs that will work on what reportedly will be nonself-propelled barges. These craft are the analogs of the Akademik Lomonosov and will be deployed in the South China Sea (SCS). It appears from the CGN presentation and official images that its FNPP has the same design as the Lomonosov.[18] Given that China lacks Russia's experience in nuclear engineering, this might be expected. China bought submarines from Russia for decades.[19] The Chinese media does not mention these facts, probably to portray an image of collective achievement and technological autarchy.

China and Russia have a history of cooperation on technological transfers, which gained momentum after 2014, when international sanctions were imposed against Russia for the invasion of Ukraine. The sanctions made Russia dependent upon China for hard currency, and China sought Russian technology. Rosatom subsidiary Rosatom Overseas and China's CNNC New Energy signed a memorandum on the construction of an FNPP in 2014, which China plans to use for its island territories and to develop offshore hydrocarbons.[20] China National Nuclear Corporation published an article entitled "Deep Energy

---

[16] POWER TECH., *supra* note 6.

[17] Host countries (in Europe, the Middle East and Asia) that accept Russian nuclear exports, including design, construction, management, maintenance and waste disposal, are thereby vulnerable to political influence. *See* Thomas P. Davis, *Could Generation IV Nuclear Reactors Strengthen Russia's Growing Sphere of Influence?* THE 2019 UK PONI PAPERS 19, 23–24 (Sam Dudin & Chelsey Wiley eds., 2019).

[18] Jianlin Guo, Representative of China General Nuclear Power Corporation, Address at International Atomic Energy Agency Technical Meeting: Technology Assessment of SMRs for Near Term Deployment (Oct. 3, 2017). The dimensions are the same as the Lomonosov (length approximately 140 meters, width approximately 30 meters and depth approximately 18 meters).

[19] "At the moment only the UK, US, France, Russia, China and India have nuclear powered submarines, and only the first four know how to build them (China and India bought theirs from Russia)." Andrew Hankinson, The Nuclear Submarine that Can Remain Underwater for 25 Years, Wired Mag. (U.K.), May 3, 2017.

[20] Russia and China Outline Expanded Cooperation, World Nuclear News, Nov. 8, 2016.

Observation: China will build 20 offshore nuclear power plants on the South Island and Reefs" on July 14, 2016.[21] Other media reports quote this number without citing the exact source. The article demonstrates the symbiotic relationships between FNPP, hard power projection and China's gambit for control and to commercialize the SCS.

The CGN website states that the TNPP is: "designed for the marine environment as a FNPP, will be used to provide stable, economical and green resources, such as electricity, heat and freshwater, for China's oilfield exploitation in the Bohai Sea and deep-water oil and gas development in the [SCS]. Also, it can be applied to island economies to offer residents energy and fresh water from the ocean."

If one Russian FNPP can give power to a town of approximately 200,000 people, that energy may be too much for the "residents" of the islands in the SCS, hardly justifying the costly investment from the Chinese government. Why, then, is nuclear power needed in such remote locations? In both the SCS and the Arctic Ocean, shipping diesel is difficult and costly. Diesel may be less reliable or access could be cut in case of a conflict. Ethnographic fieldwork in the SCS has shown that in the Paracel Islands, for instance, Vietnamese soldiers had to rely on solar energy,[22] an indication that shipping diesel energy was cost prohibitive.

The 20 planned Chinese FNPPs could provide energy to the 27 outposts that China occupies in the SCS – 20 in the Paracel Islands and seven in the Spratly Islands, and associated air-defense radars, ports, and airfields. Radar, in particular, requires large amounts of energy, which increases its range.[23] Satellite imagery[24] and ethnographic fieldwork confirm that solar panels and diesel generators provided energy in the area.[25]

The Chinese-state owned newspaper *Global Times* reports that China National Nuclear Power (CNNP) released in 2017 a "statement [that] said the company fits into the national strategy of building China into a

---

[21] *In-depth Report on the Nuclear Energy Industry: The Mass Construction of Hualong No. 1, the Main Force for Future Energy Increment,* SINA FIN., June 2, 2020 (Elena Bernini trans.).

[22] ELENA BERNINI, DIPLOMACY FROM BELOW: RESISTANCE OF VIETNAMESE FISHERMEN ON LY SON ISLAND 2002–2016 44–45 (2017) (M.Phil. thesis, University of Oxford) (on file with the Oxford University Research Archive).

[23] Keith Johnson, *China's Got Nuclear Power Plans for Its Fake Islands,* FOREIGN POL'Y, Apr. 22, 2016.

[24] Bernini, *supra* note 8.

[25] Bernini, *supra* note 22, at 44.

maritime power and the Belt and Road Initiatives and would help promote the civil-military integration of nuclear-powered vessels."[26]

Imagery analysis by the author shows that Huludao port where the first FNPP is being built is also where Jin-class ballistic missile submarines are constructed, and home to Chinese surface warships, suggesting the military nature of Chinese FNPPs. As a top Chinese official said in a speech, "we in the nuclear and shipbuilding industries have a call of duty to construct a 'strong maritime power.'"[27]

4.2.3   Underwater SMR on the Continental Shelf

The third example of TNPP, the cylindrically shaped Flexblue, is submerged and autonomously operated from an onshore control center.[28] The Naval Group, a French company that has built nuclear warships,[29] plans with the Flexblue "to encase an [SMR] reactor and an electricity-generating steam turbine in a steel cylinder the length of a football pitch"[30] and place it on the continental shelf at a depth of 60–100 meters, some 5–15 kilometers from the shoreline.[31] Undersea cables would bring the electricity to the shore. In addition to military purposes, Flexblue's power generation might be sold on the commercial market. There are two types of reactors within the Flexblue concept, corresponding to two market niches a 50–60 MWe reactor and a 250 MWe reactor.[32]

4.2.4   Underwater SMR on the Deep Seabed

The Arctic Underwater Sound Surveillance System (SHELF) is the second example of a submerged TNPP that will not be in the shape of a barge, like the Akademik Lomonosov, or a long cylinder, like Flexblue. NIKIET, a subsection of Rosatom, is developing the system. The SHELF

---

[26] China Announces Maritime Nuclear Power Firm, Global Times, Aug. 14, 2017.

[27] David Stanway, *China Close to Completing First Offshore Nuclear Reactor*, REUTERS, Oct. 31, 2017.

[28] Kang-Heon Lee et al., *Recent Advances in Ocean Nuclear Power Plants*, ENERGIES 11470, 11484, Oct. 14, 2015.

[29] The Naval Group is a French defense contractor and designer of warships and combat systems.

[30] Supra note 7.

[31] Lee et al., *supra* note 28, at 11471.

[32] André Kolmayer, *Blue Submarine: The Flexblue Offshore Nuclear Reactor*, POWER ENG'G INT'L, May 1, 2011.

will power a seabed sound surveillance system (HARMONY) for surveillance of foreign submarines and naval operations, accomplishing a mission similar to the Sound Surveillance System (SOSUS) realized by the United States in the Atlantic and Pacific Oceans in the early 1950s. The Russian underwater sound surveillance system, comprised of sensor arrays connected by cables, may be connected to control stations via satellites,[33] and will be powered by the SHELF or an autonomous nuclear turbine generator (ATGU).

The SHELF will contain the SMR in a cylindrical *Energykapsule* that is 14 meters long and 8 meters in diameter. The SHELF will not only be submerged, like Flexblue, but emplaced at a significant depth of 1,000 meters (compared to Flexblue's 100 meter depth) on the Arctic seabed. The new submarine *Belgorod*, launched in 2019, will carry midget submarines to emplace the cylindrical TNPPs on the seabed.

The power generated from a single *Energykapsule* is only 44 kW with pumped circulation and about 28 kW with natural circulation.[34] Yet this level is sufficient to operate the underwater sensors to capture acoustic signals of subsurface and surface ships.

Russia's largest design center for nuclear submarines, Rubin Design Bureau, reportedly is building another SMR (ATGU) capable of placement on the deep seabed to power a drilling complex to extract oil in the Arctic. The 24 MW unit could also power unmanned submarines and other unmanned underwater vehicles.[35] In comparison, each of the two reactors on board Russia's nuclear-powered icebreakers is 171 MW.[36] The Ministry of Defense of Russia, Rosatom, Gazprom and United Shipbuilding Corporation support the project.

4.2.5 Poseidon

Russia's Poseidon autonomous, nuclear-powered torpedo is the fourth emerging technology to use nuclear propulsion.[37] It uses an SMR

[33] H. I. Sutton, *Spy Subs: Project 09852* Belgorod, COVERT SHORES: BLOG, Oct. 18, 2019.
[34] H. I. Sutton, *Russia Seeks Submarine Advantage in Arctic,* COVERT SHORES: BLOG, Sept. 20, 2016.
[35] David Hambling, Why Russia Is Sending Robotic Submarines to the Arctic, www.bbc .com/future/article/20171121-why-russia-is-sending-robotic-submarines-to-the-arctic (last visited Nov. 21, 2017) (online).
[36] Thomas Nilsen, *Russia Mulls Underwater Nuclear Reactors for Arctic Oil,* BARENTS OBSERVER, Sept. 12, 2016.
[37] An unmanned submarine would require significantly less energy, as 30 percent of a submarine's power consumption, not including propulsion, is dedicated to crew survival

combined with AI in a dual role as attack submarine and ballistic missile submarine. The Poseidon reportedly reaches underwater speeds of 108 knots, which is at least 35 percent faster than the North Atlantic Treaty Organization's spearfish torpedo.[38] The small size decreases displacement and the lack of a human crew obviates the need for radiation shielding.

4.2.6   On the Horizon Applications of SMRs and TNPPs on Land and in Space

Two future applications of SMRs and TNPPs in space and on land, the Kilopower reactors and the Pele reactors, will have major implications and raise more questions in international law in the years to come. For space, NASA is developing the "Kilopower reactors" that may "power human outposts on the Moon and Mars"[39] by providing up to 10 kW of electrical power, sufficient to powering, for example, several households for at least ten years.[40]

On land, the US Pele Project may equip remote military operating bases with SMRs that could fit on the back of a truck. This concept would decrease reliance on diesel fuel and mitigate supply risks, including from improvized explosive device (IED) attacks on vehicle convoys needed to deliver the diesel.[41] During the Iraq war, for example, fuel at times composed over one-third of the transported tonnage for military operations. More than half of US casualties in Iraq and Afghanistan from 2001 to 2010 resulted from land-transport missions, including fuel deliveries to remote (forward operating bases.[42] Nuclear power generated from SMRs would solve this dilemma and provide long-term energy to military assets on land, as it already does at sea.

and comfort. H. I. Sutton, *Submarine Game Changer: Russian Atomic Drones?*, COVERT SHORES: BLOG, Feb. 5, 2020.

[38] "The Pentagon reports confirmed the existence of the UUV in 2016. It can reportedly carry a nuclear warhead with a blast yield of two megatons (MT)." Peter Suciu, *This New Russian Submarine Carries the Ultimate Doomsday Weapon*, NAT'L INTEREST: BUZZ BLOG, May 17, 2020.

[39] Press Release, NASA, Demonstration Proves Nuclear Fission System Can Provide Space Exploration Power, May 2, 2018.

[40] *Id.*

[41] Under the Skin of a Made-for-Military Microgrid, Army Tech., Mar.12, 2017.

[42] Nuclear Power Plants Are Coming to the Battlefield, The Economist, Mar. 14, 2020.

4.3 The Legal Regime Applicable

The legal framework applicable to the applications of SMRs on TNPPs is multilayered, lying at the intersection of the United Nations (UN) Convention on the Law of the Sea (UNCLOS),[43] legal instruments adopted under the auspices of the International Atomic Energy Agency (IAEA), the Organization for Economic Co-operation and Development (OECD), the International Maritime Organization (IMO) and other conventions. The legal framework of nuclear power deriving from the IAEA and the OECD are especially vexing within the context of UNCLOS due to conflicting legal definitions.

4.3.1   Nuclear Regime

The member states of the IAEA adopted several conventions to regulate nuclear safety of TNPPs, which apply if the latter are characterized as "nuclear facilities."[44] These conventions are:

- The 1997 Convention on Safety of Spent Fuel Management and on Safety of Radioactive Waste Management.
- The 1987 Convention on the Physical Protection of Nuclear Material (CPPNM) and its 2005 Amendment.
- The 1986 Convention on Early Notification of a Nuclear Accident, which adds to Article 198 of UNCLOS that deals with state notification requirements in case of "imminent or actual damage" to the marine environment by pollution.
- The 1986 Convention on Assistance in the Case of a Nuclear Accident or Radiological Emergency.
- The 1994 Convention on Nuclear Safety (CNS), which sets benchmark standards (siting, design, construction and operation of nuclear installations).[45]

---

[43] United Nations Convention on the Law of the Sea, Dec. 10, 1982, 1833 U.N.T.S. 397.

[44] All of the aforementioned conventions in the first paragraph (on nuclear safety) have been ratified by many more states compared to the nuclear liability conventions mentioned here. In fact, as of the time of writing, averaging the ratifying parties of the nuclear safety conventions, we see that around ninety states versus around twenty-seven ratifying parties for the nuclear liability conventions. The stark difference is explained in this chapter.

[45] Article 2 of the CNS explicitly states that it only applies to land-based small nuclear reactors, which would include the Pele project and TNPPs that fit on top of trucks. Article

All of the aforementioned conventions, with the exception of the CNS, can be applied without much doubt to the civilian TNPPs.

Under the IAEA and the OECD, there are also liability conventions that apply to TNPPs if characterized as "nuclear installations":

- The 1960 Paris Convention on Third Party Liability in the Field of Nuclear Energy (hereinafter the Paris Convention), and its 2004 Amending Protocol that, however, is not yet in force.
- The 1963 Vienna Convention on Civil Liability for Nuclear Damage and the 1997 Protocol to Amend the Vienna Convention (hereinafter the Vienna Convention).
- The 1997 Convention on Supplementary Compensation for Nuclear Damage (hereinafter the CSC).

Under the auspices of the IMO are the following instruments relevant to this chapter that apply to TNPPs if characterized as "ships":[46]

- The Convention for the Safety of Life at Sea (SOLAS), and in particular Chapter VIII, is dedicated to nuclear ships.
- The 1981 Code of Safety for Nuclear Merchant Ships.
- The 1962 Convention relating to Civil Liability in the Field of Maritime Carriage of Nuclear Material, which is not yet in force.[47]
- The Convention for the Prevention of Pollution from Ships ((MARPOL).

Transportable nuclear power plants pose unique new legal questions in terms of the nuclear regime and law of the sea since they may be excluded from these conventions for three reasons: they do not fit within the scope of "land-based nuclear power plants"; are not characterized as "nuclear installations"; and are not classified as "ships."

4.3.2   Law of the Sea Regime

The legal status of TNPPs raises legal conundrums. Most scholarship on SMRs and TNPPs arises from the nuclear engineering, so the legal

---

2 might then exclude FNPPs from its scope. U.N. Convention on Nuclear Safety, art. 2, June 17, 1994, S. Treaty Doc. No. 104-6, 1963 U.N.T.S. 293.

[46] UNCLOS, art. 91, recognizes that flag states have competence to fix conditions for vessels that fly their flag. Yet the IMO conventions may not be applied by coastal states that do not recognize nonself-propelled TNPPs as "ships," thus presenting legal gaps.

[47] Additionally, there are different IAEA regulations, and a regime for nuclear weapons and nuclear free zones that fall outside the scope of this chapter, as do the aforementioned IMO instruments.

status of these units, both floating and submerged varieties, has not been addressed.

4.3.2.1   TNPPs: Ships or Installations?

There is no definition of a "ship" or of a "vessel" in UNCLOS, generating some amount of debate and confusion.[48] While there is growing legal scholarship and state practice that recognizes unmanned systems as "ships,"[49] which is for instance reflected in the positive official answers of numerous coastal states to the Comité Maritime International (CMI), the same cannot be said for TNPPs. Scholarship has not yet delved into whether TNPPs should be considered "ships."[50]

Removing murkiness around the legal status of the Akademik Lomonosov and the future Chinese FNPPs, together with all the other TNPPs, is fundamental since many important provisions in UNCLOS, IMO instruments and admiralty law revolve around the concept of "ships" or "vessels." If the Akademik Lomonosov is not a "ship," then SOLAS and other IMO do not apply, potentially imposing fewer duties on the units but also offering the master and crew fewer legal protections.

The current design of the Russian floating power plant is that of a nonself-propelled barge, and the Chinese design will likely be the same. Both have the potential to be self-propelled, but a top Rosatom official related that, for economic costs, an engine was not installed, given that it would only be used once in twelve years.[51] Lack of propulsion, however,

---

[48] In particular, the terms "ship" and "vessel" can be used interchangeably in the law of the sea, as the scholar Walker notes that "the terms were viewed as identical at UNCLOS III." *See* DEFINITIONS FOR THE LAW OF THE SEA: TERMS NOT DEFINED BY THE 1982 CONVENTION 56 (George K. Walker ed., 2011).

[49] *See* COMITÉ MARITIME INTERNATIONAL, SUMMARY OF RESPONSES TO THE CMI QUESTIONNAIRE ON UNMANNED SHIPS 10–12, 14 (2018) (discussing the growing state practice of different coastal states that recognize unmanned systems as "ships" in their replies to the CMI). Of particular importance for naval operations and Chinese standing on the legal status of UUVs is the China Maritime Law Association (CMLA) official response to *id.*, which signaled that most likely they can be considered as "ships."

[50] *But see* CATHERINE REDGWELL & EFTHYMIOS PAPASTAVRIDIS, *International Regulatory Challenges of New Developments in Offshore Nuclear Energy Technologies: Transportable Nuclear Power Plants.* INNOVATION IN ENERGY LAW AND TECHNOLOGY: DYNAMIC SOLUTIONS FOR ENERGY TRANSITIONS 103, 110 (Donald Zillman et al. eds., 2018) (characterizing, a priori, offshore TNPPs as "installations"). Only Redgwell and Papastavridis' book chapter, to the author's knowledge, has characterized the Russian and French TNPPs as "installations," however, without discussing the definitions of "ships" and comparing and applying the test of "ship" to any of the TNPPs.

[51] E-mail from Aleksander V. Bychkov, *supra* note 9.

does not necessarily mean craft are not considered "vessels" or "ships." In Lozman v. City of Riviera Beach, the US Supreme Court clarified that "not *every* floating structure is a 'vessel.'" "[A] washtub, a plastic dishpan, a swimming platform on pontoons, a large fishing net, a door taken off its hinges, or Pinocchio (when inside the whale) are not 'vessels,' even if they are 'artificial contrivance[s] capable of floating, moving under tow.'"[52] Instead, the Court held that "transportation" involves movement of people or things from one place to another from a practical rather than theoretical standpoint. "But for the fact that it floats," the Court observed, "nothing about Lozman's home suggests that it was designed to any practical degree to transport persons or things over water."[53] It could not be steered, had an unraked hull and rectangular bottom, and no capacity to generate or store electricity. While the Court concluded that Lozman's houseboat was not considered a "vessel," its lack of propulsion was not dispositive.[54]

The Convention for the Prevention of Pollution from Ships (MARPOL)[55] defines "ship" in Article 2 as "a vessel of any type whatsoever operating in the marine environment and includes hydrofoil boats, air-cushion vehicles, submersibles, floating craft and *fixed or floating platforms*" (italics added). This would potentially include not only traditional installations such as oil rigs, or offshore wind turbines, but TNPPs. Similarly, Rule 3 of the Convention on the International Regulations for Preventing Collisions at Sea (COLREGs) states that "[t]he word 'vessel' includes every description of watercraft, including non-displacement craft, WIG craft and seaplanes, used or capable of being used as a *means of transportation on water*" (italics added).[56] This definition also covers TNPPs. Also relevant to the question of self-propulsion, Article 1 of the London Dumping Convention states that the term "vessels" means "waterborne or airborne craft of any type

---

[52] Lozman v. City of Riviera Beach, 568 U.S.115, 121 (2013). *See also*, MARITIME LAW ASSOCIATION OF THE UNITED STATES, RESPONSE OF THE MARITIME LAW ASSOCIATION TO THE COMITÉ MARITIME INTERNATIONAL QUESTIONNAIRE RE: SHIP NOMENCLATURE 6 (Dec. 20, 2017).

[53] Lozman, *supra* note 52, at 121–22.

[54] *Id.*

[55] Protocol of 1978 Relating to the International Convention for the Prevention of Pollution from Ships, 1973, Feb. 17, 1978, 34 U.S.T. 3407, 1340 U.N.T.S. 61.

[56] Convention on International Regulations for Preventing Collisions at Sea, Oct. 20, 1972, 28 U.S.T. 3459, T.I.A.S. No. 8587, 1050 U.N.T.S. 16.

whatsoever ... [and] includes air-cushioned craft and floating craft, *whether self-propelled or not*" (italics added).[57]

These treaties suggest that the Chinese and Russian FNPPs can be characterized as "ships" or "vessels." It is more challenging, however, to outrightly consider submerged fixed TNPPs such as the Flexblue and the SHELF as "ships" or "installations."[58] Under the London Dumping Convention and under the definition of MARPOL, which includes fixed platforms, they could be characterized as "ships," but likely not under the Convention for the Suppression of Unlawful Acts against the Safety of Maritime Navigation. The UUV Poseidon may be more easily character-ized as a "ship," given the growing state practice in autonomous vessels and submarines.

Russia's domestic law of the Merchant Shipping Code explicitly recog-nizes a vessel that is nonself-propelled as such (Article 7).[59] The Rosatom representative at the IAEA has stated that the Akademik Lomonosov is a "ship."[60] China's domestic law has two major definitions but they both leave room to recognize nonself-propelled crafts as "ships," including FNPPs. In particular, Article 56 of the Ships Registration Regulations (SRRs) defines a "ship" as "*any self-propelled or non-self-propelled vessel and any other mobile unit on water with the exception of lifeboats and life rafts equipped on board ships and boats or rafts of less than five metres in length*" (italics added).[61] The elements of "usage" (whether a ship is military or commercial) and the tonnage are dispositive for a craft to be considered a "ship" for China. China's official response to the CMI states that its Maritime Code and SRR definitions of "ships" only

---

[57] Convention on the Prevention of Marine Pollution by Dumping of Wastes and Other Matter, Aug. 30, 1975, 26 U.S.T. 2403, 1046 U.N.T.S. 120 (hereinafter LDC).

[58] UNCLOS does not define "installations." The major distinctive right of "installations" compared to "ships" under UNCLOS is that the first are entitled to safety zones under Article 60(4) of UNCLOS and "all ships must respect these safety zones" under Article 60 (6) of UNCLOS. *See generally* Hossein Esmaeili, The Legal Regime of Offshore Oil Rigs in International Law 31 (2016) (discussing whether oil rigs can be classified as ships).

[59] Kodeks Torgovogo Moreplavaniia Rossiĭskoĭ Federatsii [KTM RF] [Code of Merchant Shipping], art. 81 (Russ.).

[60] E-mail from Aleksander V. Bychkov, Representative of Russian State Atomic Corp. "Rosatom" to the International Atomic Energy Agency, to author (June 10, 2020) (on file with author).

[61] *See* Maritime Law and Policy in China 206 (Sharon Li & Colin Ingram eds., 2002) (discussing and presenting the English translations of all the major maritime laws of the People's Republic of China [PRC] and the rationale behind some of the laws).

mentions that they do not include military ships (usage test),[62] but then does not clarify the legal status of warships. China also stated that it accepts the definitions of "ships" contained in COLREGs.[63]

Thus, both Chinese and Russian domestic law recognize barge design FNPPs as "ships," given that they include nonself-propelled craft in their definition. Regardless of domestic law, however, conventional international law accommodates these FNPPs, as well as the UUV Poseidon, as "ships" or "vessels." A single universal definition of ship would be "undesirable and unworkable."[64] By not defining those terms, UNCLOS leaves space for a continuous and intertwined coevolution of maritime law and the technology of craft such as TNPPs and UUVs. The issues of interpretation and legal status will persist given the transboundary and modular nature of the SMRs.

4.3.2.2   Navigational Rights

Having assessed that most TNPPs may be characterized as ships, what are their navigational rights? Under Article 23 of UNCLOS, nuclear-powered ships of all nations enjoy the right of innocent passage regardless of whether they are warships or merchant ships. This rule applies to TNPPs. Article 23 of UNCLOS affirms that nuclear-powered ships and ships carrying nuclear, or other inherently dangerous or noxious substances, enjoy the right of innocent passage in the territorial sea if they "carry documents and observe special precautionary measures established for such ships by international Agreements." Such provision would not apply to sovereign immune vessels, therefore also to TNPPs if characterized as such.

Numerous coastal states have impinged on the freedom of navigation guaranteed by UNCLOS by requesting prior notification or authorization to foreign-flagged nuclear-powered warships or ships containing nuclear material.[65] Article 22(2) of UNCLOS provides coastal states the right to limit the passage of foreign nuclear-powered ships transiting in the

---

[62] CHINA MARITIME LAW ASSOCIATION (CMLA), THE CMLA RESPONSE TO THE COMITÉ MARITIME INTERNATIONAL QUESTIONNAIRE RE: SHIP NOMENCLATURE 6–7 (2017), (citing the Maritime Code of the PRC and the SRR, and including in the definition of "ships" all "ships that can navigate regardless of their self-propelled or non-self-propelled character").

[63] Id., at 25.

[64] ANDREW NORRIS, LEGAL ISSUES RELATING TO UNMANNED SYSTEMS 25 (2013).

[65] See Raul A. F. Pedrozo, Transport of Nuclear Cargoes by Sea, 28 J. MAR. L. & COM. 207, 210–11 (1997) (identifying a list of coastal states that have requested prior notification).

territorial sea and ships carrying dangerous or noxious substances by
"confining [their] passage" into different sea lanes and traffic separation
schemes. Some coastal states however have taken bolder actions and
denied a priori innocent passage of foreign-flagged nuclear-powered
ships and notably of warships by arguing that it is "prejudicial to the
peace, good order or security of the coastal state" under Article 19(1) of
UNCLOS. Coastal states may attempt to impose similar restrictions on
TNPPs. Navigational rights of a nuclear-powered UUV such as the
Poseidon compared to floating TNPPs differ mainly in that Article
20 of UNCLOS requires submarines and underwater vehicles "to navigate on the surface and to show their flag" when exercising innocent
passage in the territorial sea. On the other hand, if crafts such as the
Flexblue or SHELF are "installations," they would not be concerned with
navigational rights but with issues of jurisdiction and lawful placement
on coastal states' continental shelf.

4.4   Civil Liability for Nuclear Damage from TNPPs and SMRs

4.4.1   General Principles of the Nuclear Liability Conventions

Given that SMRs run on highly enriched uranium (HIEU) and release
radioactive isotopes, TNPPs carry civil liability and risk. Civilian reactors
of TNPPs are enriched to a maximum level of 20 percent, the stage before
the material becomes fissile for use in a nuclear weapon. Even if enriched
below that level, however, TNPPs risk nuclear damage to the environment. A meltdown, natural disaster or attack against TNPPs could cause
long-lasting radiation damage to the marine ecosystem and human life,
and may include transboundary effects, such as in the case of Chernobyl.
Damage from a nuclear accident can occur in all phases of the nuclear
fuel cycle of a TNPP: during its transport; at the site; during its decom-
missioning; or even during the storage of spent nuclear fuel.

The nuclear liability regime that provides compensation in case of
nuclear damage is formed by the following international conventions
previously outlined: the Paris Convention; the Vienna Convention;[66] and
the CSC. Many states have not signed or ratified these agreements,
impeding recognition of a global, uniform civil nuclear liability regime.

---

[66] In 1988, the Paris and the Vienna Conventions were linked by the Joint Protocol relating
to the Application of the Vienna Convention and the Paris Convention. Parties to the
1988 Joint Protocol are treated as if they are parties to both conventions.

Even some of the most important nuclear states such as China, India, Japan and the Republic of Korea do not adhere to the Vienna and Paris Conventions.[67] The United States only adheres to the CSC and is pushing for its wider adoption.[68] About half of all nuclear installations worldwide are not covered by the regime of nuclear conventions.[69] Japan is only party to the CSC, while the UK and France are party only to the Paris Convention. Russia is party only to the Vienna Convention.[70] The United States has legislation for nuclear civil liability and in the past negotiated agreements with other states to facilitate the offshore movement of its nuclear-powered ships.[71]

4.4.1.1   Comparing the Nuclear Liability Conventions with UNCLOS

Only OECD countries can immediately access the Paris Convention,[72] while the Vienna Convention can be accessed by all member states of the UN. In contrast to UNCLOS, the Vienna and Paris Convention regimes are not a "package deal," so states joining the agreement must accept all of its provisions.[73] On the contrary, states have added numerous reservations to their acceptance of nuclear civil liability conventions.[74]

---

[67] This chapter will only focus on the first two conventions to better suit hypothetical scenarios of nuclear damage.

[68] For a summary of the nuclear power states and liability conventions to which they are party, *see* MOHIT ABRAHAM, NUCLEAR LIABILITY: A KEY COMPONENT OF THE PUBLIC POLICY DECISION TO DEPLOY NUCLEAR ENERGY IN SOUTHEAST ASIA 16 (2014).

[69] INTERNATIONAL EXPERT GROUP ON NUCLEAR LIABILITY (INLEX), CIVIL LIABILITY FOR NUCLEAR DAMAGE: ADVANTAGES AND DISADVANTAGES OF JOINING THE INTERNATIONAL NUCLEAR LIABILITY REGIME 1 (2012) [hereinafter INLEX Position Paper].

[70] Duncan E. J. Currie, *The Problems and Gaps in the Nuclear Liability Conventions and an Analysis of How an Actual Claim Would Be Brought under the Current Existing Treaty Regime in the Event of a Nuclear Accident*, 35 DENV. J. INT'L L. & POL'Y 85, 100 (2006).

[71] For instance, in the 1960s, the United States made numerous bilateral agreements with European countries to facilitate port visits by US nuclear-powered merchant vessel *N. S. Savannah*. *See* Peider Kronz, *The 1962 Brussels Convention on the Liability of Operators of Nuclear Ships*, 57 AM. J. INT'L L. 100, 110 (1962).

[72] More precisely, "non-OECD member states require the consent of the contracting parties to the Paris Convention in order to join the Paris/Brussels Convention regime." *Nuclear Liability in the UK: Implementation of the 2004 Protocol*, SHEARMAN & STERLING: BLOG, Sept. 13, 2016.

[73] UNCLOS, *supra* note 43, art. 309.

[74] It is peculiar that the nuclear civil liability conventions allow for reservations while most environmental treaties deposited at the Secretary-General (e.g., the Montreal Protocol, Kyoto Protocol, Rotterdam Convention, Stockholm Convention and Cartagena Protocol) and many disarmament treaties deposited with the Secretary-General (e.g.,

Sometimes the amending protocols are not ratified by states once they join the underlying treaty. Consequently, the nuclear liability regime does not enjoy the same level of uniformity and effectiveness as UNCLOS.

The general principles of these treaties are: (1) strict liability (the victim/s do not need to prove fault or negligence against the operator of the nuclear installation); (2) channelling and exclusive liability of the operator of a nuclear installation; (3) compulsory financial insurance of the operator's liability,[75] compensation without discrimination based on nationality, domicile or residence; and (4) limitation of liability in amount and in time, and exclusive jurisdiction (victims may file claims within a certain period, and only courts of the *situs* of nuclear damage have jurisdiction, if they are states parties). For example, Article 3 of the Paris Convention and Article II of the Vienna Convention state that liability is exclusively channelled to the operator of the nuclear installation. This principle of "channelling liability" exclusively to the "operator" of the installation[76] is a particular feature of the tort law of nuclear civil liability conventions.[77] In contrast, fault liability in general tort law permits victims to bring a claim against any entity that may consider liable for the accident, so long as there is a causal link between fault or negligence and the accident.[78] Fault liability would be helpful in the case of FNPPs that typically involve leasing floating FNPPs to other countries and layers of actors and parties. In the event of a nuclear accident, a fault liability regime would expose private industry and states alike to liability, even if states were not operating the nuclear reactor but were nonetheless overseeing or sponsoring it. The exclusive channelling of the liability to the operator of a nuclear reactor may clash with the principle of exclusive

---

Comprehensive Nuclear-Test-Ban Treaty, Chemical Weapons Convention and Anti-personnel Mines Convention) do not allow for reservations and thus constitute a uniform global regime.

[75] For instance, the Akademik Lomonosov is covered by "SOGAZ ... and in 2014 it won the tender to insure the first floating nuclear power plant, covering it for RUR 22.6 billion, and also covering third party liability to RUR 500 billion." World Nuclear Association, Liability for Nuclear Damage, www.world-nuclear-news.org/Articles/Sogaz-insures-Russia-s-nuclear-power-plants (last visited Mar. 6, 2022) (online).

[76] The "operator of the installation" that can be held liable can be an individual but also a state as per the nuclear liability conventions.

[77] The strict liability principle is the standard of the environmental liability regime (e.g., the 1992 Civil Liability and Fund Conventions) for activities that are considered high-risk so as to deter damage to the environment.

[78] OECD, *Progress towards a Global Nuclear Liability Regime*, 93 NUCLEAR LAW BULLETIN 9, 13 (2014).

flag state jurisdiction in Article 94 of UNCLOS, in which the flag state is responsible for enforcement of vessel source pollution of its ships regardless of where they are located.

4.4.2   Are TNPPs Nuclear Installations? Does the Nuclear Liability Regime Apply?

This section explores whether the nuclear liability regime applies in case of damage from a TNPP. For example, what if uranium is released by the Russian FNPPs (Russia being a contracting party to the Vienna Convention) and results in damage to the territory of Lithuania (a contracting party to the Vienna Convention)? The basic tenet of the civil nuclear liability conventions is that they apply to nuclear damage suffered from a "nuclear installation" (nuclear reactor). The IAEA's conventions revolve around the concept of "nuclear installations," hence the question is not whether TNPPs are "ships" or "installations" (such as a fixed structure like an oil rig) in UNCLOS, but whether TNPPs can fall under the definition of "nuclear installation" in the IAEA regime.

Unlike UNCLOS, the term installation is synonymous with nuclear reactors in the civil nuclear liability regime. This chapter refers to nuclear installations as nuclear reactors and defines installation in accordance with UNCLOS. Note that terms like coastal state, flag state and port state do not appear in the nuclear liability conventions, which instead use terms such as installation state, host state and operator (all referring to nuclear reactors).

The definition of nuclear installation (reactor) is the fulcrum to answer the question that was posed at the beginning of this section. Notwithstanding, the nuclear liability conventions have different definitions. For instance, under Article I.1(j) of the 1997 Vienna Convention, nuclear installation means:

> (i) any nuclear reactor other than one with which *a means of sea or air transport is* equipped for use as a source of power, whether for propulsion thereof or for any other purpose; (ii) any factory using nuclear fuel for the production of nuclear material, or any factory for the processing of nuclear material, including any factory for the reprocessing of irradiated nuclear fuel; and (iii) *any facility where nuclear material is stored,* other than storage incidental to the carriage of such material. [italics added]

One school of thought suggests that the nuclear reactor of a TNPP installed on a barge, such as the Akademik Lomonosov, which in this view is a means of transport, and which uses such a reactor to power the local electric grid, would not be characterized as a nuclear installation. The Paris Convention leaves a broader interpretation of application to nuclear reactors than the Vienna Convention as it defines nuclear installations as "reactors *other than those* comprised in *any means of transport*" (italics added).

However, the opinion recently expressed by the IAEA International Expert Group on Nuclear Liability (INLEX) sheds some light on this debate. According to that body, TNPPs fall under the definition of a nuclear reactor. With respect to TNPPs, INLEX concluded at its meeting of May 2018 that "[a] transportable TNPP in a fixed position (that is, in the case of a floating reactor, anchored to the seabed or the shore, and attached to shore by power lines) would fall under the definition of a 'nuclear installation [reactor]' and therefore be covered by the nuclear liability regime."[79] INLEX's meeting also concluded that "in case of transport of a factory-fuelled reactor, the TNPP would also be covered by the nuclear liability conventions just as any other transport of nuclear material."[80]

In the opinion of INLEX, a transportable power plant would qualify as a nuclear installation and not a means of transport only if it was in a *fixed* position, per the Paris or Vienna Conventions. INLEX considers anchored and fixed TNPPs and its reactors that are not used as a means of transport. INLEX is correct in this view. Additionally, TNPPs are included as installations because they act as storage for nuclear fuel, which is included in the scope of the civil liability conventions under Article I.1(j) of the 1997 Vienna Convention. Therefore, TNPPs that are permanently moored and not a means of transport, such as the SHELF (with its capsules) or the Flexblue, are in fact nuclear reactors per the

---

[79] The opinion of INLEX was expressed in a report at its eighteenth meeting (May 15–17, 2018) [hereinafter the 2018 INLEX Meeting]. Report of the 2018 INLEX Meeting from the IAEA to author, para. 140 (May 22, 2020) (unpublished report on file with the author). INLEX is a group of independent experts advising the IAEA on nuclear liability issues and whose views, though not binding on the states parties to those conventions, are considered as carrying some weight, *see* IAEA, THE 1997 VIENNA CONVENTION ON CIVIL LIABILITY FOR NUCLEAR DAMAGE AND THE 1997 CONVENTION ON SUPPLEMENTARY COMPENSATION FOR NUCLEAR DAMAGE: EXPLANATORY TEXTS (2020) (the IAEA's EXPLANATORY TEXTS refer, usually in footnotes, to the INLEX's views, interpretations and recommendations. The Second Revision of those EXPLANATORY TEXTS, which was finalized in September 2020, refers to the views expressed by INLEX on transportable nuclear power plants) [hereinafter IAEA EXPLANATORY TEXTS].

[80] The 2018 INLEX Meeting, *supra* note 79, at 30.

Paris and Vienna Conventions. However, given that the SHELF is not used for a "peaceful purpose," it will likely not be covered under the nuclear civil liability conventions as analyzed in this chapter.

One scholar has expressed the view that TNPPs are not covered by the nuclear liability regime. His scholarship argues that such conventions are applicable to only land-based reactors.[81] But the text of the conventions makes no explicit mention of the term land-based. Given that these instruments were formulated in the 1960s, it would be erroneous to think that they forgo mention nuclear reactors at sea because the drafters were unaware of nuclear-powered ships. Instead, the treaties do not apply to ships because the superpower did not want to limit the operations of military nuclear-powered ships, which were and are essential for their naval operations and strategic deterrence.[82]

Another limitation of the TNPP scholarship is that it has suggested excluding civil liability conventions only by taking as the term of reference SMRs on floating TNPPs with the design of the Akademik Lomonosov (a floating TNPP) in mind, without looking more closely at other types of TNPPs (such as the submerged one). However, the preceding INLEX statement about TNPPs leaves room to broadly include different TNPPs and of nuclear reactors, not only floating ones, as technology evolves.[83] This approach mirrors the far-sighted principle found in both the two major nuclear liability conventions when they state that the definition of nuclear installations (reactors) can evolve. To reinscribe this, Article I of the 1963 Vienna Convention was amended in the 1997 Protocol and a provision included as follows: "such other installations in which there are nuclear fuel or radioactive products or waste as the Board of Governors of the International Atomic Energy Agency *shall from time to time determine*" (italics added). The same principle is stated in the 1960 Paris Convention.[84] This critical point

---

[81] Handrlica Jakub, *Transportable Nuclear Power Plants: An Enigma of International Nuclear Liability Law*, 12 J. WORLD ENERGY L. & BUS. 1, 4–5 (2019).

[82] IAEA EXPLANATORY TEXTS, *supra* note 79, at 26.

[83] This is expressed when INLEX says "transportable NPP in a fixed position (*that is, in the case* of a floating reactor)" (italics added). The 2018 INLEX Meeting, *supra* note 79, at 30.

[84] Paris Convention on Third Party Liability in the Field of Nuclear Energy, art. 1(a)(ii), July 19, 1960, 956 U.N.T.S. 251 (as amended) (determinations on the inclusion of a nuclear reactor to be made by the Steering Committee of the Nuclear Energy Agency); *cf.* Vienna Convention on Civil Liability for Nuclear Damage, May 21, 1963, 1063 U.N.T.S. 265 (as amended) (determinations on the inclusion of a nuclear reactor to be made by the Board of Governors of the IAEA).

has been left out of the scholarship on whether TNPPs can be considered nuclear reactors, but it nonetheless informs an understanding of the extent emerging technologies can fit within the existing nuclear liability regime.

SMRs on TNPPs meet the test of nuclear reactors and are covered by the nuclear liability regimes. TNPPs act as a storage of nuclear fuel and as a transport of nuclear material. The fact that the TNPPs are fixed, or not "in motion," does not affect their characterization as ships or vessels per admiralty law or the law of the sea.

4.4.3   Do Nuclear Civil Liability Regimes Apply to Military Nuclear Reactors at Sea?

The exclusion of military activities or warships in the nuclear liability conventions has implications for nuclear damage arising from TNPPs, but also for nuclear-powered ships. Nuclear power at sea is primarily a feature of warships rather than civilian ships.

Nuclear damage at sea involving military ships was common during the Cold War era, yet there are few remedies. For instance, the Soviet Union suffered fifty-two accidents involving nuclear submarines during the Cold War. The country's submarine program imposed considerable environmental costs, including the dumping of spent nuclear fuel, reactors and submarines into the Barents Sea.[85] Because of the interests of states in keeping their nuclear warships immune from a nuclear liability regime, the Convention on the Liability of Operators of Nuclear Ships of 1962 promoted by the IMO has not entered into force. The instrument may never enter into force because it applies to nuclear-powered warships even during peacetime. The Convention may be an ideal instrument to assess liability damage arising from TNPPs or nuclear-powered ships.

A paper written by INLEX claims warships or military activities may be excluded in the nuclear liability conventions, yet there is no explicit text or open exclusion in them.[86] The only reference that is mentioned is found in Article IB of the Vienna Convention, which states that the civil liability conventions "shall not apply to nuclear installations used for

---

[85] Justin Mellor, *Radioactive Waste and Russia's Northern Fleet: Sinking the Principles of International Environmental Law*, 28 Denv. J. Int'l L. & Pol'y 51, 54 (2020).
[86] INLEX Position Paper, *supra* note 69, at 3.

non-peaceful purposes."[87] This approach merely reflects the widespread view that all military activities are peaceful so long as they are consistent with the Article 2(4) of the Charter of the UN.[88]

4.4.4   Geographical Scope of Application and Jurisdiction

The 2004 Amending Protocol to the Paris Convention offers more clarity regarding the geographical scope of application and jurisdiction. The Protocol has not entered into force, but it underscores the trajectory of the nuclear liability law. Both the 1960 Paris Convention and the 1997 Vienna Convention apply to damages suffered in the territory of a contracting party. This area presumably includes the territorial sea. Furthermore, are ships be considered part of the territory under the nuclear liability regime? Ships presumably may be considered as such. Although the 1960 Paris Convention and the 1963 Vienna Convention were limited to the territories of parties only, the 2004 Paris Convention and the 1997 Vienna Convention cover nuclear damage wherever suffered.[89]

The 1997 Vienna Convention, like the 2004 Paris Convention, includes damages suffered in the maritime zones of a state party to it or on board of one of its ships or of an aircraft as it states that it applies to "nuclear damage wherever suffered" (Article IA).[90]

The 1960 Paris Convention was silent on such issues until its amendment in 2004. The provision of the 2004 Amending Protocol is summarized by the *Exposé des Motifs* of the OECD, which states use to interpret the nuclear liability conventions. It says: "the Convention applies to nuclear damage suffered *in the territory or in any maritime zones* of a Contracting Party or, subject to the exception referred to in paragraph 11, *on board a ship or aircraft* registered by a Contracting Party *regardless of where the damage is suffered including on the high seas*" (italics

---

[87] *See also* Paris Convention on Third Party Liability in the Field of Nuclear Energy, art. 1(a) (ii), July 19, 1960, 956 U.N.T.S. 251 (as amended).

[88] 3 UNITED NATIONS CONVENTION ON THE LAW OF THE SEA 1982: A COMMENTARY 88–89 (Satya N. Nandan & Shabtai Rosenne, eds., 1995).

[89] NORBERT PELZER, Nuclear Accidents: Models for Reparation. 3 Nuclear Non-Proliferation in International Law: Legal Aspects of the Use of Nuclear Energy for Peaceful Purposes 355, 381 (Jonathan L. Black-Branch & Dieter Fleck eds., 2016).

[90] This was an important article that was added from the 1963 Vienna Convention.

added).[91] When and if the 2004 Protocol will enter into force, this amendment will constitute a *lex posterior*.

The second important point from the aforementioned amendment is that the Paris Convention would also apply if nuclear damage was suffered "*on board (of) a ship* or aircraft registered by a Contracting Party regardless of where the damage is suffered including on the high seas" (italics added). This means that if a British ship sailing in the EEZ of France (both states are states parties to the Paris Convention) was damaged by the nuclear accident of Flexblue, the Paris Convention would apply, and the UK would have standing to seek redress against the French operator of the TNPP. Likewise, the Paris Convention would also apply if the British ship suffered nuclear damage in the high seas, but such damages came from the French TNPP (Flexblue).

The civil nuclear liability regime has not been sufficiently explored in cases in which states sued for nuclear damage waive their possible right of state immunity,[92] which is a departure from domestic law in the UK (the Sovereign Immunity Act)[93] and in the United States (the Foreign Sovereign Immunities Act [FSIA]).[94] Therefore, if the nuclear reactors that cause damage were operated by states or state-owned, like the Chinese and Russian FNPPs, such states would be barred from invoking sovereign immunity under the nuclear liability conventions. China, however, is not party to any of these instruments, thus leaving a gap in the law of remedies for injured parties. (In such case, of course, the general international law of state responsibility still applies.)

If the EEZ or continental shelf of a coastal state was affected by a nuclear accident, such as in the SCS, the application of liability is less certain, especially in the case of overlapping claims. However, amendments to the Vienna and Paris Conventions seek to harmonize with UNCLOS. Article 12 of the 1963 Vienna Convention was amended to permit liability for nuclear damage in the EEZ of a contracting party only

---

[91] The OECD's *Exposé des Motifs* is the authoritative source used to interpret the nuclear conventions and is equivalent to the IAEA's EXPLANATORY TEXT. OECD, Exposé des Motifs 4 (2020); *see* IAEA EXPLANATORY TEXT, *supra* note 79.

[92] *See* Paris Convention on Third Party Liability in the Field of Nuclear Energy, art. 13(c)(i), July 19, 1960, 956 U.N.T.S. 251 (as amended); Vienna Convention on Civil Liability for Nuclear Damage, art. XIV, May 21, 1963, 1063 U.N.T.S. 265 (as amended).

[93] State Immunity Act 1978, c. 33, § 1(1) (U.K.).

[94] Foreign Sovereign Immunities Act of 1976, 28 U.S.C. §§ 1330, 1391(f), 1441(d), 1602-11 [hereinafter FSIA].

in the courts of the coastal state, even where there was lack of precise delimitation of the outer boundaries of the zone.

4.4.5   Do the Nuclear Civil Liability Conventions Apply to Injured Nonparties?

The third important issue regarding geographic scope is that both the "[t]he 2004 Paris Convention and the 1997 Vienna Convention extend their geographical scope of application also to non-Contracting States if certain conditions are met and thus may be applicable."[95] This is a particular feature of the nuclear liability conventions, as usually only states parties to a treaty are bound by its provisions.[96]

The first condition for the 2004 Paris Convention and the 1997 Vienna Convention to extend their coverage for damage for injured noncontracting states is not to have nuclear reactors in their territories;[97] or in other words they apply to noncontracting nonnuclear states and their maritime zones. For instance, a state that is not party to any of the nuclear liability conventions like Vietnam, and which does not have nuclear installations on its territory, could be covered in case of damage from a Russian FNPP. This would also be an important provision for Southeast Asian countries surrounding the SCS who are not party to any of the nuclear liability regimes but that nonetheless will face increasing risks from the deployment of the Chinese TNPPs in the maritime domain.

One thing is certain: Making more states join the nuclear civil liability conventions would involve an effort in achieving a Pareto efficiency that would be a gargantuan effort to achieve given the interests at stake of states.

---

[95] Pelzer, *supra* note 89, at 395.

[96] *See* Vienna Convention on the Law of Treaties, art. XXXIV, May 23, 1969, 1155 U.N.T.S. 331 ("A treaty does not create either obligations or rights for a third State without its consent."); *Id.*, art. XXXVI ("A right arises for a third State from a provision of a treaty if the parties to the treaty intend the provision to accord that right either to the third State, or to a group of States to which it belongs, or to all States").

[97] The second condition is that such noncontracting states need to afford "equivalent reciprocal benefits." It is open to interpretation what these "reciprocal benefits" are. Also note that the conditions in Article 2 of the 2004 Paris Conventions are slightly different than in Art. I A.2 and 3 of the Vienna Convention. *See, e.g.,* IAEA EXPLANATORY TEXTS, *supra* note 79, at 30.

4.4.6   Alternative Remedies in Cases of Accidents by Nonparty States

Consider a hypothetical scenario in which a Chinese FNPP stationed in China's territorial sea caused a transboundary nuclear accident that affected a state party to one of the nuclear liability conventions. How can the injured state or states seek remedies given that China is not party to any international nuclear liability conventions?[98] There are two recourses for the injured state: seek remedies in domestic courts; or use an international court or tribunal.[99] First, if there are no contrary bilateral or other agreements between the parties, the *lex fori*, and specifically the domestic tort law, applies. Since China has no domestic nuclear civil liability regime, this resource is unsatisfying. One of the limitations of *lex fori* in authoritarian countries is that it hampers efforts to seek redress and show proof of causation. Injured states may then forum shop to locate a competent court that can exercise extraterritorial jurisdiction over a foreign defendant.

Foreign sovereign governments are normally immune from lawsuits in foreign courts. In narrowly specified exceptions, US federal courts are sometimes venues for foreign injured parties to seek remedies against wrongful acts by foreign states and corporations under the FSIA.[100] Cases may circumvent foreign sovereign immunity, foreign government commercial activities and foreign government noncommercial activities that cause injury, death or damage occurring in the United States from tortious acts.[101] Belgium, the UK and Spain have a regime for extraterritorial jurisdiction so that injured individuals and states would have standing in seeking redress in their domestic courts against a Chinese TNPP even if the damage happened in Chinese territory. But prescriptive and enforcement jurisdiction for liability is relatively weak in the case of

---

[98] In the case of the 1986 Chernobyl nuclear disaster, for instance, the civil nuclear liability regime could not be applied as the Soviet Union was not party to any convention.

[99] MATTHEW HENDERSON ET AL., CORONAVIRUS COMPENSATION? ASSESSING CHINA'S POTENTIAL CULPABILITY AND AVENUES OF LEGAL RESPONSE 23 (2020).

[100] FSIA, *supra* note 94.

[101] To circumvent the FSIA, on April 21, Missouri filed a lawsuit in US District Court against the PRC for damage arising from COVID-19. Missouri not only sued China but also the Chinese Communist Party (CCP), which, it was argued, is not a foreign state or an agency or instrumentality of a foreign state and is therefore not entitled to any form of sovereign immunity. Note also that other parties were sued to circumvent the FSIA, such as the Wuhan Institute of Virology, under the "commercial activity exception" of the FSIA. *See* Complaint, Missouri *ex rel.* Schmitt v. People's Republic of China, No. 1:20-cv-00099 (E.D. Mo. filed Apr. 21, 2020).

transboundary environmental pollution.[102] Paradoxically, it is easier to seek remedies for nuclear accidents with the civil liability space regime, where there are far fewer nuclear-powered items compared to the sea. For example, compensation was paid by the Soviet Union in the case of Cosmos 954, its nuclear-powered satellite that caused damage after it crashed in Canada in 1978. The CA\$3 million payment was made pursuant to the Convention of Liability for Damage Caused by Space Objects.[103] The international law of state responsibility also might provide relief for nuclear damage in our hypothetical scenario involving a Chinese FNPP.

4.4.6.1   Law of State Responsibility

Article 1 of the International Law Commission's 2001 Articles of State Responsibility says that states are responsible for their internationally wrongful acts.[104] Acts are "wrongful" when they constitute a breach of an international obligation and are attributable to the state.[105] The law of the sea contains broad proscriptions against damaging the marine environment. Article 192 of UNCLOS enshrines the obligation on all states to prevent marine pollution from *any source*, therefore nuclear damage would be included, and "to protect and preserve the environment."[106] States are also required to ensure that activities under their jurisdiction do not cause damage to other states – the no-harm principle reflected in

---

[102] The civil liability regime of oil pollution developed under the auspices of the IMO has yielded successful cases and been relatively more effective compared to the nuclear liability regime in seeking remedies.

[103] Alexander F. Cohen, *Cosmos 954 and the International Law of Satellite Accidents*, 10 YALE J. INT'L L. 78, 80 (1984).

[104] Report of the International Law Commission to the General Assembly, 53 U.N. GAOR Supp. No. 10, U.N. Doc. A/56/10 (2001), reprinted in [2001] 2 YB INTERNATIONAL LAW COMMISSION 32, U.N. Doc. A/CN.4/SER.A/2001/Add.1 (Part 2).

[105] *Id.,* art. 2.

[106] Article 236 of UNCLOS says that such provisions on environmental protection do not apply to "any warship, naval auxiliary, other vessels or aircraft owned or operated by a State and used, for the time being, only on government non-commercial service." Again, as discussed before, we can see how relevant it is to determine whether TNPPs are merchant ships or warships to allow prescriptive and enforcement jurisdiction. One potential environmental drawback in the admissibility of this hypothetical suit would arise if Chinese FNPPs were deemed to be sovereign immune vessels and hence UNCLOS provisions on the environment would not apply. However, other customary international law principles such as the no-harm principle could apply as demonstrated. *See* UNCLOS, *supra* note 43, art. 236.

the landmark Trail Smelter Arbitration.[107] This principle is also reiterated in Principle 21 of the 1972 Stockholm Declaration[108] and in the 1992 Rio Declaration.[109]

In the last hypothetical scenario, nuclear damage emanating from a Chinese FNPP would be "attributable to the state," given its open civil–military integration of FNPPs. It would also violate the obligation of the no-harm principle and the UNCLOS obligation, under Article 192, to "protect and preserve the environment."

China is a state party to UNCLOS and has a duty to ensure that its FNPP does not breach these obligations. This overcomes the impasse of the current nuclear liability regime for an effective litigation. The injured party would then be able to choose between the four dispute resolution processes that UNCLOS makes available: (1) Annex VII arbitration; (2) Annex VIII arbitration; (3) International Tribunal for the Law of the Sea; and (4) the International Court of Justice. Moreover, importantly, according to Article 32 of the Articles of State Responsibility, China cannot "rely on the provisions of its internal law as justification for failure to comply with its obligations." The principles of no-harm and protection of the marine environment are reflective of customary international law and apply outside the treaty as well.

Adding a piece to our hypothetical scenario: would the United States be able to seek remedies under this scenario if it suffered nuclear damage from a Chinese FNPP? Such a hypothetical lawsuit could be admissible even if filed in the United States since China has declared that it is conducting commercial activities with the FNPPs and hence the commercial activity exception under FSIA may be invoked and given the status of international obligations in UNCLOS as reflective of customary law, the United States could move forward as a matter of general law rather than treaty law to enforce environmental obligations.

In case of a nuclear accident, the injured party or parties could suffer from long-lasting damage that would require reparations.[110] Article 31 of

---

[107] Trail Smelter (U.S. v. Can.), 3 R.I.A.A. 1905 (1941).
[108] United Nations Conference on the Human Environment, Stockholm Declaration of the United Nations Conference on the Human Environment, U.N. Doc A/CONF.48/14/Rev.1 (June 16, 1972).
[109] United Nations Conference on Environment and Development, Rio Declaration on Environment and Development, U.N. Doc. A/CONF.151/5/Rev.1 (June 14, 1992).
[110] For another legal avenue that could be used in case of nuclear damage from a nuclear state nonparty to the nuclear liability conventions, see UNCLOS, *supra* note 43, art. 211. Douglas John Steding has argued,

the Articles of State Responsibility requires states to make full reparation for the injury caused by their internationally wrongful acts. Furthermore, under Article 235(2) of UNCLOS and the polluter-pays principle in customary law, the injured party must receive reparations. Article 235 (2) of UNCLOS affirms the obligation that states establish a domestic forum and international liability instruments with compensation: "States shall ensure that recourse is available in accordance with their legal systems for prompt and adequate compensation or other relief in respect of damage caused by pollution of the marine environment by natural or juridical persons under their jurisdiction."

4.5   Conclusion

Resources are finite, especially in peripheral areas where nuclear power and the application of SMRs and TNPPs are becoming critical enablers for economic and military competition. Likewise, as worldwide demand rises for clean energy, how to ensure the provision of inexpensive nuclear power to service remote populations is emerging as one of the greatest challenges. To compete in World War II and the Cold War, the great powers invested in industrial policy to facilitate technological advancements. Now, they are doing the same to reduce carbon and address climate change, bringing nuclear power to the fore, which may be viewed as offering advantages over other forms of energy.

While emerging technologies are susceptible to legal conundrums and liability lacunae in the maritime domain and the law of the sea, the greater simplicity of SMR and TNPP design results in economies of production, including shorter construction times and reduced siting

[a]s a party to the UNCLOS, Russia is also obligated to follow generally accepted international rules and standards in the operation of floating reactors. Although Russia is not directly bound by the IAEA treaties, UNCLOS Article 211 may indirectly bind Russia to the standards set forth in such Treaties. Pursuant to Article 211, guidelines adopted by Russia to protect the environment must "at least have the same effect as that of generally accepted international rules and standards established through the competent international organization or general diplomatic conference.

Douglas John Steding, *Russian Floating Nuclear Reactors: Lacunae in Current International Environmental and Maritime Law and the Need for Proactive International Cooperation in the Development of Sustainable Energy Sources*, 13 PAC. RIM L. & POL'Y J. 711, 733 (2004). Moreover, the same legal rationale that Steding applies to Russia could be applied to China in our hypothetical scenario, which would not directly be bound by the IAEA conventions, but indirectly bound by Article 211 of UNCLOS.

costs. Yet the prospect of large numbers of small reactors in the oceans raises environmental and legal conundrums in the law of the sea, while resurrecting older debates about the definitions of various kinds of ships and vessels, and giving them greater salience. Scholarship on SMRs and TNPPs has only recently emerged from the nuclear engineering field, and hence the legal problems presented in this chapter have been underexplored.

This chapter has highlighted problems of concurrent jurisdiction of the law of the sea and the nuclear law regime concerning TNPPs and the lacunae over a lack of applicable and correlative definitions of TNPPs (the term installation being a clear example). TNPPs therefore risk not being covered by the existing legal instruments.

Chinese and Russian FNPPs, with the current design, can be covered by the civil nuclear liability conventions and also be characterized as ships, even without self-propulsion. Self-propulsion is not dispositive for a craft to be considered a ship. Moreover, Chinese and Russian FNPPs can be characterized as ships under Chinese and Russian domestic law, where nonself-propelled ships are expressly included in their statutory definition of ships. By contrast, the other TNPPs can be characterized as ships on a case-by-case basis. The Poseidon, for example, would likely be characterized as a ship, while the Flexblue and the SHELF would likely be considered as installations. Unlike UUVs, the legal status of TNPPs has been unexplored question. State practice has not crystallized. Innocent passage of TNPPs is likely to be challenged by some coastal states. Yet, the means of propulsion or the lack of it cannot be used to exclude innocent passage a priori of TNPPs.

On the other hand, the nuclear liability conventions are seeking harmonization with UNCLOS by having certain provisions or having added provisions during the years by including maritime zones (with express reference to UNCLOS) and including damage suffered on ships as within the geographical scope of the nuclear conventions. Furthermore, the conventions reference application for areas including, "an area not exceeding the limits of an exclusive economic zone," even if such a zone has not been established, such as in the case that can arise in maritime boundary disputes. These provisions underscore a synergistic approach between the two regimes.

Vis-à-vis TNPPs, the civil nuclear law regime achieves a suboptimal outcome and degree of uniformity by being open only to certain states (in the case of the Paris Convention) and also by allowing reservations. Both features are inconsistent with UNCLOS's 'package deal. Moreover, through strict liability and exclusively channelling of liability to the operator, no proceedings can be instituted against other parties of a nuclear reactor regime. This approach is in contrast with domestic tort liability. Some of the most important nuclear states are not part of the nuclear liability conventions. All of these factors increase the risk of injured parties being left without adequate remedies under the nuclear liability conventions, more so in the case of TNPPs.

Notwithstanding this finding, even if the state that causes nuclear damage was not liable for damage under the civil nuclear liability conventions, it could still owe damage for a breach of an international duty to prevent environmental harm under customary international law, under the environmental legal regime or under UNCLOS. On the other hand, unique or peculiar features of the civil nuclear liability regime mean that states parties forfeit state immunity if they caused nuclear damage, even noncontracting states are covered by nuclear damage under certain conditions, and military nuclear reactors are not excluded a priori from the nuclear liability conventions. Finally, distinguishing the military or commercial nature of Chinese and Russian FNPPs and their coverage by the nuclear liability regime will be difficult since FNPPs provide energy to both commercial activities, such as oil and gas exploration projects, and militarized assets.

This chapter enters the conversation over these issues, but additional research is required to clarify the applicability of civil nuclear liability conventions to SMRs and TNPPs on the sea, in outer space and on land. Presciently, the civil nuclear law regime adopts a far-sighted approach by expressly allowing the definitions of nuclear reactors in the conventions to evolve with societal and technological advances. In an era of exponential technological change, better international law is not in having more detailed definitions of technology, but in allowing for living treaties that are sufficiently flexible to evolve with the quickly changing environment.

5

Shipping, Distributed Ledgers and Private Maritime Law

ANDREW TETTENBORN

If you ask the CEO of any large or medium corporation which part of the law has the biggest impact on their company's operations, there is little doubt about the answer you will get. It is public and regulatory law, and the need to spend more and more time on compliance issues. This is as true of shipping as of anything else. For that reason, much of this book rightly concentrates on such regulatory law and how far it will be impacted by new technology (the answer being, as one might expect, very considerably: for instance, in container monitoring;[1] crew certification;[2] and low-sulfur fuel assurance[3]). But this is by no means the only relevance of new technology. Private law is almost as strongly affected by it. In particular, blockchain and distributed ledgers, in combination with

---

[1] In 2016, the International Maritime Organization (IMO) amended the 1965 Facilitation of Maritime Traffic (FAL) Convention to require ships and ports to exchange data through a single portal by 2019. Blockchain technology is also used to store the nowmandatory verified gross mass (VGM) data on containers. *See, e.g.*, Kuehne + Nagel, Kuehne + Nagel Deploys Blockchain Technology for VGM Portal, https://newsroom.kuehne-nagel.com/kuehne–nagel-deploys-blockchain-technology-for-vgm-portal/ (last visited Sept. 10, 2020) (online).

[2] For example, the Lloyd's Register Group in December 2018, through its associate Hanseaticsoft, outlined plans to digitize crew certification using blockchain. *See* Maximilian Hagemann, Blockchain Pilot Launched for Crew Certification, Hanseaticsoft: Blog, Dec. 13, 2018.

[3] For example, in tracing the origin and provenance of bunkers to make sure they are compliant with the 2020 legal position, *see* Ledger Insights, Marfin Shipping Fleet to Use Blockchain DNA Tagging to Track Clean Fuel, www.ledgerinsights.com/blockchain-dna-tagging-marine-fuel-bunkertrace/ (last visited Mar. 19, 2021) (online).

monitoring technology, and also the progressive replacement of paper documentation with digital records, is likely to be almost as significant here in the medium to long term.

In this area, the use of paper raises three classic problems. One is the authentication of documents, in particular protection against the use of duplicates or forgeries. A second is their safe storage and making available to those (and only those) with a need to see them, and the prevention of unauthorized or illegal tampering. A third is difficulties in fast and secure transmission; paper in the hands of a post office or courier is inherently slow and vulnerable.

Although widespread digitization has been with us for nearly thirty years, until recently it has not really addressed any of these difficulties. Computer storage and email have always been relatively hackable, and joint control of documents difficult. Copy protection of documents on an ordinary server is available, but still fairly rudimentary when faced with an accomplished fraudster. Furthermore, in recent years, carriers' and shippers' desire for speed of turnaround inconsistent with extensive checks of documents, together with the ready availability of sophisticated printing software, has if anything eased the forger's task.

However, much more promise is shown in this respect by distributed ledger technology, and by its offshoot blockchain.[4] When applied properly, these techniques make the production of usable forgeries extremely difficult, unlawful tampering with an existing instrument almost impossible, and the interception or unlawful copying of a document in transmission a vastly harder enterprise. Hence this chapter. It concentrates on three areas: cargo care; payment; and shipping documentation.

5.1   Sea Cargo Documentation

Cargo documentation, in the shape of bills of lading and (increasingly in recent times) sea waybills, has traditionally been paper-based. Everyone

---

[4] "Blockchain" and "distributed ledger" are often used synonymously. But technically the former is a subset of the latter. "Distributed ledger" is any system in which a ledger and changes to it are distributed over a number of participants and not dependent on any centralized server or database. "Blockchain" is a distributed electronic ledger system in which each ledger is readable by all participants and all ledgers can be securely and indelibly updated virtually simultaneously, the vital feature being that all additions and their timing are themselves permanently preserved. *See* IMRAN BASHIR, MASTERING BLOCKCHAIN: DISTRIBUTED LEDGER TECHNOLOGY, DECENTRALIZATION, AND SMART CONTRACTS EXPLAINED ch. 1 (2d ed. 2018).

agrees that, at least as regards bills of lading, this reliance on physical paper is problematic.[5] The problems are not hard to spot. For one thing, now that everyone has access to sophisticated word-processing software, convincing-looking documents of title are easily forgeable, necessitating increasing efforts to secure them by way of special paper, security printing, identity checks and so on.[6] Again, even where a bill of lading is genuine, its need for physical toting by post or courier between traders, and between traders and financial institutions, makes dealings with it a logistical nightmare. This is made even worse by a triple cocktail of fast ships, a slow postal service and bureaucratic banks. When combined with the document of title function of the bill of lading, all this leads to a need for costly and time-consuming indemnities when (as frequently happens) goods arrive before documents. The sheer expense generated by this constant exercise in meticulous paper-shuffling is difficult to reckon but has been estimated at between 5 and 10 percent of the value of goods traded.[7]

Attempts to digitize bills of lading have a long history.[8] The problems arise not so much with their functions as contracts or receipts, which can be performed just as well in paper or nonpaper forms, but with their use as documents of title.[9] Matters started nearly forty years ago in this connection with Seadocs, a cumbersome (and ultimately unsuccessful) 1983 scheme thought up by Intertanko for the oil trade under which

---

[5] See, e.g., David A. Bury, *Electronic Bills of Lading: A Never-Ending Story?*, 41 Tul. Mar. L.J. 197 (2016); *see also* Anthony Lloyd, *The Bill of Lading: Do We Really Need It?*, Lloyd's Mar. & Com. L.Q. 47 (1989).

[6] The risk of such forgery is currently borne by carriers under American and English law. *See* King v. Barbarin, 249 F. 303 (6th Cir. 1917); David Crystal, Inc. v. Cunard S.S. Co., 339 F.2d 295, 298 (2d Cir. 1964); *see also* Motis Exports Ltd. v. Dampskibsselskabet Af 1912 Aktieselskab [2001] EWHC (Admlty) 499, [2001] 1 Lloyd's Rep. 211 (Eng. & Wales); *but see* Allied Chemical International Corp. v. Companhia de Navegação Lloyd Brasileiro, 775 F. 2d 476 (2d Cir. 1985) (holding that, under the Harter Act (46 U.S.C. § 190), liability cannot be excluded, at least where the misdelivery is negligent).

[7] See Sally-Ann Underhill & William Bibby, Electronic Bills of Lading, Reed Smith: Blog, www.shiplawlog.com/2016/01/14/electronic-bills-of-lading/ (last visited Feb. 28, 2022) (online); *see also* Laura Starr, E-bills of Lading Come of Age, Maritime Risk International, www.i-law.com/ilaw/doc/view.htm?id=383381 (last visited Mar. 2, 2022) (online).

[8] Bury, *supra* note 5, at 212; Nick Gaskell, *Bills of Lading in an Electronic Age*, Lloyd's Mar. & Com. L.Q. 233, 260 (2010).

[9] See Christian Albrecht, *Blockchain Bills of Lading: The End of History? Overcoming Paper-Based Transport Documents in Sea Carriage Through New Technologies*, 43 Tul. Mar. L.J. 251 (2019).

physical bills of lading were issued, but then, pursuant to an agreement between all participants, they were left with a depositary and from that time on notionally transferred by exchange of electronic messages.[10] The 1990 Comité Maritime International (CMI) Rules for Electronic Bills of Lading,[11] under which the carrier agreed with the shipper to issue a notional electronic document of title that could then be notionally "transferred" to someone else by use of a private key, were slightly better, but equally unsuccessful.

The first breakthrough came with Bolero in 1999,[12] involving genuine electronic bills issued and stored in a central registry under the aegis of a multilateral umbrella agreement among a number of carriers, traders and financiers known as the Bolero Rulebook. Under this agreement all parties agreed to recognize the efficacy of the electronic bill as equivalent to a paper one, with any need for transfer satisfied through a mechanism of deemed attornment by the carrier. The year 2009 saw the introduction of essDocs,[13] a platform without any central registry, trading as CargoDocs, which works by setting up a secure communications bridge between would-be participants. It allows for the issue, manipulation and endorsement of electronic bills of lading; to deal with cases of third-party enforcement and the need for transfers of possession it provides facilities for novation and attornment. Active since 2011 in addition to this from has been the system known as e-title,[14] a decentralized high-security peer-to-peer network involving elaborate systems of message verification backed by a framework agreement that must be signed by all parties. Both are still developing.

There are obviously possibilities of combining electronic bills of lading with distributed ledger technology here. If large numbers of shippers, consignees, carriers and financial institutions participate, the problem of transmission time almost disappears, and forgery and alteration become

---

[10] Hugh Beale & Lowri Griffiths, *Electronic Commerce: Formal Requirements in Commercial Transactions*, LLOYD'S MAR. & COM. L.Q. 367, 477 (2002).

[11] *See* PAUL TODD, *Dematerialisation of Shipping Documents*. CROSS-BORDER ELECTRONIC BANKING: CHALLENGES AND OPPORTUNITIES 78 (Chris Reed et al. eds., 2d. ed. 2000); Miriam Goldby, *The CMI Rules for Electronic Bills of Lading Reassessed in the Light of Current Practices*, LLOYD'S MAR. & COM. L.Q. 56 (2008).

[12] *See* Malcolm Clarke, *Transport Documents: Their Transferability as Documents of Title; Electronic Documents*, LLOYD'S MAR. & COM. L.Q. 256 (2002).

[13] Gaskell, *supra* note 8, at 261–62.

[14] *See* Mark Holford, A Tricky Problem in Brief, Maritime Risk International, www.i-law .com/ilaw/doc/view.htm?id=266013 (last visited Mar. 2, 2022) (online).

vastly more difficult. Not surprisingly, this gap in the market has been spotted; and schemes of this kind are in course of development by organizations such as Wave,[15] Edox[16] and others.[17]

If electronic bills of lading operating under schemes of this sort can be guaranteed to have the same legal effect as paper bills, then this solution, virtually eliminating the problems currently plaguing paper instruments, is a "no-brainer." But can they? As regards the relations between shipper and carrier,[18] it seems the answer is yes. A contractual or bailment relationship fundamentally depends on agreement, and in the vast majority of legal systems, this agreement will be just as valid whether embodied in paper or in patterns of electrons. Indeed, bills of lading in the latter form logically ought to be preferable, in that they are potentially more secure, and no issues arise of loss or theft. The problem lies in the other functions of a bill of lading: the creation of rights as between carrier and transferee, and operation as a document of title. Here, unfortunately, there is no such certainty, and jurisdictions will vary.

Some have legislation to deal with the point, including importantly New York, perhaps the most significant US jurisdiction in this respect. In 2014, the state finally enacted the 2003 alterations to Article 7 and other connected provisions of the Uniform Commercial Code (UCC). Essentially,[19] these changes give electronic documents issued pursuant to distributed ledger schemes full effect. Thus, the definition of a "document of title" now expressly includes an electronic document of title, meaning a "document of title evidenced by a record consisting of information stored in an electronic medium."[20] In addition, New York provides for an electronic "holder" in control of the document,[21] and for

---

[15] Israeli shipowners Zim successfully completed a container shipment from China to Canada in 2017 using blockchain technology that Wave developed. Nick Blenkey, *Zim Completes Pilot of Blockchain Based Paperless Bills of Lading*, MARINE LOG, Nov. 21, 2017.

[16] Edox is owned by Argentinian company Globalshare, which specializes in agricultural cargo.

[17] *E.g.*, CargoX. See Press Release, *CargoX and Europacific Partner to Innovate in Logistics Processing*, CargoX, Aug. 31, 2018.

[18] Including both the strictly contractual function of the bill of lading and its function as a receipt. The comments in the text apply to both.

[19] It is technically subject to the Pomerene Bills of Lading Act (49 U.S.C. § 80101) and the Carriage of Goods by Sea Act (COGSA) (46 U.S.C. § 30701), but these statutes do not exclude the possibility of an electronic bill of lading. *See* Sea-Land Serve. v. Lozen Int'l, 285 F. 3d 808, 814–15 (9th Cir. 2002).

[20] U.C.C. § 1-201(b)(16) (AM. L. INST. & UNIF. L. COMM'N 1977).

[21] U.C.C. § 1-201(b)(21)(C) (AM. L. INST. & UNIF. L. COMM'N 1977).

electronic signature.[22] The holder is defined as, in essence, the person in control in circumstances typified by the existence of a distributed ledger: namely, where reliable electronic means exist to ensure that there is only one authoritative copy of the relevant document and a means whereby that person can securely transfer it.[23] Constituting someone else as a "holder" in this connection is sufficient to transfer all rights to the goods where this is intended,[24] plus rights under the contract,[25] or to create a security interest in a lender.[26]

Others do not, however, do this. England is a case in point. The rule that a carrier must deliver, and deliver only, to a bill of lading holder is, it seems, conditioned on the latter being a physical holder.[27] Again, to sue on a bill of lading a nonoriginal party has under s.2 of the English Carriage of Goods by Sea Act 1992 to show that they are a "lawful holder," which involves both endorsement and physical delivery.[28] Again, because a valid pledge requires a transfer of possession to the pledgee,[29] a financier needing to be assured of a valid security may feel they need to make sure that they take actual delivery of a bill of lading relating to a particular cargo.[30] In sale of goods, in so far as a person dealing with a bill of lading wishes to take advantage of negotiability, or defeat a lien or right of stoppage, once again they must have the bill of lading transferred (i.e., delivered) to them;[31] and so on. It is no doubt because of this, and the prevalence of English law and jurisdiction clauses

---

[22] U.C.C. § 7-102(a)(11)(B) (Am. L. Inst. & Unif. L. Comm'n 1977).

[23] U.C.C. § 7-106 (Am. L. Inst. & Unif. L. Comm'n 1977).

[24] U.C.C. § 7-102(a)(11)(B) (Am. L. Inst. & Unif. L. Comm'n 1977).

[25] U.C.C. § 7-502(4) (Am. L. Inst. & Unif. L. Comm'n 1977).

[26] U.C.C. § 9-203(b) (Am. L. Inst. & Unif. L. Comm'n 1977).

[27] At least until a mercantile custom to the contrary can be established. But here we have a chicken-and-egg problem. A mercantile custom depends on widespread use of electronic bills and an acceptance that delivery may be effected against them; but carriers will not use them in this widespread way until their efficacy is assured.

[28] See Standard Chartered Bank v. Dorchester LNG (2) Ltd. (the "Erin Schulte") [2014] EWCA (Civ.) 1382, [2015] 1 Lloyd's Rep. 97 (Eng. & Wales); Keppel Tatlee Bank Ltd. v. Bandung Shipping Pte. Ltd. [2003] 1 SLR(R) 295, [2003] 1 Lloyd's Rep. 619 (Sing.).

[29] England has no equivalent to UCC, art. 9. See Inglis v. Robertson & Baxter [1898] UKHL 2, [1898] 1 AC (HL) 616 (U.K.).

[30] There are probably ways of getting round this, but they can be complex. See Andrew Tettenborn, Lending on Waybills and Other Documents: Banker's Dream or Financier's Nightmare? International Trade and Carriage of Goods 208 (Barış Soyer & Andrew Tettenborn eds., 2017).

[31] See, e.g., Sale of Goods Act, (1979) §§ 24–25, 47 (U.K.); Sale of Goods Ordinance, (1898) §§ 27, 49 (H.K.).

in many shipment and sale contracts, that the schemes mentioned have felt compelled to introduce fairly complex provisions about matters such as attornment and novation, in order artificially to reproduce the effects of a transfer of possession in a document that, existing only in electronic ether, cannot be possessed in the first place.

Furthermore, even if England (and other jurisdictions applying what is essentially English law, such as Singapore) in practice accepts the validity of electronic bills of lading, difficulties may arise, on the basis that some conservative jurisdictions in which the goods might find themselves may have difficulties recognizing rights to cargo arising out of unwritten bills of lading.[32]

Nevertheless, distributed ledger and similar schemes are making progress. One reason for this is that P&I interests, who in practice are expected to pick up the tab when something goes wrong, have decided that if carefully controlled, the risks are manageable. Since 2010, the International Group of P&I Clubs has approved the use by shipowners of Bolero, essDocs and e-title; in 2020, Edox was added.[33] Indeed, in 2017, it was reported that 61 percent of the world tanker fleet was signed up, at least in principle, to the essDocs CargoDocs system.[34] Moreover, such documents are now being combined with electronic payment methods, such as those governed by the eUCP though innovators such as R3 or Voltron so as to render as much of a transaction paperless as possible.[35]

---

[32] Three years ago, international law firm Norton Rose Fulbright mentioned India and Indonesia as doubtful in this respect. This may matter, not only in respect of goods consigned to such places, but also where (for example) a party based in such a jurisdiction becomes insolvent and it is sought to have the rights of the relevant insolvency practitioner recognized in England under the Model Law on Cross-border Insolvency. See Charlotte Winter & Matthew Plaistowe, E-bills of Lading on the Move, Maritime Risk International, www.i-law.com/ilaw/doc/view.htm?id=382732 (last visited Mar. 2, 2022) (online).

[33] P&I cover is generally available on an equal basis whether or not paper documents are used. See International Group of P & I Clubs, International Group Circular: Bills of Lading and Blockchain Based System, www.igpandi.org/article/international-group-circular-bills-lading-and-blockchain-based-system (last visited Mar. 2, 2022) (online).

[34] Winter & Plaistowe, *supra* note 32.

[35] In May 2018, a shipment of soybeans from Argentinian sellers to Malaysian buyers was experimentally performed and financed entirely through blockchain technology developed by R3. The banks involved were HSBC and ING. A similar exercise was undertaken in respect of a cargo of Australian iron ore sold to China in November 2018 using essDocs. See Don Weinland, HSBC Claims First Trade-Finance Deal with Blockchain, Fin. Times, May 13, 2018; essDOCS: Blog, essDOCS Enables First Fully Integrated Paperless Trade in Iron Ore, www.essdocs.com/blog/essdocs-enables-first-fully-integrated-paperless-trade-iron-ore (last visited Mar. 2, 2022) (online).

Another reason may be that, while traditional negotiable bills of lading may cause difficulties, they are in any case in decline. Most sea cargo travels under other forms of contract, such as a form of nonnegotiable bill of lading (known as a sea waybill in England and Europe[36]): a trend long ago approved and encouraged by the CMI[37] and now well acknowledged in such matters as letter of credit law,[38] not to mention INCOTERMS 2020.[39] And where a document is – as is the case with a sea waybill – neither a document of title nor a document whose presentation is necessary to obtain goods, a great many of the difficulties with disembodied documents disappear. We are talking here of what is essentially just a contract between shipper and carrier to carry and deliver to the consignee against presentment of identification.[40] Unlawful copying is possible but pointless, since possession of the document gives no right to the goods anyway; and transfer raises few if any difficulties where no onsale of goods afloat is contemplated or even permitted. Admittedly, some issues could arise with dematerialized documentation over

---

[36] The waybill developed from the straight bill of lading, to which it is still very similar. The main difference lies in the fact that the former does not need to be presented to obtain the goods. Two of the earliest instances appeared in 1970 and 1971, respectively. The first standard-form General Council of British Shipping and SITPRO waybills dated from 1977. The first mention in a legal work of sea waybills seems to be by UNCITRAL in 1978. See NICK GASKELL, BILLS OF LADING: LAW AND PRACTICE para. 22.1 (2d ed. 2012); see also 9 UNITED NATIONS COMMISSION ON INTERNATIONAL TRADE LAW, U.N. DOC. A/CN.9/SER.A/1978, Y.B. 198 (1978); William Tetley, Waybills: The Modern Contract of Carriage of Goods by Sea, 14 J. MAR. L. & COM. 465 (1983).

[37] Since its 1983 colloquium in Venice, where a resolution was passed that the practice of issuing a bill of lading when a negotiable document was not required should be discouraged. See also, UNITED NATIONS ECONOMIC COMMISSION FOR EUROPE, RECOMMENDATION NO. 12: MEASURES TO FACILITATE MARITIME TRANSPORT DOCUMENTS PROCEDURES, U.N. DOC. ECE/TRADE/240 (2d ed. 2001).

[38] Which, since 1993, has happily contemplated presentation of sea waybills to operate letters of credit. These provisions do not appear in UCC, art. 5, even though the latter is largely based on UCP600's precursor. See U.C.P. 600, art. 24 (INT'L CHAMBER OF COM. 2007); cf. U.C.C. § 5 (AM. L. INST. & UNIF. L. COMM'N 1977).

[39] Which, in a reform dating from 1990, refer even-handedly to bills of lading and sea waybills even in connection with CIF contracts, which used to be one of the strongholds of the marine bill of lading. See INTERNATIONAL CHAMBER OF COMMERCE, INCOTERMS 2020, at A8 (2019).

[40] Admittedly, the risk of nonnegligent misdelivery here is almost always placed on cargo. Typical is this term from BIMCO's GENWAYBILL 2016: "The Carrier shall exercise due care ensuring that delivery is made to the proper party. However, in case of incorrect delivery, the Carrier will accept no responsibility unless due to fault or neglect on his part."

contractual rights and liabilities as between carrier and consignee, and how far the latter, not being the shipper, could exercise such rights. But these are largely theoretical. Under the UCC, since a nonnegotiable bill of lading is a bill of lading, it follows that the provisions allowing the consignee under a bill of lading to sue equally apply.[41] English law is slightly more awkward, since there a nonnegotiable bill of lading is not a bill of lading, and furthermore the English legislator, while empowered to legislate for electronic documents, has studiedly never done so. But there nevertheless seems a straightforward workaround here that in practice prevents problems arising.[42] No doubt this is why in 2014 an unnamed Greek carrier estimated that it was using electronic sea waybills transmitted by email in connection with some 20 percent of its transactions.[43]

5.2   The Payment Process

How to avoid credit risks by ensuring that payment is made only against goods or the means of access to them, and not otherwise, is one of the oldest problems as regards goods sent by sea. The original solution, the documentary bill, worked well enough with honest consignees who by bad luck then became insolvent, but gave little protection to sellers against unscrupulous or fraudulent buyers who took advantage of an opportunity to increase their cash-flow at the sellers' expense by selling the goods on before becoming insolvent and leaving the original sellers in the lurch. Not surprisingly, it was superseded in the twentieth century by forms of payment against documents, notably in the form bank collections under the Uniform Rules for Collections.[44]

---

[41] U.C.C. § 7-502(4) (Am. L. Inst. & Unif. L. Comm'n 1977).

[42] The Carriage of Goods by Sea Act 1992 gives a consignee the right to sue if they are "the person who (without being an original party to the contract of carriage) is the person to whom delivery of the goods to which a sea waybill relates is to be made by the carrier in accordance with that contract." If a sea waybill in electronic form is indeed not within the Act, while a paper exemplar is, the person named as consignee who only has the former faces no serious obstacle. They need merely to head to the nearest Staples and print out a copy. Eureka! *See* Carriage of Goods by Sea Act 1992, s.2(1)(b).

[43] *See* S. Deehan et al., Report on Activity 1: Electronic Sea Waybill Interoperability, Arising from the EU-Sponsored B2MOS (Business to Motorways of the Sea) Project 11. This was presented at the B2MOS mid-term conference in Valencia, Spain, on October 30–31, 2014.

[44] *See* International Chamber of Commerce, URC 522: ICC Uniform Rules for Collections, Supplement for Electronic Presentation (eURC) Version 1.0 (2019) (hereinafter eURC 522).

But all these required tiresome and expensive paper handling. Today, the need for this has largely disappeared. The effectuation of the payment side in such transactions is today nearly always electronic by bank transfer, and indeed in practice secured, like any other electronic money transfer worth the name, by some sort of blockchain arrangement. So too, the actual undertaking to pay against a presentation can just as well be electronic as written. There has, for example, never been any legal need for letters of credit to be in written form, whether under UCC, Article 5[45] or the UCP600,[46] and today electronic letters of credit, notified to correspondent banks in almost real-time and printed out only if there is a need for a record to be filed, are commonplace. Furthermore, it is now made clear that formal presentation may equally be made electronically: witness protocols like the International Chamber of Commerce's (ICC's) eUCP[47] allowing for electronic presentations under letters of credit and at last, in 2019, the new eURC[48] for similar use with URC522 in the case of bank collections. Both of these are likely in practice to make use of some kind of distributed ledger arrangements between financial institutions.[49]

Even here, however, digitization is not complete. The assumption is still that, even if presentation and payment are electronic, the connection between the two is emphatically not; the intervention of human agency remains necessary before the decision to honor is made. Something closer to a wholly automated payment process triggered by computer-generated "documents" is SWIFT's bank payment obligation (BPO)[50] regime, governed by the Uniform Rules for Bank Payment Obligations (URBPO).[51] This provides scope for setting up genuine smart payment contracts in the form of entirely paperless irrevocable payment

[45] The UCC requires a letter of credit to take the form of a "record," which may be electronic as much as paper. U.C.C. §§ 5-102, 5-104 (AM. L. INST. & UNIF. L. COMM'N 1977).
[46] Article 2 defines a *credit* expansively as "any arrangement, however named or described, that is irrevocable and thereby constitutes a definite undertaking of the issuing bank to honour a complying presentation." U.C.P. 600, art. 2 (INT'L CHAMBER OF COM. 2007).
[47] *I.e.*, The Electronic Uniform Customs and Practice (currently the eUCP 2.0 (2019)).
[48] The ICC Uniform Rules for Collections (URC522) Supplement for Electronic Presentation (eURC), currently in the form of eURC 1.0 (2019).
[49] *See* eURC 522, *supra* note 44, arts. e1, e4; INTERNATIONAL CHAMBER OF COMMERCE, UCP 600: EUCP VERSION 2.0, art. e3 (2019).
[50] Bank Payment Obligation. *See* Roberto Bergami, *Bank Payment Obligation: A Commentary*, 16 VINDOBONA J. INT'L COM. L. 1 (2012).
[51] Uniform Rules for Bank Payment Obligations (ICC, 2013).

obligations triggerable electronically by submission of agreed electronic documents in the form of files in a particular form. Yet this automation of the entire process from creation to submission to payment is so far in its infancy. The BPO platform, combined with the TSU[52] protocol aimed at unifying the electronic creation of purchase orders, the preparation and transmission of agreed documents, and payment against those documents, for a time seemed to represent the future. However, BPOs never created much enthusiasm (perhaps because they only operated between banks and did not allow for direct payment to sellers), and the TSU side of this project was retired in December 2020.

Other distributed ledger–based consortia have been seeking to take up the slack. One example is Marco Polo, a blockchain-based platform aimed at easing the creation and integration of sales agreements, documentary presentations and payment against those presentations, which has been successfully tested on a consignment of German machinery sent to China.[53] Another is we.trade, set up on the basis of proprietary IBM-provided blockchain to do something similar;[54] yet another, European-based, is Tradeshift.[55] But these suffer from difficulties. In particular, while they may operate as well over a public ("permissionless") blockchain as a proprietary one, they often not only require both parties to subscribe to the same platform, but also are geared to open account trade rather than strict payment against the means of access to goods aimed at providing the seller with watertight protection. As a result, while they have some reference to goods sent by sea, they only in practice cover a fairly small part of it.

What is needed is a project combining facilities for electronic payment, or the issue of electronic letters of credit, with the presentation of entirely electronic shipment documents providing – or at least getting as near as possible to providing – the same protection and rights as full-blown bills

---

[52] trade services utility.
[53] *See* Oliver Smith, Marco Polo Blockchain to Solve Trade Finance Woes Goes Live, AltFi, www.altfi.com/article/5196_marco-polo-blockchain-trade-finance-live (Mar. 28, 2019; last visited Mar. 2, 2022) (online).
[54] This is a blockchain arrangement that small to medium enterprises can join, if their banks approve, and which a number of European banks, including HSBC and UBS, participate in.
[55] Which experimentally eventuated an entirely automated payment in Euros in December 2019. *See* Tradeshift Frontiers, World's First Euro Transactions Settled via Smart Contracts on Permissionless Blockchain: Part 1, https://hub.tradeshift.com/global-trade/world-s-first-euro-transactions-settled-via-smart-contracts-on-permissionless-block chain-part-2 (Dec. 18, 2019; last visited Mar. 2, 2022) (online).

of lading, sea waybills or other transport documents. In other words, to
some extent, the whole transaction must turn into one large smart
contract.[56] There have been a number of projects of this sort. More
importantly, however, have been projects specifically to digitize shipping
documents and integrate them with payment arrangements such as
letters of credit. The Letter of Credit Network (connected with
Voltron) has seen HSBC and ING take steps to integrate Bolero's solution for issuing and managing electronic bills of lading; it has already
arranged an experimental shipment of wool from Australia to the China
SDIC International Trade Nanjing Co., with HSBC China issuing the
electronic letter of credit on behalf of the importer,[57] and a shipment of
oil from Thailand to Singapore with the letter of credit issued by
Standard Chartered.[58] Another similar project, aiming to integrate
shipping documents with letter of credit issue, is the Indian 2017 start-
up Finacle Trade Connect, to which several Indian and a few non-Indian
banks subscribe. It is here that distributed ledger technology can in
principle come into its own; where carrier, forwarder, shipper, bank,
buyer and issuers of other documents are members of an open or
proprietary system, the gains from automation, and from the near
impossibility of falsification of either the letter of credit or the documents
to be presented under it, are clear and undeniable.

There are of course some further issues. If payment is to be genuinely
automated, and human intervention eliminated in favor of smart contracts, shipping documents will have to be standardized. A simple stipulation for generic on-board bills of lading or sea waybills for a given
quantity of goods will not do. A computer, however powerful or tamper-
proof, cannot scrutinize shipping documents for legal or other pitfalls, or
make nice judgments about what will, and will not, do as a presentation
for the purposes of the UCP600 and the eUCP; in such a case, we will

---

[56] *See generally* Dakota A. Larson, *Mitigating Risky Business: Modernizing Letters of Credit
with Blockchain, Smart Contracts, and the Internet of Things*, 2018 MICH. ST. L. REV. 929
(2018).

[57] *See* Sanne Wass, Voltron Blockchain Consortium to Create Independent Company
Ahead of Commercial Launch, Global Trade Review, www.gtreview.com/news/fintech/
voltron-blockchain-consortium-to-create-independent-company-ahead-of-commercial-
launch/ (Apr. 3, 2019; last visited Mar. 2, 2022) (online).

[58] *See* Daniel Palmer, Standard Chartered Completes First Transaction on Blockchain Trade
Platform Voltron, CoinDesk, www.coindesk.com/markets/2019/08/07/standard-char
tered-completes-first-transaction-on-blockchain-trade-platform-voltron/ (Aug. 7, 2019;
last visited Mar. 2, 2022) (online).

therefore still require a large back-office operation to scrutinize what is presented and exercise human judgment as to whether the presentation is good. Instead, the stipulation will have to refer to a particular form and precise wording of digitized carriage document, such as CONGENBILL 2016. (This is a matter that may well be helped by BIMCO's own practice of digitizing all new, and a number of existing, standard documents.) Moreover, this is not limited to shipping documents proper. In order to reap the benefits of smart contracts in the shipping and international trade context, all of the relevant documents will have to be harmonized, including such uninteresting but vital things as packing lists and certificates of origin or quality, all of which will have to be specified to take a particular standard form of wording that cannot then be altered. Moreover, the issuers of such documents will also have to be participants in whichever blockchain system is used. The making of these arrangements will clearly be a major logistical operation; nevertheless, it is suggested that these are not insuperable problems.

5.3   Cargo Care and Monitoring

Carriage contracts such as bills of lading or sea waybills, and documentary payments, raise issues about the *legal* replaceability of paper documents with electronic impulses. *Ex hypothesi* one cannot have a documentary payment without documents to pay it against (and indeed letter of credit law presumptively tells banks specifically to ignore any nondocumentary conditions); similarly, without specific legislation, it remains unclear, and certainly variable among jurisdictions, whether a disembodied bill of lading is or is not a contradiction in terms.

By contrast, questions of cargo care do not directly raise any formal legal issues relating to documents. Cargo damage claims, it is true, exist against the background of a number of legal presumptions and other provisions (e.g., the rule that a bailee is liable for damage occurring while in charge of goods unless it proves some excepted peril, with the shipping documents being strong evidence as to state and quantity of goods originally entrusted to it). Nevertheless, claims against carriers and P&I clubs remain essentially fact-specific; in the vast majority of cases, the issue is simply what went wrong, where and when. The same goes for disputes between seller and buyer over short or damaged delivery at the time of outturn. In nearly all such cases, the question is whether the goods were defective at a particular time or stage of the journey, when damage occurred and how it eventuated, all of which are matters to be

proved by evidence in the ordinary way. So too in the converse case
where damage is allegedly caused by cargo to a vessel or other cargo on
board during a voyage, what we need in order to know whether a
dangerous cargo claim is feasible can be vital to know when and how
the damage happened. Once again, this is simply a matter of evidence.
Distributed ledger technology nevertheless has the potential to be highly
significant here, especially when combined with existing means of continuous nonhuman cargo monitoring.

It must be remembered that the continuous surveillance of cargo en
route, especially container cargo, is rapidly turning into the norm.[59] This
is particularly true with containers, which are progressively becoming not
simply sealed boxes, but smart machines equipped with a remarkably
wide range of sensors.[60] The latter are able to detect the temperature of a
freezer or reefer container and any changes in it; watch the humidity in a
dry container; or detect sudden movement in any container. They can
equally check for weight,[61] listen for footsteps, detect door openings and
film interior events. They can also give a precise geolocation. In the
longer term, it may be possible for them to detect the nature of a given
cargo. The practical applications go in step.[62] Precise geolocation means
shippers and consignees can be provided with real-time information as to
where their goods are and when they are likely to get them (not to
mention enabling the tracing of stolen containers that are in the hands
of fraudsters).[63] Sudden changes in temperature or atmosphere can be
fairly precisely timed, thus implicating the carrier if the goods should
arrive damaged or deteriorated (or for that matter exonerating it in the

[59] See Forbes Insights, Opinion, *Logistics 4.0: How IoT Is Transforming the Supply Chain*, FORBES, June 14, 2018 (describing the tendency toward continuous monitoring using blockchain to ensure the data emanating from it is reliable and tamper-proof).
[60] See, e.g., Frank Stevens, *Smart Containers: The Smarter, the More Scope for Liability?* MARITIME LIABILITIES IN A GLOBAL AND REGIONAL CONTEXT 72 (Barış Soyer & Andrew Tettenborn eds., 2019).
[61] This is important in any case for another reason, since the introduction in July 2016 of the requirement to ascertain a VGM for all containers prior to loading. International Convention for the Safety of Life at Sea ch. VI, r. 2, 1974, Nov. 1, 1974, 32 U.S.T. 47, 1184 U.N.T.S. 2 (as amended) (hereinafter SOLAS).
[62] UNITED NATIONS ECONOMIC COMMISSION FOR EUROPE, U.N. DOC. ECE/TRADE/C/CEFACT/2019/10, SMART CONTAINERS: REAL-TIME SMART CONTAINER DATA FOR SUPPLY CHAIN EXCELLENCE 9 (2019).
[63] Mediterranean Shipping Company v. Glencore International [2017] EWHC (Civ) 365, [2017] 2 Lloyd's Rep. 186 (Eng. & Wales) (involving the hacking of access codes in the port of Antwerp, allowing fraudsters to hitch up their trucks and drive off with containers of immensely valuable and saleable cobalt briquettes).

case of through or multimodal carriage, in so far as it indicates that the problems actually occurred at some other stage). Sensors can equally be programmed to avoid problems in the first place by triggering compensating adjustments – for example, changing the ambient atmosphere in a container full of fruit, or dehumidifying a cargo of coffee to ensure its arrival in perfect condition – or in extreme cases, by initiating such things as fire precautions. Theft and pilferage from a container become more difficult when door opening is constantly monitored and there are cameras inside; fraudulent removal of the container itself (i.e., in the course of discharge) becomes more problematic if those doing it know that geolocation may be active. As and when accurate identification of cargo in a container becomes possible, carriers will be able more effectively to deal with the problem of undeclared dangerous cargo, and so on. Such developments are most clear with containers, but it should not be forgotten that bulk cargoes such as oil or grain are equally subject to increasing automatic monitoring by equipment on board, and most of the following comments on containerized cargo will apply at least to some extent to them too.

Viewed on their own, it must be admitted that electronic information gathering largely benefits shipowners and bareboat charterers acting as physical carriers. Being in control of the vessel, they will receive the relevant information, where appropriate take advantage of it[64] and be ultimately responsible for ensuring that necessary measures are taken. But there is no reason why it should be made available to them exclusively. Distributed ledger technology makes it possible for information not only to be proofed against manipulation and falsification, but also to be distributed on a selective basis, as in the case of electronic bills of lading discussed earlier. And here it may well be to the benefit of all parties for reliable and unmanipulable cargo data to be shared between two or more of, say, carriers, charterers, shippers, consignees and container suppliers.

The point is that in many cases they may share a common interest in receiving it in order to avoid uncertainty.[65] A great deal of the expense of cargo litigation, for example, results from argument over when damage occurred – especially in the case of serial carriers, which feature in almost

---

[64] One advantage seen by carriers as stemming from information about the contents of containers is valuable marketing intelligence as to their customers' wants and needs.
[65] This point is not lost on some entrepreneurial companies. See, e.g., Announcing the Launch of ShipChain Mainnet, SHIP Staking Open, SHIPCHAIN: BLOG, July 30, 2020.

every case of multimodal transport – and what its immediate cause was. A sharing of reliable cargo monitoring data between carrier or carrier and shipper will normally avert argument over the former and will often help with the latter. Similarly, with arguments between shippers and consignees, which will not infrequently turn on issues of whether damage occurred before or after risk passed (i.e., before or after shipment). In so far as a smart container will have the capacity to begin monitoring at the time of stuffing, the prospect of being able to establish whether damage occurred after that moment, and if so when, is attractive. And so also with dangerous cargo claims, especially if and when reliable technology becomes available to identify otherwise invisible hazardous cargo, as well to monitor such matters as combustion.

5.4   Vessel Monitoring

Quite apart from issues connected with cargo, when it comes to the monitoring of the well-being and progress of vessels themselves, human oversight – already more difficult because of reduced crew numbers – is now heavily supplemented by machine surveillance. For some twenty years, all vessels of any size[66] have been bound under SOLAS to carry an electronic voyage data recorder (VDR),[67] and there are various other requirements and recommendations: for example, hull stress monitoring machinery on bulk carriers.[68] Not only is this required as a matter of regulatory law, but in some jurisdictions, it has also made an impact in civil litigation. For example, in an English collision suit, all VDR data must be exchanged at an early stage between the parties.[69] In practice, it is not unknown for such suits to be decided on the basis of little other evidence apart from it.[70] The importance of this in collision cases is obvious, and there is also scope for extending it further, for example to grounding cases[71] or possibly others, such as product liability suits arising out of a marine casualty.

---

[66] That is, over 3,000 GRT.

[67] SOLAS, *supra* note 62, ch. V, r. 20.

[68] *See* Int'l Mar. Org., Recommendations for the Fitting of Hull Stress Monitoring Systems, U.N. Doc. MSC/Circ.646 (1994).

[69] CPR 61.4(4A) (Eng. & Wales).

[70] *See, e.g.,* Nautical Challenge Ltd. v. Evergreen Marine (U.K.) Ltd. [2017] EWHC (Admlty) 453, [2017] 1 Lloyd's Rep. 666 (Eng. & Wales).

[71] *See, e.g.,* Alize 1954 v. Allianz Elementar Versicherungs [2019] EWHC (Admlty) 481, [2019] 1 Lloyd's Rep. 595 (Eng. & Wales).

There is much to be said for blockchaining data of this sort, on the basis that its preservation in the hands of shipowners, registry port states and others (e.g., cargo owners in the case of a bulk carrier) can be vital not only for full and proper accident investigation but also for the efficient conduct of litigation. Facilities exist to do this, for example through Inmarsat's Fleet Data System and offerings from other private enterprise operators.[72] Unfortunately, the take-up of these seems to be small. No doubt this is because the incentives may not be present here that are present in the case of cargo surveillance. If a vessel is involved in a collision, sinking or other casualty, it can often in practice be difficult to avoid a finding of at least some degree of fault on the part of those on board; it may well not be in the shipowner's interests to make public any recording under their control of what has gone on. Although all port states on principle tend to demand the handover of VDR and other data after a casualty, there is at least something to be said for a specific regulatory requirement that such material be regularly updated to some central location operated by the relevant port state, subject to the necessary requirements of confidentiality.

---

[72] Press Release, *Inmarsat Unveils Major New IoT Service for the Shipping Industry*, INMARSAT, Sept. 4, 2018.

6

Maritime Cyber Security

BRIAN WILSON

6.1 Introduction

In 2017, malicious NotPetya code struck a computer in the seaport of Odessa, Ukraine, and quickly disabled the world's largest shipping company.[1] The electronic virus did more than disrupt commerce and corrupt

---

[1] The event began in Ukraine on June 27, 2017, as chronicled by Andy Greenberg in SANDWORM: "[O]ne single infection would become particularly fateful for the shipping giant Maersk. In an office in Odessa, a port city on Ukraine's Black Sea coast, a finance executive for Maersk's Ukraine operation had asked IT administrators to install the accounting software M.E.Doc on a single computer. That gave NotPetya the only foothold it needed." ANDY GREENBERG, SANDWORM: A NEW ERA OF CYBERWAR AND THE HUNT FOR THE KREMLIN'S MOST DANGEROUS HACKERS 189 (2019). "The shipping giant would soon be dead in the water." *Id.*, at 153. "Because the NotPetya malware was designed to spread to connected networks belonging to other victims, the attacks also rendered inoperable computer systems belonging to victims in other countries, including in the United

the information systems of A. P. Møller–Mærsk A/S (Maersk). The malware exposed some of the most pressing contemporary maritime challenges: technology outstripping regulations; competing stakeholders scrambling to respond to crisis without full information; and an inability to control enormous, unforeseen losses. While the Internet seamlessly connected the Copenhagen headquarters to Maersk offices on six continents, as well as to numerous ships and port facilities, the cyber links created vulnerability. This chapter focuses on state, multinational organization and private-sector efforts to ensure safety at sea amid expanded digital reliance. As maritime cyber security challenges mount, however, actions to prevent or counter them have lagged.

Regarding terminology, there is no universally recognized definition of maritime cyber security. The UK's Maritime and Coastguard Agency's examination of this concept – that it is more than preventing unauthorized access to systems and includes information integrity and maintenance to support business continuity – acknowledges the broad array of considerations and provides a beneficial framing for this chapter.[2]

The NotPetya attack is the most visible in a series of malicious activities impacting maritime industry. In recent years, operations were impaired at another major shipping company and hackers sought to electronically breach the port of San Diego.[3] Similarly, the largest cruise line operator on earth reported numerous instances of malicious cyber activities.[4] Even the specialized United Nations (UN) agency for regulating shipping, the International Maritime Organization (IMO),

---

States." Indictment ¶ 31, United States v. Adrienko, No. 20-316 (W.D. Pa. filed Oct. 15, 2020). NotPetya was designed "to masquerade as ransomware, a type of malware that encrypts and blocks access to a victim's computer system and/or files until the victim pays a ransom . . . however, the purported ransomware purpose of NotPetya was a ruse [and even after payment], the Conspirators would not be able to decrypt and recover the victims' files." *Id.*, ¶ 33.

[2] UK Mar. & Coastguard Agency, Marine Information Note 647(M): Incorporation of Cyber Security measures within Safety Management Systems ¶ 1.2 (2021).

[3] "Mediterranean Shipping Company (MSC) . . . admitted it was hit by a malware resulting in much of its IT infrastructure going offline for five days around the Easter weekend." Sam Chambers, *MSC Admits Malware Attack*, Splash247.com, https://splash247.com/msc-admits-malware-attack/ (Apr. 16, 2020; last visited Mar. 2, 2022) (online); Indictment ¶ 2(b), United States v. Savandi, No. 18-CR-704(BRM) (D.N.J. filed Nov. 26, 2018); *Ransomware Attack Cripples Systems of Island Port in Washington State*, Mar. Exec., Nov. 19, 2020.

[4] Carnival Corp., Form 8-K: Current Report Pursuant to Section 13 or 15(d) of the Securities Exchange Act of 1934, para. 2 (Aug. 15, 2020).

experienced a sophisticated intrusion of its Internet website, causing it to temporarily shut down.[5] In each case, multiple organizations and countries were affected.

Cooperation in cyberspace is a current priority for businesses and governments, though such focus is not new. In 1984, President Ronald Reagan signed a directive that recognized that the response to emerging technology requires a comprehensive and coordinated approach.[6] In 1997, the European Commission acknowledged that "electronic commerce is inherently a global activity," and that cybercrime was a global concern.[7] In 2000, the government of Australia connected cyber protection with national security, one of the first countries to do so.[8] And, numerous US Congressional hearings have examined issues associated with protecting cyber infrastructure.[9]

Resources and personnel now widely flow into digital security. J. P. Morgan Chase, for example, annually spends US$600 million and devotes 3,000 employees to cyber security efforts.[10] This tremendous amount is only a fraction of the billions of dollars spent by private-sector entities and governments to address cyber security, which includes the maritime sector.[11] Such investments make even more sense on the water, where electronic disruptions can disable a vessel plying the high seas. Ships are reliant on technology, yet often operate in geographic isolation and beyond the reach of assistance. Ships at the pier are dependent on port facilities that rely on software programs to control the movement of millions of freight tons of cargo.

[5] UN Shipping Agency Says Cyber Attack Disables Website, Reuters, Oct. 1, 2020.
[6] Exec. Off. of the President, National Security Decision Directive No. 145, National Policy on Telecommunications and Automated Information Systems Security (1984).
[7] Commission Communication on a European Initiative in Electronic Commerce, ¶¶ 21–22, COM (1997) 157 final (Apr. 4, 1997); id., ¶ 32 ("benefits of electronic commerce will only be achieved if interoperability is ensured at a global level").
[8] Australian Department of Defence, Defence 2000: Our Future Defence (2000).
[9] Stmt Sen. John McCain, Cybersecurity, Encryption and United States National Security Matters: Hearing Before the S. Comm. on Armed Services, 114th Cong. 1–3 (2016) (hereinafter McCain Hearing); see also Executive Office of the President, National Cyber Strategy of the United States of America 1–2 (2018).
[10] Bruce Sussman, JPMorgan Chase Cybersecurity: We Spend Nearly $600M a Year, SecureWorldExpo.com, July 9, 2019.
[11] Steve Morgan, Global Cybersecurity Spending Predicted to Exceed $1 Trillion from 2017–2021, Cybercrime Mag., June 10, 2019; Rachel Covill, Cybersecurity Firm to Use £1.8m Boost to Lead New Growth in Maritime Sector, TheBusinessDesk.com, April 27, 2020.

Maritime cyber issues are guided by international instruments, private-sector guidance and domestic enforcement. The cyber jumble in shipping, which is largely transnational, underscores why the status quo is unacceptable.[12] This chapter explores existing laws and regulations and proposes new frameworks for improving the response to cyber threats. Expanding collaboration is the foundation for changing the status quo.

6.2   Technology, Systems and the Maritime Environment

Technology has driven the trajectory of vessel operations and shipping. The evolution of navigation began with rudimentary piloting based on the "fish, the color of the water, the type of terrain, the birds, and the rocks," and celestial navigation.[13] Approximately a thousand years ago, compasses were employed with "a magnetized needle floating in a bowl of water," followed by the chronometer, which provided an ability to plot positions within "tens of miles."[14] While each advancement improved navigation and expanded trade opportunities, the shift from piloting based on a zodiac dial and the stars placed ships farther from shore and added uncertainty and risk. Despite these advances, the high seas would remain "radically free [of regulations ...] at a time when every last patch of land is claimed by one government or another, and when citizenship is treated as an absolute condition of human existence."[15]

Telecommunication advances over a century ago presaged the need for states to collaborate in technology. "After Samuel Morse sent his first public message over a telegraph line between Washington and Baltimore on May 24, 1844, telegraphy became a service widely accessible to the public."[16] Telegraph lines were not managed cross-border, but instead

---

[12] At a 2018 Senate Armed Services Committee hearing, Chairman Sen. John McCain stated that "there is a growing recognition that the threat posed by the status quo is unacceptable and that we need the public and private sectors to come together to eliminate cyber safe havens for terrorists and criminals." McCain Hearing, *supra* note 9, at 2 (stmt of Sen. McCain).
[13] Andrew K. Johnston et al., Time and Navigation: The Untold Story of Getting from Here to There 16 (2015).
[14] "About 1040 CE, Chinese navigators began to use the compass ... and ... Emperors in the Yuan Dynasty (c. 1271–1368) built a trade network with posts as far away as Sumatra and India." *Id.*, at 19; *see also Id.*, at 44 (noting that the chronometer "had demonstrated its ability to fix positions at sea routinely within tens of miles ... and ... better timekeeping and star positions brought better navigation").
[15] William Langewiesche, The Outlaw Sea 3 (2004).
[16] Sabine von Schorlemer, Telecommunications, International Regulation. 9 Max Planck Encyclopedia of Public International Law 818 (Rüdiger Wolfrum ed., 2009);

maintained by each country at a national level. States were connected through numerous international telegraph links developed by agreements.[17] The expansion of telegraphy may have been the most important advance in communications in the nineteenth century, but cooperation was necessary to unleash its global benefits.[18] Along with contributing to the expansion of shipping, nineteenth-century telegraphy agreements serve as a model for multinational collaboration today.[19]

Another seminal event occurred approximately a century later, when a trucker from North Carolina became dissatisfied with how inefficiently cargo moved through port facilities. Transporting commodities on the water has been a lynchpin of commerce for centuries, yet the interface between ships and ports was complicated and chaotic well into the 1950s.[20] At the warehouse,

> freight would be loaded piece by piece onto a truck or railcar. The truck or train would deliver hundreds or thousands of such items to the waterfront [where each was] unloaded separately, recorded on a tally sheet, and carried to storage in a transit shed, a warehouse stretching alongside the dock. Containers included . . . paperboard cartons . . . wooden crates . . . casks . . . and steel drums . . . alongside . . . bales of cotton and animal skins.[21]

Following this lengthy process, the cargo was ready for yet another move onto vessels. Malcolm McLean, who started in local shipping with a single flatbed trailer for local shipping, grew his business into a trucking fleet. He viewed the disorganization at the pier firsthand while delivering cargo to ports. McLean's plan involved significantly expanding the use of steel-box containers, which existed at the time, but were not frequently

---

International Telecommunication Convention, pmbl., ¶¶ 1, 3, Dec. 9, 1932, 49 Stat. 2393, T.S. No. 867.

[17] Von Schorlemer, *supra* note 16.

[18] Marc Levinson, The Box: How The Shipping Container Made the World Smaller and the World Economy Bigger (2006) (hereinafter The Box);
   Marc Levinson, Outside The Box: How Globalization Changed from Moving Stuff to Spreading Ideas 29 (2020) (hereinafter Outside The Box).

[19] Von Schorlemer, *supra* note 16; International Telecommunication Convention, *supra* note 16, International Telecommunication Union Constitution, art. 1; Convention for the Protection of Submarine Telegraph Cables, Mar. 14, 1884, 24 Stat. 989, T.S. No. 380.

[20] Levinson, The Box, *supra* note 18, at 16-35. "By the early 1950s, there was little dispute that freight terminals were a transportation choke point." *Id.* at 33.

[21] *Id.*, at 16-17. *See also*, "Unloading could be just as difficult. An arriving ship might be carrying 100-kilo bags of sugar or 20-pound cheeses nestled next to 2-ton steel coils. Simply moving one without damaging the other was hard enough." *Id.*, at 17-18.

employed.[22] His innovation, and enduring legacy, was to view maritime commerce as being about "moving cargo, not ships," and approach that meant that "each node in the system, from ports, ships, cranes, storage facilities, trucks, and trains, had to accommodate containers of the same size and dimension."[23] By 1966, three carriers were actively transporting containers with stunning efficiency. Shipping costs plummeted from US$16.00 per ton to US$2.25 per ton.[24]

It is not hyperbole to suggest that the shift pioneered by McLean changed the world.[25] In 2019, almost 800 million containers moved through ports worldwide, measured as 20-foot equivalent units, or TEUs.[26] Like the adoption of telegraphy, nobody anticipated the seismic influence of containers.[27] The digitization of this process in recent decades was overwhelming.[28] Both the container expansion and telecommunication advances occurred well before regulations governing their employment and use were implemented.[29]

The 1990s represent a turning point for addressing electronic capabilities in the maritime environment. During this period, regulations, initially to prevent ship collisions, were developed by member states of the IMO to monitor and track ships that weighed over 300 metric tons, among other requirements.[30] Adopted under the International Convention for the Safety of Life at Sea (SOLAS),[31] designated vessels

---

[22] *Id.* at 36–53.

[23] *Id.* at 53.

[24] *Id.* at 164–65.

[25] Gary Hoover, *Malcolm McLean: Unsung Innovator Who Changed the World*, AMERICANBUSINESSHISTORY.ORG. Jan. 21, 2021.

[26] UN Doc. UNCTAD/ RMT/2019/Corr.1, REVIEW OF MARITIME TRANSPORT 2019, at 2 (Jan. 31, 2020).

[27] LEVINSON, OUTSIDE THE BOX, *supra* note 18, at xii–xiii, 29.

[28] JOSEPH KRAMEK, THE CRITICAL INFRASTRUCTURE GAP: U.S. PORT FACILITIES AND CYBER VULNERABILITIES iv (2013);

P. W. SINGER & ALLAN FRIEDMAN, CYBERSECURITY AND CYBERWAR: WHAT EVERYONE NEEDS TO KNOW 1–2 (1st ed. 2014);

DAVID E. SINGER, THE PERFECT WEAPON: WAR, SABOTAGE, AND FEAR IN THE CYBER AGE xx (2018).

[29] LEVINSON, OUTSIDE THE BOX, *supra* note 18, at 63–64. *See also*, Hariesh Manaadiar, My Name is Container 42, the Smartest Container on the Planet, Shipping and Freight Resource, bit.ly/3s17KG6 (May 31, 2019; last visited Mar. 2, 2022) (online).

[30] ROSE GEORGE, NINETY PERCENT OF EVERYTHING: INSIDE SHIPPING, THE INVISIBLE INDUSTRY THAT PUTS CLOTHES ON YOUR BACK, GAS IN YOUR CAR, AND FOOD ON YOUR PLATE 3 (2013).

[31] International Convention for the Safety of Life at Sea, 1974, Nov. 1, 1974, 32 U.S.T. 47, 1184 U.N.T.S. 278 (as amended) (hereinafter SOLAS).

engaged in international voyages are required "to carry an automatic identification system (AIS) capable of providing information about the ship to other ships and to coastal authorities automatically [that include] the ship's identity, type, position, course, speed, navigational status, and other safety-related information automatically to appropriately equipped shore stations, other ships, and aircraft, as well as to receive automatically such information."[32] This system was implemented for its safety benefits, but introduced a potential area of cyber vulnerability that could be exploited.

In 2005, the legal landscape was altered further when member states at the IMO required the use of the satellite-based long-range identification and tracking (LRIT) system for designated vessels.[33] Data from AIS (including satellite AIS) transmissions and LRIT, along with the vessel monitoring system (VMS)[34] for fishing boats, collectively support shipping safety. These systems also improve maritime awareness, helping hold polluters accountable.[35]

Combined with port automation, the Global Positioning System (GPS) and other tracking, navigational and vessel[36] systems[37] underscore an electronically reliant environment. Despite inherent vulnerabilities associated with these new systems, the digital transformation is occurring because of the significant benefits that these technologies provide.[38]

6.3 Electronic Interference, Disruptions and Malicious Cyber Activities

Maritime cyber threats before and after NotPetya exposed weaknesses in operating systems as well as regulatory gaps. A report published in

[32] Verified Complaint for Forfeiture ¶ 34, United States v. Bulk Cargo Carrier Known as the "Wise Honest," No. 1:19-CV-04210 (S.D. N.Y. filed May 9, 2019).
[33] IMO, Long-range identification and tracking (LRIT), www.imo.org/en/OurWork/Safety/Pages/LRIT.aspx (last visited Apr. 9, 2021) (online).
[34] Global Fishing Watch, Vessel Tracking Data, https://bit.ly/3gZhfj6 (last visited Apr. 9, 2021) (online).
[35] Stmt of Brian M. Salerno, Maritime Domain Awareness: Hearing before the H. Subcomm. on Coast Guard & Mar. Transp. of the H. Comm. on Transp. & Infrastructure, 111th Cong. p.1 (2009).
[36] Chris Parker & Dinos A. Kerigan-Kyrou, A Decade of Disruption: Cyber in the Maritime Environment, 20 NMIOTC MAR. INTERDICTION OPERATIONS J. 13, 14 (2020).
[37] Container xChange: Blog, Container Terminal Automation and Its Benefits Explained, bit.ly/3BBVZcI (last visited Apr. 9, 2021) (online).
[38] IMO Doc. MSC 95/4/2, Submission to the Maritime Safety Committee (Canada) (2015).

2013 noted "little attention has been paid to the networked systems that undergird port operations."[39] That lament remains accurate across the entirety of the maritime spectrum, as interference, ransomware, systems failure/disruption and denial-of-services exploit systems[40] designed to improve shipping efficiencies and navigational fidelity. This section notes several – though certainly not all – cyber breaches affecting the maritime sector.

Automatic identification system data acquired from ocean-going vessels across the globe are voluminous and instructive.[41] Electronic systems expand awareness of illicit activity that may not otherwise be known, such as vessel loitering, shadowing, operations just outside the 200-mile exclusive economic zone (EEZ) or tracks from the same vessel at simultaneous times across the globe. But AIS is based on VHF transmission and it is the least secure protocol, with a large number of false positives.[42] Even signals from satellites can be intercepted, and passwords remotely reset.[43] Malicious cyber activities can cause ships to report incorrect locations or fuel levels, false environmental readings, transmit inaccurate data or deny service altogether, disrupting data that is essential for safe operations.[44] One maritime industry study found that ports had a 900 percent increase in malicious activities over a three-year period, further noting that the actual number of incidents and intrusions is likely higher due to underreporting.[45] A reluctance to disclose cyber

---

[39] KRAMEK, *supra* note 28, at iv.
[40] NICOLE van der MEULEN, EUN A. JO & STEFAN SOESANTO, CYBERSECURITY IN THE EUROPEAN UNION AND BEYOND: EXPLORING THE THREATS AND POLICY RESPONSES (2015).
[41] Nathan A. Miller et al., *Identifying Global Patterns of Transshipment Behavior*, 5 FRONTIERS MARINE SCI. 1 (2018) (examining 32 billion AIS messages from 2012 to 2017 and identifying "694 cargo vessels capable of transshipping and transporting fish … mapping 46,570 instances where these vessels loitered at sea long enough to receive a transshipment and 10,233 instances where [they could see] a fishing vessel near a loitering transshipment vessel long enough to engage in transshipment."); *id.*, at 8 (concluding, based on AIS data, that "transshipment behavior clusters along EEZ boundaries in the high seas, is common in regions of challenging or limited regulation and oversight, and often involves vessels registered to flags of convenience").
[42] Matt Coyne, Intentional or Unintentional? US Reliance on AIS Creates Pitfalls for Shipping; Trade Winds, bit.ly/3v0l9xN (Aug. 6, 2020; last visited Mar. 2, 2022) (online).
[43] Dan Goodin, Insecure Satellite Internet Is Threatening Ship and Plane Safety, ARS Technica, bit.ly/3gWTCrl (Aug. 5, 2020; last visited Mar. 2, 2022) (online).
[44] *Id.*
[45] Jasmina Ovcina, Ports Increasingly Targeted by Cyberattacks as Maritime Incidents Surge, Offshore Energy, bit.ly/3s1nucg (July 20, 2020; last visited Mar. 2, 2022) (online) (noting 301 significant cyber breaches in 2019 and only 50 in 2017).

breaches could be based on a difficulty in describing "something unfamiliar," no explicit requirement to report an incident, a lack of awareness that a system has been compromised, or for competitive or propriety business reasons.[46] The study found that hackers can directly attack crane operations and storage systems, sometimes even with just a cellular connection.[47] Such exploitation is no longer a theoretical danger. A 2020 US Federal court indictment charged two hackers with the penetration of computers around the world and the theft of terabytes of data from a shipbuilding firm that included source code and engineering schematics from a defense contractor.[48]

Moreover, the US government has issued warnings regarding GPS interference against ships in port and underway[49] that have disrupted bridge navigation, timing and communications.[50] GPS interference has occurred in the Eastern and Central Mediterranean Sea, the Persian Gulf,

---

[46] "Unlike IT infrastructure, there is no 'dashboard' for the OT network allowing operators to see the health of all connected systems. Operators rarely know if an attack has taken place, invariably writing up any anomaly as a system error, system failure, or requiring restart." *Id.*

[47] The consequences of electronic reliance are that "if just one piece of this meticulously-managed operation goes down it will create unprecedented backlog and impact global trade, disrupting operations and infrastructure for weeks if not months, costing tens of millions of dollars in lost revenue." *Id.*

[48] Indictment ¶¶ 1 and 17, United States v. Li Xiaoyu and Dong Jiazhi, No. 4:20-CR-6029-SMJ (E.D. Wash. filed July 7, 2020); *see also* Press Release, U.S. Cybersecurity & Infrastructure Security Agency, Chinese Ministry of State Security-Affiliated Cyber Threat Actor Activity (Sept. 14, 2020) (alerting that "[t]he continued use of open-source tools by Chinese MSS-affiliated cyber threat actors highlights that adversaries can use relatively low-complexity capabilities to identify and exploit target networks").

[49] U.S. Maritime Advisory 2021-004: Various GPS Interference (Mar. 19, 2021); U.S. Maritime Advisory 2020-016: Various GPS Interference (Sep. 22, 2020); U.S. Maritime Advisory 2019-013 Eastern/Central Mediterranean Sea and Suez Canal-GPS Interference (Sep. 24, 2019); and U.S. Maritime Advisory 2018-004B: Port Said, Egypt, GPS Interference (Apr. 6, 2018), among others. US maritime alerts and advisories are transmitted by the National Geospatial-Intelligence Agency in accordance with the US Maritime Advisory System of the Maritime Security Communications with Industry (MSCI) program.

[50] *Id.*, U.S. Maritime Advisory 2019-013 further noted, "Satellite communications equipment may also be impacted." *See also*, background on US government–issued alerts and advisories, "The *U.S. Maritime Advisory System* serves as the consolidated U.S. government system for communication with U.S. maritime industry stakeholders regarding . . . maritime security threats. This system involves cooperation between U.S. government maritime security partners from the Departments of State, Transportation, Defense, Homeland Security, the Intelligence Community, and the Global Maritime Operational Threat Response Coordination Center (GMCC)." US Department of Transportation, Maritime Security Communications with Industry (MSCI) Web Portal, www.maritime

Chinese ports, in the vicinity of the Suez Canal[51] and the Black Sea,[52] among other areas. US government–issued warnings further reported that electronic tampering has resulted in "inaccurate positions or no position,"[53] as well as "jammed, lost or ... altered GPS signals."[54]

In 2020, DESMI, a Danish pump maker, was forced to restore its network after suffering a cyberattack.[55] The impact of this breach to a firm with annual revenue in excess of US\$200 million that supplies pumps for naval and coast guard vessels is unknown.[56] Also in 2020, the operating system of the world's second largest container line, MSC, was inoperable for five days.[57] The fourth largest carrier, CMA CGM, had to shut down its systems following malicious cyber activities against two of its Asia-Pacific subsidiaries.[58]

Participants from the private sector play an influential role in cyber prevention and response that can include control of critical infrastructure facilities.[59] They have powerful financial incentives to ensure the safe navigation of their vessels. That said, the private sector includes diverse stakeholders, with varied priorities. Their efforts, as well as legal authorities, national regulations and member state efforts at the IMO are discussed in the following.

.dot.gov/msci/maritime-security-communications-industry-msci-web-portal (last visited July 12, 2021) (online).

[51] U.S. Maritime Advisories 2021-004, 2020-016, 2019-013, *supra* note 49.

[52] U.S. Maritime Alert 2017-005A: Black Sea GPS Interference (June 22, 2017).

[53] U.S. Maritime Alert 2018-008A: Jeddah Port, Saudi Arabia, GPS Interference (Oct. 23, 2018).

[54] U.S. Maritime Advisory 2018-004B, *supra* note 49.

[55] Harry Papachristou, Danish Pump Maker Reveals Cyber Attacks as Virus Lockdown Raises Hacking Threat, Trade Winds, bit.ly/3JInML1 (Apr. 10, 2020; last visited Mar. 2, 2022) (online).

[56] *Id.*

[57] "The MSC malware news means the world's top three container lines have all been hit by cyberattacks in the space of the last three years. Maersk suffered hundreds of millions of dollars of losses when it was hit by the NotPetya malware in June 2017, while Cosco was hit the following year by malware in an attack that started at its US west coast operations." Chambers, *supra* note 3.

[58] Costas Paris, Container Line CMA CGM Hit by CyberAttack, Wall St. J, Sept. 28, 2020; Press Release, CMA CGM Group, The CMA CGM Group (excluding CEVA Logistics) Is Currently Dealing with a Cyber-attack Impacting Peripheral Servers, on.wsj.com/3JDdZpz (Sept. 28, 2020; last visited Mar. 2, 2022) (online).

[59] GOV'T ACCOUNT. OFF. PUB. NO. GAO-16-152, CRITICAL INFRASTRUCTURE PROTECTION: MEASURES NEEDED TO ASSESS AGENCIES' PROMOTION OF THE CYBERSECURITY FRAMEWORK 7 (2015).

6.4   Legal Authorities

Maritime cyber activities are regulated, albeit inconsistently, through international instruments, domestic regulations and private-sector protocols. They are infrequently presented collectively.[60] Enforcement is fragmentary. This cluster of distributed authorities has nevertheless resulted in norms[61] that may be enforced by a state as a condition of port entry, by the flag state of the vessel or privately through P&I clubs, owners, operators and shippers.[62]

6.4.1   The International Maritime Organization (IMO)

IMO member states have adopted several instruments related to electronic systems and cybersecurity. Collectively, these documents provide frameworks for assessing both regulation and response.

6.4.1.1   Maritime Cyber Risk Management

IMO Maritime Safety Committee, Resolution MSC.428(98) (2017), Maritime Cyber Risk Management in Safety Management Systems, encourages "Administrations to ensure that cyber risks are appropriately addressed in safety management systems no later than the first annual verification of the company's Document of Compliance after 1 January 2021." The resolution recommends that cyber risks be addressed as part of a ship's safety management system under the International Safety Management (ISM) code.[63]

---

[60] *See* IMO Doc. MSC-FAL.1/Circ. 3, Guidelines on Maritime Cyber Risk Management 4 (July 5, 2017) (hereinafter IMO Guidelines) (noting that "additional guidance standards may include but are not limited to: The Guidelines on Cyber Security Onboard Ships drafted by BIMCO, CLIA, ICS, INTERCARGO, INTERTANKO, OCIMF and IUMI") (Version 4) (2020); International Organization for Standardization, Pub. No. ISO/IEC 27001, Information Technology – Security Techniques – Information Security Management Systems – Requirements (2013);
US National Institute of Standards and Technology, Framework for Improving Critical Infrastructure Cybersecurity (2018).

[61] Liisi Adamson, *International Law and International Cyber Norms: A Continuum.* Governing Cyberspace: Behavior, Power, and Diplomacy 19, 29 (Dennis Broeders & Bib van den Berg eds., 2020).

[62] United Nations Convention on the Law of the Sea, Dec. 10, 1982, arts. 92, 94, 1833 U.N.T.S. 397.

[63] IMO Res. 428(98), Maritime Cyber Risk Management in Safety of Management Systems ¶ 2 (June 16, 2017).

IMO Facilitation Committee, MSC.FAL.1/Circ. 3 (2017), *Guidelines on Maritime Cyber Risk Management*, provides a nonbinding framework to identify, protect, detect, respond and recover, as well as implement, best practices.[64] The guidelines recognize that "cybertechnologies have become essential to the operation and management of numerous systems critical to the safety and security of shipping and protection of the marine environment."[65] Maritime vulnerabilities include bridge systems; cargo handling and management systems; propulsion and power control systems; access control systems; and communication systems.[66]

Systems supervision is unquestionably important, though holistically evaluating contemporary maritime vulnerabilities must also include technology. Yet in earlier discussions at the IMO, China contended that because, "[c]ybersecurity is a highly technical issue and evolves very quickly ... it will be more efficient and effective to focus ... on the management aspects of maritime cybersecurity rather than on the specific cybertechnical requirements."[67] China's intervention is emblematic of the uncertainty surrounding regulation of maritime cyberspace.

6.4.1.2 SOLAS and the ISPS Code

The International Ship and Port Facility Security (ISPS) code, developed at the IMO as an amendment to SOLAS,[68] provides a comprehensive regime for security measures.[69] The ISPS code ensures a consistent approach to vessel and port security by providing – with mandatory requirements and nonmandatory guidance – the standards by which audits are measured, representing the benchmark for security assessments. The ISPS code focus areas include screening containers, cargo and baggage; compliance with ship security standards; the security management program of the port; and other measures to deter terrorism.[70]

---

[64] IMO Guidelines, *supra* note 60, ¶ 3.5; *see also* IMO Doc. MSC 96/4/2, Submission to the Maritime Safety Committee (China) ¶ 3 (2016).

[65] IMO Guidelines, *supra* note 60, ¶ 2.1.1.

[66] *Id.,* ¶ 2.1.3.

[67] IMO Doc. MSC 96/4/3, Submission to the Maritime Safety Committee (China) (2016); IMO, Measures to Enhance Maritime Security, Proposals for Guidance on Maritime Cybersecurity ¶ 4.

[68] SOLAS, *supra* note 31; IMO Res. 5/34, International Ship and Port Facility Security code, Annex (Dec. 17, 2002) (hereinafter ISPS Code).

[69] ISPS Code, *supra* note 68.

[70] *Id.*

While unadorned with precise cyber security requirements, the ISPS code encourages security officers to consider computer systems and networks when conducting security assessments.[71] Facility security plans developed from such assessments should include the development of procedures for responding to security threats or breaches of security on vessels and in ports, including provisions for maintaining critical operations of the port facility or ship/port interface and measures designed to ensure effective security of cargo and the cargo handling equipment at the port facility.[72]

During discussions on ISPS code implementation challenges at the IMO, Canada submitted drafting recommendations that sought to reduce confusion stemming from ambiguous or inconsistent provisions related to cyber security.[73] While the ISPS code includes imprecise text, and the Canadian intervention was helpful, the code also contains broadly worded sections that allow flexibility regarding security measures. For example, Regulation XI-2/6 of the ISPS code requires vessels to be equipped with a ship security alert system (SSAS). When activated, the SSAS "shall initiate and transmit a ship-to-shore security alert to a competent authority designated by the administration of the flag State, identifying the ship, its location and indicating that the security of the ship is under threat or it has been compromised."[74]

The US Coast Guard advises US-flagged ships to immediately activate the SSAS if they are attacked or boarded by pirates.[75] This advisory is notable because ISPS does not explicitly identify the threats that would be considered a transportation security incident (TSI) that would require ships to activate their SSAS, correctly opting for flag states to provide clarity and implementing guidance. There is no legal restriction to likewise including cyber incidents that compromise the security of the ship.[76] The United States defines a TSI as a "security incident resulting in

---

[71] Id., ¶¶ 8.2, 16.2.

[72] Id., ¶¶ 16.3.3; 16.3.12.

[73] Id.; ¶ 9.

[74] Id., Reg. XI-2/6.

[75] U.S. COAST GUARD & U.S. DEP'T OF HOMELAND SEC., PORT SECURITY ADVISORY (9-09): EXPECTED COURSES OF ACTION FOLLOWING ATTACKS BY PIRATES IN THE HORN OF AFRICA REGION 1 (2009).

[76] IMO Res. 147(77), Adoption of the Revised Performance Standards for a Ship Security Alert System § 1.1 (May 29, 2003); IMO Doc. MSC/Circ. 1111, Guidance Relating to the Implementation of SOLAS Chapter XI-2 and the ISPS Code (June 7, 2004); IMO Res. A.1106(29), Revised Guidelines for the Onboard Operational Use of Shipborne Automatic Identification Systems (Dec. 2, 2015).

a significant loss of life, environmental damage, transportation system disruption, or economic disruption in a particular area,"[77] which could include electronics and computer systems. An owner or operator is required to have a security plan and shall, without delay, report suspicious activities that may result in a TSI to the National Response Center and notify the US Coast Guard of a TSI.[78]

6.4.1.3   Automatic Identification System (AIS)

In 2015, IMO member states amended AIS requirements in a resolution that clarified that the system "is intended to enhance [the] safety of life at sea; the safety and efficiency of navigation [and] the protection of the marine environment."[79] Moreover, the resolution provided that AIS can "help identify ships, assist in target tracking, assist in search and rescue operation, simplify information exchange and provide additional information to assist situational awareness."[80]

Importantly, this resolution provides that AIS should always be in operation when ships are underway or at anchor. If the master believes that continuing to operate AIS might compromise the safety or security of the ship or where security incidents are imminent, transmissions may be switched off. Unless it would further compromise the safety or security, if the ship is operating in a mandatory ship reporting system, the master should report this action and the reason for doing so to the competent authority. Actions of this nature should always be recorded in the ship's logbook together with the reason for doing so. The master should restart AIS as soon as the danger has passed.[81] Thus, this system's requirement is binding, but its continuous use has exceptions that may be invoked at the discretion of the master.

6.4.1.4   International Safety Management (ISM) Code

The IMO resolution, Maritime Cyber Risk Management in Safety Management Systems, expressly references the ISM code.[82] The ISM code was developed to facilitate the safe management and operation of

---

[77] 46 USC § 70101(7) (2018).
[78] 33 C.F.R. § 101.305, Reporting (2008).
[79] IMO Res. A.1106(29), *supra* note 76, ¶ 4.
[80] *Id.*
[81] *Id.*, ¶ 22.
[82] IMO Res. 428(98), *supra* note 63, pmbl.

ships.[83] Amended on multiple occasions over several decades, the ISM
code requires "a safety management system to be established by the
company (defined as the owner or any other organization or person
who has assumed responsibility for operating the ship)" and further
requires that the company "establish and implement a policy for achieving these objectives."[84] Compliance with ISM code obligations in the
United States, for example, provide insight into its potential relevance in
civil proceedings for cyber breaches.

A longshoreman who was injured when a piece of timber broke
through a faulty sling sought damages against the owner and operator
of the ship on which the accident occurred.[85] The suit in Revak
v. Interforest Terminal UMEA was grounded in the Longshore and
Harbor Workers' Compensation Act, and the US Federal court denied
the defendant's motion for summary judgment.[86] Portions of the judgment have relevance to cyber breaches, particularly in the context of a
vessel's duty regarding potential "hazards that are not known to the
stevedore and that would be neither obvious to nor anticipated by a
skilled stevedore in the competent performance of his work. The duty
encompasses only those hazards that are known to the vessel or should
be known to it in the exercise of reasonable care."[87] While there may not
be unanimity on the parameters of reasonable care for the protection and
safeguarding of cyber systems aboard a vessel, sufficient guidance exists.

The faulty sling may have caused the injury, but the case turned on the
duty of care. The court in Revak noted "defendant's practice of inspecting
the slings prior to turning them over to a stevedore; and the ISM Code
requirement that slings be maintained in conformity with industry
standards."[88] A comparable case remarked that "any analysis ... must

---

[83] IMO Res. A.741(18), International Management Code for the Safe Operation of Ships
and for Pollution Prevention, annex (Nov. 17, 1993) (hereinafter ISM Code); IMO
Res. 1022(26), Guidelines on the Implementation of the International Safety
Management (ISM) Code by Administrations, annex (Jan. 18, 2010) (hereinafter
Guidelines on Implementation of the ISM Code).
[84] Id.
[85] Revak v. Interforest Terminal UMEA, No. 03-4822, 2009 WL 1362554, at 1-2 (E.D. Pa.
May 14, 2009).
[86] Id.; see 33 U.S.C. §§901–50 (2018).
[87] Revak, No. 03-4822, ¶ 5.
[88] The court further noted that the Plaintiff asserted "that a reasonable jury could find that
Defendant did not exercise reasonable care by delegating its inspection duty to a third
party ... because Defendant (1) did not provide [the third party] with any criteria or
standards to utilize in inspecting and rejecting slings; (2) did not know whether [the third

begin by resolving the scope of defendant's duty to plaintiff."[89] Separately, a US Federal court in Oregon, which also denied a defendant's motion for summary judgment, addressed assertions that an unsecured grating that caused an accident was inherently unsafe and in violation of the ISM code.[90] And the US Supreme Court in Howlett v. Birkdale Shipping Co. held a "vessel's turnover duty to warn of latent defects … is narrow. As a rule, the duty to warn attaches only to hazards that are not known to the stevedore and that would be neither obvious to, nor anticipated by, a skilled stevedore in the competent performance of its work."[91] The court in Howlett also held, "a vessel must exercise ordinary care under the circumstances."[92]

The ISM code, as applied domestically, could provide a basis for damages from injuries where a vessel has not taken adequate actions consistent with IMO guidance and industry standards. State enforcement of international standards along with providing access to civil redress could be catalysts for increased attention on the protection of systems and technology.

6.4.2   European Union

The European Union (EU)–promulgated Security of Network and Information Systems (NIS Directive) represents the "first piece of EU-wide legislation on cybersecurity" and entered into force in 2016 along with imposing national-level obligations by 2018.[93] This legislation sought to instill a "culture of security across sectors … such as energy, transport, water, banking, financial market infrastructures, healthcare and digital infrastructure."[94]

In addition, the EU Council in Decision 2019/797 further addressed digital breaches.[95] The earlier EU Cyber Diplomacy Toolbox provides a

---

party] had expertise or skills with regard to inspecting slings; and (3) did not know who was actually inspecting the slings." *Id.*, ¶ 9.

[89] Schnapp v. Miller's Launch, Inc., 150 A.D.3d 32, ¶¶ 1-2 (N.Y. App. Div. 2017).

[90] Gilstrap v. Lakhi Maritime, Inc., No. 03-1503-KI, 2005 WL 1113839, ¶ 2 (D. Or. May 6, 2005).

[91] Howlett v. Birkdale Shipping Co., 512 U.S. 92, 105 (1994), *citing* Scindia Steam Nav. Co. v. De los Santos, 451 U.S. 156, 167 (1981).

[92] *Id.*, ¶ 98.

[93] EU Council Directive 2016/1148, 2016 O.J. (L 194) (EC); *see also* Press Release, European Commission, NIS Directive (Mar. 26, 2021).

[94] EU Council Directive 2016/1148, *supra* note 93.

[95] EU Council Decision 2019/797, 2019 O.J. (L 129) (EC).

framework for a joint diplomatic response to malicious cyber activities.[96] The 2019 decision emphasized "cyber-attacks are actions involving any of the following access to information systems; information system interference; data interference; or [unauthorized] data interception."[97] Further, EU Regulation 2019/881 (2019) set forth the mandate of ENISA (European Network and Information Security Agency), underscoring the importance of a "common approach" to a European cybersecurity.[98] This authoritative document noted the fundamental challenge is that although malicious cyber activities cross borders, the policy responses and law enforcement authorities are generally national.[99]

6.4.3   United States

In 2003, the United States released the *National Strategy to Secure Cyberspace* as well as *Homeland Security Presidential Directive 7: Critical Infrastructure Identification, Prioritization, and Protection.*[100] The National Strategy recognized the need for public–private partnerships, highlighting the interdependence among cyber security, economic

[96] EU Council of the European Union, June 7, 2017, 9916/17, Draft Council Conclusions on a Framework for a Joint EU Diplomatic Response to Malicious Activities ("Cyber Diplomacy Toolbox"). The Council affirmed "that malicious cyber activities might constitute wrongful acts under international law and emphasizes that States should not conduct or knowingly support ICT (information and communication technology) activities contrary to their obligations under international law, and should not knowingly allow their territory to be used for internationally wrongful acts using ICTs." COUNCIL OF THE EUROPEAN UNION, PUB. NO. 9916/17, DRAFT COUNCIL CONCLUSIONS ON A FRAMEWORK FOR A JOINT EU DIPLOMATIC RESPONSE TO MALICIOUS CYBER ACTIVITIES, annex ¶ 2 (2017).

[97] EU Council Decision 2019/797, *supra* note 95, art. 1(3).

[98] EU Council Regulation 2019/881, 2019 O.J. (L 151), 15, 25 (EC); *Id.*, art. 7(1) (providing that the European Union Agency for Cybersecurity [ENISA] "shall support operational cooperation among Member States, Union institutions, bodies, offices and agencies, and between stakeholders."); *see also* id., art. 6(1)(i) (further providing that ENISA shall assist "relevant public bodies by offering trainings regarding cybersecurity, where appropriate in cooperation with stakeholders"). *See also*, ATHANASIOS DROUGKAS, ET AL., CYBER RISK MANAGEMENT FOR PORTS, GUIDELINES FOR CYBERSECURITY IN THE MARITIME SECTOR, ENISA 7 (2020).

[99] EU Council Regulation 2019/881, *supra* note 98, pmbl. ¶ 5.

[100] US Department of Homeland Security, National Strategy to Secure Cyberspace, www.cisa.gov/national-strategy-secure-cyberspace (Feb. 2003; last visited Mar. 2, 2022) (online); US Department of Homeland Security, HSPD-7, www.cisa.gov/homeland-security-presidential-directive-7 (Dec. 17, 2003; last visited Mar. 2, 2022) (online); Presidential Decision Directive 63, Critical Infrastructure Protection (May 22, 1998).

prosperity and national security. Ten years later, a presidential order sought to "enhance the security and resilience of the nation's critical infrastructure and to maintain a cyber environment that encourages efficiency [and] innovation."[101] In 2018, the National Strategy sought to refine roles and responsibilities and improve incident reporting and response actions to enhance "transportation and maritime cybersecurity."[102]

In 2020, the White House released the National Maritime CyberSecurity Plan, prioritizing collaboration and the protection of ports and the commercial shipping sector.[103] Along with policies and strategies, US laws include 46 U.S.C. § 70114: implementing AIS requirements;[104] and 33 C.F.R. 161.2: defining "hazardous conditions" as the absence or malfunction of AIS equipment, which triggers a reporting requirement to the Captain of the Port (COTP).[105] Moreover, AIS data must be made available to an investigator in the event of a marine casualty investigation and may be subpoenaed if necessary.[106]

Earlier action includes the 2002 Maritime Transportation Security Act (MTSA), which created requirements for port security, sought to improve communication among law enforcement officials responsible for port security, and addressed physical and personnel security standards onboard vessels and at maritime transportation facilities.[107] Further authorities include MTSA implementing regulations, which oblige facility owners and operators to address cybersecurity vulnerabilities to communication systems, computer systems and networks.[108] MTSA amendments implemented under the Maritime Security Improvement

---

[101] E.O. 13636, Improving Critical Infrastructure Cybersecurity, 3 Fed. Reg. 217 (Feb. 12, 2013).

[102] EXECUTIVE OFFICE OF THE PRESIDENT, supra note 9, at 9–10.

[103] Office of the President of the United States, National Maritime Cyber Security Plan, bit .ly/3v35kce (Dec. 2020; last visited Mar. 2, 2022) (online).

[104] 46 U.S.C. § 70108 (2018); see also 33 C.F.R. § 164.46 (2021).

[105] 33 CFR 160.216 and 161.12(d) and 33 CFR 160.111, which allows the COTP to direct the movement of a vessel that has a "hazardous condition."

[106] 46 CFR 4.07-5, as amended by 46 U.S.C. § 70116, Port, Harbor and Coastal Facility Security.

[107] Maritime Transportation Security Act of 2002, 46 U.S.C. §§ 70101-70117) (2018); see also id., §70108(b) (providing that that the assessment shall ensure: effective screening of containers, cargo and baggage; restrict access to cargo, vessels and dockside property; additional security aboard vessels; certification of compliance with appropriate security standard; the overall security management program of the port; and other appropriate measures to deter terrorism [also referred to as the Super 6]).

[108] 33 C.F.R. Parts 105 and 106.

Act in 2018 require facility owners and operators to include cybersecurity risks in their facility security assessment and security plans.[109]

In 2018, the National Institute of Standards and Technology (NIST), a US government laboratory within the US Department of Commerce, promulgated an updated *Framework for Improving Critical Infrastructure Cybersecurity*. The framework provides guidance to align and prioritize cybersecurity activities with business requirements, risk tolerances and resources.[110] The framework also includes metrics to assess cybersecurity risk management activities.

The Department of Treasury's Office of Foreign Assets Control (OFAC) released an advisory on *Potential Sanctions Risks for Facilitating Ransomware Payments* as an additional accountability measure to combat criminal acts.[111] This document cites domestic authorities, such as the International Emergency Economic Powers Act (IEEPA) and the Trading with the Enemy Act (TWEA).[112] The Government Accountability Office (GAO) has published several impressive reports on maritime cyber efforts,[113] including *Cybersecurity: National Strategy, Roles, and Responsibilities Need to Be Better Defined and More Effectively Implemented* and *Maritime Critical Infrastructure Protection: DHS Needs to Enhance Efforts to Address Port Cybersecurity*.[114]

---

[109] Maritime Security Improvement Act of 2018, Pub. L. No. 115-254, §§ 1801–1816, 132 Stat. 3186 (codified as amended in scattered sections of 46 U.S.C.); *see also* 46 U.S.C. § 70102(b)(1)(C) (including "security against cyber risks" for development of facility security assessment and facility security plans. Cybersecurity risk was defined as "threats to and vulnerabilities of information or information systems and any related consequences caused by or resulting from unauthorized access, use, disclosure, degradation, disruption, modification, or destruction of such information or information systems," which is the same definition as in 6 U.S.C. § 148(a)(1)(A) (Domestic Security and National Cybersecurity and Communications Integration Center)).

[110] US National Institute of Standards and Technology, *supra* note 60, at v.

[111] US Department of the Treasury, Advisory on Potential Sanctions Risks for Facilitating Ransomware Payments 1 (2020).

[112] *Id.*, at 3 (noting OFAC may impose civil penalties for sanctions violations based on strict liability). 50 U.S.C. §§ 4301–41, 1701–06.

[113] Office of Commercial Vessel Compliance, U.S. Coast Guard, Pub. No. CVC-WI-027(2), Vessel Cyber Risk Management Work Instruction (2021).

[114] US Government Accountability Office, Pub. No. GAO-13-187, Cybersecurity: National Strategy, Roles, and Responsibilities Need to Be Better Defined and More Effectively Implemented (2013);

US Government Accountability Office , Pub. No. GAO-16-116T, Maritime Critical Infrastructure Protection: DHS Needs to Enhance Efforts to Address Port Cybersecurity (2015).

6.4.4   National Strategies

National-level efforts are crucial in responding to maritime cyber challenges, including reporting, notification systems, reporting requirements and strategies. At least six countries have released national cyber strategies,[115] including Denmark.[116] The Danish strategy references the EU Council NIS Directive that addresses legal requirements in the maritime environment.[117] Other beneficial approaches include the New Zealand government's statement on "The Application of International Law to State Activity in Cyberspace."[118] This insightful, and remarkably brief, four-page document addresses use of force, due diligence, human rights and responding to malicious cyber activity, among other substantive areas, but not the law of the sea.[119] The increased development of guidance to support an expanding maritime cyber environment in the coming years is probable.[120]

6.5   Other Potential Legal Approaches and Industry Guidance

The Convention for the Suppression of Unlawful Acts (SUA) against the Safety of Maritime Navigation (1988),[121] as well as the European Convention on Human Rights could provide states with a basis to pursue those who have installed malware on ships and potentially oblige countries to conduct investigations into breaches.

6.5.1   SUA Convention

States working at the IMO negotiated the SUA Convention (1988), which entered into force in 1992, and as of April 2021, the Convention had

---

[115] These include the United States (2011), the Russian Federation (2013), the Netherlands (2015), Norway (2017), Australia (2017), and China (2017). *See* ENEKEN TIKK, INTERNATIONAL LAW IN CYBERSPACE: MIND THE GAP 16 (2020).

[116] DANISH MARITIME CYBERSECURITY UNIT, DANISH MARITIME AUTHORITY, CYBER AND INFORMATION SECURITY STRATEGY FOR THE MARITIME SECTOR: 2019–2022 §§ 4.1.6-4.1.7 (2019).

[117] *Id.*, at 5.

[118] Press Release, New Zealand Ministry of Foreign Affairs and Trade, The Application of International Law to State Activity in Cyberspace (Dec. 1, 2020); *see also* NEW ZEALAND MINISTRY OF TRANSPORT, MARITIME SECURITY STRATEGY: GUARDIANSHIP OF AOTEAROA, NEW ZEALAND'S MARITIME WATERS 84, 87 (2020).

[119] Press Release, New Zealand Ministry of Foreign Affairs and Trade, *supra* note 118.

[120] ASTAARA CO. LTD. & BRITISH PORTS ASSOCIATION, WHITE PAPER: MANAGING PORTS' CYBER RISKS 4 (2019).

[121] Convention for the Suppression of Unlawful Acts against the Safety of Maritime Navigation, Mar. 10, 1988, 1678 U.N.T.S. 22 (hereinafter SUA Convention).

166 states parties. This treaty has led to at least a dozen national-level prosecutions across the globe.[122] The SUA Convention applies to commercial ships of states parties conducting an international transit or that are scheduled to conduct an international voyage. Provisions in SUA that might be applied to address a cyber event include: incidents causing damage to a ship or to its cargo that is likely to endanger the safe navigation of that ship; emplacement of a device or substance that is likely to destroy that ship or damage to the ship or its cargo and thereby endangers navigation of that ship; or damage or destruction of maritime navigational facilities that endangers the safety of navigation.[123] Though a national-level prosecutorial decision must be judicially validated, it is reasonable to assert malware and viruses that endanger the safe navigation of ships constitute a "device" or "substance" to enable a criminal prosecution.

6.5.2   Industry Guidance

In 2020, BIMCO, along with a consortium of shipping-related organizations, updated guidelines for cyber security onboard ships.[124] Maritime protection is inherently difficult because of emerging cyber capabilities, data availability, processing and data transfer speeds that increase connectivity but create cyber vulnerabilities.[125] Likewise, ISO standards provide a code of practice for information security controls and security of digital information.[126] The ship classification society, Nippon Kaji Kyokai (ClassNK) also drafted maritime cyber guidelines,[127] along with the Digital Container Shipping Association (DSCA) in 2020.[128] Separately, the American Club in October 2020 provided an

---

[122] Brian Wilson, *The Turtle Bay Pivot: How the United Nations Security Council Is Reshaping Naval Pursuit of Nuclear Proliferators, Rogue States, and Pirates*, 33 EMORY L. REV. n. 356 (2016); Landgericht Hamburg [LG] [Hamburg Regional Court] Oct. 19, 2012, 603 KLs 17/10 (2012) (Ger.); Press Release, US Attorney's Office, Central District of California, US Department of Justice, Filipino Seaman Who Allegedly Stabbed to Death Fellow Crewmember on Container Ship Faces Federal Charges (Sept. 28, 2020).

[123] SUA Convention, *supra* note 121, art. 3.1.

[124] BIMCO, THE GUIDELINES ON CYBER SECURITY ONBOARD SHIPS: VERSION 4 (2020).

[125] *Id.*, at 1.

[126] The International Organization for Standardization (ISO) "is an independent, non-governmental international organization with a membership of 165 national standards bodies," and has published a series of standards for information security management. *See generally*, INTERNATIONAL ORGANIZATION FOR STANDARDIZATION, *supra* note 60.

[127] ClassNK, GUIDELINES FOR DESIGNING CYBER SECURITY ONBOARD SHIPS (2d ed. 2020).

[128] DIGITAL CONTAINER SHIPPING ASSOCIATION, IMPLEMENTATION GUIDE FOR CYBER SECURITY ON VESSELS: v.1.0 (2020).

overview of cyber risk issues from the perspective of a P&I club.[129] In contrast to most other forms of marine insurance, international group P&I clubs "do not exclude claims arising from cyber incidents, unless they are acts of war or terrorism."[130] The ABS guidance also provides cybersecurity best practices.[131] The increasingly influential role of ship classification societies as well as P&I clubs in developing as well as ensuring implementation of cyber protection measures underscores the imperative for public–private partnerships, discussed in more detail in the following section.

6.6   Conclusion: Partnerships Are the Key

The number of maritime cybersecurity instruments developed between 2015 and 2020 underscores the need to take action to prevent as well as identify and respond to cyber threats. Collaboration at all levels of the prevention and response spectrum is key. Governments must coordinate internally;[132] states must cooperate externally; and both must collaborate with industry daily. The foundation for substantive cooperation is the exchange of information. This is challenging because the private sector may have competitive business reasons to withhold information, investigators may seek details for criminal prosecution, and industry representatives may seek substantive details on malware tactics and other

---

[129] AMERICAN CLUB, MANAGING CYBER RISKS AND THE ROLE OF THE P&I CLUB: AN OVERVIEW (2020).

[130] *Id.*, at 1. *See further*, "regular Group club P&I cover would be available for the consequences of a nonwar or terrorism related cyber incident. This might arise, for example, from a simple onboard computer malfunction, from a breakdown unintentionally caused by remote intervention in onboard systems, or even from an act of sabotage by a disgruntled former employee." *Id.*

[131] *Id.*, at 5–12.

[132] An interview with Rear Admiral Enrique Arnáez, Commander Cyber Defence Command of the Peruvian Navy, provides an exceptional overview of the scope of coordination. Admiral Arnáez discussed coordination, and separately, the status of the Peruvian Navy Cyber Command, which he noted, "cannot reach full operational capability ... due to the permanent evolution of technology and cyber threats. Consequently, constant modifications, improvements and adjustments to our techniques, procedures and equipment are required." The admiral further noted, "during the PanAm Games, we identified about *five million incidents* and we were able to deal, block and control all of them." Interview by Guy Toremans with Enrique Arnáez, Commander, Peruvian Cyber Defence Command, 1 MAR. SEC. & DEF. 10 (2020) (emphasis added).

malicious activities.[133] There is not a single solution for overcoming these challenges though effective models include developing a trusted, inclusive and networked approach.

The UK study on Russian cyber breaches acknowledged the value of interagency cooperation.[134] Regarding multiple government agencies involved in the response spectrum, the report noted, "cyber is a crowded domain – or a 'complex landscape.' There are a number of agencies and organizations across the Intelligence Community which have a role ... and it was not immediately apparent how these various agencies and organizations are coordinated and indeed complement each other."[135] The report concluded by noting the variety of involved departments "makes for an unnecessarily complicated wiring diagram of responsibilities."[136]

The NATO Cooperative Cyber Defence Centre of Excellence's *Cyber Commanders' Handbook* also discussed the importance of cooperation.[137] "Coordination is essential and can act as a force multiplier in this domain due to its interconnectivity and interdependency."[138] Moreover, "cooperation between the military, industry and academia is probably the best way to supply operational needs with the required resources to develop them, both financial and intellectual."[139] The *Cyber Commanders' Handbook* also emphasized the value of national-level, or interagency, alignment. And, collaborative efforts extend into the private

---

[133] *See* U.S. Maritime Advisory 2021-004, *supra* note 49; U.S. Maritime Advisory 2020-016, *supra* note 49; U.S. Maritime Advisory 2019-013, *supra* note 49; U.S. Maritime Advisory 2018-004B, *supra* note 49; U.S. Coast Guard, Pub. No. 19-20, Marine Safety Information Bulletin: Malicious Email Spoofing Incidents (Sept. 30, 2020) (discussing technical controls, user awareness and training, and collaboration with IT staff).

[134] Intelligence and Security Committee of Parliament (United Kingdom) (ordered by the House of Commons, July 21, 2020).

[135] *Id.*, ¶ 17.

[136] *Id.*, ¶ 18.

[137] NATO Cooperative Cyber Defence Centre of Excellence, Cyber Commanders' Handbook 46–48 (A. Dalmjin et al. eds., 2020). *See also*, The White House, Executive Order on Improving the Nation's Cybersecurity (May 12, 2021) (after noting "persistent and increasingly sophisticated malicious cyber campaigns," the Executive Order asserted "the Federal Government must improve its efforts to identify, deter, protect again, detect, and respond," and that such efforts must include the private sector. The Executive Order further directed the development of a "standard set of operational procedures (playbook) to be used in planning and conducting a cybersecurity vulnerability and incident response activity").

[138] Cyber Commanders' Handbook, *supra* note 137, at 46.

[139] *Id.*

MARITIME CYBER SECURITY 181

sector, such as the International Maritime Cyber Centre of Excellence in Singapore, launched in 2018 involving a Maritime Cyber Emergency Response Team and a "cyber academy."[140]

Cooperation in the maritime cyberspace is ongoing, active and, at times, productive. Notable organizations and initiatives include the Computer Emergency Readiness Team (CERT) in the United States as well as the Cybersecurity and Infrastructure Security Agency and the FBI-run program, InfraGard, "a public–private partnership with over 30,000 members."[141] Other beneficial constructs include the European Maritime Safety Agency–run SeaSafeNet, a vessel traffic monitoring and information system that includes AIS data, ENISA, the Danish Maritime Authority's Centre for Cyber Security, GLANCY+, and NYA24, among others.

Collaborative efforts in multiple venues to better protect electronic networks in the maritime environment is a positive development. That said, more can be done, and as such, it is useful to distill lessons from responses to security challenges across the globe that are unrelated to cyber.

- A nonbinding declaration is a good starting point to both identify common goals and open communication channels. One example, a declaration by port authority officials in 2020 addressed COVID-19 and the importance of sharing information and collaboration.[142] This nonbinding declaration included commitments by signatories to "work together and strive to ... facilitate closer coordination ... so that like-minded port and maritime authorities can share experiences/ exchange information in combating COVID-19 while safeguarding unimpeded maritime trade."[143]
- In addition, the New York Declaration (2009) reflected a commitment to avoid, or delay, acts of piracy.[144] The governments of the Bahamas, Cyprus, Japan, Liberia, Marshall Islands Panama, Singapore, the UK and the United States agreed to promulgate internationally recognized best practices for the self-protection of vessels within their registries.

---

[140] The Maritime Executive, Wärtsilä Opens World's First International Maritime Cyber Centre, bit.ly/3sS4n3N (Oct. 16, 2018; last visited Mar. 2, 2022) (online).

[141] John P. Carlin, Assistant Attoney General for National Security, US Department of Justice, Address at Harvard Law School (Dec. 3, 2015).

[142] Declaration by Port Authorities Roundtable (PAR) Members in View of the Global COVID-19 Situation (May 29, 2020).

[143] Id.

[144] Press Release, US Department of State, the Bahamas, the Republic of Liberia, the Republic of Marshall Islands and the Republic of Panama Announce Their Commitment to Best Practices to Avoid, Deter or Delay Acts of Piracy (May 29, 2009).

The signatories further underscored their commitment to the ISPS code, including obligations regarding self-protection measures in ship security plans.

- Integrate the private sector and government representatives in informal, though regularly scheduled, discussions. Lessons from countering piracy include the creation in 2009 of the Contact Group on Piracy off the Somali Coast.[145] This innovative ad hoc construct brought together diplomats, military officials, international organizations, attorneys and the private sector, proving remarkably durable, with meetings ongoing as of 2020. Each of the working groups within this construct – information sharing, judicial capacity, financial flows and strengthening shipping self-awareness – has resonance in maritime cyberspace collaboration.

- Draw on lessons from across the globe. Cooperation in the response to migration and human trafficking includes the creation of Shared Awareness and Deconfliction in the Mediterranean Sea (SHADE MED). The SHADE construct in the Persian Gulf to combat Somali piracy informed the development of SHADE MED. Even though the specific threat and the geographic regions were different, the concept of putting military officers and civilians in the same room for informal, trusted discussions on primarily operational issues provides a model for collaborating in the response to other threats, including cyber.

- A formal agreement, where possible, may be preferable. Lessons from countering piracy and armed robbery at sea in Asia include the Regional Cooperation Agreement on Combating Piracy and Armed Robbery against Ships in Asia (ReCAAP) and the ReCAAP Information Sharing Center (ISC). Operating from a facility in Singapore, ReCAAP has produced timely reports and facilitated information dissemination. Since 2006, ReCAAP has remained focused exclusively on piracy and armed robbery. Thus far, it has avoided delving into other challenges, such as human trafficking, weapons smuggling or drug trafficking.

- Consistent coordination benefits from designated points of contact – focal points. Multiple instruments require that participants include a single point of contact, a designated competent authority, to facilitate discussions and ensure there is consistency in reporting,

---

[145] US Department of State, Fact Sheet: Contact Group on Piracy off the Coast of Somalia, https://2009-2017.state.gov/t/pm/rls/fs/2016/255175.htm (Jan. 20, 2009; last visited Mar. 2, 2022) (online).

correspondence and collaboration. One example is the Vienna Drug Convention, which provides, "At the time of becoming a Party to this Convention, each Party shall designate an authority or, when necessary, authorities to receive and respond to such requests. Such designation shall be notified through the Secretary-General to all other Parties within one month of the designation."[146] Designation of a point of contact for formal requests and correspondence, generally at a level below a ministry chief, has dramatically influenced the effectiveness of this instrument and must be considered in cyber collaboration activities. Another example is ReCAAP, discussed earlier, which includes designated "focal points" for each member that is authorized to receive and convey requests for information and/or action.

Other considerations include prioritizing training and collaborative exercises, investigative efforts that recognize cyber security is transnational, and a whole-of-port approach. Cyber vulnerability will inevitably expand as facilities continue to rely on wireless connectivity and increase automation and incorporate remote monitoring capabilities, as well as expand the supply chain by integrating third-party stakeholders. Software that tracks cargo further adds to digital exposure. Addressing these challenges requires more than just deploying additional resources or promulgating further authorities. While legislation along with regulations and threat assessments are important, cooperation – *provided that stakeholders seek to collaborate, have focused leadership, and find benefit* – will be the enduring difference in a resilient approach to cyber threats.

---

[146] United Nations Convention against Illicit Traffic in Narcotic Drugs and Psychotropic Substances, art. 17.7, Dec. 20, 1988, 1582 U.N.T.S. 95.

International Standards for Hull Inspection and Maintenance of Robotics and Autonomous Systems

TAFSIR JOHANSSON*

7.1 Introduction

Artificial intelligence (AI)–integrated robotic technologies, commonly referred to as robotics and autonomous systems (RAS), provide innovative – perhaps even revolutionary – new solutions for cutting-edge industries that offer great potential for the maritime sector. Specific present and potential applications of RAS will enhance both safety and efficiency by allowing the completion of tasks that are otherwise risky and onerous. This chapter focuses on standardization of rules and

* This chapter derives from the findings from project *BUGWRIGHT2: Autonomous Robotic Inspection and Maintenance on Ship Hulls and Storage Tanks* (Task 1.4) – funded by the European Union's Horizon 2020 research and innovation program under grant agreement No. 871260. The views and opinions expressed are those of the authors and do not reflect the official policy or position of BUGWRIGHT2 consortium members, the International Maritime Organization or any of the classification societies. The author would like to thank the Nippon Foundation, staff members of the World Maritime University-Sasakawa Global Ocean Institute, especially, Professors Ronán Long and Clive Schofield, and Dr. Jon Skinner, Mr. Thomas Klenum, Mr. Sean Pribyl and Mr. George Giazlas for their invaluable support.

requirements for RAS involved in ship survey and maintenance, with a sharp focus on bulk carriers.[1]

Evolving RAS refinements are undoubtedly progressing at an extraordinary pace. An illustrative precedent was the then "revolutionary" introduction of autonomous automotive technologies to the global industry. Automotive automation can be traced back to the mid-1920s and continues to transition from semiautonomous vehicles to state-of-the-art fully autonomous vehicles in the land-based transport sector.[2] Technological breakthroughs via RAS to advance autonomous or self-piloting platforms in the ocean domain gained momentum much later, most notably through the initiation of the Norwegian project, Maritime Unmanned Navigation through Intelligence in Networks (MUNIN).[3] Current efforts are focused on combining the concepts of "autonomy" and "unmanned" into a holistic concept to guide future ocean-based transport modes.[4]

While work on developing fully autonomous vessels progresses, the last decade has seen more conspicuous success integrating RAS within the maritime sector – especially with "service robotics." The services provided by these robots have numerous and significant advantages, safety being foremost, over conventional methods that require strenuous, if not at times extreme, human effort. Designed and programmed to complete tangible actions by combining the best of two worlds (robotics and AI), the vision behind the deployment of service robots is similar to that of "autonomous vessels," achieving optimum safety, reliability and efficiency with less human intervention, as well as anticipated cost-savings.

Service robots in the shipping industry provide a wide range of other practical marine services. A noteworthy contemporary area of this application involves visual inspection and maintenance of commercial vessel hulls. These tasks enhance vessel upkeep and maintenance – an unavoidable obligation for ship owners and operators, and one required by IMO instruments. Scientists and engineers are also introducing reconfigured

---

[1] The discussion touches upon both primary and secondary application domains of BUGWRIGHT2: outer hull and storage tanks (in relation to bulk carriers).

[2] KESHAV BIMBRAW, *Autonomous Cars: Past, Present and Future – A Review of the Developments in the Last Century, the Present Scenario and the Expected Future of Autonomous Vehicle Technology*. PROCEEDINGS OF THE 12TH INTERNATIONAL CONFERENCE ON INFORMATICS IN CONTROL, AUTOMATION AND ROBOTICS 191 (2015).

[3] ØRNULF JAN RØDSETH, *From Concept to Reality: Unmanned Merchant Ship Research in Norway*. IEEE UNDERWATER TECHNOLOGY 1–4, 6–10 (2017).

[4] *Id.*, at 1, 3–4, 6, 8–10.

service robots into maintenance practices to alleviate the need for humans to work in dangerous or dirty environments, as well as "to improve its image into one with productive and cost saving elements requiring the need for highly skilled, tech-savvy engineers."[5]

Outer hull inspection and maintenance of commercial vessels is a niche area where service robots are being tested and introduced to ship owners and operators to replace traditional methods of survey that are time consuming. Service robots engineered to perform outer hull and storage inspections and benefit from advances in "metamorphic" RAS capabilities.[6] Holistically, RAS capability have transitioned from limited to multifaced functions requiring both specific and diverse standards, such as for micro aerial vehicles (MAVs), autonomous underwater vehicles (AUVs) and magnetic-wheeled crawlers (MWCs).[7] As manufacturers move from single-use to polyfunctional service robots, standardization became a concern.[8] RAS should embrace and adhere to critical safety, quality, performance and efficiency standards developed in a cooperative and common effort; the earlier in the life cycle the better.

The emergence of service robots has attracted attention at the European Union (EU). Meeting standards tailored for RAS is a priority emphasized by recognized organizations (ROs), including the European Committee for Standardization (CEN), the European Committee for Electrotechnical Standardization (CENELEC) and the European Telecommunications Standards Institute (ETSI). The EU High-Level Expert Group on AI has explored elements for reliable and trustworthy AI, and envisions the creation of a necessary horizontal foundation that

---

[5] MICHAEL JOHN FARNSWORTH ET AL., *Autonomous Maintenance for Through-Life Engineering.* THROUGH-LIFE ENGINEERING SERVICES 395, 397 (Louis Redding & Rajkumar Roy eds., 2014); *N.B.* "ship" and "vessel" are used interchangeably and follows the definition of "ship" found in Marine Environmental Protection Committee Res. MEPC.207(62), annex 26 (July 15, 2011) (hereinafter 2011 Guidelines).

[6] Luigi Pagliarini & Henrik Hautop Lund, *The Future of Robotics Technology*, 3 J. OF ROBOTICS NETWORKING & ARTIFICIAL LIFE 270 (2017); *see* KASPER STOY ET AL., SELF-RECONFIGURABLE ROBOTS: AN INTRODUCTION 5–7 (2010); *see also* N. A. STRAVPODIS ET AL., *An Integrated Taxonomy and Critical Review of Module Designs for Serial Reconfigurable Manipulators.* ADVANCES IN SERVICE AND INDUSTRIAL ROBOTICS: PROCEEDINGS OF THE 28TH INTERNATIONAL CONFERENCE ON ROBOTICS IN ALPE-ADRIA-DANUBE REGION 3–4 (Karsten Berns & Daniel Görges eds., 2020).

[7] *Id.*

[8] GURVINDER S. VIRK ET AL., *ISO Standards for Service Robots.* ADVANCES IN MOBILE ROBOTICS: THE ELEVENTH INTERNATIONAL CONFERENCE ON CLIMBING AND WALKING ROBOTS AND THE SUPPORT TECHNOLOGIES FOR MOBILE MACHINES 1–2 (2008).

could topple current regulatory, ethical and societal barriers with a singular innovation of establishing trust between manufacturer and the end-user.[9] To achieve this objective, particularly in the business-to-consumer domain, the High-Level Expert Group promotes the value of universal designs and the need to remain in conformity with specific technical standards for safety and transparency.[10]

At the international level, the International Organization for Standardization (ISO) has been active in RAS standardization since 1947.[11] Classification societies today operate in tandem with the ISO and other ROs. In the maritime domain, the procedural rules developed through consultation with international bodies assist integrating RAS applications in mandatory surveys under international law. Similar to land-based technologies, the functionality of technologies applied in the ocean domain are evaluated on standard safety and performance standpoints. For international provisions on safety and performance standards, it is a common practice to turn to the International Maritime Organization (IMO) and recognized classification societies. While it is important to understand the implications of new service emerging technologies on the law of the sea, there is also a need to observe how other international governmental and nongovernmental organizations impact innovation, safety and protection of the marine environment.

The previous discussion highlights the central work of the IMO, which details biofouling and the pertinent international regulatory arrangements covering operational and procedural standards pertinent to introducing new shipping technologies in specific niche areas. Hereafter, the discussion focuses on identifying the crucial barriers – followed by an expository analysis of international technology-based standards within the framework of the safety and environmental protection aspects of the law of the sea. The chapter concludes by considering some strategic tools that may assist and enable a much-needed harmonization process.

7.1.1   Setting the Scene: RAS Terms and Concepts

The term RAS is of recent origin. In defining the term "robots," the ISO *Vocabulary* utilizes scientific terms referring to mechanical systems that

---

[9] Ethics Guidelines for Trustworthy AI, Report of the High-Level Expert Group on Artificial Intelligence, at 1–36, European Commission (2019).

[10] *Id.*, at 19, 22.

[11] VIRK ET AL., *supra* note 8, at 2.

can move "within its environment, to perform intended tasks."[12] In its definition, ISO keeps the performance aspect open-ended respecting the degree of autonomy or level of a systems' dependency on human interaction when performing intended tasks.[13] The ISO defines "service robots" as those that "perform useful tasks for humans" (except those that are used in industrial automation applications).[14] The ISO/TC 184 Technical Committee further classifies service robots into personal service robots and professional service robots with the latter comprised of those that are used in commercial tasks and operated and monitored by a properly trained operator. While the definition of "professional service robot" acknowledges the integration of human intervention to initiate and stop an operation, it does not clarify what "monitor" entails.[15] Professional service robots have image sensors that convert photons into electrical signals that are then analyzed by inspectors. Therefore, according to section 2.12 (professional service robot) when read together with section 2.17 (operator), "monitoring" may pertain to actions undertaken by the operator to observe how the robot "itself" is performing, or alternatively, the "inspection function" being undertaken by the robot. The word "monitor" is imprecise and may create confusion.

7.1.2   Biofouling Degrades Vessel Performance

About 100,000 commercial vessels of more than 100 tons constitute the global maritime shipping industry, which is the cornerstone of global trade and commerce.[16] Among this number, some 9,734 large ships and 4,759 very large ships in operation are over the age of five years.[17] This global shipping fleet depends on efficiency and optimal vessel performance. "Hull resistance" is a primary issue that degrades hull performance, hindering the ship's capacity to operate efficiently.[18] Hull fouling or

---

[12] INTERNATIONAL ORGANIZATION FOR STANDARDIZATION, ROBOTS AND ROBOTIC DEVICES: VOCABULARY § 2.6 (2012).

[13] Id., § 2.2.

[14] Id., § 2.10.

[15] Id., § 2.17.

[16] UN Conference on Trade and Development, Review of Maritime Transport, at 4, U.N. Doc. UNCTAD/RMT/2019/Corr.1, U.N. Sales No. E.19.II.D.20 (2020); see also JEAN-PAUL RODRIGUE & THEO NOTTEBOOM, Maritime Transportation. THE GEOGRAPHY OF TRANSPORT SYSTEMS 151, 171 (Jean-Paul Rodrigue ed., 5th ed. 2020).

[17] Id., at 9, table 3 (ships by age and size).

[18] Panos Deligiannis, Ship Performance Indicator, 75 MARINE POL'Y 204, 205 (2017).

biofouling makes ships less efficient and contributes substantially to increased emissions.[19] In technical terms, hull fouling increases water resistance to the hull, thereby increasing energy usage and affecting scheduling and maintenance costs.[20]

Hull inspection and maintenance are cost interlinked with energy efficiency improvements and can curb emissions.[21] While the IMO's efforts to control invasive species through the International Convention for the Control and Management of Ship's Ballast Water and Sediment, 2004 heralds a new era for marine environmental protection, transportation of invasive species through biofouling with ships as vectors has drawn the IMO's attention on the importance on hull inspection and maintenance.[22]

7.2   The International Legal Regime

7.2.1   IMO 2011 Guidelines

At the international level, the primary forces driving outer hull inspection cleaning and maintenance are twofold: (1) to inspect the biofouling status of a ship; and (2) to address elevated risks that could result in safety and environmental concerns. These twofold motivations reside at the crux of the IMO's work reflected in the *2011 Guidelines for the Control and Management of Ship's Biofouling to Minimize the Transfer of Invasive Aquatic Species* (hereinafter 2011 Guidelines).

The 2011 Guidelines are designed to facilitate the implementation of the International Convention for the Control and Management of Ships' Ballast Water and Sediments, 2004 ("BWM Convention") and the International Convention on the Control of Harmful Anti-fouling

---

[19] *Id.*, at 204; *see also* Roar Adland et al., *The Energy Efficiency Effects of Periodic Hull Cleaning*, 178 J. OF CLEANER PROD. 1, 2 (2018).

[20] *See* U.S. COAST GUARD, Pub. No. CG-D-15-15, VESSEL BIOFOULING PREVENTION AND MANAGEMENT OPTIONS REPORT, at v (2015); *see* M. P. Schultz et al., *Economic Impact of Biofouling on a Naval Surface Ship*, 27 BIOFOULING 87–89 (2011); H. WANG & N. LUTSEY, LONG-TERM POTENTIAL FOR INCREASED SHIPPING EFFICIENCY THROUGH THE ADOPTION OF INDUSTRY-LEADING PRACTICES 3–8 (2013).

[21] "Fouling of the hull can increase fuel consumption up to 15 percent." *See* ANTHONY F. MOLLAND ET AL., SHIP RESISTANCE AND PROPULSION (2017); *see* also Adland et al., *supra* note 19, at 2. *See also* INTERNATIONAL MARITIME ORGANIZATION, THIRD IMO GREENHOUSE GAS STUDY 2014 (2015).

[22] U.S. COAST GUARD, *supra* note 20, at v.

Systems on Ships, 2001 ("AFS Convention") in conjunction with
Guidance for the Development of a Ship Energy Efficiency
Management Plan (SEEMP). Recognizing the significance of evidence-
based studies that concluded that all ships contribute to some degree to
biofouling after immersion in water, the 2011 Guidelines prescribe "in-
water" inspection, cleaning and maintenance procedures as additional
measures for antifouling installation and maintenance.[23]

Specific provisions of in-water inspection, cleaning and maintenance
can be found in section 7 of the 2011 Guidelines. As the first step, the
2011 Guidelines prescribe the inspection of niche areas of the ship that
have a high probability of prolific build-up of hard-shell fouling, allowing
operators to optimize target zones for cleaning and maintenance.[24] In
this context, the 2011 Guidelines suggest two options for conducting
inspections: human divers and remotely operated vehicles (ROVs;
Figure 7.1).[25] Considering the absence of a preset definition of ROV
within the framework of the 2011 Guidelines, it is reasonable to assert
that ROVs deployed in hull inspections belong to "inspection-class
ROVs" that are consistent with the ISO definition of "professional service
robots" that are monitored by an operator. These types of robots are real-
time "acoustic eyes" with a smaller footprint compared to "intervention-
class ROVs" that are not typically equipped with tooling equipment.[26]

Post inspection, member states are advised to perform risk assessments prior to cleaning and maintenance to minimize environmental
threats associated with cleaning actions, such as biological, toxic effects
from employed substances.[27] While the 2011 Guidelines did not anticipate the use of ROVs for those tasks, if there had been such a provision,
the high operational costs associated with deploying "intervention-class

---

[23] Section 2.1 defines "biofouling" as "the accumulation of aquatic organisms such as microorganisms, plants, and animals on surfaces and structures immersed in or exposed to the
aquatic environment," and "in-water cleaning" as the "physical removal of biofouling
from a ship while in the water." See 2011 Guidelines, supra note 5, § 2.1.

[24] "Niche areas" are defined as "mean areas on a ship that may be more susceptible to
biofouling due to different hydrodynamic forces, susceptibility to coating system wear or
damage, or being inadequately, or not, painted, e.g., sea chests, bow thrusters, propeller
shafts, inlet gratings, dry-dock support strips, etc." See 2011 Guidelines, supra note 5, §§
2.1, 6.9.1 ("niche areas").

[25] Id., § 7.4.

[26] Romano Capocci et al., Inspection-Class Remotely Operated Vehicles: A Review, 5 J. OF
MARINE SCI. & ENG'G 1, 4–6 (2018).

[27] 2011 Guidelines, supra note 5, § 7.6.

Figure 7.1   Underwater inspection using ROV.
Source: Diving Status (permission to use image granted by copyright holder)

ROVs" would likely be debated.[28] All in all, the 2011 Guidelines emphasize the need to exercise due diligence to provide a continuous cycle of cleaning and maintenance.[29]

7.2.2   *International "Standards" and the Regulatory Regime*

Among the three relevant international organizations, the ISO is chartered with mandating and developing standards.[30] The widely accepted definition of "standard" can be found in one of the earliest ISO publications *The Aims and Principles of Standardization*, published in 1972. This publication defines "standard" as "[t]he result of a particular standardization effort, approved by a recognized authority" that "may take the form of: (1) a document containing a set of conditions to be fulfilled (*norme* in French); and (2) a fundamental unit or physical constant, for example, ampere, meter, absolute zero (Kelvin)(*étalon* in French)".[31] The same definition is incorporated verbatim by the American National

---

[28] Capocci et al., *supra* note 26, at 3.
[29] 2011 Guidelines, *supra* note 5, § 7.10.
[30] The two other organizations are the International Electrotechnical Commission (IEC) and the International Telecommunication Union (ITU).
[31] Terrence Robert Beaumont Sanders, The Aims and Principles of Standardization 18 (1972).

Standard Institute (ANSI) and is commonly referred to by other national standard developing organizations.[32]

The development of product standards is predominantly private-sector driven.[33] But what is remarkable about this phenomenon is the coexistence of mandatory and voluntary standards, which stems from a complex private–public relationship that blurs organizational boundaries and creates legal ambiguity.[34] This begs the question: Where do standards fit into the hierarchy of the regulatory governance regime? To answer this question, Lindøe and Baram address voluntary "soft" standards as well as regulatory "binding" standards, illustrating the usefulness of both types within a given national framework.[35]

The pyramidal diagram proposed by Lindøe and Baram depicts a transcending pyramidal model with three distinct layers: (1) a "soft" private standards making up the bottom foundational layer (with embedded methodological and behavioral); (2) a middle layer composed of private technical and administrative standards adopted by regulators that forms the compliance regime (this layer is characterized as "authoritative" and therefore, according to authors "constitute *de jure* or *de facto* requirements that must be heeded by the targeted set of private actors");[36] and (3) a top layer entitled "law, orders and regulations" that forms the "command and control" domain comprised of government-mandated regulations.[37]

---

[32] NATIONAL BUREAU OF STANDARDS, NBS SPECIAL PUBLICATION 74 (1977).

[33] Eduardo Fosch Villaronga & Angelo Golia, Jr., *Robots, Standards and the Law: Rivalries between Private Standards and Public Policymaking for Robot Governance*, 35 COMPUT. L. & SEC. REV. 35, 129–30 (2019); *see* Charles Sabel et al., *Regulation under Uncertainty: The Coevolution of Industry Regulation*, 2 REGUL. & GOVERNANCE 1, 2 (2017); *see also* MAHA SALEM ET AL., *Towards Safe and Trustworthy Social Robots: Ethical Challenges and Practical Issues.* INTERNATIONAL CONFERENCE ON SOCIAL ROBOTICS 584, 589 (Adriana Tapus et al. eds., 2015).

[34] JEAN-CHRISTOPHE MAUR & BEN SHEPHERD, *Product Standards.* PREFERENTIAL TRADE AGREEMENT POLICIES FOR DEVELOPMENT: A HANDBOOK 197, 199 (Jean-Pierre Chauffour & Jean-Christophe Maur eds., 2011).

[35] PREBEN H. LINDØE & MICHAEL S. BARAM, THE ROLE OF STANDARDS IN HARD AND SOFT APPROACHES 236 (2020).

[36] *Id.*, at 236–37; *see also* LAN AYRES & JOHN BRAITHWAITE, RESPONSIVE REGULATION 39 (1992).

[37] *N.B.*, the authorities of the "top layer" determine whether the regulatory regime in question will enact hard law or soft law on the subject matter, and depending on that decision, this layer is composed of enacted laws, orders and regulations. LINDØE & BARAM, *supra* note 35, at 236–37.

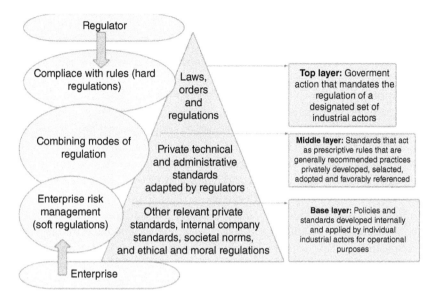

Figure 7.2   "Standards" in the regulatory governance regime.
Source: Adapted from Preben H. Lindøe and Michael S. Baram[38] (used with permission)

This transcending model underlines the importance of standards derived from private-industry forces. Private prompted standards, guidelines and norms serve as external nongovernmental forces paralleling and supporting the regulatory regime (Figure 7.2). Adherence and compliance boost the economic value of those industries while also serving the public interest.[39] Since the public interest is one of the core mandates of government, regulators are encouraged to incorporate international industrial and private standards, whenever applicable, as a means to enhance the efficiency and optimization of the regulatory regime. Capitalizing on industry-based standards developed by both international nonprofit and industry organizations enables member state regulators to maintain a robust regulatory regime as well as maneuver in a landscape that is shared with other stakeholders.[40]

---

[38] PREBEN H. LINDØE & MICHAEL S. BARAM, *The Role of Standards in Hard and Soft Approaches to Safety Regulation*. STANDARDIZATION AND RISK GOVERNANCE: A MULTI-DISCIPLINARY APPROACH 236 (Odd Einar Olsen, Kirsten Voigt Juhl, Preben H. Lindøe & Ole Andreas Engen, eds., 2020).

[39] *Id.*, at 239, 250.

[40] *Id.*, at 250.

7.2.3   State-of-the-Art International Standards and RAS Integration

Condition, statutory and classification surveys comprise the typical inspection regime that enable issuance of recommendations for maintenance and repairs during the operational lifetime of a ship. Of the three types, condition surveys are nonperiodic surveys and are generally conducted by surveyors at the request of ship owners, cargo owners, charterers, insurance companies, port state authorities, flag state authorities or P&I clubs to determine the overall condition of the vessel, including the ship's statutory and class certification status. In certain instances, P&I condition surveys can be viewed as a check and balance to surveys performed by class and flag states by revealing deficiencies.[41]

Statutory and classification surveys follow the statutory and class rule requirements (for all ship types), and lead to the issuance of statutory and classification certificates, respectively. For statutory surveys, the scope and intervals are determined by international conventions, codes ratified by flag states, and rules and requirements of flag states and port states. In other words, statutory rules detail stipulations by member states' flag administrations in accordance with international regulations ratified by the flag state. Adherence requires ship owners to obtain certificates attesting compliance with these standards.[42] Until the end of the twentieth century, survey and certification procedures were diffused in a wide range of international instruments. These procedures, although generally sharing a common content and intent, gave rise to nonstandardized survey approaches and dates under the many IMO conventions in force since 1966.[43]

Moving toward a harmonized synchronized method, the IMO's Harmonized System of Survey and Certification (HSSC) has addressed

---

[41] Gard, Experiences from Condition Surveys of Bulk Carriers, www.gard.no/web/updates/content/52989/experiences-from-condition-surveys-of-bulk-carriers (last visited Feb. 15, 2022) (online).

[42] It is important to note that "[p]ort state control and flag state inspections cover the statutory requirements. Classification Societies perform most of the surveys based on the statutory requirements and by authorization of a flag state." *See* SABINE KNAPP & PHILIP HANS FRANSES, ANALYSIS OF THE MARITIME INSPECTION REGIMES: ARE SHIPS OVER-INSPECTED? 3 (2016).

[43] *See*, for example, International Convention for the Safety of Life at Sea, 1974, Nov. 1, 1974, 32 U.S.T. 47, 1184 U.N.T.S. 2 (as amended) (hereinafter 1974 SOLAS); International Convention on Load Lines, 1966, Apr. 5, 1966, 18 U.S.T. 1857, 640 U.N.T.S. 133 (as amended) (hereinafter CLL 66/88); International Convention for the Prevention of Pollution from Ships, 1973, Nov. 2, 1973, 34 U.S.T. 3407, 1340 U.N.T.S. 61 (as amended) (MARPOL); International Convention for the Control and Management of Ships' Ballast Water and Sediments, 2004, Feb. 13, 2004, (IMO, BWM/CONF/36) (BWM Convention).

future survey procedural matters that have for a considerable period of time resulted in duplication of effort (for individual survey requirements imposed under different conventions for different niche areas of a vessel).[44] Patently, the harmonization objective of the HSSC achieves seamless procedural standards governing inspection and maintenance tasks through a set of uniform surveys that better address various convention requirements.[45] Considering the advanced age of large and very large vessels in the current world fleet, harmonized statutory surveys (periodic survey, intermediate survey, annual survey, underwater inspection of ship's bottom and additional survey) are necessary for effective monitoring to enhance compliance with maritime safety and environmental rules. These harmonized statutory surveys found in the HSSC are accompanied by references to schemes developed by classification societies and are considered to be at the cutting edge of standards in the maritime world.[46] Additionally, ISO standards on service robot performance developed by the ISO/TC 299 Technical Committee on Robotics establishes international standards for the determination of performance criteria that contain technical specifications as well as operational procedures.[47] Those ISO standards are primarily developed taking into account indoor environments, and therefore do not apply to verification or validation of environmental or safety requirements.[48] As such, the discussion on ISO standards is left outside the scope of this section.

---

[44] The first "Global and Uniform Implementation of the Harmonized System of Survey and Certification" adopted by the IMO entered into force on February 4, 2000. In 2019, the 2017 HSSC was amended and updated to reflect amendments to the BWM Convention, MARPOL and 1974 SOLAS. No survey-specific changes were made during the amendment. The amendments are set out in annex XX to IMO Document III 6/15. International Maritime Organization Res. A.1120(30) (Dec. 6, 2017) (as amended) (Survey Guidelines under the Harmonized System of Survey and Certification, 2017).

[45] N.B. HSSC is an attempt to unify survey requirements under mandatory conventions including 1974 SOLAS. See also International Maritime Organization Res. 1049(27) (Nov. 30, 2011) (International Code on the Enhanced Programme of Inspections during Surveys of Bulk Carriers and Oil Tankers, 2011).

[46] HSSC, supra note 43, §§ 4.3.2.2, 5.9.2, annex 1.

[47] With reference to ISO 18646-1:2016 (Robotics – Performance Criteria and Related Test Methods for Service Robots – Part 1: Locomotion for Wheeled Robots); ISO 18646-2:2019 (Robotics – Performance Criteria and Related Test Methods for Service Robots – Part 2: Navigation) etc. developed by the ISO/TC 299 Technical Committee.

[48] International Standards Organization, Robotics: Performance Criteria and Related Test Methods for Service Robots, www.iso.org/committee/5915511/x/catalogue/p/1/u/0/w/0/d/0 (last visited Dec. 20, 2020) (online).

Here, it is important to note that in this discussion on state-of-the-art, the role of classification society surfaces for two obvious reasons. First, many flag administrations are not equipped with the adequate technical, experience, resources or the broad international coverage necessary to meet the international survey requirements.[49] To this end, international conventions, such as SOLAS and CLL 66/88 have deferred to ROs to assist those administrations in the much-needed statutory surveys to comply with the objectives set by the IMO.[50] However, any attempt to narrow the role of classification societies to just "survey assistance" is likely to under-mine their positive and multifaceted influence in the "cradle-to-grave" concept of the world commercial fleet. Classification rules developed by classification societies are of paramount importance with respect to design plans, construction, sea trials and other trials – all of which are key building blocks of the maritime environment and safety regime.[51]

The second reason for referencing the work of classification societies is the significance of existing promulgated rules (i.e., bulk carrier structural rules, detailed standards rule on how to perform hull surveys and, most importantly, the manner in which these rules encompass the operational procedures for RAS integrated inspections). The work of the International Association of Classification Societies (IACS) is note-worthy as a prominent group composed of the "big 12."[52] The IACS Unified Requirements (URs) on survey and certification are supplemented

---

[49] Sean M. Holt, *Class Survey: A Former Surveyor Looks at the Origins and Current Status of Classification Societies*, MARITIME EXEC., July 30, 2017.

[50] *Id. N.B.* This includes conducting "minimum two inspections of the outside of the outside of the ship's bottom during any five-year period (*see* 5.7), except where SOLAS 74/88, regulation I/14(e) or (f) is applicable. One such inspection should be carried out on or after the fourth annual survey in conjunction with the renewal of the Cargo Ship Safety Construction Certificate or the Cargo Ship Safety Certificate." *See* HSSC, *supra* note 43, § 4.6.1.

[51] Classification societies serve two distinct roles. The public role is assumed as an IMO RO, and the private role is assumed when conducting inspections on behalf of the ship owner. International Association of Classification Societies, Classification Societies: What, Why and How? www.iacs.org.uk/media/7425/classification-what-why-how.pdf, at 5 (last visited Sept. 20, 2020) (online); *see* International Maritime Organization Res. MEPC.2385(65) (May 17, 2013) (amendments to the annex of the Protocol of 1978 Relating to the International Convention for the Prevention of Pollution from Ships); International Maritime Organization Res. MSC.350(92) (June 21, 2013) (amend-ments to SOLAS 74/88); International Maritime Organization Res. MSC.349(92), pt.1 §§ 2.4–2.5 (June 21, 2013) (Code for Recognized Organizations).

[52] Lloyd's Register (LR), American Bureau of Shipping (ABS), Bureau Veritas (BV), China Classification Society (CCS), Croatian Register of Shipping (CRS), Det Norske Veritas (DNV), Korean Register (KR), Nippon Kaiji Kyokai (NK), Registro Italiano Navale

by a number of recommendations in the form of guidelines coupled with twenty-six documents amalgamated under the label of UR Z family-of-requirements.[53] Briefly stated, the UR Z requirements are seen as a positive reflection on the IACS's expertise in advanced detailed requirements and recommended procedures for hull surveys designed to identify structural defects or corrosion that might compromise a ship's structural integrity, inter alia.[54]

The UR Z7 titled *Hull Classification Surveys* is most relevant as it supports intervention procedures for special surveys, annual surveys and intermediate surveys, which are aligned with the IMO's HSSC requirements.[55] An examination of the different sections of UR Z7 reveals attention to detail. For example, section 1.4 stresses that all subsequent surveys following repairs should include taking thickness measurements of structures in specific areas where close-up survey is required.[56] Other useful standards include precise guidelines for hull inspection and maintenance, elaborately explained in the texts of several UR Z, including Z7.1, Z7.2, Z10.2, Z10.4, Z10.5, Z13 and Z16.

In terms of RAS procedural recommendations, IACS Recommendation 42 titled *Guidelines for Use of Remote Inspection Techniques for Surveys* sets the stage for acceptable remote inspection techniques (RITs) via RAS platforms that are followed by specific conditions and procedures that need to be considered in the survey process.[57] Recent literature published by Laura Poggi et al. considers the incorporation of a group-based non-exhaustive list of RITs as a positive attribute of Recommendation 42.[58] For example, while technologies under "drone" category could be used for visual examination during flight-mode, and even enable visual inspection

---

(RINA), Polish Register of Shipping (PRS), and the Indian Register of Shipping (IRS), The IACS revoked the membership of the Russian Maritime Register of Shipping (RMS).

[53] INTERNATIONAL ASSOCIATION OF CLASSIFICATION SOCIETIES, REQUIREMENTS CONCERNING SURVEY AND CERTIFICATION, INTERNATIONAL ASSOCIATION OF CLASSIFICATION SOCIETIES (2017).

[54] *Id.*

[55] *N.B.* A special survey is one that is carried out every five years for renewal of Classification Certificate.*Id.*,at 13, 19.

[56] *Id.*, at 51.

[57] INTERNATIONAL ASSOCIATION OF CLASSIFICATION SOCIETIES, RECOMMENDATION 42 GUIDELINES FOR USE OF REMOTE INSPECTION TECHNIQUES FOR SURVEYS § 1.1 (2016) ("Remote inspection techniques may include the use of: - Divers; - Unmanned robot arm; - Remote Operated Vehicles (ROV); - Climbers; - Drones; and - Other means acceptable to the Society") (Recommendation 42).

[58] Laura Poggi et al., *Recent Developments in Remote Inspection of Ship Structures*, 12 INT'L J. OF NAVAL ARCHITECTURE & OCEAN ENG'G 881, 882 (2020).

in enclosed spaces, such as, ballast tanks and cargo holds, "crawlers" would have the capability of inspecting structures through direct contact with the structure.[59] As per Recommendation 42, survey results via RAS could be obtained through the performance of two tasks: close-up surveys and gauging.[60] In addition to close-up surveys and gauging, Recommendation 42 prescribes that "means thickness-gauging and non-destructive testing could be required in conjunction" with the use of RIT.[61] As a follow-up to these RAS tasks, and should the RIT reveal damage or deterioration requiring attention, the surveyor is prescribed to conduct another close-up survey to verify the results obtained through the RAS platform as a part of the monitoring and compliance system.[62]

Invaluable standards in relation to procedures corresponding to interventions utilizing RAS can be found in UR Z17 titled *Procedural Requirements for Service Suppliers*.[63] As of 2019, twelve classification societies have implemented UR Z17 (which came into effect as of July 1, 2020) and considered tacit acceptance of the procedural standards developed by IACS.[64] It is important to note that procedural standards under UR Z17 primarily govern the approval and certification processes of service suppliers that provide a *broad* range of services of practical value.[65] This includes both statutory and classification services provided by firms that carry out "in-water survey on ships, mobile offshore units by divers or remotely operated vehicles," as well as firms that engage in "thickness measurement using RITs as an alternative means for close-up survey of the structure of the ships."[66]

As a part of the general procedure, UR Z17 emphasizes that the service provider needs to be approved by the concerned society prior to operations, especially in instances where the surveyor of the society uses the results provided by the service provider to reach decisions affecting both

---

[59] *Id.*

[60] Recommendation 42, *supra* note 56, § 1.2.

[61] *Id.*, § 3.2.

[62] *Id.*, § 1.2.

[63] International Association of Classification Societies, Z17: Procedural Requirements for Service Suppliers (online) (hereinafter UR Z17).

[64] UR Z17 has been implemented by the CRS, PRS and the IRS as well as nine out of the ten members of IACS: LR, ABS, BV, CCS, DNV, KR, NK, RINA and RMS. International Association of Classification Societies, Unified Requirements, www.iacs.org.uk/publications/unified-requirements/ (last visited Sept. 21, 2020) (online).

[65] UR Z17, *supra* note 62.

[66] *Id.*, § 4.12.

classification and statutory services.[67] The approval and certification procedure entails submission of an exhaustive list of documents outlined in section 5.1.1 of UR Z17. Subsequent to approval, the service supplier should maintain the "general requirements" on training and demonstrate competence of the "human element" comprised of operator, technical personnel and inspector.[68] Data control is an important aspect covered under the general requirements to the extent that service suppliers are under an obligation to demonstrate the ability of computer software used for the "acquisition, processing, recording, reporting, storage, measurement assessment, and monitoring of data".[69] With a view to ensuring good-quality services provided by suppliers, UR Z17 prescribes the maintenance of a documented system covering codes of conduct for: maintenance and calibration of equipment; training programs for operators, technicians and inspectors; supervision and verification to ensure compliance with operational procedures; and recording or reporting of information.[70]

Under the UR Z17 procedural requirements, the scope of engagement for firms or service suppliers using ROVs is limited to in-water survey and/or internal hull survey of compartments filled with water.[71] As the title indicates, the main objective of section 3 of annex I is to govern surveys using ROVs should the ship owner seek an alternative to a dive-survey. The requirements found in this part of annex I can be classified into seven principal building blocks that range from procedures governing the human element, to procedures covering reporting and verification of results. With regard to the human element, important criteria for ROV requisite supervisors and ROV operators is a minimum two-years and one-year experience, respectively, in know-how on handling ROVs.[72] When maneuvering equipment (outlined in section 3.6.1), the service supplier has an explicit obligation to follow documented operational procedures and guidelines with reference to: "guidance for the operation and maintenance of the ROV, if applicable, and methods and equipment to ensure the ROV operator can determine the ROV's

[67] Id., §§ 4.3–4.4.
[68] Id., § 5.2.
[69] Id., § 5.2.6.
[70] Id. §§ 5.5.1, 2.1 (defining "service supplier").
[71] Id., § 3.1.
[72] Id., §§ 3.4.1, 3.5.2.

location and orientation in relation to the vessel."[73] In doing so, ROV operators must have knowledge of inter alia the ship's underwater structure, nondestructive testing in accordance with recognized national or international industrial standards, underwater communication system and bearing clearance measurements. Postoperation provisions include documentation of results in the form of a report produced by the firm or supplier followed by verification and signature of the attending surveyor.[74]

Finally, provisions for using RIT applications in close-up surveys of a ship's structure rest in a distinct section under annex I of UR Z17. Section 16 of annex I is dedicated to procedural and operational requirements and is deemed as a theoretical extension of IACS Recommendation 42. In theory, a close-up survey is an examination "where the details of structural components are within the close visual inspection range of the surveyor" and is an integral formality satisfied, if required, during annual, intermediate and special (or renewal) surveys for detecting fractures, buckling, substantial corrosion and other types of structural deterioration.[75] Accordingly, a close-up survey may be performed in association with thickness measurements.[76] The extent of a close-up survey may also serve as an additional task, which could be determined after completion of the overall examination on the hull structure.[77]

Traditionally, the agenda for close-up surveys are included in a planning document alongside other particulars and conducted via physical access in selected holds and tanks of the ship under survey.[78] Within the same operational framework, RITs are now integrated into IACS international standards to serve as *alternatives* that come with an obligation to provide information that one would generally obtain from a close-up survey through physical access.

Focusing on the human element, UR Z17 prescribes requirements to be satisfied by the supplier. These include training and qualification of operators, practical work experiences for supervisor and operator,

---

[73] Id., § 3.7.2.
[74] Id., § 3.8.
[75] Id., § 1.4.1.
[76] Id.
[77] INTERNATIONAL ASSOCIATION OF CLASSIFICATION SOCIETIES, RECOMMENDATION 76: IACS GUIDELINES FOR SURVEYS, ASSESSMENT AND REPAIR OF HULL STRUCTURE § 3.2.1 (2008).
[78] Id., at 15, § 4.3.4.

documented procedures and guidelines containing planning preliminaries (plan), operational specifics (handling/operating equipment) and postoperational requirements (collection and storage of data).[79] Similar to section 3 of annex I, section 16 of annex I concludes with a verification clause whereby the supplier is under a procedural duty to have the surveyor's verification for each job that is conducted using one or more of the RITs referred to in section 16.1.[80]

The permissible limits of RAS application are succinctly embedded within the international standards. The work of IACS in developing international standards for survey and maintenance, and the functional integration of RAS into the survey agenda is commendable because of the pragmatic benefits. As rightly noted by Laura Poggi et al., the many recommendations issued by IACS over the years is a glimpse into the perplexities of on-board surveys that anticipate "a series of preventive operations" for allowing safe entrance into spaces and "reaching significant heights and inaccessible zones." These tasks translate into an "increase in risks, time and costs of inspection."[81] However, when analyzing UR Z17 requirements against individual classification society rules, there appear to be limitations in the international standards set by IACS. While the basic instructive building blocks for using ROVs in in-water surveys and RITs for close-up surveys are visible, UR Z17 neither covers the safety details, such as risk management system and safety assurance, nor the "third-party liability" clause. Those are important segments that require meaningful coverage given that IACS now allows the integration of RAS technologies – all of which require individual safety and liability considerations.

Notably, a majority of the provisions found in sections 3 and 16 of annex I of UR Z17 are focused on ROVs that are maneuverable underwater machines or tethered submersibles.[82] With the caveat that suppliers should have documented operational and procedural guidelines, UR Z17 supplements a handful of UAV-related requirements spread across section 16 of annex I in a brief manner. Clearly, the features related to RITs for RAS operating on water surfaces or underwater differ from unmanned aerial vehicles (UAVs) and require a proper delineation

---

[79] UR Z17, *supra* note 62, § 16.8.

[80] *Id.*, at 40, § 16.8.

[81] Poggi et al., *supra* note 57, at 881.

[82] ROBERT D. CHRIST & ROBERT L. WERNLI, SR., THE ROV MANUAL: A USER GUIDE FOR REMOTELY OPERATED VEHICLES 53–54, 536–45 (2d. ed. 2014).

of procedural and operational guidance in a more organized fashion. Significantly, section 16.1 incorporates two separate terms, "drones" and "UAVs," under the overarching definition of "remote inspection techniques," creating confusion by raising the question as to the differences between those two technologies.

Moving forward, individual classification societies have developed individual guidance notes that serve as best practice for class surveys requiring the use of UAVs.[83] These individual efforts also cover in scope robotic crawlers or magnetic crawlers that are "tethered or wireless vehicles designed to 'crawl' along a structure by means of wheels or tracks," and have the technical capacities to operate both in the air and underwater.[84] Nevertheless, in developing recommendation and requirements, classification societies consider the three basic international standards, IACS Recommendation 42, UR Z7 and UR Z17.[85]

7.3   Perceived Barriers and the Way Forward

Achieving regulatory excellence is complex and difficult. For success, four distinct but interrelated constraints must be addressed: (1) the intrinsic, specific and unique architecture requiring regulation; (2) the social norms surrounding the subject matter; (3) the rules of the market; and (4) the law.[86] Lessig views these four elements as regulatory blocks. The law stands out as the most readily available and has the most influence on the other three.[87] Further complications achieving RAS regulatory excellence is the plurality of existing laws in the form of class rules corresponding to RAS statutory standards, published by IACS, as

---

[83] *E.g.*, AMERICAN BUREAU OF SHIPPING, GUIDANCE NOTES ON USING UNMANNED AERIAL VEHICLES (2018); CHINA CLASSIFICATION SOCIETY, GUIDELINES FOR USE OF UNMANNED AERIAL VEHICLES FOR SURVEY (2018); *see also* Germanischer Lloyd Aktiengesellschaft, RULES FOR CLASSIFICATION AND CONSTRUCTION (2009). Also note that Germanischer Lloyd Aktiengesellschaft has gone further by developing rules on the design and construction of ROVs and AUVs. Those comprise the technical requirements, which are not covered by IACS.

[84] AMERICAN BUREAU OF SHIPPING, GUIDANCE NOTES ON THE USE OF REMOTE INSPECTION TECHNOLOGIES (2019).

[85] *Id.*, at ii.

[86] BRIDGET M. HUTTER, *A Risk Regulation Perspective on Regulatory Excellence.* ACHIEVING REGULATORY EXCELLENCE 101–04 (Cary Coglianese ed., 2016); *see* LAWRENCE LESSIG, CODE: AND OTHER LAWS OF CYBERSPACE, VERSION 2.0, at 124 (2006).

[87] LESSIG, *supra* note 85, at 124.

well as those of individual classification societies. While UR Z17 could be viewed as a concrete step toward harmonization of operational proced-ures for outer hull inspection and maintenance, it is noteworthy that there are no rules that bar other societies outside the "big 11" from developing their own class rules. In fact, that is the tradition for both IACS members and non-IACS members, resulting in numerous subject matter documents.

The development of de facto standards is not universally considered desirable and there is a school of thought that notes the negative impact of standards on innovation.[88] This perspective underscores four characteristic features (of standards) to show the casual nexus between *standards* and *innovation* that can result in both positive and negative effects.[89] Of the four noteworthy features, "variety" is deemed casual to negative effects on innovation by reducing choice, deterring market concentration and pro-moting premature selection of technologies.[90] Therefore, the reduction of variety allows the exploitation of economies of scale.[91] However, the reality of maritime RAS technologies is one of continuous innovation that enables manufacturers and service providers to table dozens of products able to perform the same tasks for an end-user's convenience.

Companies are introducing leading-edge dual-purpose service drones that include aerial inspection micro drones and drones with depth sensing. Depending on the size of the vessel, these drones can measure defects such as metal corrosion, metal erosion, wear and tear and even design flaws. The same trend can be observed in other professional service robots such as magnetic crawlers and ROVs. A methodology to establish standards based on product categorization could reduce variety and thereby serve as a foundation to guide future technology *without inhibiting innovation*.[92] Technological innovation therefore should not be hindered from setting standards because they can guide the standards and attract investment in complementary technologies.[93] This barrier

---

[88] KNUT BLIND, THE IMPACTS OF STANDARDIZATION AND STANDARDS ON INNOVATION 10 (2013).

[89] *Id.*, table 2.

[90] The four features are: compatibility/interoperability, minimum quality/safety, variety reduction and information. *See id.*

[91] G. M. PETER SWANN, THE ECONOMICS OF STANDARDIZATION 6 (2000).

[92] *Id.*, at 7. *N.B.* UR Z17 does not cover operational and safety procedures for drones and other means for inspection and cleaning tasks, as indicated in the list found in IACS Recommendation 42.

[93] BLIND, *supra* note 88, at 9.

would greatly be reduced by revising UR Z17, which references only a single professional service robot (i.e., ROVs). Further discussion among IACS members is warranted with due consideration given to other types of standard equipment found in IACS Recommendation 42.[94] This process would promote development of safety requirements for other categories of service robotic products that could added to UR Z17 alongside existing ROV requirements.

At present, biofouling hazards and future concepts are already covered under IMO's 2011 Guidelines as well as in the harmonized HSSC rules. Using IMO requirements as a basis, IACS developed class rules that embrace RAS and characterizes the organization as forward-thinking. Despite differences in strategic direction, there is some alignment between relevant IMO provisions and UR Z17 standards. For example, both IMO and IACS endorse the usage of divers and ROVs for outer hull in-water survey. The principal thread that helps align the two is section 7.4 of the 2011 Guidelines.[95] Yet this section remains inadequate, as ROVs are not the only marketed equipment that has the potential to perform hull surveys on bulk carriers. Bureau Veritas reportedly has already conducted the first close-up inspections and ultrasonic thickness measurements via aerial drones, confirming that this type of professional service robot is mature.[96] Accordingly, section 7.4 of the *2011 Guidelines* needs to remain open-ended to ensure there is no ambiguity.

Regulatory symmetry between IMO standard recommendations and IACS requirements could be achieved by incorporating the term "remote inspection technique" in the text of section 7.4. Moreover, considering that RAS emerges as an alternative to physical access to structures, an amendment should be directed at aligning the definition of close-up survey found in the international code on the enhanced program of inspections during surveys of bulk carriers and oil tankers (2011 ESP Code) after consultation between IMO and IACS.[97] As a recognized technical advisor body within the framework of IMO, IACS is in privileged position to facilitate dialogue, such as on the types of technologies

[94] Recommendation 42, *supra* note 56, § 1.1.
[95] *See* 2011 Guidelines, *supra* note 5, § 7.4 (permitting usage of both "diver" and "ROV," both of which are recognized by IACS for in-water inspection).
[96] Bureau Veritas, Press Release, Seeing Remotely: Bureau Veritas Performs First Survey by Drone (Mar. 4, 2020).
[97] Poggi et al., *supra* note 57, at 883.

permitted by the IMO and performance evaluation schemes for regulators.

Establishing a solid international foundation would ensure professional service robots are categorized by either the level of control or the level of autonomy. RAS experts envision a future where the different operational modes of service robots will rest on autonomous systems (i.e., a system capable of making decisions by direct interaction with the environment). Although outside the present scope of service robots, the IMO Maritime Safety Committee (MSC) is conducting a regulatory scoping exercise for a maritime autonomous surface ship (MASS), defined as: "a ship which, to a varying degree, can operate independently of human interaction."[98] As a first step in this scoping exercise, experts have adopted four degrees of autonomy:

- First degree: A ship with automated processes and decision support
- Second degree: A remotely controlled ship with seafarers on board
- Third degree: A remotely controlled ships without seafarers on board
- Fourth degree: A fully autonomous ship[99]

Although the current RAS control paradigm adopted for professional service robots is supervised autonomy, experts are exploring the full potential of the current system that may evolve into unmanned autonomy.[100] Recalling the supportive role of IACS in IMO's MASS scoping exercise, it would be beneficial to include categorized equipment or equipment classified according to autonomy (taking into account the levels of autonomy for RAS platforms endorsed by IACS). This classification highlights the level of complexity of the individual tasks (inspection/cleaning/maintenance) required by the control platform and informs the precise levels where human intervention might be required. An analysis of the five types of equipment found in IACS Recommendation 42 raises the question: What are the risks of deploying an "unmanned robot arm" or "ROV" or "drones" in the close-up survey process? Clearly, the use of an "unmanned" platform for inspecting a ship's bottom cannot be deemed as semiautonomous given that it is a not

---

[98] International Maritime Organization, Press Release, IMO Takes First Steps to Address Autonomous Ships (May 25, 2018).

[99] International Maritime Organization Res. MSC 100/20/Add.1, annex 2 (Dec. 7, 2018) (Framework for the Regulatory Scoping Exercise for the Use of Maritime Autonomous Surface Ships).

[100] Lloyd's Register, UNMANNED MARINE SYSTEMS CODE 1–2 (2017).

a "system that can be operated without personnel."[101] But as full autonomy is on the horizon, further work is required to comprehend risks of
AI-based interventions. In short, the essential issue that needs to be
addressed by IACS is the risk factor connected with different degrees of
autonomy in light of the control paradigms, similar to the scoping
exercise conducted by IMO.

Collateral safety standards for all of the different inspection and
maintenance RAS product types are also an important factor. Product
safety standards are intrinsically related to the product information sheet
(PIS) that covers technical or engineering specifications for every product. All products are prone, to some degree, to defects or technical
glitches. For service providers, design defects and manufacturing defects
could invoke liability (because in-water surveys are statutory in
nature).[102] In the long run, this issue complicates the relationship
between ship owners and charter parties.[103] This type of defective product liability is separate from the liability regime governing the relationship between a buyer and seller in sales *of goods*. Rather, the international
liability seeks to rationalize regional and national laws governing manufacturer liability and consumer protection, as in Product Liability
Directive 85/374/EEC.[104]

Professional service robots endorsed by the UR Z and individual
classification societies are labeled "equipment" – a term that is synonymous with "product."[105] Each component that goes into making a product
needs to be of high quality, especially the ones that are marketed for
services involving RITs that are statutory in nature. The quality of those
components needs to be assured at the design and manufacturing level.
In product liability cases arising in the automotive sector, courts take into
account quality and design defects.[106] Therefore, developing the basic PIS

---

[101] *Id.*, at 3.

[102] Woodrow Barfield, *Liability for Autonomous and Artificially Intelligent Robots*, 9
PALADYN: J. OF BEHAV. ROBOTICS 193, 196 (2018).

[103] Julie Mangiante, Hull Fouling Clauses and Prolonged Stays, Skuld, Dec. 18, 2019.

[104] Council Directive 85/374/EEC, art. 6(1), 1985 O.J. (L 210) 29, 31 (EC).

[105] From a manufacturer's perspective, robots are products manufactured through an action
or a process and refined for sale.

[106] With reference to the automotive sector, Professor Bertolini stresses that "different
standards of safety required from products can – at least in part – be determined by
decisions of specific bodies, called upon to define the characteristic a given object needs
to present ... [s]uch criteria are normally taken into account by the courts." *See* Andrea
Bertolini, *Robots as Products: The Case for a Realistic Analysis of Robotic Applications
and Liability Rules*, 5 L. INNOVATION & TECH. 214, 241 (2013).

standards specifying the quality of individual components could help manufacturers not only address defects at the design level, but could also prove to be a strong legal defense. Yet UR Z17 does not contain PIS standards. This also holds true for guidance documents produced by classification societies, although organizations such as the China Classification Society and the American Bureau of Shipping (ABS) have made commendable efforts to provide detailed recommendations on equipment standards. There is, however, a regulatory vacuum at the international level with the potential to leave both ship owners and service providers without a safety net. The way forward is not easy. The development of international PIS standards requires a technical mandate. Prima facie, the scope of this work falls under the mandate of ISO/TC 299. Taking this mandate into account, a joint collaboration among IACS, ISO and product manufacturers could develop performance criteria and PIS standards for professional service robots. The result would be valuable and help professional service robots syn-chronize with the regional and national product liability regime.

Finally, matters related to data storage or data preservation requires special attention lest they create legal concerns on data protection. Image and data gathering tasks are accomplished through machine learning, sensors and algorithms. Once the tasks are completed, the operator shall then deliver those images and data in a format acceptable to the attending surveyor, and survey reports are submitted to the classification society for certification.[107] This process is governed by a contractual agreement between ship owners and service providers or ship owners and a classification society. However, IACS as well as many of the "big 11" classification societies are silent on post data acquisition steps. This could later prove problematic from a data privacy perspective.[108]

In due course, further questions will require clarification in consultation with ship owners. Who is responsible for data and image preservation? How long should survey data and image be preserved? What protection do service providers require against third-party liability? How could classification societies complement regional and national laws on end-user data privacy?

---

[107] This process is clearly laid out in guidance documents issued by classification societies. See, e.g., AMERICAN BUREAU OF SHIPPING, supra note 83, at 18; see also CHINA CLASSIFICATION SOCIETY, supra note 82, at 17.

[108] This has been confirmed in an interview conducted with a service provider company known as Diving Status.

7.3.1   Implications for the Law of the Sea

The forgoing issues raise two distinctly different strands of analysis – the legal status of professional service robots in the United Nations Convention on the Law of the Sea (UNCLOS) and the affect harmonized standards governing new technology may have on the treaty.

Part XIII of UNCLOS concerns "marine scientific research" (MSR).[109] Although MSR is undefined in the texts of part XIII, the term is important to protect the marine environment.[110] Assessment of data sets gathered through surveys acquired via technology is included in MSR. Examples of this are ripe in ocean research: the surveying of the ocean floor by submarines; ocean data collection with the help of floaters and gliders launched by ships or planes; and sensor-based platforms incorporating advanced modeling systems that gather highly complex data sets. Historically, the greater portion of MSR has been moored to areas under national jurisdiction, underscoring the importance of the "consent" regime.[111] Coastal state competence is sometimes unclear, such as whether the legal status of gliders and floaters constitute "operational oceanography."[112] Fortunately, however, the equipment used in vessel inspection and maintenance, while arguably within the ambit of MSR, are generally deployed when the vessel is berthed, anchored or dry-docked within internal waters.[113]

---

[109] *See* United Nations Convention on the Law of the Sea pt. XIII, Dec. 10, 1982, 1833 U.N.T.S. 397 (UNCLOS). MSR is "any study or related experimental work designed to increase man's knowledge of the marine environment." ALFRED H. A. SOONS, MARINE SCIENTIFIC RESEARCH AND THE LAW OF THE SEA 6 (1982).

[110] TARA DAVENPORT, *Submarine Communications Cables and Science: A New Frontier in Ocean Governance?* SCIENCE, TECHNOLOGY AND NEW CHALLENGES TO OCEAN LAW 226 (Harry N. Scheiber, James Kraska & Moon-Sang Kwon eds., 2015); *see* SOONS, *supra* note 109, at 14. *See also* Tafsir Johansson, Ronan Long & Dimitrios Dalaklis, *The Role of WMU-Sasakawa Global Ocean Institute in the Era of Big Data*, 14 J. OF OCEAN TECH. 22, 28–29 (2019).

[111] James Kraska et al., *Bio-logging of Marine Migratory Species in the Law of the Sea*, 51 MARINE POL'Y 394, 399 (2015).

[112] Tobias Hofman & Alexander Proelss, *The Operation of Gliders under the International Law of the Sea*, 46 OCEAN DEV. & INT'L L. 167, 168 (2015); *see also* Katharina Bork et al., *The Legal Regulation of Floats and Gliders: In Quest of a New Regime?* 39 OCEAN DEV. & INT'L L. 298, 307, 311 (2008).

[113] For operation of UAVs beyond twelve nautical miles or the territorial sea, it is important to observe the civil aviation rules. *See* SEAN T. PRIBYL, *Regulating Drones in Maritime and Energy Sectors.* HANDBOOK OF UNMANNED AERIAL VEHICLES 1, 14 (Kimon P. Valavanis & George J. Vachtsevanos eds., 2018).

Ronán Long has noted that from a human rights perspective, technology is a tool that can be used to improve compliance with law and policy.[114] Could technology help improve compliance with safety law and policy? The answer is contingent on the intended purpose of deploying such technology and the benchmarking of performance over a defined period. "Intentionality" occurs when operational objectives become aligned with international objectives. Whether compliance improves can only be determined by comparing vessel performance and energy efficiency levels between two bulk carriers: one that has been surveyed and maintained manually with one that has used service robots. Until such a comparison has been conducted, the use of new technology should not disrupt the duties and obligations in international law.

International safety standards could not be clearer. The flag state must take necessary measures under UNCLOS for ensuring "safety at sea." Article 94 of UNCLOS provides a detailed but nonexhaustive list of flag state responsibilities, including construction and seaworthiness.[115] The integration of professional service robots into the survey and maintenance aspects of article 94 are subject to the same, if not higher, expectations.

Writing, sensing and shaping are subset indicators of intentionality or terraforming practices that continuously shape and structure the desired environment.[116] Published standards form a part of the writing "subset" and are rooted in the governing dynamics of "environing technology."[117] Therefore, both normative published international technology-based standards and informative detailing RAS procedures impact the modern technological environment. Equipment endorsed by the IMO and classification societies is deployed with clear and precise objectives. The regional and national objectives are deeply ingrained in the environmental objectives of UNCLOS. This bolsters support for the proposition that UNCLOS promotes the application of international harmonized

---

[114] RONÁN LONG, *A European Law Perspective: Science, Technology, and New Challenges to Ocean Law*. SCIENCE, TECHNOLOGY AND NEW CHALLENGES TO OCEAN LAW 63, 78 (Harry N. Scheiber, James Kraska & Moon-Sang Kwon eds., 2015).

[115] *See* UNCLOS, *supra* note 108, art. 94(3).

[116] Sverker Sörlin & Nina Wombs, *Environing Technologies: A Theory of Making Environment*, 34 HIST. & TECH. 101, 105–08 (2018).

[117] "[O]ften these technologies are also connected to writing, as documenting is intrinsic to many activities, especially those which are circulated in society and over time. UNCLOS or the IPCC Fifth Assessment Report are examples of writing (documents) that environ." *See id.*, at 7.

standards on niche technologies, supporting the second strand of this discussion.

Shipping is intrinsically a global enterprise and is therefore best regulated at the international level. Currently, the maritime international regime is "based on two interdependent bodies consisting of an umbrella framework formed by customary law, UNCLOS, and Chapter 17 of Agenda 21, and a regulatory regime consisting of instruments adopted by the member states of the IMO."[118] The *Code for the Implementation of Mandatory IMO instruments* is a bridge to connect this "interdependency," requesting flag state administrations to give UNCLOS and IMO instruments "full and complete effect" to ensure that "a ship is fit for the service for which it is intended."[119]

Part XII of UNCLOS sets forth an obligation for member states to take all measures to prevent pollution of the marine environment from any source. In this endeavor, states shall use the "best practicable means at their disposal and in accordance with their capabilities."[120] Pollution prevention measures under part XII should ideally include all potential sources including "pollution from vessels" by regulating "design, construction, equipment," inter alia.[121] Part XII establishes a global and regional cooperation regime with reference to "competent international organizations" to facilitate development of "international rules" consistent with UNCLOS.[122]

General accepted international rules and standards (GAIRS) fits within the UNCLOS framework as a legal mechanism for safeguarding the marine environment.[123] GAIRS are the gateway to synergistic integration with other international treaties and agreements, allowing "new concepts, such as precaution and biodiversity to become part of UNCLOS normative structure."[124] GAIRS embraces standards developed by competent

---

[118] Proshanto Kumar Mukherjee & Abhinayan Basu Bal, The Status of International and Regional Conventions Relating to Ship Source Marine Pollution in States in the Baltic Region 8 (2011).
[119] International Maritime Organization Res. A.973(24), § 4 (Dec. 1, 2005) (Code for the Implementation of Mandatory IMO Instruments).
[120] UNCLOS, *supra* note 108, art. 194(1).
[121] *Id.*, art. 194(3).
[122] *Id.*, art. 197.
[123] *See Id.*, arts. 21(2), (4); 39(2)(a)–(b); 41(3); 53(8); 60(3),(5), (6); 94(2)(a); 94(5); 211(2), (5), (6)(c); 226(1)(a); 271.
[124] Richard Barnes, The Continuing Validity of UNCLOS. The United Nations Convention on the Law of the Sea: A Living Instrument 459, 472 (Jill Barrett & Richard Barnes eds., 2016), *citing* David Freestone, *International Fisheries Law*

international organizations compatible with the scope, intent and object-ives of UNCLOS. This rule of reference is spread across a number of articles throughout UNCLOS, including article 211, pollution from vessels, which is an implicit reference for cooperation through the IMO.[125] Moreover, article 237 adopts an approach of "openness and complementarity" to all other regimes with respect to protection of the marine environment.[126] Thereby, the rules of reference via GAIRS not only offer consistency with IMO regulatory instruments but also includes IMO ROs and their rules and requirements. Conversely, through their respective functions, classification society standards complement the rules of IMO, which in turn ensures the effective and efficient implemen-tation of environmental provisions of UNCLOS.

7.4   Conclusion

The most obvious manifestation behind the surge in the use of professional service robots for survey and maintenance of niche areas embodies is the same as the use of autonomous vessels more generally: enhanced performance maintaining world-class safety and environmen-tal standards. There are promising prospects for integrating RAS into niche areas that have been traditionally accessed through physical pres-ence. Whether or not there will be universal consensus to replace

---

Since Rio: The Continued Rise of the Precautionary Principle. INTERNATIONAL LAW AND SUSTAINABLE DEVELOPMENT: PAST ACHIEVEMENTS AND FUTURE CHALLENGES 135 (Alan Boyle & David Freestone eds., 1999).

[125] This is reflected in numerous provisions of UNCLOS that require states to "take account of," "conform to," "give effect to" or "implement" the relevant international rules and standards developed by or through the "competent international organization" (*e.g.*, IMO). *See, e.g.,* UNCLOS, *supra* note 108, arts. 22; 39; 41(4)–(5); 53(9); 60(3), (5); 61(2), (5); 119(2); 197–202; 204–05; 207(4); 208(5); 210(3); 211(1)–(6); 212–14; 216; 217(1), (4), (7); 218(1); 220(7); 222–23; 238–39; 242–44(2); 246(3), (5), (5)(d); 248–49; 251–53 (1)(b), (4), (5); 254(1)–(4); 256–57; 262–63(3); 265; 266(1); 268–273; 275(1)–(2); 276(1); 278; 297(1)(c); 319(2)(a); *see also* Report of the Secretariate of the International Maritime Organization, Implications of the United Nations Convention on the Law of the Sea for the International Maritime Organization, U.N. Doc. LEG/MICS.8, at 8 (Jan. 8, 2014); AGUSTIN BLANCO-BAZAN, *The Environmental UNCLOS and the Work of IMO in the Field of Prevention of Pollution from Vessels.* INTERNATIONAL MARITIME ENVIRONMENTAL LAW, INSTITUTIONS, IMPLEMENTATION AND INNOVATIONS 31, 32–37 (Andree Kirchner et al. eds., 2003).

[126] SELINE TREVISANUT et al., *Introduction.* REGIME INTERACTION IN OCEAN GOVERNANCE: PROBLEMS, THEORIES AND METHODS 1, 12 (Seline Trevisanut et al. eds., 2020).

traditional human-centric techniques with RAS, the demand for remote services will only increase, highlighting the need for harmonized rules.[127] Under the auspices of IACS, a governance framework has emerged for both manufacturers and service providers that will harmonize RAS within the maritime industry. Discussions segue into the world of international technology-based standards and raise questions about robustness in the face of product variety, better performance and improved compliance.

Analysis of current technology-based standards for in-water survey and maintenance indicate that they are spatially uneven. In fact, IACS RAS integrated standards as a whole tend to be inadequate compared to the standards developed by IACS members, such as, ABS, Lloyd's Register (LR), Korean Register (KR) and Det Norske Veritas (DNV). Management of change system (by LR, BV, ABS and KR), certifying multisite organizations (by ABS), approval database (by LR), safety management system (by ABS), liability (by ABS), and reporting and data storage (by DNV) are the noteworthy provisions that are covered by individual IACS members.

Gray areas pertaining to operational and technical information likely will hamper integration of technology into the class survey and maintenance regime. To remove those barriers, constructive dialogue is required among the "big 11" and other classification societies. Attention must be drawn to the discrepancies delineated to move forward with the necessary harmonizing of the plethora of existing advisory documents issued by individual classification societies.

Classification societies need to coordinate strategic efforts to standardize the technical and engineering specifications for all equipment approved for conducting inspection and maintenance of a vessels structure. The existing operational procedures, risk-management assessments and new provisions (including product technical specifications should those be developed) should then be added as a subset IACS requirement titled Z-17.1 under the existing UR Z17. If this were achieved, the revision process would be made easier without disrupting the natural flow of UR Z17.

Presently, efforts are duplicative. Guidelines on RITs have been issued by IACS members and it is likely that other classification societies will follow to increase financial gain. All existing guidelines could be

---

[127] See *Class Societies and Remote Inspection Techniques*, SEADRONEPRO, Aug. 24, 2020.

streamlined into a standard guideline, unifying approved procedures that concern the usage and deployment of technology for services on ship's outer hull. Furthermore, because the economic value of class rules on hull survey is substantial, it is conceivable that governments as well as national standardization bodies will turn to IACS or individual classification societies for guidance and best practices.[128] However, in its current form, the standards remain disparate, incomplete and insufficient. Without uniformity, at the core of the term "standard," the current landscape only enhances existing criticisms of classification societies.[129]

There are readily available tools that could be applied to resolve these issues. Whatever pathways that are eventually developed, it is advisable that international organizations keep the IMO informed of progress since technology-based standards for hull inspection and maintenance are intertwined with the spirit of the IMO's HSSC and the 2011 Guidelines that adhere to the basic tenets of safety and environment in UNCLOS. For professional service robots that influence vessel performance and reduce emissions, it is undoubtedly a catalyst for positive change.

---

[128] JURGEN BASEDOW & WOLFGANG WURMNEST, THIRD-PARTY LIABILITY OF CLASSIFICATION SOCIETIES: A COMPARATIVE PERSPECTIVE 7 (2005).

[129] Notably, how conflict of interest may question the efficiency of classification societies. It is also noted that both the *Prestige* and the *Erika* were classed by BS and RINA, respectively – two members of the IACS "big 12". *See* JOHN N. K. MANSELL, FLAG STATE RESPONSIBILITY: HISTORICAL DEVELOPMENT AND CONTEMPORARY ISSUES 131–32 (2009); *see also* Commission Communication on the Applicability of Article 101 of the Treaty on the Functioning of the European Union to Horizontal Co-operation Agreements, 2011 O.J. (C 11), ¶ 316, n.128.

Functionalism and Maritime Autonomous Surface Ships

ALEXANDROS X. M. NTOVAS

8.1   Introduction

Autonomous ships may be used for noncommercial purposes, such as for naval activities and marine scientific research,[1] as well as international shipping.[2] Smaller craft under the threshold (500 gross tons) for most International Maritime Organization (IMO) instruments are being validated through technical projects that could scale up to full-size

---

[1] See James Kraska, *Oceanographic and Naval Deployments of Expendable Marine Instruments under US and International Law*, 26 Ocean Dev. & Int' L. 311, 313 (1995); James Kraska, *The Law of Unmanned Naval Systems in War and Peace*, 5 J. Ocean Tech. 44, 45 (2010).

[2] See Alexandros X. M. Ntovas et al., Liability for operations in Unmanned Maritime Vehicles with Differing Levels of Autonomy 1ff. (2016); New Technologies, Artificial Intelligence and Shipping Law in the 21st Century 65–162 (Barış Soyer & Andrew Tettenborn eds., 2020); Autonomous Ships and the Law 56–82 (Henrik Ringbom et al. eds., 2020).

commercially operated ships.[3] Yet the requirement for manning of ships in Article 94 of the United Nations (UN) Convention on the Law of the Sea (UNCLOS) and IMO instruments poses the most challenging legal issue for widespread use of unmanned ships.[4] The manning requirement in UNCLOS has led to calls for "a thorough overhaul" of the convention[5] to more narrowly prescribed amendments to accommodate autonomous ships.[6] Similarly, international contributions to a Comité Maritime International (CMI) study on the use of autonomous ships present a similar divergence in views.[7] Most national maritime law associations (MLAs) conclude that potential inconsistencies between legal regulations developed for manned ships and autonomous ships may be resolved through IMO measures, although the Irish and French associations believe nothing less than amendment to UNCLOS is necessary. The IMO is engaged in a project to assess the required regulatory framework for maritime autonomous surface ships (MASSs).[8] The MASS exercise is proceeding but not without delays.[9]

This chapter offers an interpretative account that functionally constructs the requirement of manning in UNCLOS, Article 94. Part 2 views UNCLOS as a timeless constitution for the world's oceans with textual integrity and coherence that should be protected against the ill-advised, if not entirely unrealistic, prospect of unwarranted amendments. However, the possibility of modifications ought not to be precluded with a view to

---

[3] GLENN WRIGHT, UNMANNED AND AUTONOMOUS SHIPS passim (2020).

[4] United Nations Convention on the Law of the Sea, art. 94(3), Dec. 10, 1982, 1833 U.N.T.S. 397 (hereinafter UNCLOS); see also MÅNS JACOBSSON, What Challenges Lie Ahead for Maritime Law? MARITIME LAW IN MOTION 257, 274–79 (Proshanto Mukherjee et al. eds., 2020); Joel Coito, Maritime Autonomous Surface Ships: New Possibilities and Challenges in Ocean Law and Policy, 97 INT'L. L. STUD. 259, 303–4 (2021).

[5] Eric van Hooydonk, The Law of Unmanned Merchant Shipping – An Exploration, 20 J. OF INT'L MAR. L. & COM. 403, 410 (2014).

[6] DANISH MARITIME AUTHORITY, ANALYSIS OF REGULATORY BARRIERS TO THE USE OF AUTONOMOUS SHIPS 58 (2017).

[7] As of February 13, 2018, the CMI International Working Group had received responses from the MLAs of Argentina, Brazil, Britain, Canada, China, Croatia, Denmark, the Netherlands, Finland, France, Germany, Japan, Malta, Panama, Singapore, Spain, the UK and the United States. IMO Doc. MSC 99/INF.8, work conducted by the CMI International Working Group on unmanned ship (Feb. 13, 2018).

[8] IMO Res.A/1110/30, Strategic Plan for the Organization for the Period 2018–2023, §§17–19 (Dec. 6, 2017).

[9] IMO Doc. MSC 98/20/2, Maritime Autonomous Surface Ships Regulatory Scoping Exercise (MASS RSE) (Feb. 27, 2017). The present chapter has captured the developments and reflected thereon as until May 5, 2021.

facilitating the conduct of coastal operations within the national jurisdiction of interested states. The specialized international treaties under IMO will need to evolve but in a manner that maintains their symmetry with UNCLOS. While IMO is the competent international organization to regulate autonomous ships, it should avoid creating tension with the wording of UNCLOS, Article 94.[10] Throughout parts 4–8, the analysis argues that technological progress is best promoted by viewing the manning requirement in light of functional flexibility. The IMO must constitute the principal forum for the regulation of autonomous ships at the international level within the boundaries of UNCLOS and through its remit to adopt generally accepted international rules and standards, regulations, procedures and practices (GAIRS).

Part 3 suggests the definition of term ship should remain generic in the conventional language as it has not been predicated on the presence of a human element onboard. Part 4 explores the construction of UNCLOS, Article 94(3)(b) and recounts the drafting intentions to that the requirement of manning is to be functionally qualified. The legal rationale underlying the argument in favor of functional flexibility is further advanced in part 5 through the perspective of IMO consideration of the MASS regulatory scoping exercise (RSE) and by comparison with the emerging new regulatory philosophy of setting goal-based standards (GBSs) discussed in Part 6.

The main elements of the functionality test in parts 7 and 8 consider that the flag state obligation to take measures are within its discretion to achieve and maintain comprehensive safety at sea for autonomous ships. Substantial parts of this approach rely on the principles and methodology of general international law, and therefore can be applied by analogy to GAIRS produced in the context of UNCLOS.

8.2   The Constitutional Nature of UNCLOS

UNCLOS has emplaced the constitutional foundations of an international legal order for the oceans that emerged for humanity to uphold "peace, justice and progress" toward the "realization of a just and equitable international economic order."[11] This social, economic and

---

[10] Henrik Ringbom, *Regulating Autonomous Ships - Concepts, Challenges and Precedents,* 50 OCEAN DEV. & INT.L L. 141, 161–2 (2019); Henrik Ringbom, *Legalizing Autonomous Ships,* 34 OCEAN Y.B. 429, 442–3 (2020).

[11] UNCLOS, *supra* note 4, preamble; TOMMY KOH, BUILDING A NEW LEGAL ORDER FOR THE OCEANS 1 et seq. (2020).

political *order public* at sea was crafted to encompass the comprehensive restatement of the law, incorporating elements of codification and the progressive development of new law. The claim to its constitutional nature nonetheless is made mostly with respect to the visible aspects of the regime featuring the accomplishments pertaining to the jurisdictional zones, the expansion of sovereign rights through a careful balance of competing interests, new institutions and the inclusion of compulsory dispute settlement procedures.

Two paramount normative conditions underlay the negotiations at the Third UN Conference on the Law of the Sea: the "package deal" principle and the "theory of interrelatedness" among the topics and respective agendas. These principles drove the procedural work of the conference to adopt a single comprehensive text. In addition, the decision-making process was governed throughout the proceedings by a "gentlemen's agreement" that required every effort to reach an agreement on substantive matters by way of consensus. No votes were taken "until all efforts at consensus [had] been exhausted."[12]

8.2.1   The Prospect of Amending UNCLOS

The principles that governed the Third UN Conference persist, raising a high bar to amending the treaty.[13] Calls to amend UNCLOS on the sole account of accommodating autonomous ships shall be treated lightly as they tend to reflect industry convenience rather than legal or political reality. For the foreseeable future, the prospect of autonomous navigation for commercial ships will be restricted in safe waters, including inland waterways,[14] in conducting shortsea coastal navigation between fixed points.[15] Operations in confined geographical seas within the exclusive economic zone will facilitate the evolution of autonomous ships in two important and interrelated ways. First, the ships will operate within a

---

[12] UN Doc. A/Conf.62/WP.2, Appendix to the Rules of Procedure, 13 I.L.M. 1 (1974).

[13] UNCLOS, *supra* note 4, arts. 312–13.

[14] As in the case of the M/V *American Courage* becoming in January 2021 the largest ship to perform automatic dock-to-dock operations and transit along the Cuyahoga River in the United States, *see* Wärtsilä, www.wartsila.com/insights/article/sailing-straight-and-true-on-crooked-river (Jan. 13, 2021; last visited Mar. 3, 2022) (online).

[15] MASS UK INDUSTRY CONDUCT PRINCIPLES AND CODE OF PRACTICE (version 4 2020) (autonomous ships are likely to operate within a 3 nautical mile [M] radius from a nominated departure point, and in the future up to a maximum of 150 M from a safe haven).

presumptively safer and more secure cyber domain in employing compatible systems to fix their location proximate to littoral shore control
centers and benefit from vessel traffic services, aids to navigation, and
infrastructure and port services.[16] Second, in terms of law, the ships will
be in waters under the jurisdiction of both a flag and coastal state with a
shared interest in a common regulatory framework.[17] Modification of
IMO instruments rather than amendment of UNCLOS best facilitates the
operation of autonomous ships. UNCLOS allows states to conclude inter
se agreements modifying or suspending rights, duties and obligations,
insofar as they do not relate to a provision derogation from which is
incompatible with the effective execution of its purposes, and provided
that such agreements shall not affect the application of its basic principles
or the enjoyment by other states parties of their rights or the
performance of their obligations. Provisions of this nature typically relate
to freedom of navigation.[18]

8.2.2   Interpreting UNCLOS

UNCLOS may be considered a "living tree," undergoing continuing
development and flexible adaptation over time.[19] The emergence of
autonomous ships benefits from the evolutionary interpretation of
oceans law. This should be a relatively limited task to avoid constant
revision, however.[20] Broader provisions in UNCLOS, such as human
rights, are more amenable to an expansive approach in interpretation.
In seeking to make allowances for autonomous ships, however, care must
be taken to avoid the fragmentation of terms, such as crew and ship.[21]

---

[16] For example, see the M/V *Yara Birkeland*, designed for short-range, fully autonomous
coastal operations in Norway. Kongsberg Autonomous Shipping, www.kongsberg.com/
maritime/support/themes/autonomous-shipping/ (last visited Mar. 2, 2022) (online).

[17] GOVERNMENT OF NORWAY, BLUE OPPORTUNITIES: THE NORWEGIAN GOVERNMENT'S
UPDATED OCEAN STRATEGY 31, 47 (2019).

[18] UNCLOS, *supra* note 4, art. 311(3); *see* David Galligan, *Wrapping up the UNCLOS III
Package: At Long Last the Final Clauses*, 20 VA J. INT'L L. 347, 363–64 (1979).

[19] Separate Opinion of Judge Lucky, Request for Advisory Opinion submitted by the Sub-
regional Fisheries Commission, Case No. 21, Advisory Opinion of April 2, 2015, ITLOS
Rep. 2015 p. 88, §§ 9–11.

[20] ALAN BOYLE, *Further Development of the 1982 Convention on the Law of the Sea:
Mechanisms for Change.* THE LAW OF THE SEA: PROGRESS AND PROSPECTS (David
Freestone et al. eds., 2006), 45–47.

[21] Anna Petrig, *La "Révolution Robotique" en Mer et la Convention de Montego Bay: Un Défi
Interprétatif pour ses Dispositions Relatives à la Criminalité Maritime?*, 23 ANNUAIRE DU
DROIT DE LA MER 17, 32–42 (2018).

For that reason, a functionally dispositive approach to the manning requirement in UNCLOS, Article 94 is optimal,[22] although the methodology of such a construction has not been defined so far in the bibliography.

Deliberations during the Third UN Conference considered the application of unmanned submersibles for marine scientific research.[23] Consequently, there is a presumption that the operational technology in question was not beyond legal contemplation but rather of limited application at the time. The view that "one cannot study modern findings in cybernetics without arriving at the conclusion that there is nothing in such fields of activity as navigation that an electronic device will not eventually be able to do as well as and more reliably than a human being" predates the conference by at least a decade.[24] The functional construction of the manning requirement thus can be best served by an effective interpretation to dispose questions pertaining to ship manning, which in this context arise from technical rules rather than originating internally to the whole treaty normative dynamic.[25]

In following this paradigm, there may be opportunities to consider the possible effect of subsequent state practice concerning the interpretative implementation of treaty provisions, and there is already a positive bilateral precedent set with regards to the uniform interpretation of UNCLOS.[26] The effect of this practice as a wider process nonetheless remains uncertain. Commenting on this, the UN International Law Commission (ILC) concluded that "the possibility of amending or modifying a treaty by subsequent practice of the parties has not been generally recognized."[27] However, if in the future there is a movement toward a

---

[22] Aldo Chircop, *Testing International Legal Regimes: The Advent of Automated Commercial Vessels*, 60 GERMAN YB INT'L L. 109, 137–41 (2017).

[23] UN Doc. A/Conf.62/C.3/L.22, Description of Some Types of Marine Technology and Possible Methods for Their Transfer: Report of the Secretary-General, §31, §47 (Feb. 27, 1975).

[24] Leonard LePage, *The Nature of the Information to be Displayed at Sea*, 13 NAVIGATION J. 39, 46 (1960).

[25] PIERRE-MARIE DUPUY, *Evolutionary Interpretation of Treaties: Between Memory and Prophecy*. THE LAW OF TREATIES: BEYOND THE VIENNA CONVENTION 123 (Enzo Cannizzaro ed., 2011).

[26] Joint Statement with Attached Interpretation of Rules of International Law Governing Innocent Passage, U.S.–U.S.S.R., Sept. 23, 1989, 28 I.L.M. 1444.

[27] International Law Commission, *Draft Conclusions on Subsequent Agreements and Subsequent Practice in Relation to the Interpretation of Treaties*, 2 Y.B. INT'L L. COMMISSION art. 7(3) (2018).

concentrated reinterpretation of UNCLOS, this will more likely transpire as a process from within the IMO.[28]

8.2.3   Implementation of UNCLOS and the Modality of GAIRS

UNCLOS is indispensable as a framework regime that is not self-contained but rather inextricably connected to external law-making. Especially in shipping, UNCLOS has established symbiotic synergies with the IMO specialized treaty instruments either by various references to those predating its adoption in the area of safety of life at sea,[29] marine pollution[30] and prevention of collisions at sea,[31] or in general by references being made collectively to GAIRS. Undeniably, without these instruments, many of the UNCLOS provisions relevant to these matters would be hollow exhortations.[32] How should IMO adapt and further develop GAIRS pertinent to autonomous ships? In conducting the MASS RSE for instruments within its purview, the IMO Legal Committee (LEG) has started to explore the most appropriate ways of addressing the operations of autonomous ships, taking into account the human element, by considering the options of developing new instruments, amending existing instruments, developing interpretations or pursuing none of these efforts, as a result of the analysis.[33] While this work is underway, a brief comment on these means highlights the importance of my argument in favor of functional flexibility.

While legislative intervention through development of new hard law may augment the present regime it may not be an expeditious method or assure a successful outcome. In principle, the IMO Assembly has consistently reiterated that new instruments, and amendments to existing ones, should be considered only if there is a clear and well-documented

---

[28] Raul Pedrozo, *Is It Time for the United States to Join the Law of the Sea Convention?*, 41 J. MAR. L. & COM. 151, 164 (2010).

[29] International Convention for the Safety of Life at Sea, 1974, Nov. 1, 1974, 32 U.S.T. 47, 1184 U.N.T.S. 2 (as amended) (hereinafter SOLAS).

[30] Protocol of 1978 Relating to the International Convention for the Prevention of Pollution from Ships (with Annexes, Final Act and International Convention), Feb. 17, 1978, 1340 U.N.T.S. 61 (hereinafter MARPOL).

[31] Convention on the International Regulations for Preventing Collisions at Sea, Oct. 20, 1972, 28 U.S.T. 3459, T.I.A.S. No. 8587, 1050 U.N.T.S. 16 (hereinafter COLREGs).

[32] RICHARD BARNES et al., The Law of the Sea: Progress and Prospects. THE LAW OF THE SEA: PROGRESS AND PROSPECTS 9 (David Freestone et al. eds., 2006).

[33] IMO Doc. LEG/106/16, Report of the Legal Committee on the Work of its 106th Session (May 13, 2019).

compelling need.[34] Provided that such a need exists, a legally binding new international instrument can be concluded in the form of a free-standing treaty focused on autonomous ships by a conference convened by the IMO. Alternatively, the member states of the IMO may develop optional supplementary protocols that amend *mutatis mutandis* and in a uniform way all of the necessary instruments under its administration. However, the long wait for the entry into force of numerous IMO instruments, or even at important ones remaining unratified, indicate how diplomatic and legal intricacies of treaty practice can hinder international legislation from taking effect in a timely fashion. Amendments ad hoc may also prove difficult for a synchronized entry into force. Procedures in each instrument have varying formalities, including time requirements, or require a different method to be employed for the consideration of amendments depending on the technical or legal nature of a specific provision.

Given the hurdles associated with a hard-law process, soft-law steps developing interpretations in the form of circulars recording *procès-verbal* that can mature into interpretative resolutions based on consensus may be a better direction for the incremental development of a timely and efficient regulatory scheme for autonomous ships. Nevertheless, merely the development of an interpretation should not fulfill regulatory aims, but all of these steps need to be undertaken with the intent of gradually building toward the adoption of guidelines to clarify the requirements of the relevant IMO instruments.

Irrespective of the specific option, or likely combination of options, to carry forward the regulation of autonomous ships, it must be beyond any doubt that all of the previously mentioned IMO processes, either relating to hard-law instruments or to soft-law outputs, shall operate within the constitutional reach of UNCLOS. The incorporation of GAIRS by reference in its text enables the states parties under UNCLOS to comply with international rules and standards that evolve over time to meet the changing environmental needs and technological advancements. IMO exercises a "quasi-legislative function" to implement UNCLOS through the adoption of such measures by means of specialized treaties, codes and guidelines.[35] In being thus open to further developments in the

---

[34] IMCO Res.A/500/XII, Objectives of the Organization in the 1980s §3 (Nov. 20, 1982); IMO Res.A/998/25, Need for Capacity-building for the Development and Implementation of New, and Amendments to Existing, Instruments, preamble (Jan. 3, 2008).
[35] Robert Beckman & Zhen Sun, *The Relationship between UNCLOS and IMO Instruments*, 2 Asia-Pacific J. Ocean L. & Pol'y 201, 218, 225, 235 (2017).

regulation of substantive matters, the integrity of UNCLOS's text preserves its normative authority by prohibiting reservations, and even more so by finding application "without prejudice" to any other treaty, past or future, while at the same time is binding these agreements to its general objectives and principles.[36] To that normative superiority are gravitated all of the IMO instruments in their application. When necessary, this is further explicitly attested by the inclusion into the latter of specific confirmation clauses indicating that they should not be interpreted as prejudicing the codification and progressive development of the law in UNCLOS.[37]

This approach has been reaffirmed in relation to the MASS RSE with LEG stressing that the topic has been included in the agenda of its work without prejudice to the member states' position on whether autonomous ships are permissible under international law and especially UNCLOS.[38] Future regulatory developments under the aegis of the IMO to furnish GAIRS will abide to the constitutional normative reach of UNCLOS. The need is quintessential in areas such as safety at sea, maritime security and marine environmental protection, whose regulation increasingly demands elements of accountability to be performed as international task to the benefit of public interest and international community at large. This task, as it has perceptively described through a more generic approach elsewhere, will come to be seen as "an inextricably complex systemic interaction of science, technology, economics and human values that cannot be organized simply by occasional text-centered law-making."[39] On the question of autonomous ships, this is precisely the legal interrelationship in UNCLOS, Article 94 that will control the evolving regulatory process for any determination over the requirement of manning. The analysis in consequence will next examine two important links between UNCLOS and the future development of

---

[36] UNCLOS, *supra* note 4, arts. 237, 309–11.

[37] IMO Doc. LEG/MISC.8, Implications of the United Nations Convention on the Law of the Sea for the International Maritime Organization (Jan. 30, 2014); *see, e.g.,* the standard clause featuring in MARPOL, Article 9(2), *supra* note 30, explicitly stating that "Nothing ... shall prejudice the codification and development of the law of the sea by [UNCLOS] ... nor the present or future claims and legal views of any State concerning the law of the sea and the nature and extent of coastal and flag State jurisdiction."

[38] IMO Doc. LEG/105/14, Report of the Legal Committee on the Work of its 105th Session (May 1, 2018).

[39] Phillip Allott, *Mare Nostrum: A New International Law of the Sea*, 86 AM. J. INT'L L. 764, 782 (1992).

GAIRS, namely that of the legal concept of a ship as a term not being predicated on the presence of humans onboard, and the indeterminate scope of the manning requirement in UNCLOS, Article 94(3)(b).

8.3 Elusive Definitions and Autonomous Navigation

An important preliminary question is whether autonomous ships come under the scope of UNCLOS in lack of a legal definition on ship and vessel. It will suffice here to note that both terms are used interchangeably in UNCLOS, with their ordinary meaning to be amenable to a construction based on the general rule of interpretation,[40] including by having recourse to other specialized treaties as these may be applicable, and for any other matter in absence of a conventional definition by reference to internal law.[41] This is consistent with a functional interpretation considering that the relevant definitions at the international level do not address the human element, which may be nonetheless a prescriptive requisite in terms of manning by reference to the shipmaster and crew for the purpose of national jurisdiction. In the latter case, this does not suggest that a definition stemming from domestic legal orders, which are marked by an even more disparate statutory and jurisprudential attitudes,[42] takes precedence ipso facto and ab initio at the international plane, where rights and obligations are being primarily asserted and contested. Should that have been the case, then a consequential implication, for example, with respect to international navigation, would have made the exercise of passage rights by a foreign ship contingent upon the coastal state's own interpretation.[43]

Human agency represented by the shipmaster and crew, with those to be considered present in the future either physically or constructively, should not form a constituent criterion at all, insofar as the requirement of manning is not an intrinsic characteristic of a ship's legal status for the technical purpose of the craft's designation. By way of illustration, this is

---

[40] Vienna Convention on the Law of Treaties, art. 31, May 23, 1969, 1155 U.N.T.S. 331.

[41] 2 UNITED NATIONS CONVENTION ON THE LAW OF THE SEA 1982, A COMMENTARY 45–6 ¶ 1.28(b) (1993); 3 UNITED NATIONS CONVENTION ON THE LAW OF THE SEA 1982, A COMMENTARY 101 ¶ 90.8(b) (1995).

[42] Gotthard Gauci, *Is It a Vessel, a Ship or a Boat, Is It Just a Craft, or Is It Merely a Contrivance?*, 47 J. MAR. L. & COM. 479, 499 (2016).

[43] Passage through the Great Belt (Finland v. Denmark) Provisional Measures, Order of July 29, 1991, I.C.J. Rep. 1991 p.12.

evident when a ship is being assigned to a class within the registration process once the requisite specifications of the flag state are met at the shipyard. The human element has been necessarily present in the service of the ship to ensure it can complete operational tasks and concomitant duties. Consequently, the requirement of manning will need to be functionally approached. The analysis turns toward this is an important question later. First, however, the chapter addresses the obscurity surrounding technical concepts that already are in the law.

The legal analysis appears confused by the erratic use of some terminology, such as technical terms smart and intelligent, to other designations such as uncrewed and crewless, unmanned, automated and autonomous. These terms suggest an established legal content or can be susceptive to gaining legal currency. The obscurity of these terms may be inevitable semantics at the intersection of science and the law, but resolving the legal analysis requires first that these terms carry some legal precision if they are to guide regulation.

Consequently, the most suitable term is this of the generally inclusive autonomous ship for the following reasons. The unmanned concept originally described a ship that could execute voyages being remotely operated either for the entirety or for certain phases. Its use is mainly promoted in the assumption that the conduct of operations will meet legal requirements that traditionally have been done with a human presence onboard.[44] Although now the technology may allow these requirements to be discharged remotely, a legal argument based on a constructively notional human element will be still restrictive. Further, such an approach does not evade the human-centric approach and later will require revision to cover fully autonomous ships. The same conclusion applies to gender-inclusive terms uncrewed or crewless.[45] To begin with, the term crew on the one hand mainly subsumes the entire complement of the human element onboard and in the service of the ship,[46] and

---

[44] In the context of COLREGs, *supra* note 31, *see also* DONALD LIU, *Autonomous Vessel Technology, Safety, and Ocean Impacts.* THE FUTURE OF OCEAN GOVERNANCE AND CAPACITY DEVELOPMENT 490, 491–93 (Dirk Werle et al. eds., 2019).

[45] This is an important aspect for the longevity of the term to be chosen as the introduction of automation technology in the maritime sector aspires also to increase gender parity in the era of autonomous shipping; *see* Tae-Eun Kim et al., *Impact of Automation Technology on Gender Parity in Maritime Industry*, 18 WMU J. OF MAR. AFF. 579, 592 (2019).

[46] UNCLOS, *supra* note 4, arts. 73 and 292.

it distinguishes that altogether with others, such as passengers, being present onboard.[47] On the other hand, and in spite of this term fitting in cases of fully autonomous ferries,[48] it fails to differentiate among the shipmaster, officers and crew, who fill distinctive roles regulated by the flag state.[49] Moreover, where the legal position of the shipmaster is not only set apart from the crew but surpasses even the vicarious liabilities of the shipowner, the shipmaster may be subject to penal or disciplinary responsibility.[50] Shipmasters have a duty to act in accordance with their professional judgment[51] and engage with foreign authorities and respond to information requests.[52]

The use of the term autonomous ship is preferable for its flexible conceptual depth across the technological and legal fields. The term lends itself to a varying adaptation from a technical perspective in both temporal and process parameters and does not preclude overlap with the levels of the ships' autonomy. It applies to a wide spectrum of situations, ranging from a remotely controlled ship with or without humans onboard, to a ship that performs autonomously without human intervention.[53] At the same time that this term has technical elasticity, it can also acquire a distinctive legal usage. This will be important where the parameters of the autonomous system will need to be examined in the context of delegable authority. In particular, liability, accountability and operational responsibility have to be allocated for negligence accrued by the use of artificial intelligence in ships that have a combined of autonomous and human decisions.[54]

---

[47] UNCLOS, *supra* note 4, art. 98 and 101(a) in referring to "the crew or the passengers."

[48] See the trials conducted with the M/F *Folgefonn* ferry on fully autonomous dock-to-dock operations, Wärtsilä, www.wartsila.com/media/news/28-11-2018-wartsila-achieves-notable-advances-in-automated-shipping-with-latest-successful-tests-2332144 (Nov. 28, 2018; last visited Mar. 3, 2022) (online).

[49] Contrast provision (4)(b) where "the master and officers" are distinguished from the "crew", with (4)(c) where the same distinction is diluted in UNCLOS, *supra* note 4, art. 94.

[50] UNCLOS, *supra* note 4, art. 97.

[51] *Id.*, art. 98(1)(a)–(b).

[52] *Id.*, art. 211(3).

[53] The term maritime autonomous surface ship (MASS) is defined as "a ship which, to a varying degree, can operate independently of human interaction." IMO Doc. MSC.99/WP.9, Regulatory Scoping Exercise for the Use of Maritime Autonomous Surface Ships (MASS); Report of the Working Group (May 23, 2018). *See also* IMO Doc. MSC/99/22, Report of the Maritime Safety Committee on its Ninety-Ninth Session (June 5, 2018).

[54] EUROPEAN UNION EXPERT GROUP ON LIABILITY AND NEW TECHNOLOGIES, LIABILITY FOR ARTIFICIAL INTELLIGENCE AND OTHER EMERGING DIGITAL TECHNOLOGIES 37–46 (2019).

8.4   Functional Flexibility in the Requirement
for Ship Manning

The requirement of manning appears in references to GAIRS in the context of balancing the exercise of jurisdiction between navigational freedoms on the one hand, and their safe exercise, including the protection and preservation of the marine environment, on the other.[55] The central provision on manning is contained in UNCLOS, Article 94(3)(b), which specifies that all states "shall take such measures" for its ships that are necessary to ensure their safety at sea. This remit includes the manning of ships, labor conditions and the training of crews, under UNCLOS and other international instruments. Although the provision was finalized early in the negotiations,[56] there are important aspects of the structure and substance that have been left unnoticed and they should be borne in mind for its application and interpretation. The word "shall" denotes a compelling tone of express obligation and it is immediately followed by the qualifying proviso "such ... as are necessary to ensure." The intended effect of the proviso "such ... as are necessary to ensure" has not been commented upon, in spite of the lengthy proceedings of the Third UN Conference, and the wealth of information captured by the Virginia Commentary on UNCLOS,[57] which provides an accurate account of the negotiation of each article in the treaty.[58] Likewise, the UNCLOS commentary edited by Alexander Proelß does not shed additional light.[59] The effort by the CMI is also vague, stating that:

> UNCLOS ... avoids the need to formulate more precise obligations of flag States by referring to an abstract, and continuously changing, set of international rules to be developed elsewhere. In this way it avoids "freezing" the requirements at a given point in time or at a given technical level, while still preserving the international character of the rules in

---

[55] UNCLOS, *supra* note 4, arts. 21(2); 193(3)(b); 211(6)(c); 217(1).

[56] UN Doc. A/Conf.62/WP.8/Part II, Informal Single Negotiating Text, art. 80 (1975).

[57] 3 United Nations Convention on the Law of the Sea, *supra* note 41, at 135–52.

[58] JOHN NOYES, *Memorializing UNCLOS III, Interpreting the Law of the Sea Convention, and the "Virginia Commentary."* PEACEFUL ORDER IN THE WORLD'S OCEANS 218, 219–20 (Michael Lodge & Myron Nordquist eds., 2014).

[59] THE UNITED NATIONS CONVENTION ON THE LAW OF THE SEA: A COMMENTARY 707–14 (Alexander Proelß ed., 2017). The section is titled "Measures ... Necessary to Ensure Safety at Sea" but the adjacent commentary only repeats that Article 94(3) obliges states to take measures "necessary to ensure safety at sea."

question. The more precise extent of flag States' obligations is hence left to be developed by the IMO in particular.[60]

I disagree with the generalization by the CMI. The IMO through the modality of GAIRS aims to set relevant standards for the sake of uniformity and consistency in shipping. The proviso "such ... as are necessary to ensure" in UNCLOS, Article 94 is founded upon a functional flexibility that rests with the states individually. The obligation to take measures as set forth in UNCLOS, Article 94(3)(b) should be functionally construed to fulfill the material objective of attaining safety at sea, and this sequentially forms an obligation of conduct within the margin of the flag state's regulatory discretion. This interpretation is also supported by the available *travaux préparatoires*, which on the point of the manning requirement, are traced back to the ILC Articles concerning the Law of the Sea[61] and the First UN Conference on the Law of the Sea (1958) that produced the corresponding provisions in Article 10 of the 1958 High Seas Convention.[62] More specifically, the ILC, Article 34(1)(b), titled "Safety of navigation," provided that: "[e]very State is required to issue for ships under its jurisdiction regulations to ensure safety at sea with regard inter alia to: ... The crew, which must be adequate to the needs of the ship and enjoy reasonable labour conditions." It is thus plain that the requirement of manning, being subsumed under the term crew is functionally established "to ensure safety at sea" and on the basis of being "adequate to the needs of the ship." In doing so, the ILC suggested that this was to lay down general principles and not to settle any technical questions in detail regarding any of the standards under the proposed article.[63] The approach of introducing a formal rule in principle regarding manning was accepted without any substantial changes at the ensuing negotiations of the 1958 UN Conference. Based on the ILC proposed Article 34, adopted Article 10 reads in part, "[e]very State shall

---

[60] Comité Maritime International, Position Paper on Unmanned Ships, released following the Assembly of 2018 in London; the position on UNCLOS, Article 94 is recorded on page 4.

[61] UN Doc. A/CN.4/104, Report of the International Law Commission on the Work of its Eighth Session, Apr. 23–July 4, 1956, Official Records of the General Assembly, Eleventh Session, Supplement No. 9 (A/3159) (1956).

[62] Convention on the High Seas, Apr. 29, 1958, 13 U.S.T. 2312, T.I.A.S. No. 5200, 450 U.N.T.S. 11.

[63] ARTICLES CONCERNING THE LAW OF THE SEA, WITH COMMENTARIES, adopted by the ILC at its eighth session in 1956 [UN Doc. A/CN.4/104]; available in 1956 2 YEARBOOK OF THE INTERNATIONAL LAW COMMISSION 265 (hereinafter ILC Yearbook).

take such measures for ships under its flag as are necessary to ensure safety at sea with regard, inter alia, to: ... The manning of ships and labour conditions for crews taking into account the applicable international labour instruments."

At this point of the provision's drafting history, the functional requirement of crew's adequacy for the needs of the ship evolved into the provision, "such measures ... as are necessary to ensure." This change in the text is reflected in an amending proposal by the UK in which the introduction of the article clearly stressed the flag state's discretion. The change replaced the opening words of paragraph 1 with "[e]very State shall satisfy itself concerning, and take such measures as are necessary to ensure, safety at sea for ships under its jurisdiction with regard, inter alia, to."[64] The amended text was further improved in a joint proposal with the Netherlands to render the final version as "[e]very State shall take such measures for ships under its flag as are necessary to ensure safety at sea."[65] This text was adopted without any prolonged deliberation, and the only statement on record was made by the UK delegation as a joint sponsor, in clarifying its position on internationally accepted standards. In doing so, it conveyed a functional approach to the requirement of manning in stating: "[The UK] has never found it practicable or desirable to legislate as to the adequacy of a ship's crew, but maintains a sufficient control by means of the power to detain a ship which is unseaworthy as a result of undermanning."[66] A similar mindset had been revealed previously by the Special Rapporteur Jean Pierre Adrien in proposing to the ILC for inclusion a definition in which a commercial ship was considered to be "Un navire est un engin apte à se mouvoir dans les espaces maritimes à l'exclusion de l'espace aérien, avec l'armement et l'équipage qui lui sont propres en vue des services que com port e l'industrie à laquelle il est employé."[67] While the definition was not taken forward, the

---

[64] UN Doc. A/Conf.13/C.2/L.82, Gambia, Ghana, Ivory Coast, Kenya, Lesotho, Liberia, Libyan Arab Republic, Madagascar, Mali, Mauritania, Morocco, Senegal, Sierra Leone, Sudan, Tunisia, United Republic of Cameroon, United Republic of Tanzania and Zaire: draft articles on the exclusive economic zone (1958).

[65] UN Doc. A/Conf.13/C.2/L.114, Netherlands and United Kingdom of Great Britain and Northern Ireland: proposal (Article 34) (Apr. 8, 1958) (every state shall take such measures to ensure safety at sea for ships under its flag with regard to, inter alia, signals and communication, and construction, equipment and seaworthiness of ships).

[66] 4 UNITED NATIONS CONVENTION ON THE LAW OF THE SEA OFFICIAL RECORDS 58 (1958). The UK national MLA response to CMI retains this position.

[67] UN Doc. A/CN.4/79, Sixth Report on the Regime of the High Seas by Mr. J. P. A. François, Special Rapporteur (1954) ("a ship is a craft capable of moving in maritime

text of the provision states the view that the manning requirement is determined by the purpose of the ship.

Further support is lent to my argument in favor of the functional flexibility in the manning requirement by UNCLOS, Article 94(4), which provides that a state shall take such measures for ships flying its flag. The requirement that "such measures shall include those necessary to ensure," creates flexibility by entrusting the flag state to determine the appropriateness of the level as well as the form of those measures.[68] Referring to subparagraph (3)(b), the article directs states when fulfilling such necessary measures to "[t]ake into account the applicable international instruments." Upon that direction for the requirement of manning, there have been adopted specialized technical standards under the International Convention for the Safety of Life at Sea (SOLAS) that require the state to maintain measures for the purpose of ensuring that all seagoing ships flying its flag are "sufficiently and efficiently manned."[69] These measures are to be considered in the subsequent reading of UNCLOS, Article 94(3)(b).[70]

Distinctively, the regulatory approach is based on the functional flexibility of these requirements while avoiding any prescriptive constraint either in the form or the number of the humans on board the ship.[71] Specifically, the determination of safe manning is considered as a function, to which the application of the guidelines explicitly recommend the adoption of a GBS approach,[72] for the ship's performance in taking into account relevant factors such as, inter alia, the level of ship automation and the construction and equipment of the ship.[73] The language can therefore be considered permissive for autonomous ships as further to the substantive functional attributes of the technical requirement of manning, the general standards are formed as a recommendation for "international acceptance of broad principles as a framework for [flag

---

spaces to the exclusion of air space, with its own equipment and crew for the services provided by the industry to which it is employed").

[68] UNCLOS, *supra* note 4, art. 94(4)(b)–(c).

[69] Article 2 SOLAS, in conjunction with chapter V (Safety of navigation) regulation 14(1) (Ship's manning) of the annex.

[70] 3 UNITED NATIONS CONVENTION ON THE LAW OF THE SEA 1982, A COMMENTARY 147–8 §94.8(f) (1995).

[71] IMO Res.A/1047(27), Principles of Minimum Safe Manning (Nov. 30, 2011).

[72] *Id.* Annex 1 "Guidelines for the Application of Minimum Safe Manning"; Annex 5 "Framework for Determining Minimum Safe Manning."

[73] *Id.* Annex 2 "Guidelines for the Determination of Minimum Safe Manning," §1.1 (3)–(4).

State] administrations."[74] Correspondingly, states have pursued this approach by articulating along functional terms the objective of safe manning in domestic legislation,[75] driven by the innovations in the design and operating technology of the ship, that among other aspects may address both the number and organization of the crew.[76] Manning levels without doubt are going to be reduced commensurately to the phased adoption of ship automation technologies. This dynamic will eliminate the necessity of the human element as it is currently perceived.

8.5   The IMO MASS Regulatory Scoping Exercise

As part of its work toward integrating new and advancing technologies in the regulatory framework, the IMO has included the question of the operation of autonomous ships in its strategic plan. To this end, the organization introduced the MASS RSE to assess IMO instruments relating to safety at sea, maritime security, and liability and compensation.[77] The Maritime Safety Committee (MSC) has been especially active in this regard.

Prompted by member states with a keen interest to include the issue immediately on its agenda,[78] the MSC was the first committee to initiate the MASS RSE in embarking on the task of determining how the safe, secure and environmentally sound operation of autonomous ships may be introduced in the context of a preliminary selection of IMO specialized treaties. The framework of the MASS RSE endorsed a two-step methodology. First, pertinent treaty provisions were identified following an initial review considering their prima facie application. Second, analysis of the provisions was examined, taking into account the human element, technology and operational factors, with a view to ascertaining the need for equivalence in the treaties under consideration or

---

[74] *Id.*, preamble.
[75] The Australian Navigation Act 2012 No. 128/2012 is an example of a GBS approach to minimum safe manning.
[76] *See* the US practice since 1980s in Effective Manning of the US Merchant Fleet (1984).
[77] The full list can be accessed at Autonomous Shipping on the IMO, www.imo.org/en/MediaCentre/HotTopics/Pages/Autonomous-shipping.aspx (last visited Mar. 2, 2022) (online).
[78] IMO Doc. 98/20/2, Maritime Autonomous Surface Ships: Proposal for a Regulatory Scoping Exercise. Submitted by Denmark, Estonia, Finland, Japan, the Netherlands, Norway, the Republic of Korea, the UK and the United States (Feb. 27, 2017).

developing interpretations, amendment of existing instruments or development of new instruments.[79]

While the conclusion of the MASS RSE is pending, the release of the interim guidelines during this process covers testing in operational trials for the evaluation of alternative methods of performing specific functions or satisfying regulatory requirements by ships with varying degrees of automation.[80] Although serving to provide a temporary legal framework for the trials, the interim guidelines have already proved in principle the feasibility of a regulatory structure to facilitate the future operation of autonomous ships. This principle envisages that the operations "should be conducted in a manner that provide at least the same degree of safety, security and protection of the environment as provided by the relevant [treaty standard]."[81] To accommodate this principle of equivalency, the interim guidelines demonstrated a functional formulation based on the GBSs, which is to be pursued by appropriate safeguards against the cause of significant harm. Regarding the latter, the principle of equivalency has been established in conjunction with the general principle of "no-harm," as the interim guidelines envisaged that "risks . . . should be appropriately identified . . . to reduce the risks, to as low as reasonably practicable and acceptable."[82]

8.6 Toward a Goal-Based Standard Setting Approach

The legal argument on the functional flexibility inherent in UNCLOS, Article 94(3)(b) is also reflected in IMO practice and GAIRS and arises from a purely technical standpoint. The IMO has been gradually applying a goal-based philosophy to the development of new technical requirements, often by means of equivalents and alternatives as provided for in various specialized treaties in the areas of safety at sea, including the prevention and control of pollution.[83] The goal-based notion aims at setting high-level goals, which are composed of at least one functional

---

[79] MSC/100 (Dec. 3–7, 2018), with Legal (LEG) and Facilitation (FAL) following the same approach minorly adjusted as approved in LEG/106 (Mar. 27–29, 2019) and FAL/43 (Apr. 8–12, 2019), respectively, www.imo.org/en/MediaCentre/MeetingSummaries/ (last visited Mar. 3, 2022) (online).

[80] IMO Doc. MSC.1/Circ.1604, Interim Guidelines for MASS Trials (June 14, 2019).

[81] *Id.*, annex, ¶1.

[82] *Id.*, annex, ¶2§1(1).

[83] IMO Doc. MSC.287/87, Adoption of the International Goal-Based Ship Construction Standards for Bulk Carriers and Oil Tankers (May 20, 2010).

requirement to be met through the development and implementation of detailed regulations, rules and standards for ships. These are then subject to verification procedures by independent auditors within a framework that comprises maritime administrations including, where allowed by each treaty, classification societies acting as recognised organizations. This approach enables the move from the traditional prescriptive-based regulation toward one that is goal driven and performance oriented, considering the sophisticated nature of the maritime industry.[84]

For example, the concept of safety is conceived predominately as a functional state or condition in which a structured application of risk-based methodologies can ensure the absence of unacceptable levels of risk. A generally prescriptive regulatory regime thus will be unsuitable for autonomous ships, especially taking into account the rapid pace of technological advancements.[85] In fact, the industry standards being already employed to support the new level of technical requirements of marine applications with increasing autonomy signify a strong trend toward a GBS approach to safety and operational performance requirements.[86]

Shifting the regulatory paradigm in the direction of the GBS approach will be essential to accommodate efficiently novel technologies and effectively address the associated safety risks, including maritime security threats.[87] Many of these are gradually transforming into critical hazards in the cyber domain, where commercial shipping interests can be targeted throughout a spectrum of activities, ranging from the instalment of malicious software and fraud to intervention in geopolitical conflicts. In response, the *Guidelines on Maritime Cyber Risk Management* (2017) set a GBS approach to safeguard shipping from emerging cyber threats and related vulnerabilities by recommending functional elements to support effective risk management. These received the form of high-level recommendations to facilitate their flexible incorporation into the existing risk management processes that are complementary to the safety

---

[84] IMO Doc. MSC.1/Circ.1394/Rev.2, Generic Guidelines for Developing IMO Goal-Based Standards (Aug. 7, 2019).

[85] Steven Mallam et al., *The Human Element in Future Maritime Operations – Perceived Impact of Autonomous Shipping*, 63 ERGONOMICS 334, 341 (2020).

[86] International Association of Classification Societies, Position Paper on MASS (2018).

[87] Although originally the concepts of safety at sea and maritime security were developed independently, now they are to be seen in many respects intertwined in making their fusion unavoidable. JAMES KRASKA & RAUL PEDROZO, INTERNATIONAL MARITIME SECURITY LAW 5 (2013).

and security management practices under the IMO treaty regime, and especially the International Safety and Management Code of SOLAS (ISM code).[88] In this framework, the MSC reaffirmed that an approved safety management system should take into account cyber risks in accordance with the objectives and functional requirements of the ISM code. Domestic implementation has been encouraged to ensure that cyber risks are appropriately addressed, since January 1, 2021.[89]

Even more important questions are bound to feature in the context of autonomous ships given the increasing reliance of their information and operational technology shipboard systems on digitization, automation and integration within a highly interactive cyber domain system. It must be expected that a goal-based approach will apply to autonomous ships for matters requiring functional flexibility in terms of regulation to achieve the material objective of safety at sea. For safety aspects in which a holistic perspective is essential, such as this of assuring cyber resilience,[90] the existing treaty regime applicable to commercial shipping is reflected in the goal-based regulatory philosophy. In furtherance of the regime, industry-leading technical stakeholders have opted for the development of requirements within a goal-based framework to guide the implementation of remotely controlled and autonomous functions.[91]

The interim guidelines reflect the GBS and already have influenced the first outputs of domestic and regional legislation to promote development of autonomous ships without compromising the interests of safety at sea, maritime security and the protection of the marine environment.[92] The discussions at the MSC have emphasized that the operational trials should be undertaken against goals being set for the scoping of reliability, robustness, resiliency and redundancy to test safety aspects in the operations of autonomous ships. This approach is expected to afford the flexibility required to move forward in the development of a regulatory framework, while balancing the benefits derived from new and advancing technologies against safety and security concerns, the

---

[88] IMO Res.A/741/18, International Management Code for the Safe Operation of Ships and for Pollution Prevention (Nov. 4, 1993).

[89] IMO Doc. MSC.428/98, Maritime Cyber Risk Management in Safety Management System (June 16, 2017), annex 10.

[90] See BIMCO et al., GUIDELINES ON CYBER SECURITY ONBOARD SHIPS (2020).

[91] AMERICAN BUREAU OF SHIPPING, ADVISORY ON AUTONOMOUS FUNCTIONALITY (2020).

[92] As demonstrated in the adoption of the "goal-based approach, as far as possible" within the scope and application of the EUROPEAN UNION, OPERATIONAL GUIDELINES ON TRIALS OF MARITIME AUTONOMOUS SURFACE SHIPS ¶2 (v1 2020).

impact on the environment and to advance international trade, balancing the potential costs to the industry, and their impact on personnel, both onboard and ashore.[93]

8.7   Procedural Obligations and Functional Flexibility

In the light of the foregoing analysis over the emerging GBS safety-level approach and the call for functional flexibility to its regulation, UNCLOS, Article 94(3)–(4) does not impede the introduction of fully autonomous ships. Certainly, the technological restraints had until recently premised the practice of the relevant rules upon human presence and control onboard ships. But what shall be the case when the ship has reached the edge of technology where the human element can be entirely removed? Then it may not be necessary to implement human-based rules. The requirement of manning does not raise an insurmountable substantive difficulty since the standard exists only to functionally ensure the safety of navigation without purporting to acquire the authority of a generally prescriptive condition either in terms of physical presence or a numerical minimum complement as prerequisite. However, there are two correlative and successively operating procedural obligations to be discharged primarily by the flag state that immediately follow from this functional interpretation.

First, there is a general obligation of observance for each state "in taking the measures called for in paragraphs 3 and 4 . . . to conform to [GAIRS]."[94] The scope and practical utility of this obligation not only differs among the distinct rules and standards but it should moreover be measured against the underlying regulatory goals, such as universality, precision and their adaptability to change.[95] Thus, the extent of this obligation is not clear. When it comes down to the application of the manning requirement, in relation to which subparagraph (3)(b) constitutes the lex specialis field of reference within the interpretative boundaries of UNCLOS, Article 94, the scope of observance appears to reside within the confines of the flag state obligation to "[t]ake into account the

---

[93] MSC/98 (June 7–16, 2017), as well as the opening speech by IMO Secretary-General at the MSC/99, www.imo.org/en/MediaCentre/MeetingSummaries/ (May 16, 2018; last visited Mar. 2, 2022) (online); indicative of this approach is the broad formulation on the "cyber risk management" objective in the interim guidelines, annex, ¶ 2 §10.

[94] UNCLOS, *supra* note 4, art. 94(5).

[95] Bernard Oxman, *The Duty to Respect Generally Accepted International Standards*, 24 NYU J. INT'L L. & POL'Y 109, 129, 144ff. (1991).

applicable international instruments," rather than being "[r]equired to conform to" a particular standard. Certainly, these are two different stipulations concerning the scope of observance sought and they are not necessarily coextensive. In relation to the requirement of manning and in the absence of a prohibitive rule,[96] a flag state is not prevented from forging ahead to develop and register an autonomous ship by fixing, as in any other case, the conditions for the grant of its nationality.[97]

Second, by entertaining exclusive flag jurisdiction,[98] the state assumes the international responsibility for the fulfillment of an explicit obligation to pay "due regard" to the legitimate interests, rights and freedoms of other states as set forth in UNCLOS, Articles 58(3) and 87(2). To meet this obligation, the flag state shall effectively exercise jurisdiction and control in order to secure the implementation of its duties,[99] including to ensure safety of navigation by autonomous ships flying its flag,[100] and in this context by having determined in domestic legislation the manning requirements within its "margin of discretion."[101] Once the flag state decides to exercise its discretion, and this may take the form of legislative or administrative modalities, the obligation of observance changes under the function of the operating provision "such ... as are necessary to ensure" into an obligation of conduct toward the attainment of the material objective of safety at sea and protection of the marine environment by implication of the specialized treaty regime.

For instance, consider the case of an event that is attributable to the performance of an autonomous ship – operational discharges, navigational accident or any other similar incident – resulting in marine pollution. UNCLOS makes a direct reference to regulatory aspects regarding " design, construction, equipment, operation and manning" within the context of the measures designed to ensure the safety at sea

---

[96] The Case of the SS *Lotus* Judgment 1927 PCIJ, A/No. 10, 18–19.
[97] ASV *C-Worker 7*, a below 5 ton deadweight craft engaging in geographically restricted operations for subsea positioning, surveying and environmental monitoring is the first autonomous ship that was signed in the UK. *See* UK Ship Register.
[98] Special provision of 94(6) in conjunction with the broader rule on legal status in UNCLOS, art. 92(1).
[99] M/V Saiga No. 2 (St. Vincent v. Guinea), Case No. 2, Judgment of July 1, 1999, ITLOS Rep. 1999 p.10, at §§ 41-2 §§ 82-3.
[100] The obligation of due regard has been unambiguously reiterated regarding the protection of the environment in the "Aim" of the interim guidelines, Annex, ¶ 1 § 1.
[101] Yoshinobu Takei, *Assessing Flag State Performance in Legal Terms: Clarifications of the Margin of Discretion*, 28 INT'L J. MAR. & COAST. L. 97, 118 (2013).

and prevention of vessel source pollution and emergency response.[102] In these circumstances, the flag state may have exposure to international responsibility on several grounds regarding a wide range of acts or omissions to prevent, reduce and control pollution of the marine environment. In the absence of an applicable international regime, it may be unclear whether the state has ensured an effective system to discharge its obligations.[103] Can registration, classification, survey and any other process to attest technical requirements, including those being normally expressed in innominate terms, manifest elements of sovereign authority to the extent of being undertaken, or otherwise allowed, within the margin of the state's discretion?[104] It may be unclear what recourse is available in accordance with its domestic legislation for prompt and adequate compensation, reparations or other relief for civil and criminal damages caused by a ship under its exclusive jurisdiction.[105]

8.8   Functional Flexibility and Standard of Review

These questions open the prospect of third-party review through dispute settlement,[106] to examine such actions or omissions by the flag state in exercising its discretion. The need for this usually arises when an international norm or obligation is so open-ended or indeterminate as to create critical scope for its interpretation and application. The category of rules demonstrating such intrinsic legal disposition comprise also these requiring states to take "necessary" measures in order to achieve certain

---

[102] UNCLOS, *supra* note 4, art. 194(3)(b).

[103] As in any other occasion of ship-source pollution, the flag state's performance will be questioned in terms of any failure to exercise its extensive jurisdiction to prevent pollution; *see* BRIAN SMITH, STATE RESPONSIBILITY AND THE MARINE ENVIRONMENT 147–66 (1988).

[104] By reflecting on the conduct of entities exercising elements of governmental authority as envisaged by the ILC in Article 5 of the Draft Articles on Responsibility of States for Internationally Wrongful Acts (2001). *See* the controversies over the classification process coming within the scope of *acta jure imperii* by relying on *lato sensu* governmental functions emanating through UNCLOS, arts. 90, 91 and 94 featuring in *Rina* [2020] EUECJ C-641/18.

[105] UNCLOS, *supra* note 4, arts. 235(2); 304.

[106] ROBERT BECKMAN, *Responsibility of Flag States for Pollution of the Marine Environment: The Relevance of the UNCLOS Dispute Settlement Regime.* FREEDOM OF NAVIGATION AND GLOBALIZATION 257, 272–76 (Myron Nordquist et al. eds., 2015).

policy goals.[107] The provisions on manning, such as a crew or master are "necessary to ensure" represents this category of rules. This requirement applies especially within the context of autonomous ships, as the adoption of international standards, especially those being set through a goal-based approach, will increase the flag state's margin of discretion for a decision on the determination of safe manning in UNCLOS, Article 94. On that account, the flag state's responsibility is confined in the "due regard" obligation, which insofar as not being formulated as a universal rule of conduct, falls under the test of due diligence.[108] Two important matters on the applicable standard of review merit further consideration: the expected content of the reviewing standard to apply and the level on which the standard is to be set for autonomous ships.

The content of a standard to review the regulatory discretion of the flag state in having functionally determined the level of manning will need to be commensurable to the substantive obligation of "[t]aking such measures as are ... necessary to ensure safety at sea" under UNCLOS, Article 94(3). The meaning of "ensure" does not entail the achievement of a result in every case, but rather it is one of conduct, as evidenced in the measures being of a "regulatory or administrative" nature,[109] aiming to "[d]eploy adequate means, to exercise best possible efforts, and to do the utmost to obtain this result."[110] However, the substance of this obligation will materially integrate the adjoining duty of preventing safety risks. This prospect will afford a critical expanse for the general legal principle of prevention and its future regulation of autonomous ships. Although the principle of prevention in its contemporary form is mostly invoked in the context of environmental jurisprudence,[111] it originates from a much broader area regarding the exercise of due diligence in the performance of state obligations at large.[112] Germane obligations also encompass matters connected to safety obligations under

---

[107] Jin-Hyun Paik, *Standard of Review in the Law of the Sea: Reflections from the Bench.* Ocean Law and Policy: 20 Years under UNCLOS 359 (Carlos Espósito et al. eds., 2017).

[108] *Supra* note 19, at p. 40, §129.

[109] Pulp Mills on the River Uruguay (Argentina v. Uruguay), Judgment, I.C.J. Rep. 2010 p.14, 67 §187.

[110] Responsibilities and Obligations of States with Respect to Activities in the Area, Advisory Opinion of Feb. 1, 2011, ITLOS Rep. 2011 p.10, 41 §110.

[111] Trail Smelter Arbitration (US v. Canada) 3 U.N. RIAA 1905, 1965 (1938 and 1941); UNCLOS, art. 194(2).

[112] Alabama Claims of the United States of America against Great Britain, 19 U.N. RIAA 125 (1872). The Tribunal offered a broad definition of the "due diligence" standard.

the exclusive jurisdiction or control of a state,[113] as in the area of safety of international navigation.[114] Approaching the content of the reviewing standard this way requires a balancing exercise for the introduction and advancement of new but risky technologies within the remit of UNCLOS. Although it is unreasonable to make the state liable for each and every violation "committed by persons under its jurisdiction," it is also unsatisfactory to rely on the simple application of a principle that the conduct of private individuals is never attributable to the state as a matter of international law.[115]

Following the analysis on the substantive obligation to take "such measures as are … necessary to ensure safety at sea," the second consideration in the context of autonomous ships should be the benchmark level to assess the acts and omissions of the flag state within its regulatory discretion to functionally determine the level of manning. Given that the "obligation to ensure" envisions conduct rather result, the standard for autonomous ships should be set through the principle of equivalency on the level of operating at least as safely as human.[116] This threshold may be either variant or *de minimis*. Setting a comparable threshold standard does not represent an extraneous practice for UNCLOS. The formula requiring that a state's domestic legislation "shall at least have the same effect" as those set under an international regime also applies to the prevention, reduction and control of pollution of the marine environment from ships.[117]

Moreover, in the context of safety per se, the model of technical equivalence has been progressively utilized in SOLAS regulations to enable states to demonstrate that the level of safety achieved through alternative arrangements is at least equivalent to the prescriptive

---

[113] *See* Christopher Weeramantry commenting *ex cathedra* on the burden of proving safety for acts related to environmental damage in its polysemous dissenting opinion in Legality of the Use by a State of Nuclear Weapons in Armed Conflict, Advisory Opinion, I.C.J. Rep. 1996 p.66, 280–81.

[114] Corfu Channel Case (Merits) (UK v. Albania), (1949) I.C.J. Rep. 1949, at 4 (Grave omissions of a state in failing to prevent within its jurisdiction safety hazards that resulted in damage and loss of human life on foreign ships).

[115] Responsibilities and Obligations of States with Respect to Activities in the Area, *supra* note 110, 41 §112.

[116] Alexandros X. M. Ntovas, *Full Steam Ahead for Unmanned Ships? (Interview)*, THE GREAT CIRCLE, *reprinted in* Safety 4 Sea, https://safety4sea.com/full-steam-ahead-for-unmanned-ships (Jan. 28, 2016; last visited Mar. 3, 2022) (online).

[117] UNCLOS, *supra* note 4, art. 211(2).

criteria.[118] Guided by the goal-based philosophy, these allowances are made to support the advancement of technological innovations as long as following a holistic assessment determines that the risk introduced by the novel arrangements is no more than is guaranteed by the prescriptive regulations. In similar terms, functionally equivalent situations are being contemplated for the gradual development of a liability framework to include artificial intelligence aspects of autonomy, either directly or by way of analogy.

While there is a strong belief that the advancing technology will minimize the risks associated with human errors, the safety level to induce confidence in the shipping industry may need to be even higher.[119] This uncertainty was identified during the deliberations of the RSE undertaken by the MSC, in acknowledging that autonomous ships could also introduce new risks to maritime safety, security and environment that are not yet understood. Therefore, innovations in autonomy should be treated as an evolving technology so that requirements can be maintained with greater agility, and in this regard, "[t]he next steps should be based on the principles of flexibility, integrity and efficiency".[120] Bearing that in mind, it is doubtful whether the currently conceptual approach employed to adjudge the promise of increased safety of autonomous ships in making comparisons to the factor of "human error"[121] will be sufficient to enable the development in law of a general *de minimis* threshold.

For the foreseeable future, the level to review safety standards applicable on autonomous ships should be set on a case-by-case basis. This model accords with the standards of diligence under the duty of prevention that in principle assesses the state conduct against what is generally considered to be appropriate and proportional to the degree of risk at a given circumstance. Practically, this means that the threshold standard

---

[118] IMO Doc. MSC.1/Circ.1455 Guidelines for the Approval of Alternatives and Equivalents as Provided for in Various IMO Instruments (May 24, 2013).

[119] Hadi Ghaderi, *Autonomous Technologies in Short Sea Shipping: Trends, Feasibility and Implications*, 39 TRANSPORT REV. 152, 169 (2019).

[120] *See* the outcomes of the first intersessional MASS RSE Working Group, Sept. 2–6, 2019 as recorded in the briefing released by the Institute of Marine Engineering, Science and Technology (2019), www.imarest.org/policy-news/technical-leadership (last visited Mar. 3, 2022) (online).

[121] ÅSA HOEM ET AL., *At Least as Safe as Manned Shipping? Autonomous Shipping, Safety and "Human Error."* SAFETY AND RELIABILITY – SAFE SOCIETIES IN A CHANGING WORLD 417, 421 (Stein Haugen et al. eds., 2018).

applicable, for instance, to an incident involving the allision of an autonomous barge transporting perishable cargo will be set lower compared to that of an autonomous tanker against the duty of preventing damage to the environment, and that of an autonomous passenger ship against the prevention of injury or loss of life. The threshold standard therefore will need to be kept variable to respond to the risks of the evolving technology. The ILC commentary on the concept of prevention is quite relevant, providing that "what would be considered a reasonable standard of care or due diligence may change with time; what might be considered an appropriate and reasonable procedure, standard or rule at one point in time may not be considered as such at some point in the future."[122] An even more opportune direction regarding the flag state's regulatory discretion, as advanced here, is afforded by the ILC finding that "hence, due diligence in *ensuring safety* requires a State to keep abreast of technological changes and scientific developments."[123]

8.9 Conclusion

A recent study posed two favorable scenarios for the adoption of autonomy in maritime transports by considering technical feasibility, social boundary conditions (including legislation, policy and social acceptance) and economic benefit. The "revolutionary" scenario envisages the adoption of autonomous ships at a fast pace driven by increasing business and trade demands on a large geographical scale that will require filling existing gaps in regulation at the national and international level. Conversely, the "evolutionary" scenario predicts a slow adoption process induced by projects continuing to be implemented under domestic legislation, based on the assumption that economic benefits are low while technical or legal boundaries remain high.[124] The latter postulation seems more plausible and accords with the trajectory of the current developments.

On the legal aspects, an evolutionary pace, although not precluding limited and carefully chosen modifications for the application of

---

[122] International Law Commission, *Draft Articles on Prevention of Transboundary Harm from Hazardous Activities*, 2 Y.B. INT'L L. COMMISSION 153–55 (art. 3, Prevention) Commentary (2001).

[123] *Id.* (emphasis added).

[124] WORLD MARITIME UNIVERSITY, TRANSPORT 2040 – AUTOMATION, TECHNOLOGY AND EMPLOYMENT – THE FUTURE OF WORK 16 (2019).

UNCLOS within waters under national jurisdiction, will be guided mainly by soft-law steps.[125] Shipping has always been an industry conducive to technological progress, and the prospect of full autonomy, as distant as it may be, may be leading the maritime sector toward unprecedent changes with ramifications that will be disruptive to the traditional shipping environment require careful management.[126] It is crucial that this progress fully respects the global rule of law and *order public* in regulating the autonomous ships in a manner that will not attempt to circumvent established methods for making, amending and interpreting treaties.[127] To this end in the preceding analysis, I broached an interpretative account of the functional construction of UNCLOS, Article 94(3)(b) that embraces the introduction of innovatory technologies for autonomous shipping in affording to the flag state the regulatory discretion to determine the manning requirement without conceding its responsibility to assure safety at sea. As the developments will continue apace, the interpretation on functional flexibility can provide the essentially organic scope of the manning requirement to evolve alongside the effective safety levels that can be assured by the technology. This can be best sustained by reference to the emerging technical philosophy at the IMO and considering the early signs from the MASS RSE. Further, shifting the law-making paradigm on autonomous ships in the direction of an exploratory approach based on GBS is consistent with the expectations of the stakeholders to exploit and advance technology without compromising the safety interests of the society.[128]

In conclusion, this argument applies equally well on either of the two postured scenarios in confirming that UNCLOS will ever remain the milieu of the perennial winds ascribed to the cardinal direction of technological progress in the law of the sea. The arrival of autonomous ships reflects the next fundamental innovation in the shipping industry

---

[125] Natalie Klein et al., *Maritime Autonomous Vehicles: New Frontiers in the Law of the Sea*, 69 Int'l & Comp. L. Q. 719, 734 (2020).

[126] Marine Insight, Autonomous Shipping: Small Steps Not a Giant Leap, www .marineinsight.com/shipping-news/autonomous-shipping-small-steps-not-a-giant-leap/ (July 29, 2019; last visited Mar. 3, 2022) (online).

[127] Craig Allen, *Determining the Legal Status of Unmanned Maritime Vehicles: Formalism vs Functionalism*, 49 J. Mar. L. & Com. 477, 513–14 (2018).

[128] Exploiting Autonomy Will Require More Agile Approaches to Regulation and Safety, www.maritimeuk.org/media-centre/blog-posts/blog-exploiting-autonomy-will-require-more-agile-approaches-regulation-and-safety/ (Aug. 1, 2020; last visited Mar. 2, 2022) (online).

with a question as to "when," not anymore of "if." Although the scenario of a fully autonomous ship engaging in unrestricted geographical navigation may still be beyond reach, when all of the required conditions are met, a substantial part of international seaborne trade may shift in the context of multimodal global transport networks toward fixed sea routes for point-to-point voyages by robotic shuttles, resembling the ones that once were called ships.

Artificial Intelligence to Facilitate Safe Navigation of Ships

STEVEN GEOFFREY KEATING

9.1 The Sea and AI

This chapter proposes that artificial intelligence (AI) can improve maritime domain decision-making in the areas of hydrographic services and safety of navigation, subject to the legal regimes in the broad corpus of the international law of the sea. Like the sea, AI has unknown potential and compels our curiosity. The tantalizing promise of AI has motivated scientific investigation for decades.[1] AI can improve hydrographic charting and safety of navigation at sea. The following sections examine what aspects of AI may be employed within the framework of the international law of the sea to maximize safe and sustainable use of the oceans. At present, AI is neutral, and it will support cooperative activities as well as competitive ones.

Successful, sustainable use of the maritime domain necessitates effective maritime domain awareness (MDA), defined as "the effective understanding of anything associated with the maritime domain that could impact the security, safety, economy, or [the] environment."[2] MDA is maximized by using geospatial intelligence (GEOINT), an intelligence discipline defined as "the exploitation and analysis of imagery and geospatial information to describe, assess, and visually depict physical features and geographically referenced activities on or about the earth. GEOINT consists of imagery, imagery intelligence, and geospatial information."[3] Outside of a statutory construct, GEOINT is "the perception, cognition, computation, control, reaction, and understanding of physical features and geographically referenced activities."[4] Both states and private entities use GEOINT to better understand the oceans, using both remote sensing and direct observations to analyze physical features, processes and potential outcomes as well as to study geographically referenced activities on the Earth.[5]

Following this introductory section, this chapter contains four additional sections: "Defining Concepts in AI"; "Legal Duties Relating to

---

[1] English mathematician and computational pioneer Alan Turing's 1950 article "Computing Machinery and Intelligence" introduced "arguably established artificial intelligence as a modern field of study." *See* MARTIN FORD, ARCHITECTS OF INTELLIGENCE: THE TRUTH ABOUT AI FROM THE PEOPLE BUILDING IT 13 (2018).

[2] The White House, NATIONAL STRATEGY FOR MARITIME SECURITY: NATIONAL MARITIME DOMAIN AWARENESS PLAN iv (2013). This document defines the maritime domain as being all areas and things of, on, under, relating to, adjacent to or bordering on a sea, ocean or other navigable waterway, including all maritime-related activities, infrastructure, people, cargo, vessels and other conveyances. *Id.*

[3] 10 U.S.C. § 467(5) (2021).

[4] Juergen Dold & Jessica Groopman, *The Future of Geospatial Intelligence*, 20 GEO-SPATIAL INFO. SCI. 151 (2017).

[5] Steven Geoffrey Keating, *Rock or Island? It Was an UNCLOS Call: The Legal Consequence of Geospatial Intelligence to the 2016 South China Sea Arbitration and the Law of the Sea*, 9 J. NAT'L SEC. L. & POL'Y 514, 519–22 (2018).

Hydrography and Safe Navigation"; "AI and Disaster Prevention"; and "Final Thoughts and Conclusion."

9.2   Defining Concepts in AI

This section defines foundational AI concepts to give legal practitioners a working understanding of how the virtual AI domain intersects with the maritime domain.

9.2.1   Definitional Building Blocks

9.2.1.1   Intelligence

Any analysis of the impact of AI on the oceans and international maritime law should first define the term intelligence. There is not a universally accepted definition of intelligence,[6] but there are necessary elements – "[t]he ability to learn, understand and make judgments or have opinions that are based on reason."[7] Legg and Hutter offer this definition: "[i]ntelligence measures an agent's ability to achieve goals in a wide range of environments."[8] Intelligence is not merely the ability to deal with the known environment, it also includes the ability to adapt to the unanticipated.[9] Such agile adaptability to changing environments is essential for AI to optimally support legally sufficient decision-making at sea, especially in high-risk circumstances such as vessels operating in close proximity to hazardous features, other vessels or heavy weather.

9.2.1.2   Algorithms

Algorithms are fundamental to AI. These are sets of complex mathematical actions or instructions expressed as a formula to answer a problem.[10] Computer scientists envision algorithms that will self-assimilate information in an adaptive manner similar to how humans improve decision

---

[6] *See* SHANE LEGG & MARCUS HUTTER, A COLLECTION OF DEFINITIONS OF INTELLIGENCE 2 (2007)

[7] *Id.*, at 2; *see also* Cambridge Dictionary, Intelligence, https://dictionary.cambridge.org/dictionary/english/intelligence (last visited Feb. 17, 2022) (online).

[8] SHANE LEGG & MARCUS HUTTER, UNIVERSAL INTELLIGENCE: A DEFINITION OF MACHINE INTELLIGENCE, 391, 401 (2007).

[9] *Id.*, at 402.

[10] JOHN C. BUYERS, ARTIFICIAL INTELLIGENCE: THE PRACTICAL LEGAL ISSUES 10 (2018); Cambridge Dictionary, Algorithm, https://dictionary.cambridge.org/dictionary/english/algorithm (last visited Feb. 17, 2022) (online).

processes by experimentation.[11] Simply, the goal of AI is to create algorithms that improve themselves through iterative, recursive processes.

9.2.1.3   Artificial Intelligence

John Frank Weaver said there is "an open secret in the field of AI that there is no widely accepted definition of 'artificial intelligence.'"[12] Weaver recognizes that the accepted definition of AI is a moving target, and agrees with Moshe Y. Vardi's pithy assertion that "[a]s soon as it works, no one calls it AI anymore."[13] This observation echoes Tesler's theorem, which states: "AI is whatever hasn't been done yet."[14] Therefore, the definition of AI is evolutionary, paralleling the advance of technology. This chapter contributes to the scholarship and state practice to better discern the potential impact of AI upon the components of oceans governance, including the competence of coastal states, flag states and their shared responsibilities for promoting free, peaceful and safe use of the sea.

The US Defense Innovation Board defined AI "to mean a variety of information processing techniques and technologies used to perform a goal-oriented task and the means to reason in the pursuit of that task."[15] The British government has offered another definition of AI, as "the analysis of data to model some aspect of the world. Inferences from these models are then used to predict and anticipate possible future events."[16] In this context, the British construct contemplates the analysis of Big Data, meaning "high-volume, high-velocity and high-variety information assets that demand cost-effective, innovative forms of information processing for enhanced insight and decision making."[17] Recognizing the

---

[11] "We spent a lot of time trying to make algorithms learn more efficiently from data." Interview by Martin Ford with Gary Marcus, Founder and CEO, Geometric Intelligence, in Ford, *supra* note 1, at 305, 313.

[12] RESEARCH HANDBOOK ON THE LAW OF ARTIFICIAL INTELLIGENCE 156 (Woodrow Barfield & Ugo Pagallo eds., 2018).

[13] *Id.*, n.13 (citing Moshe Y. Vardi, *Artificial Intelligence: Past and Future*, 55 COMMUNICATIONS OF THE ASS'N FOR COMPUTING MACHINERY 5 (2012)).

[14] DOUGLAS R. HOFSTADTER, Gödel, Escher, BACH: AN ETERNAL GOLDEN BRAID 601 (1979) (publishing Larry Tesler's theorem).

[15] US DEFENSE INNOVATION BOARD, AI PRINCIPLES: RECOMMENDATIONS ON THE ETHICAL USE OF ARTIFICIAL INTELLIGENCE BY THE DEPARTMENT OF DEFENSE 5 (2019).

[16] UK GOVERNMENT OFFICE FOR SCIENCE, ARTIFICIAL INTELLIGENCE: OPPORTUNITIES AND IMPLICATIONS FOR THE FUTURE OF DECISION MAKING 5 (2016).

[17] Gartner Glossary, Big data, www.gartner.com/en/information-technology/glossary/big-data (last visited Feb. 17, 2022) (online).

immense scope of the maritime domain in terms of the variety and volume of data sets, one can see opportunity for better comprehension of the physical environment and the multitude of dynamic interdependent variables to manage for maximizing the beneficial use of the sea[18] and minimizing the harmful effects of weather events and tsunamis.[19]

Computers are efficient at goal-oriented tasks. In contrast, humans can be brilliant at creativity and making cognitive leaps. The persistent question is whether computers can be liberated from the determinism of a program. In his 1979 seminal work, *Gödel, Escher, Bach: An Eternal Golden Braid*, Douglas R. Hofstadter observed that "[c]omputers by their very nature are the most inflexible, desireless, rule-following of beasts. Fast though they may be, they are nonetheless the epitome of unconsciousness. How, then, can intelligent behavior be programmed?"[20] The challenge for AI is to combine the optimal computational speed and stamina of a machine with the genius of human intuition.

9.2.2   Manifestations of AI

The following concepts represent a manifold set of present and aspirational AI capabilities, ranging from the directed to potentially fully autonomous:

Machine learning (ML) is "a subset of AI devoted to algorithms that learn from data."[21] It includes subcategories of supervised learning (which includes backpropagation), unsupervised learning and reinforcement learning.

Supervised learning "involves an algorithm presented with prior, labelled examples (sometimes in the millions) and has the benefit of identifying associations between the data and the labeled outcome, or classification."[22] An example of supervised learning in the maritime domain is iSharkFin, described as "an expert system that uses machine

---

[18] "World per capita fish consumption has risen to 16.4 kg from a per capita average of 9.9 kg in the 1960s." Brandon Gaille, 27 Notable Seafood Consumption Statistics, SMALL BUS. & MKTG. ADVICE: BLOG, May 28, 2017; Melina Kourantidou, Artificial Intelligence Makes Waves in Seafood Traceability, GREENBIZ, July 24, 2019.

[19] BRUCE PARKER, THE POWER OF THE SEA: TSUNAMIS, STORM SURGES, ROGUE WAVES, AND OUR QUEST TO PREDICT DISASTERS 76–78, 161–79 (2010).

[20] HOFSTADTER, *supra* note 14, at 26.

[21] FORD, *supra* note 1, at 10.

[22] AMIR HUSSEIN, THE SENTIENT MACHINE: THE COMING AGE OF ARTIFICIAL INTELLIGENCE 21 (2017).

learning techniques to identify shark species from shark fin shapes."[23] Developed in part by the United Nations (UN) Food and Agricultural Organization (FAO) to enable sustainable fisheries, it enables identification of shark species by comparing a contemporaneous picture of the fin against an image database of thousands of shark fins.[24] Such AI techniques can support application of all dimensions of national power, or diplomatic, informational, military and economic (DIME) in the maritime domain.[25]

Unsupervised learning involves the process by which systems learn from "unstructured data" in the environment, not unlike how children observe and learn on their own.[26] Unsupervised learning is where "systems attempt to find either outliers or correlations or patterns in the data without any form of guidance."[27] According to Martin Ford, unsupervised learning is "one of the most difficult challenges facing the field" of AI, but it also "represents one of the most promising avenues for progress" in the field as an important waypoint on the road to human-level AI.[28]

Reinforcement learning is a branch of ML that involves learning from experience: "responses/actions are selected based on a combination of trial-and-error and the resulting feedback. Positive feedback (e.g., good outcomes) are reinforced (i.e., more likely to be selected in the future) whereas negative feedback means those response/actions are less likely to be selected in the future."[29] This method requires vast amounts of training data,[30] and is well-suited to competitive, game-like activities. Reinforcement learning is best remembered for the achievement of the machine system Alpha Go that defeated a world

---

[23] United Nations Food and Agricultural Organization, INTERNATIONAL PLANS OF ACTION FOR CONSERVATION AND MANAGEMENT OF SHARKS (1999).

[24] *Id.*

[25] "The 'DIME' acronym (diplomatic, informational, military, and economic) has been used for many years to describe the instruments of national power." US JOINT CHIEFS OF STAFF, JOINT DOCTRINE notes 1–18, at vii, www.jcs.mil/portals/36/documents/doctrine/ jdn_jg/jdn1_18.pdf?ver=2018-04-25-150439-540 (last visited Feb. 27, 2022) (online).

[26] FORD, *supra* note 1, at 12–13.

[27] BUYERS, *supra* note 10, at 11.

[28] FORD, *supra* note 1, at 12.

[29] Interview with Carsten K. Oertel, Principal Scientist, MITRE Corp. (Oct. 29, 2020).

[30] Deep Mind is a company that is at the forefront of AI research and development. *See, e.g.,* Jane Wang et al., Learning to Reinforcement Learn, https://deepmind.com/research/ publications/2019/learning-reinforcement-learn (Nov. 24, 2016; last visited Feb. 27, 2022).

renowned human Go champion in 2015.[31] Oil and gas exploration is a high-stakes game, so the Royal Dutch Shell oil company is using reinforcement learning to improve statistical success in drilling for energy resources.[32]

Deep learning is another branch of ML often used in association with reinforcement learning[33] that uses multiple layers of artificial neural networks designed to mimic the structure of how organic neurons function in the human brain.[34] Deep learning leverages backpropagation, a learning algorithm in which the neural network is trained so that information propagates back through the layers of the circuit neurons to cause a calibration of the "weights" for the individual neurons. This feedback algorithm allows the entire network to learn to "home in" on the correct answer.[35]

Artificial narrow intelligence (ANI) is often used to solve a specific set of problems. Deep Blue, the system that defeated chess Grand Master Gary Kasparov, is an excellent example of successful ANI.[36] Deep Blue was brilliant at chess but was unsuited for unpredictable, day-to-day decision-making.

Artificial general intelligence (AGI) is the aspirational, elusive goal of a "a true thinking machine" and is "synonymous with the terms Human-level AI or Strong AI."[37] Professor Fei-Fei Li of Stanford University and chief scientist for AI and ML at Google defines AGI as "the kind of intelligence that is contextualized, situationally aware, nuanced, multi-faceted and multidimensional – and one that has the kind of learning capability that humans do, which is not only through big data but also

---

[31] Engineering Ethics Blog, AlphaGo Defeats Human Go Champion: Go Figure, https:// engineeringethicsblog.blogspot.com/2016/03/alphago-defeats-human-go-champion-go .html (Mar. 21, 2016; last visited Mar. 6, 2022) (online).

[32] GetSmarter, The Applications of Deep Reinforcement Learning, www.getsmarter.com/ blog/market-trends/the-applications-of-deep-reinforcement-learning/ (July 23, 2019; last visited Mar. 6, 2022); see also Steven Norton, *Shell Announces Plans to Deploy AI Applications at Scale: First applications Focus on Predictive Maintenance for Valves*, GAS PRODUCTION EQUIPMENT, Wall St. J., www.wsj.com/articles/shell-announces-plans-to-deploy-ai-applications-at-scale-1537448513?tesla=y (Sept. 20, 2018; last visited Mar. 6, 2022) (online).

[33] RESEARCH HANDBOOK ON THE LAW OF ARTIFICIAL INTELLIGENCE, *supra* note 12, at 642.

[34] FORD, *supra* note 1, at 10.

[35] *Id.*

[36] GARY KASPAROV, DEEP THINKING: WHERE MACHINE INTELLIGENCE ENDS AND HUMAN CREATIVITY BEGINS 2, 187–89, 204, 212 (2018).

[37] FORD, *supra* note 1, at 13.

through unsupervised learning, reinforcement learning, virtual learning, and various kinds of learning."[38] AGI offers much promise for
attaining a sustainable maritime domain. Whereas AI ML can help
how we solve problems, AGI promises the transformative potential to
predict unforeseen problems of nth order effects. While the board
games chess and Go present billions of optional moves,[39] these games
are played on stable X and Y axes over *time*, with the variables being
the idiosyncrasies of the players. In contrast, maritime operations
involve time plus X, Y and Z axes where the axes are in constant
and sometimes unpredictable motion. Maritime activities are nonetheless subject to established rules of law. This chapter recommends that
AI deep learning and reinforcement learning could beneficially augment speed and reliability of decision-making at sea. The realization of
full AGI, however, is still on the horizon.[40] (This long-term timeframe
obviates the need to consider here the legal ramifications of "singularity," the plateau of AGI capability at which machines surpass the
intellectual capability of any human being.)[41]

Many maritime activities will improve as a result of automation and
augmentation at sea, ranging from climate forecasting and maritime
hazard warning,[42] management of offshore wind generation,[43] to
improving the sustainability of fisheries.[44] However, as ML becomes
"deeper" and approaches AGI, there may be a loss of transparency as
to how an AI system renders complex, rapid decisions, and there are
inherent risks associated with the "black box" outputs of AI systems that

---

[38] *Id.*, at 153.

[39] "[C]hess is a limited game and every position will have patterns and markers our
intuition can interpret." *See* KASPAROV, *supra* note 36, at 31. "There are over 300 billion
ways to play just the first four moves in a game of chess." *Id.*, at 34.

[40] Naveen Joshi, How Far Are We from Achieving Artificial General Intelligence?, Forbes,
June 10, 2019.

[41] Luke Dormehl, A Beginner's Guide to A.I., Superintelligence, and "the Singularity,"
DigitalTrends, Oct. 4, 2017.

[42] Machine Learning Predicts Earthquake and Tsunami with Unprecedented Accuracy,
ScienceSwitch, Oct. 16, 2018.

[43] Liz Burdock, Big Data/Artificial Intelligence, and Its Role in Offshore Wind Energy,
OffshoreWindUS, Aug. 28, 2019; *see also*
    Michelle Froese, Improving Wind-Turbine O&M with Artificial Intelligence,
WindpowerEngineering, Apr. 25, 2019.

[44] Meg Wilcox, The Future of Fishing is Big Data and Artificial Intelligence, The World,
May 10, 2018.

hinder or preclude review.[45] Should these black box systems make errors that result in maritime casualties, it may prove difficult to trace the decision processes that contributed to the loss. Humans should not become blind beneficiaries of AI systems but should be able to dissect its operational loops for compliance purposes.

9.2.3   AI–Human Interface Operational Paradigms

Three basic operational paradigms exist for AI–human interface: human-in-the-loop (HITL), human-on-the-loop (HOTL) and human-out-of-the-loop (HOOTL).

9.2.3.1   Human-in-the-Loop AI (HITL)

According to Appen, an AI company, "Human-in-the-loop (HITL) is a branch of AI that leverages both human and machine intelligence to create ML models. In HITL, people are involved in a virtuous circle where they train, tune, and test a particular algorithm."[46] Another AI company, Silo AI, defines HITL as a philosophy focused "on creating workflows where an AI learns from the human operator while intuitively making the human's work more efficient. The machine performs an action, asks a human expert for input, and learns from the response it gets."[47] Operationally, the human is part of the analytical process in HITL,[48] which is the prevalent paradigm in terms of computer-augmented human systems (and likely to remain so for some time to come).[49]

---

[45] Research Handbook on the Law of Artificial Intelligence, *supra* note 12, at 200–01.

[46] Appen, What Is Human-in-the-Loop Machine Learning?, https://appen.com/blog/human-in-the-loop/ (last visited Feb. 22, 2022) (online).

[47] Silo AI, Most Value from AI with Human-in-the-Loop Solutions, https://silo.ai/most-value-human-in-the-loop-ai/ (last visited Feb. 22, 2022) (online).

[48] Joeanna C. Arthur et al., *Human-on-the-Loop: Geospatial Intelligence in the Age of Automation, Integrating Machine Efficiency with Human-Derived Context and Experience*, Trajectory, https://trajectorymagazine.com/human-on-the-loop-geospatial-intelligence-in-the-age-of-automation/ (Apr. 28, 2020; last visited Mar. 6, 2022) (online).

[49] SWZ Maritime, *Human Will Remain in the Loop as Autonomous Shipping Advances*, https://swzmaritime.nl/news/2020/07/15/human-will-remain-in-the-loop-as-autonomous-shipping-advances/?gdpr=deny (Jul. 15, 2020; last visited Mar. 6, 2022) (online); Interview with Eero Lehtovaara, Head of Regulatory Affairs, ABB Marine & Ports (Webinar speech dated Jun. 30, 2020) (indicating a long transition time to fully autonomous vessels).

9.2.3.2   Human-on-the-Loop AI (HOTL)

The HOTL paradigm is a teaming model where the AI system does most of the work that it does best, and the human performs a regular, ongoing, supervisory role.[50] In a marine navigational scenario, this may be the situation where a ship has a very limited crew with automated bridge and engine space, but there is a human master monitoring and endorsing critical decisions. The sheer number of decision processes in the HOTL paradigm will necessitate refinement of what are critical decisions, involving an iterative, reinforcement learning process by both AI system and human oversight. For example, the first time the HOTL team encounters a new problem, the decision may be classified as "critical." However, once the problem repeats itself as a function of time or randomized variables occurring over time, the HOTL team may allow the AI system to "take over" the decision process so long as there are no outlier variables that make the problem unique.

9.2.3.3   Human-out-of-the-Loop AI (HOOTL)

The HOOTL is the operating concept in which there is no regular, ongoing human supervision. The AI or automated system receives the input directly from external sources (the environment, machinery or other digital processes) and makes decision outputs without a human. Some existing HOOTL systems are fairly predictable and have demonstrated efficiency to remove a human input where the human adds no value.

However, there are circumstances in which taking the human out of the loop may have unintended, catastrophic consequences. For example, on March 23, 2019, the MV *Viking Sky*, a passenger ship carrying 1,373 people, experienced an automatic engine shutdown when engineering sensors detected a loss of lube oil pressure (LOP). Vessel engines represent a major value of a ship, so the engineering controls were designed to automatically stop the engines when low LOP was detected. Apparently, the algorithm for automatic shutdown did not allow for timely human intercession. Pos-incident analysis showed that the *Viking Sky* had low but sufficient amounts of lube oil, but the sea-state caused the ship to roll violently, sloshing lube oil in the tank, resulting in the low LOP alarm. This engineering system did not take into account the location of the vessel, so the ship was rendered powerless even though it was

---

[50] Arthur et al., *supra* note 48, figure 1.

dangerously close to a rocky coast. Fortunately, engineers were able to restart the engines and avoid disaster, but only after the vessel issued a MAYDAY distress and 479 passengers were airlifted, some of whom required hospitalization.[51]

9.2.4   Impact of AI on the Maritime Domain

While legal scholars and practitioners have made valuable, current and predictive analysis of the potential implications of AI on transparency, reducing biases, personhood and fundamental rights for future AGI systems,[52] most of these articles focus upon the ramifications of AI in terrestrial jurisprudence.

AI can improve compliance with the law of the sea in charting and navigation. Many of the duties imposed upon vessels at sea depend upon geospatial location, either in an actual sense relating to the rights of the coastal state versus the rights of another flag state, or in a relative sense with regard to the duties of vessels under the Convention on the International Regulations for Preventing Collisions Sea (COLREGS).[53] Other duties are imposed upon agents of the flag state, most notably the vessel master, the person who commands the vessel. The time may come when ocean shipping is done by fully autonomous vessels. Even now, AI can support human crews on vessels at sea to improve compliance with the international law of the sea, including the UN Convention on the Law of the Sea (UNCLOS) and other treaties and norms that govern hydrographic charting and safe navigation.[54]

9.3   Legal Duties Relating to Hydrography and Safe Navigation

Under the law of the sea, coastal and flag state compliance depends on the agent (who), the specific activity (what) and the geospatial locus

---

[51] Lance Eliot, *Human in-the-Loop vs. out-of-the-Loop in AI Systems: The Case of AI Self-Driving Cars*, AI TRENDS, www.aitrends.com/ai-insider/human-in-the-loop-vs-out-of-the-loop-in-ai-systems-the-case-of-ai-self-driving-cars/ (Apr. 9, 2019; last visited Mar. 6, 2022) (online).

[52] RESEARCH HANDBOOK ON THE LAW OF ARTIFICIAL INTELLIGENCE, *supra* note 12; *see also* Elizabeth E. Joh, *Artificial Intelligence and the Law: Policing by Numbers: Big Data and the Fourth Amendment*, 89 WASH. L. REV. 35 (2014).

[53] Convention on the International Regulations for Preventing Collisions at Sea, Oct. 20, 1972, 28 U.S.T. 3459, T.I.A.S. No. 8587, 1050 U.N.T.S. 16.

[54] United Nations Convention on the Law of the Sea, Dec. 10, 1982, 1833 U.N.T.S. 397 (hereinafter UNCLOS).

(where) of the activities. Certain activities are also subject to a temporal (when) constraint, such as reduced visibility. Therefore, the optimal use of AI in the maritime domain should leverage GEOINT to maximize compliance with applicable law of the sea requirements. A master employs GEOINT for voyage planning, using imagery (charts from weather satellites), imagery intelligence (vessel routing analysis based upon satellite imagery) and geospatial information (charts and sailing directions) in order to safely navigate the vessel. AI can assist the coastal or flag state in meeting its duties (set forth in the following section) by informing decisions based on a wider awareness of geography, legal regimes and the nuances of operations, including weather, tides and currents, and conditions on the water.

9.3.1   UNCLOS

Recognized as a constitution for the oceans, UNCLOS contains 320 articles and nine annexes. This subsection identifies UNCLOS requirements relating to charting, providing notice of maritime features, hazards, and those for safe operation and navigation of flag state vessels.

9.3.1.1   Coastal State Duties under UNCLOS

The coastal state has the duty to show its baselines on charts of a scale or scales adequate for ascertaining their position."[55] The coastal state must give "appropriate publicity to any danger to navigation, of which it has knowledge, within its territorial sea."[56] These duties require effective MDA, which is improved by GEOINT, to geolocate features and hazards. For example, the US National Geospatial-Intelligence Agency (NGA) has the statutory mission to improve the means of navigation for vessels of the navy and merchant marine.[57] Part of this mission involves disseminating navigational warnings in furtherance of UNCLOS, Article 24(2). The NGA operates a 24-hour a day Navigational Watch that receives reports from mariners and other governmental agencies and disseminates navigational warnings as part of the World Wide Navigational Warning Service (WWNWS).[58] This watch monitors

[55] *Id.*, art. 16.
[56] *Id.*, art. 24.
[57] 10 U.S.C. § 442 *et seq.* (2021).
[58] IHO Hydrographic Dictionary, World Wide Navigational Warning Service, www.iho-ohi .net/S32/engView.php?quick_filter=world+wide+navigational+warning+service&quick_ filter_operator=Contains&order%5B0%5D=aengID (last visited Mar. 6, 2022) (online).

worldwide navigational warnings, receiving more than 1,000 maritime safety related messages a day. The NGA also fulfills the US duties under UNCLOS, Article 24(2) by publishing the Notice to Mariners,[59] which delivers periodic updates on potential hazards to navigation important to mariners. The WWNWS must be timely in its messaging, while the Notice to Mariners information is published on a near-monthly basis. The NGA is researching the use of AI to efficiently ingest and process warning messages and other foreign data that can be automatically analyzed for potential hazards to navigation and appropriately transmitted via the WWNWS or in Notice to Mariners.[60] Specifically, the NGA uses "Reinforcement Learning and Natural Language Processing" to take unstructured data from Inmarsat,[61] email and phone messages to auto-generate structured navigational warning messages. This use of AI can save thousands of human-hours a year, accelerate warning dissemination and make maritime navigation safer.

9.3.1.2   The Duties of the Flag State under UNCLOS

Article 91 of UNCLOS recognizes that a flag state must "fix the conditions for the grant of its nationality to ships, for the registration of ships in its territory, and for the right to fly its flag. Ships have the nationality of the State whose flag they are entitled to fly [and] [t]here must be a genuine link between the State and the ship."[62] Such ships are subject to the exclusive jurisdiction of the flag state. The flag state exercises plenary authority over ships that fly its flag. This authority includes jurisdiction and control over administrative, technical and social matters, and responsibility for ship masters, officers, and crews and seafarer labor. Flag states also have competence over construction, design, equipping

---

[59] IHO Hydrographic Dictionary, Notice to Mariners, www.iho-ohi.net/S32/engView.php?
quick_filter=Notice+to+Mariners&quick_filter_operator=Contains&order%5B0%5D=
aengID (last visited Mar. 6, 2022) (online).

[60] Interview with Michael J. Lenihan, Research Directorate, NGA (Aug. 6, 2020).

[61] "INMARSAT is a company providing mobile satellite communications. The only company (2011) providing services within the Global Maritime Distress and Safety System." IHO Hydrographic Dictionary, Inmarsat, www.iho-ohi.net/S32/engView.php?quick_filter=inmarsat&quick_filter_operator=Contains&order%5B0%5D=dengID (last visited Mar. 6, 2022) (online).

[62] UNCLOS, *supra* note 54, art. 91(1). There is no specific formula to determine what minimum standards are required to prove this "genuine link," only that the flag state exercise its jurisdiction effectively. *See* YOSHIFUME TANAKA, THE INTERNATIONAL LAW OF THE SEA 163 (2d ed. 2015).

and manning, and the safe operation of ships, and responsibility for the maintenance of communications and the prevention of collisions.[63]

The flag state also must ensure its vessels are surveyed by qualified surveyors, and carry appropriate charts and required systems for communications and marine engineering, machinery and equipment for safe navigation, and systems to prevent vessel source pollution.[64] Flag states further have a duty to comply with generally accepted international standards,[65] including the 1974 International Convention for the Safety of Life at Sea (SOLAS),[66] COLREGS[67] and the 1978 International Convention on Standards of Training, Certification and Watchkeeping for Seafarers (STCW).[68] In case of a maritime casualty or collision, flag States must take the appropriate action needed to remedy the situation,[69] and conduct an investigation if there is a loss of life, serious injury to nationals of another state or serious damage to ships or installations, or serious damage to the marine environment.[70]

9.3.1.3   Flag State Governance Can Benefit from AI

The duty of "effectively exercising its jurisdiction and control in administrative, technical and social matters over ships flying its flag" requires the flag state to have full cognizance of the ships registered under its flag. However, recent reports show that the issuance of fraudulent registration documents to the International Maritime Organization (IMO) without the knowledge of the flag state is a growing problem that poses a threat to the legitimacy of the ship registration regime.[71] This phenomenon came to light in 2015 and has grown in numbers. In 2019, the 106th session of the IMO Legal Committee reported fraudulent registrations in the

---

[63] UNCLOS, *supra* note 54, art. 94(3).

[64] *Id.*, art. 94(4).

[65] *Id.*, art. 94(5).

[66] International Convention for the Safety of Life at Sea, 1974, Nov. 1, 1974, 32 U.S.T. 47, 1184 U.N.T.S. 2 (as amended) (hereinafter SOLAS).

[67] Convention on the International Regulations for Preventing Collisions at Sea, Oct. 20, 1972, 28 U.S.T. 3459, T.I.A.S. No. 8587, 1050 U.N.T.S. 16 (hereinafter COLREGS).

[68] International Convention on Standards of Training, Certification and Watchkeeping for Seafarers, 1978, Apr. 28, 1984, 1361 U.N.T.S. 2 (as amended) (hereinafter STCW).

[69] UNCLOS, *supra* note 54, art. 94(6).

[70] *Id.*, art. 94(7).

[71] Cameron Trainer & Paulina Izewicz, Unauthorized Flags: A Threat to the Global Maritime Regime, Center for International Maritime Security (CIMSEC), https://cimsec .org/unauthorized-flags-a-threat-to-the-global-maritime-regime/ (Jul. 20, 2020; last visited Mar. 6, 2022) (online).

following: over 100 in the Federated States of Micronesia (FSM); 73 in the Democratic Republic of the Congo; and 91 in Fiji.[72] The audacity of such fraudulent enterprises is demonstrated by the fact that FSM did not even operate an international shipping registry.[73]

AI may provide technical solutions for the IMO, flag states and other international bodies on big data analytics to continually check the veracity and provenance of vessel registration documents to detect fraudulent registration. Blockchain technology may prove useful to reduce fraudulent paper filings.[74] In addition, AI-cued GEOINT may provide flag states and international law enforcement with evidence to discover the location of fraudulently flagged vessels.[75] AI neural networks are being developed to integrate with satellite imagery to analyze and verify that automatic identification system (AIS) data is consistent with the vessels authorized to transmit that data to avoid spoof or misleading or false transmissions.[76] AI and GEOINT may assist in leveraging diplomatic pressure against complicit nations or support international legal proceedings to ensure compliance with UNCLOS, Article 91 and support a transparent vessel flagging regime.

9.3.1.4   Duties of the Master under UNCLOS

The word "master" appears nine times in UNCLOS[77] but this convention provides no definition, yet the historic use of the term implies it is a

---

[72] Frederick Kenney, Director, IMO Legal Affairs & External Relations Division, Presentation to the 106th session of the IMO Legal Committee: Fraudulent Registries and their Impact, https://wwwcdn.imo.org/localresources/en/OurWork/Legal/Documents/IMLIWMUSYMPOSIUM/6%20Panel%202_Kenney.pdf (Mar. 28, 2019; last visited Mar. 6, 2022) (online).

[73] Trainer & Izewicz, *supra* note 71.

[74] ShipChain, How to Reduce Fraud in Logistics, https://blog.shipchain.io/how-to-reduce-fraud-in-logistics/ (Nov. 8, 2018; last visited Mar. 6, 2022) (online): *see also* Hellenic Shipping News, Blockchain at Sea: How Technology is Transforming the Maritime Industry, www.hellenicshippingnews.com/blockchain-at-sea-how-technology-is-transforming-the-maritime-industry/ (Aug. 3, 2019; last visited Mar. 6, 2022) (online).

[75] Olivia Vassalotti & Cameron Trainer, Fake Flags: At-Sea Sanctions Enforcement and Ship Identity Falsification, Fraudulent Ship Registration Makes the Already Challenge Task of Sanctions Enforcement More Difficult, The Diplomat, Sept. 26, 2018.

[76] Aristides Milios et al., *Automatic Fusion of Satellite Imagery and AIS Data for Vessel Detection*. 22nd International Conference on Information Fusion (FUSION) 1–5 (2019).

[77] UNCLOS, *supra* note 54, arts. 27(1)(c), 27(3), 94(2)(b), 94(4)(b)–(c), 97(1)–(2), 98(1), 211(3).

natural person.[78] Under UNCLOS, a master has four duties: (1) to possess appropriate qualifications for seamanship, navigation and communications;[79] (2) to observe international rules concerning the safety of life at sea, the prevention of collisions, the prevention of marine pollution and radio communications;[80] (3) to render assistance to persons or vessels in distress;[81] and (4) to cooperate with coastal states concerning vessel source pollution, when appropriate.[82]

One legitimate question is whether the master's duty to render assistance will be practically eliminated in the case of an autonomous vessel with no human master aboard. Fully autonomous vessels may create an imbalance under the law of the sea, with autonomous vessels encountering distress calls but unable to render human assistance. Will an autonomous ship be able to rescue survivors of a shipwreck? Does it have a duty to render such assistance? So long as vessels employ human crews, AI can augment and potentially correct human master decision-making. Section 4 will examine cases where an AI system could have reduced risk and avoid disaster.

AI should be integrated into ship operations with the goal of facilitating vessel compliance with the applicable, governing legal regimes, including SOLAS, STCW and COLREGS.

9.3.2   SOLAS

SOLAS, Chapter V, Safety of Navigation, applies to all ships of 500 gross tonnage or more engaged in international voyages with certain exceptions, such as warships, naval auxiliaries and other vessels engaged in government, noncommercial service.[83] Chapter V was amended on July 1, 2002, with three important updates relating to hydrographic information: the definition of nautical charts under Regulation 2; the provision of hydrographic services under Regulation 9; and the acceptance of

---

[78] "The shipmaster, usually called the master in maritime law, is a natural person hired by contract who lives on a vessel and manages it and its related matters while the vessel is navigating and carrying goods or performing services for freights or hire." JOHN A. C. CARTNER, RICHARD P. FISKE & TARA L. LEITER, THE INTERNATIONAL LAW OF THE SHIPMASTER 3 (2009).
[79] UNCLOS, *supra* note 54, 94(4)(b).
[80] *Id.*, art. 94(4)(c).
[81] *Id.*, art. 98.
[82] *Id.*, art. 211(3).
[83] SOLAS, *supra* note 66, ch. V.

an electronic charting display information system (ECDIS) as meeting the chart carriage requirements under Regulation 19.[84] AI and ML will have a direct impact on implementing these regulations.

SOLAS, Chapter V, Regulation 2 defines a nautical chart or nautical publication as "a special-purpose map or book, or a specially compiled database from which such a map or book is derived, that is issued officially by or on the authority of a Government, authorized Hydrographic Office or other relevant government institution and is designed to meet the requirements of marine navigation."[85] Section IV shows how AI can assist in the quality control process to reduce errors in electronic charts.

SOLAS, Chapter V, Regulation 9 requires contracting states to arrange for the collection and compilation of hydrographic data and the publication, dissemination and keeping up to date of all nautical information necessary for safe navigation. Contracting states must carry out effective surveying, provide timely and reliable nautical charts, publications and notices to mariners to support safe navigation.[86] Regulation 9 creates enterprise-level responsibilities for hydrographic states. Some nations have extensive hydrographic organizations while other, developing nations may lack the capacity and depend on more maritime states to provide primary charting authority.[87] AI has the potential to accelerate the hydrographic capacity of developing coastal states to independently execute their obligations in accordance with SOLAS, Chapter V, Regulation 9.[88]

Furthermore, SOLAS, Chapter V, Regulation 19, paragraph 2.4 requires

> All ships irrespective of size shall have ... nautical charts and nautical publications to plan and display the ship's route for the intended voyage and to plot and monitor positions throughout the voyage; [ECDIS] may be accepted as meeting the chart carriage requirements of this subparagraph.[89]

---

[84] Alexandros Maratos, *Regulations in Chapter V of SOLAS*, HYDRO INTL, www.hydro-international.com/content/article/regulations-in-chapter-v-of-solas (Jan. 1, 2008; last visited Mar. 6, 2022) (online).

[85] SOLAS, *supra* note 66, ch. V, regulation, 2 para. 2.

[86] *Id.*, ch. V, regulation 9.

[87] CATHY TUNKS, THE ROLE OF A PRIMARY CHARTING AUTHORITY 27 (2018).

[88] *Hydrography Is Both a Science and a Technique, 7 Questions to the New Director General of the French Hydrographic Office*, HYDRO INT'L, www.hydro-international.com/content/article/hydrography-is-both-a-science-and-a-technique (Oct. 29, 2019; last visited Mar. 6, 2022) (online).

[89] SOLAS, *supra* note 66, ch. V, regulation 19, paras. 2.1–2.4.

These requirements support adequate voyage planning so that the navigational watch of the vessel be informed on potential hazards to navigation in the voyage. Additionally, this same regulation imposes a redundancy requirement for "back-up arrangements to meet the functional requirements of subparagraph .4, if this function is partly or fully fulfilled by electronic means."[90] Backup systems are essential for human-crewed vessels, and such backup capabilities are necessary for those vessels that become increasingly autonomous.

Under SOLAS, Chapter V, contracting governments are the responsible actors and ship masters are responsible agents for the flag state. For example, under SOLAS, "contracting governments shall take all steps necessary to ensure that, when intelligence of any dangers is received from whatever reliable source, it shall be promptly brought to the knowledge of those concerned and communicated to other interested Governments."[91] These duties lend well to the application of AI and ML, especially as more vessels and platforms operate in the maritime domain. The US NGA is investing in research and development to leverage AI to improve navigational warning messaging. In the present, the augmentation of AI to execute these duties does not appear to require a change in the law of the sea, as the technology merely enhances the state's capacity to comply.

9.3.3   STCW

STCW promotes the safety of life and property at sea and the protection of the marine environment by establishing in common agreement international standards of training, certification and watchkeeping for seafarers.[92] STCW defines the master as "the person having command of a ship."[93] The master must ensure that watchkeeping arrangements are adequate for maintaining a safe navigational watch, and that the vessels' officers of the watch are responsible for navigating the ship safely during their periods of duty to avoid collision and stranding.[94] This is a daunting

---

[90] *Id.*, para. 2.5.
[91] *Id.*, ch. V, regulation 4.
[92] STCW, *supra* note 68.
[93] *Id.*, annex, ch. 1, regulation I/I, *Definitions* (c).
[94] *Id.*, annex, ch. 2, regulation II/I, para. 2.

responsibility normally entrusted to a person with years of safely navigating vessels at sea. Because a human master must have adequate rest like any natural person, AI applications can augment situational awareness and decision quality.

The master must be aware of the serious effects of operational or accidental pollution of the marine environment and shall take all possible precautions to prevent such pollution, particularly within the framework of relevant international and port regulations.[95] However, if human masters are replaced by AI systems, and currently the STCW views the master as a "person," then either the AI master may need to be incorporated as an artificial person, or the law must adapt to allow the corporate personhood of the ship to merge with the personhood of the AI master. In either situation, the system controlling the ship must be operationally and legally tethered to the flag state.

STCW presumes a human-crewed vessel.[96] Vessels employing AI in a way that augments human decision-making would not require a major modification of STCW, but fully autonomous ships appear to require greater revision of the treaty. Nevertheless, AI can benefit human-crewed vessels by enhancing safety of navigation, voyage planning and voyage execution, as required by STCW.[97] Section IV provides specific examples from maritime casualties where AI could have identified navigational hazards and alerted the master and officers to minimize risk to vessel and crew.

9.3.4   COLREGS

COLREGS,[98] also called NAVRULES or "Rules of the Road," applies to all vessels upon the high seas and in all waters connected therewith navigable by seagoing vessels.[99] Rule 2(a) is important for reinforcing

---

[95] *Id.*, annex, ch. 2, regulation II/I, para. 11.

[96] "Seafarer" is not defined in STCW, but the term appears sixty-nine times in the text, and the context is uniformly that of a natural person. Resolution 22 of the Final Act of the Conference, which resulted in the STCW, recognized "good human relationships between the seafarers on board would greatly enhance the safety of life at sea." While the Final Act is not considered an integral part of STCW, it is instructive that the conference interpreted "seafarer" to be a natural person.

[97] STCW, *supra* note 68, annex, ch. 2, regulation, II/I, paras. 4–10.

[98] COLREGS, *supra* note 67.

[99] *Id.*, Rule 1.

accountability: "Nothing in these Rules shall exonerate any vessel, or the owner, master, or crew thereof, from the consequences of any neglect to comply with these Rules or of the neglect of any precaution which may be required by the ordinary practice of seamen, or by the special circumstances of the case."

COLREGS establishes reasonable, predictable rules to follow under specified conditions such as visibility, whether sailing or under power, ability to maneuver, meeting, overtaking and other operational experiences. Steering and Sailing rules establish rational rules for when one vessel should take action to avoid collision with another. Sound and light signals generally follow logical "if – then" action requirements. Research suggests that an explicable cause for collisions is a lack of knowledge and understanding of the regulations, leading to them being ignored or not obeyed, endangering ships and risking collision.[100] As such, AI has the potential to run the algorithms and logical processing needed to make reasonable decisions to successfully operate within the majority of circumstances involving vessels in proximity with one another. Yet, there is a "disconnect between experienced mariners and autonomous designers" – that is, system designers for marine autonomous collision avoidance algorithms lack significant experience in applying COLREGS in ocean navigation or have not yet incorporated the experience of seasoned mariners into the algorithm design and evaluation process.[101]

Future AI systems programmed for COLREGS-compliance that employ either HITL or HOTL would benefit from reinforcement learning that leverages experiential "sea sense" developed over time by prudent mariners. This experience is crucial for the AI system to function in accordance with COLREGS, Rule 2(b), which states: "In construing and complying with these Rules due regard shall be had to all dangers of navigation and collision and to any special circumstances, including the

[100] Dalibor Ivanišević, Ana Gundić & Đani Mohović, COLREGs in STCW Convention, 54 J. MARITIME & TRANSP. SCI. 23, 24 (2018). Failure to follow COLREGS was one of the causes of the August 21, 2017 collision between the USS John S. McCain and the M/V Alnic in the Straits of Singapore. See US DEPARTMENT OF THE NAVY, REPORT ON THE COLLISION BETWEEN USS JOHN S MCCAIN (DDG 56) AND MOTOR VESSEL ACX CRYSTAL, encl. 2, para 1.2 (2017); see also REZA ZIARATI ET AL., Avoiding Collisions at Sea: Pareto Analysis, IAMU CONFERENCE § 3 (2017), www.researchgate.net/publication/321314340_Avoiding_Collision_at_Sea_-_Pareto_Analysis (last visited Mar. 6, 2022) (online).
[101] KYLE L. WOERNER ET AL., COLLISION AVOIDANCE ROAD TEST FOR COLREGS-CONSTRAINED AUTONOMOUS VEHICLES (2016).

limitations of the vessels involved, which may make a departure from these Rules necessary to avoid immediate danger." The crux of Rule 2(b) is that compliance with the principles of the COLREGS (i.e., collision avoidance) may make it necessary to depart from the structured rules. This paradox is the challenge for AI – to evolve the "out-of-the-box" heuristic creativity needed to avoid collision in complex, time-dominant situations, especially those that involve multivessel, multirule variables. The creative problem-solving may also apply to those situations in extremis[102] lying outside of the context of COLREGS, which occur when collision or disaster is imminent and rapid decisive action is required.

This chapter proposes that future AI systems develop means of incorporating years of human navigational knowledge, establishing experiential reference nodes for comparison with situations that the AI system may encounter. AI systems should become corepositories for cultural maritime GEOINT, like the way that Polynesian youths once "absorbed" the knowledge of master navigators to utilize traditional knowledge.[103] In this paradigm, AI can use computer vision, temperature, and wave and swell motion to confirm geospatial location and pending weather patterns affecting navigation. This methodology may both improve the means of navigating vessels and preserve invaluable cultural knowledge at risk of extinction.

The next section examines case studies of maritime casualties in which AI could have reduced the risk of grounding and sinking.

9.4   AI and Disaster Prevention

A state's duties regarding charts, nautical publications and navigational technology fall under two broad areas: (1) the creation/publication of charts that depict specific geospatial information as required by the law of the sea; and (2) carriage/use of charts, publications and technology to ensure safe navigation. UNCLOS imposes the duties on a coastal state to prepare charts to depict baselines,[104] traffic separation schemes,[105]

---

[102] Craig H. Allen, *Admiralty's in Extremis Doctrine: What Can Be Learned from the Restatement (Third) of Torts Approach?*, 43 J. MARITIME L. & COM. 2, 155, 173 (2012).

[103] Door of Perception, Polynesian Wayfinders: The Knowledge of the Ancestors, https://doorofperception.com/2016/10/polynesian-wayfinders/ (Oct. 12, 2016; last visited Mar. 6, 2022) (online).

[104] UNCLOS, *supra* note 54, arts. 5–6, 16, 47.

[105] *Id.*, arts. 22, 41, 53.

certain lines of delimitation[106] and depictions of the outer continental shelf.[107] UNCLOS, Article 94 and SOLAS, Chapter V require a flag state to equip its vessels with such charts, nautical publications, and navigational equipment and instruments that are appropriate for safe navigation. Specifically, SOLAS, Chapter V mandates that: "All ships irrespective of size shall have ... nautical charts and nautical publications to plan and display the ship's route for the intended voyage and to plot and monitor positions throughout the voyage; [ECDIS] may be accepted as meeting the chart carriage requirements of this subparagraph."[108] This section examines specific maritime casualties from the recent past and considers how the adoption of AI integration may reduce future risk of disaster.

9.4.1   USS Guardian

While on a passage from Subic Bay, the Republic of the Philippines to Makassar, Indonesia, the USS *Guardian* (MCM-5), an Avenger-class minesweeper, ran aground on Tubbataha Reef, at 0222 local time on January 17, 2013. This grounding resulted in the total loss of the ship[109] and caused significant environmental damage to a unique UNESCO World Heritage site. The United States paid the Philippines US$1.9 million in damages.[110]

The US Navy Pacific Fleet conducted an extensive command investigation to determine the cause of the grounding. The first endorsement of the investigation determined that cause of the grounding was:

[106] *Id.*, arts. 74–75.
[107] *Id.*, arts. 76, 84.
[108] SOLAS, *supra* note 66, ch. V, regulation 19, para. 2.1.4.
[109] The calculated cost of replacing the USS *Guardian* in 2013 was approximately US$211,971,974. *See* US Department of the Navy, Command Investigation into the Grounding of USS *Guardian* (MCM 5) on Tubbataha Reef, Republic of the Philippines that Occurred on 17 January 2013 110 (2013) (hereinafter *Guardian* Command Investigation).
[110] Tubbataha Reefs Natural Park, https://whc.unesco.org/en/list/653 (last visited Mar. 6, 2022) (online); Press Release, Republic of the Philippines Department of Foreign Affairs, Statement on US Government Compensation for Tubbataha Reef, https://dfa.gov.ph/index.php/newsroom/dfa-releases/5418-statement-on-us-government-compensation-for-tubbataha-reef (Feb. 18, 2015; last visited Mar. 6, 2022) (online).

the failure to reconcile the known difference between Digital Nautical Chart[111] (DNC) GEN11A, the "general" chart,[112] and DNC COA11D, the "coastal" chart.[113] The Commanding Officer (CO) and Executive Officer/Navigator (XO/NAV), and Assistant Navigator (ANAV) all had an affirmative duty to use all available means to ensure the safe navigation of *Guardian*. After determining there was a difference between the general chart and the coastal chart, the CO, XO/NAV, and ANAV had a duty to verify the position of Tubbataha Reef using Publication 112 List of Lights and Publication 162 Sailing Directions and to make the chart difference known to the National Geospatial-Intelligence Agency. Had the CO, XO/NAV, and ANAV taken either of the two measures that they were required to take, the grounding would not have occurred.[114]

The *Guardian* CO had chosen to rely wholly upon DNC COA11D because he believed "it is 'well known' that general charts are inaccurate."[115] In this case, however, it was the coastal chart DNC COA11D that had erroneously offset Tubbataha Reef by approximately 7.5 nautical miles (M).[116] While this error should have been discovered and corrected by the NGA as part of its hydrographic responsibilities for the Department of Defense, the command investigation did not find this error to be the proximate cause of the grounding. Rather, the final endorsement of the command investigation concluded the following on causation:

---

[111] "The Digital Nautical Chart (DNC) is produced by the National Geospatial-Intelligence Agency (NGA) and is a vector-based digital product containing maritime significant features essential for safe marine navigation. DNC, for areas in which the US is the prime charting authority, is unclassified. All other areas are limited distribution." US NGA, Digital Nautical Chart (DNC), https://dnc.nga.mil/dncp/home.php (last visited Mar. 6, 2022) (online).

[112] "General charts are intended for coastwise navigation outside of outlying reefs and shoals. The scales range from about 1:150,000 to 1:600,000." 1 NATHANIEL BOWDITCH, AMERICAN PRACTICAL NAVIGATOR: AN EPITOME OF NAVIGATION 45 (2019) (originally published 1802).

[113] "Coastal charts are intended for inshore coastwise navigation where the course may lie inside outlying reefs and shoals, for entering or leaving bays and harbors of considerable width, and for navigating large inland waterways. The scales range from about 1:50,000 to 1:150,000." *Id.*

[114] *See Guardian* Command Investigation, *supra* note 109, at 142.

[115] *Id.*, at 156–58.

[116] "Upon Initial review, we determined that the reef was displayed in the Coastal DNC approximately eight nautical miles east-southeast of its actual location. At this stage of our review, we determined the cause of this discrepancy was inaccurate source data." Memorandum from the US NGA to the Chief of Naval Operations (Jan. 18, 2013).

> USS *Guardian* leadership and watch teams failed to adhere to prudent, safe, and sound navigation principles which would have alerted them to approaching dangers with sufficient time to take mitigating action. The watch team's observations of visual cues in the hours leading up to the grounding, combined with electronic cues and alarms, should have triggered immediate steps to resolve warnings and reconcile discrepancies. Further, notwithstanding multiple, readily available sources of accurate information, the leadership and watch teams relied primarily on an inaccurate Digital Nautical Chart (DNC)® coastal chart during planning and execution of the navigation plan.[117]

The *Guardian* grounding was tragically unnecessary because the CO allowed his biased presumption that general navigation charts were inaccurate to rely on a single source of navigational information that was geospatially incorrect rather than make use of all available means, as required by a general maxim of marine navigation.[118] This human error was compounded by a lack of leadership guidance regarding establishment of a modified (i.e., enhanced) navigation detail or increased navigational fix frequency in the vicinity of Tubbataha Reef.[119]

As a result of the USS *Guardian* grounding, the NGA undertook an extensive review of its DNC charting covering more than 116 million square miles to determine whether other transpositions of hazards to navigation had occurred. The NGA discovered that there was only one other case where feature data were erroneously depicted due to errors in orthorectification of satellite imagery data used for chart updates.[120] In 2013, this review process required significant dedication of human resources over multiple shifts. Today, these procedures may be accomplished using correlational algorithms and computer vision. As hazards to navigation may be described by GEOINT in X, Y and Z coordinates, coastal states may employ AI for cross-checking the depiction of such navigational features across charts of varying scales to reduce errors in

---

[117] *See Guardian* Command Investigation, *supra* note 109, at 156.

[118] "An aid to navigation also refers to any device or structure external to a craft, designed to assist in determination of position. This includes celestial, terrestrial, and electronic means, such as Global Positioning System (GPS) and Differential GPS (DGPS). Here, too, the prudent mariner will not rely solely on any single aid to navigation." US NGA, INDEX TO SPECIAL NOTICES TO MARINERS, para. 1.

[119] *Guardian* Command Investigation, *supra* note 109, at 27.

[120] Memorandum from the US NGA to the Chief of Naval Operations ¶ 2 (Jan. 18, 2013). This memorandum was made available as a result of a Freedom of Information Act Request dated January 13, 2013, www.governmentattic.org/8docs/NGAbauticalChtsReview_2013.pdf (last visited Feb. 27, 2022) (online).

presentation and to provide adequate notice to mariners of identified hazards as required by the UNCLOS, Article 24(2) and SOLAS, Chapter V, Regulation 9.

In the event that a coastal state providing hydrographic services does not identify discrepancies in features on charts of differing scales, it is possible that improved voyage management systems (VMSs) could leverage AI algorithms to perform real-time cross-checks between accessible electronic navigational charts (ENCs) and sailing directions and other sources of information when conducting voyage planning.[121] This capability might alert a master or CO of other resources that are available for positional analysis to avoid the erroneous bias unfortunately demonstrated by the CO of the USS *Guardian*. Furthermore, VMSs could integrate AI to automatically alert the master or CO to call out additional personnel needed to respond to increased risk. These technical advancements will better enable flag state compliance with UNCLOS, SOLAS, STCW and the COLREGS.

Historically, the ship master has been accorded significant authority and accountability, called "master under God" by admiralty law and scholars.[122] Until technology obviates the need for human crews, AI can improve navigational decision-making by the master and other officers by augmenting course of action analyses and preventing data overloads at critical times – thereby reducing in extremis situations. More importantly, AI should be used to reduce human biases prejudicial to the safety of the vessel.

9.4.2   SS El Faro

At 0715 on October 1, 2015, Captain Michael Davidson, master of the Steam Ship (SS) *El Faro,* an aging RO/RO-containership[123] bound from Jacksonville, Florida to San Juan, Puerto Rico, issued distress alerts to the

---

[121] The 2018 grounding of the German-flagged Motor Tanker *Pazifik* in Indonesian waters shows similar risks where paper chart discrepancies are not accurately reflected in ENCs, and ECDIS does not automatically alert with supplemental electronic sailing directions information. *See* GERMAN FEDERAL BUREAU OF MARITIME CASUALTY INVESTIGATION, Pub. No. 241/18, GROUNDING OF THE MOTOR TANKER PAZIFIK OFF INDONESIA ON 9 JULY 2018 (2020).

[122] CARTNER ET AL., *supra* note 78, § 1.7.

[123] RO/RO is the abbreviation for a roll on/roll off vessel, a ship that has ramps that enable cars and trucks to drive on and off the ship. A RO/RO-containership carries both crane-loaded containers and wheeled vehicles.

US Coast Guard (USCG).[124] At the time, the *El Faro* was approximately 40 M northeast of Acklins and Crooked Islands, Bahamas, near the eye of Hurricane Joaquin. Approximately thirty minutes later, the ship went down with thirty-three lives lost,[125] making it one of the worst maritime disasters in US history.[126] The tragic sinking of the *El Faro* provides the sad example of how the human biases of a qualified master may have led him to steer directly into the path of a deadly hurricane. Much has been written on the specific events leading up to the sinking of the *El Faro*. Both the National Transportation Safety Board (NTSB) and the USCG issued detailed investigative reports on circumstances and causes of the sinking.[127]

The USCG Marine Board of Investigation (MBI) on the *El Faro* found twelve contributing factors that placed the ship in dangerous proximity of Hurricane Joaquin, eight of which the master had direct involvement.[128] One common theme in these factors was the master's over reliance on a single weather routing service, the Bon Voyage system (BVS), an Applied Weather Technologies product that displayed information from the National Hurricane Center (NHC) in colorful imagery rather than in text reporting as provided by the NHC. The master's dependence on BVS during Hurricane Joaquin was fateful. Analysis after the hurricane demonstrated that the NHC distributed tropical weather forecasts that proved to be inaccurate, and Applied Weather Technologies used these inaccurate forecasts to create BVS weather packages.[129] The master was not aware of the inherent latency in the BVS data compared to the NHC forecasts. Furthermore, the master was unaware that he received one BVS data package with a redundant hurricane track line.[130] The master chose not to reduce speed or take a

---

[124] The USCG Atlantic Area Command Center in Portsmouth, Virginia received *El Faro's* global maritime distress and safety system (GMDSS) and ship security alert system (SSAS) alert messages. *See* USCG, Pub. No. 16732, Marine Board's Report: Steam Ship *El Faro* (O.N. 561732) Sinking and Loss of the Vessel with 33 Persons Missing and Presumed Deceased Northeast of Acklins and Crooked Island, Bahamas on October 1, 2015 33 (2017) (hereinafter MBI SS *El Faro*).

[125] *See* US National Transport Safety Board, Pub. No. DCA16MM001, Group Chairman's Factual Report: SS *El Faro* 2–3 (2017).

[126] MBI SS *El Faro*, *supra* note 124, at 1.

[127] *See, supra* notes 124–25.

[128] MBI SS *El Faro*, *supra* note 124, at 188–90.

[129] *Id.*, at 189.

[130] *Id.*

longer route to San Juan at an earlier stage of the voyage for fear vessel owners would perceive him to be overly cautious.[131]

The USCG MBI concluded that the captain of El Faro failed to carry out his responsibilities and duties as master of the vessel by failing to download the latest BVS data package. The captain failed to act on reports from the watch officers regarding the increased severity and proximity to Hurricane Joaquin, and he ignored their suggested course changes to the south to increase the distance from the hurricane.[132]

Ironically, "El Faro" means "the lighthouse" in Spanish, an aid to navigation supposed to warn mariners of danger. The El Faro case provides a tragic warning that the sea is a dangerous environment and that a navigator must leverage emerging technologies, considering all sources of predictive weather data to balance risk. The incident occurred before broad availability of advanced AI technology for vessel navigation. However, technology exists today that could ingest diverse weather routing information to determine discrepancies in plotted locations and actual tracks of storms to alert the master and navigational officers. No change in the law of the sea would be required for such the application of this new technology.

9.5   Final Thoughts and Conclusion

Regardless of debates regarding the definition of AI, this emerging technology is on a vector toward increasingly integrated operations at sea. Given this reality, there is little doubt that AI should be employed to augment decision-making tasks of human-crewed vessels. AI should not be viewed as human against machine, but rather a human–machine symbiosis optimally leveraging the strengths of each. As hydrography and navigation are integrally related to GEOINT, the HOTL paradigm presents the most legally responsible way of developing AI systems, as technology does not always operate flawlessly.[133] Had HOTL AI been available and properly applied in the recent past, it may have been possible to avoid the disasters of the USS Guardian or the SS El Faro.

---

[131] RACHEL SLADE, INTO THE RAGING SEA: THIRTY-THREE MARINERS, ONE MEGASTORM, AND THE SINKING OF EL FARO 24 (2018); see also MBI SS El Faro, supra note 124, at 16, 128.
[132] MBI SS El Faro, supra note 124, at 189.
[133] Arthur et al., supra notes 48, 50.

However, a pressing question is whether AI should operate to situationally replace control of the master or other decision-maker is a serious one with both operational and potentially legal consequence. Even though the role of the master is an established position of trust based upon years of experience and training, AI should be incorporated to alert and limit flawed, dangerous decision-making of a master to promote the overarching aims of the law of the sea. Yet, does an AI system have the capacity to relieve a master or CO for incompetence, or should the system defer such a decision to shoreside management? The best way to examine the issue is on a continuum of possibilities. First, it is reasonable to propose that AI could be used to limit human action where the computational system incorporates MDA, informed by GEOINT that an action must not be taken given the position of the vessel and the legal requirements or prohibitions or temporal constraints. In such a case, the AI algorithms act as a governor on action, not unlike an engineering control designed to prevent system overload. An example would be AI preventing the illegal discharge of oil in a zone prohibited by MARPOL.[134]

The limitation of vessel control may be necessary to prevent vessel disaster if the AI algorithms determine that the master's or watch officer's steering or engine orders will lead to collision or grounding. For example, the disastrous capsize of the MV *Costa Concordia* on Scole Rocks near Giglio Island on January 13, 2012, was in large part caused by the illogical decisions of the *Concordia*'s master to make a hazardous passage at nighttime, close to a dangerous coast, failing to use appropriately scaled charts and navigating at unsafe speed under the circumstances. Of the 4,229 persons on board (3,206 passengers and 1,023 crewmembers), 26 passengers and 4 crew members needlessly died.[135] GEOINT-supported MDA using AI has the potential to limit erroneous or flawed decisions of the person normally in charge of a navigational watch. These AI algorithms should monitor vessel activity and record such instances for investigatory bodies and mariner training.

The IMO has undertaken a regulatory scoping exercise to examine which international conventions may need an update to support the

---

[134] International Convention for the Prevention of Pollution from Ships, Nov. 2, 1973, as modified by the Protocol of 1978, 1340 U.N.T.S. 62.

[135] ITALIAN MINISTRY OF INFRASTRUCTURES AND TRANSPORTS, REPORT ON THE SAFETY TECHNICAL INVESTIGATION: CRUISE SHIP *COSTA CONCORDIA* MARINE CASUALTY ON JANUARY 13, 2012 3–5 (2013).

transition to maritime autonomous surface ships (MASSs).[136] Amendments to treaties may be necessary, reflecting the sea change from vessels commanded by a human master to vessels controlled by AI expert systems. What must remain however, is the principle that who or what commands the vessel remains the agent of the flag State, and that the flag State is accountable for the vessel's operation under its flag.

Our understanding of AI is inchoate, like our partial knowledge of the maritime domain. Nevertheless, AI is rapidly becoming invaluable to DIME activities in the maritime domain. Technology, the law and the international regulatory structure will evolve to support some fully autonomous vessels and marine operations. Human crews on vessels and platforms will continue for some time into the future. The increasing complexity of maritime activities requires the full integration of GEOINT into MDA so that AI systems will better "understand" complex interplay of climate, weather, legal requirements and the unpredictability of human actors in geospatial place and time. As human masters command human crews, it is recommended that the HOTL paradigm be fully employed as insurance against technical errors in automated systems (e.g., avoiding repeats of the MV *Viking Sky*). Maintaining a HOTL process reinforces the learning quality of the AI systems employed.

AI can enable humans to operate in better balance with the sea. Leveraging AI can reduce unintended consequences to DIME activities in an often unpredictable maritime domain. In the meantime, admiralty and maritime law practitioners should continue studying AI to maximize legal compliance and promote the peaceful, sustainable use of the seas and oceans for the benefit of all.

---

[136] *See* IMO, Autonomous Shipping: Why Has IMO Decided to Look at the Regulation of Autonomous Ships?, www.imo.org/en/MediaCentre/HotTopics/Pages/Autonomous-shipping.aspx (last visited Mar. 6, 2022) (online).

Unmanned and Autonomous Warships and Military Aircraft

RAUL (PETE) PEDROZO

10.1   Introduction

The use of unmanned aerial and maritime systems to support military operations has grown exponentially in the twenty-first century in terms of both the number of systems employed and the complexity and lethality of the missions they are assigned. Between 2000 and 2014, the number of unmanned aerial systems (UASs) operated by the US Department of Defense (DoD) increased from 50 to over 10,000.[1] The capacity and capability of nations to deploy unmanned systems has

---

[1] US Government Accountability Office, Pub. No. GAO-09-175, Unmanned Aircraft Systems: Additional Actions Needed to Improve Management and Integration of DoD Efforts to Support Warfighter Needs 7 (2008); Military. com, Pentagon Plans for Cuts to Drone Budgets, www.military.com/dodbuzz/2014/01/02/pentagon-plans-for-cuts-to-drone-budgets (Jan. 2, 2014; last visited Mar. 6, 2022) (online).

likewise increased dramatically over time. At present, more than ninety countries and nonstate actors, including the Islamic State of Iraq and Syria (ISIS), operate surveillance or weaponized unmanned systems in support of combat operations.[2] Given that unmanned systems have proven their ability in combat to enhance situational awareness, reduce human workload and improve mission performance, at reduced risk to both civilian and military personnel and reduced cost, we can expect the proliferation of unmanned systems to continue.[3] By 2035, for example, the US DoD estimates that over 70 percent of its aviation assets will be unmanned systems, and the US Navy of 2030 will include an increased number of unmanned surface and subsurface vessels to augment and support the manned fleet.[4]

The unmanned and autonomous systems of tomorrow will fundamentally shift the way nations conduct military operations and enable commanders to counter the wide range of emerging challenges posed on the contemporary battlefield. This chapter reviews the current and future capabilities of unmanned systems at sea, as well as projected missions and tasks for these systems in times of peace and war. The chapter discusses the legal status of unmanned systems under prevailing treaties under the auspices of the International Maritime Organization (IMO), and the navigational rights and duties that these systems enjoy in peacetime under the United Nations (UN) Convention on the Law of the Sea (UNCLOS) and the Convention on International Civil Aviation (Chicago Convention). Finally, the chapter concludes with an overview of a variety of legal issues associated with unmanned system under the law of armed conflict (LOAC), also called international humanitarian law (IHL).

10.2 Unmanned Systems Capabilities and Mission Sets

The pervasive use of unmanned systems will continue as new technologies increase system persistence, stealth, mobility, versatility and

---

[2] KELLEY SAYLER, A WORLD OF PROLIFERATED DRONES: A TECHNOLOGY PRIMER 5 (2015).
[3] US DoD, Pub. No. 14-S-0553, UNMANNED SYSTEMS INTEGRATED ROADMAP: FY2013–2038 20 (2014) (hereinafter DoD INTEGRATED ROADMAP).
[4] Jon Walker, Unmanned Aerial Vehicles (UAVs) – Comparing the USA, Israel, and China, Emerj, https://emerj.com/ai-sector-overviews/unmanned-aerial-vehicles-uavs/ (Feb. 32, 2019; last visited Mar. 6, 2022) (online); Davidi B. Larter & Aaron Mehta, The Pentagon Is Eyeing a 500-Ship Navy, Documents Reveal, Defense News, Sept. 24, 2020.

survivability. Moreover, because they reduce risk to human life, unmanned systems will become the preferred alternative for dull, dirty or dangerous missions. Generally, unmanned systems:

- provide an ideal platform to conduct dull missions that "involve long-duration undertakings with mundane tasks that are ill suited for manned systems," such as intelligence, surveillance and reconnaissance (ISR) missions;
- better perform dirty missions, such as operations to detect chemical, biological and nuclear material, by significantly reducing the risk of exposure of personnel to hazardous conditions; and
- can be used to conduct missions that are inherently dangerous – such as mine clearing operations or deactivating improvized explosive devices – thereby reducing the risk exposure to personnel.[5]

The US Navy is exploring the feasibility of using unmanned systems to provide logistical support to forward-deployed forces. In mid-October 2020, the Navy conducted a successful test using a small quadcopter-type UAV to deliver supplies to the USS *Henry M. Jackson*, an Ohio-class ballistic missile submarine, while deployed near the Hawaiian Islands. The test was conducted to explore new ways to resupply submarines at sea while they are on nuclear deterrent patrols to enhance their overall readiness.[6]

The US Navy is also looking at turning commercial ocean-service barges into autonomous forward arming and refueling point (FARP) units for an amphibious maritime projection platform (AMPP).[7] Boston-based Sea Machines Robotics was awarded a multiyear contract in October 2020 to "engineer, build and demonstrate ready-to-deploy system kits that enable autonomous, self-propelled operation of . . . available barges to land and replenish military aircraft."[8] The system will enhance the effectiveness and flexibility of deployed US forces. The kit includes Sea Machines' SM300 autonomous-command and control (C2) systems, barge propulsion, sensing, positioning, communications and

---

[5] DoD INTEGRATED ROADMAP, *supra* note 3, at 20.

[6] Joseph Trevithick, The Navy Just Sent a Drone to Deliver Cargo to One of Its Ballistic Missile Submarines, TheDrive, www.thedrive.com/the-war-zone/37195/the-navy-just-sent-a-drone-to-deliver-cargo-to-one-of-its-ballistic-missile-submarines (Oct. 21, 2020; last visited Mar. 6, 2022) (online).

[7] DoD Taps Sea Machines for Autonomous VTOL Replenishment Vessels, Seapower Magazine, Oct. 6, 2020.

[8] *Id.*

refueling equipment to deploy worldwide.[9] The SM300 is a vessel intelligence system that provides "operator-in-the-loop" autonomous C2 and can adjust to remote-control operation via wireless belt back.[10] The SM300 allows shore-based operators to have remote situational awareness and C2 of the deck barge's operating system and flight deck to enhance force protection for manned warships.[11]

10.2.1 Unmanned Aerial Systems (UASs)

Over the next five years, worldwide military UAS production will grow from US$2.8 billion to US$9.4 billion. The United States accounts for more than 50 percent of this production, as well as over 77 percent of global spending for military UAS research, development, test and evaluation. Nonetheless, more than 150 different military UASs, ranging in size from the hummingbird-size Black Hornet to the 15,000-pound RQ-4 Global Hawk, are being operated by forty-seven other countries. Moreover, since the United States first used armed UASs in combat in 2001, twenty-seven nations currently have weaponized UASs in their weapons inventory. Besides the United States, eight other nations – Azerbaijan, Iran, Iraq, Israel, Nigeria, Pakistan, Turkey and the UK – have used armed UASs in combat.[12] UASs are also financially attractive to potential buyers, as they are more cost effective to purchase and operate – the MQ-9 Reaper, for example, costs about US$14.5 million, compared to US$94.6 million for a manned F-35 aircraft.

10.2.2 Unmanned Maritime Vehicles (UMVs)

The use of UMVs to support naval operations is not a new phenomenon. Unmanned surface vessels (USV) were used in 1946 during Operation Crossroads – US tests to investigate the effect of nuclear weapons on warships – to collect radioactive water samples after the two nuclear detonations at Bikini Atoll. During the Vietnam War, remotely controlled unmanned boats – 23-foot fiberglass hull powered by a V-8 inboard gas engine – were used by Mine Division 113 to conduct "chain

---

[9] Id.
[10] Sea Machines, SM300, https://sea-machines.com/sm300 (last visited Mar. 5, 2021) (online).
[11] Id.
[12] Walker, *supra* note 4.

drag" minesweeping operations. Similarly, in the 1990s, USS *Cushing* (DD-985) used the remote mine-hunting operational prototype system to conduct mine-hunting operations in the Persian Gulf. Unmanned undersea vehicles (UUVs) were also used in 2003 to clear mines and conduct ISR missions in the Persian Gulf during Operation Iraqi Freedom.[13]

The US Navy currently operates a variety of UMVs – both autonomous or remotely navigated unmanned surface vehicles (USVs) and unmanned underwater vehicles (UUVs) – that can be launched from aircraft, submarines or surface ships to perform a number of missions in support of fleet operations in times of peace and war. Varying in size and displacement, ranging from "man-portable systems to systems 40 feet in length and several thousand pounds of displacement,"[14] UMVs can operate effectively in bad weather and low visibility, thus providing a force multiplier that exceeds the capabilities of manned platforms. UMVs perform a wide range of functions, such as ISR, harbor security, minesweeping, securing critical waterways, precision strikes, scanning a ship's hull for fouling and integrity, and ocean mapping and tracking, at a reduced cost, with minimal risk to personnel, and with greater persistence, range, accuracy and speed.

10.2.3   Unmanned Surface Vehicles (USVs)

The US Navy plans to deploy USVs to augment the manned surface fleet, enhance naval and joint warfighting capabilities to support homeland defense (HLD), counterterrorism, irregular warfare and conventional campaigns.[15] The goal is to shift the fleet to a new architecture by reducing the number of large (manned) surface combatants, increasing the number of small (manned) surface combatants and significantly increasing the number of large UMVs to meet emerging challenges.[16] Shifting to a more distributed fleet force architecture offers a number of advantages. First, it complicates an adversary's targeting challenge by presenting the adversary with a larger number of navy units to detect,

[13] US Department of the Navy, The Navy Unmanned Surface Vehicle (USV) Master Plan 1–3 (2007) (hereinafter Navy USV Master Plan).
[14] DoD Integrated Roadmap, *supra* note 3, at 109.
[15] Navy USV Master Plan, *supra* note 13, at x, 7.
[16] US Congressional Research Service, Pub. No. R45757, Navy Large Unmanned Surface and Undersea Vehicles: Background and Issues for Congress 4 (2019) (hereinafter CRS Report Large USVs/UUVs).

identify and track. Second, a distributed force reduces the loss in aggregate navy capability that would result from the destruction of an individual navy platform. Third, UMVs give US leaders the option of deploying assets in wartime to sea locations that would be tactically advantageous but too risky for manned ships. Finally, the fleet becomes more adaptable with increases in modularity and reconfigurability to change as mission needs evolve.[17]

USVs will be used to augment manned platforms and perform a number of high-priority missions, including mine countermeasures (MCMs), antisubmarine warfare (ASW), maritime security (MS), surface warfare (SUW), special operations forces (SOF) support, electronic warfare (EW) and maritime interdiction operations (MIOs) support.[18] USVs will accomplish these missions using three standard and one nonstandard vehicle classes: X-class, Harbor class, Snorkeler class and Fleet class.[19]

X-class USVs are small (no more than 3 meters in length), nonstandard systems designed to support SOF and MIO missions. These systems provide a "low-end" ISR capability and are deployed from manned 11-meter rigid inflatable boats (RIBs) or the combat rubber raiding craft. X-class USVs are cheap and expendable, and have limited endurance (several hours), payload and seakeeping ability.[20]

Harbor-class (7-meter) USVs have robust ISR capabilities and are armed with both lethal and nonlethal weapons. These systems use the US Navy standard 7-meter RIB interfaces and are used to support MS missions. These USVs have moderate endurance (12 hours) and a maximum speed of 35-plus knots.[21]

The Snorkeler-class USV is a 7-meter semisubmersible vehicle (SSV) that is used to support MCM towing (search and neutralization) and ASW (maritime shield) missions. The system operates submerged with only its snorkel above the surface, which provides a more stable platform in high sea states. Its stealthy profile also allows it to be used in support of special missions. When conducting MCM search missions, the Snorkeler-class USV is capable of pulling a tow body, has stability in sea states up to Sea State 3, and an endurance of about 24 hours. The

---

[17] *Id.*, at 6–7.
[18] NAVY USV MASTER PLAN, *supra* note 13, at xi.
[19] *Id.*, at xi–xii.
[20] *Id.*, at xii, 58–59, 82.
[21] *Id.*, at xii, 58, 60, 83.

system is normally deployed from guided missile destroyers (DDGs) or littoral combat ships (LCSs) and has a maximum speed of 15-plus knots.[22]

The Fleet-class (11-meter) USV is purpose-built to support MCM sweep, protected passage ASW and "high-end" SUW missions. These systems provide moderate speed, power and endurance while towing MCM sweep gear, or high speed (32–35 knots) and very long endurance (48-plus hours) to support ASW, SUW or EW missions. Fleet-class USVs are deployable on the (LCS).[23]

In FY 2019, the US Navy began a medium USV (MUSV) program. These expendable systems have a length of between 12 and 50 meters and will initially be used for ISR and EW and will be operated with human operators in the loop or on the loop (semiautonomously), or fully autonomously.[24] The US Defense Advanced Research Projects Agency (DARPA) is working on a program called the "Sea Train" that allows a number of MUSVs to autonomously rendezvous at sea to form a convoy before navigating to their final destination. When they arrive on station, the convoy separates, with each MUSV going its own way to conduct an independent mission. Once these missions are complete, the MUSVs will reunite and return to their home port.[25]

The US Navy also plans to purchase two large USVs (LUSVs) per year from FY 2020 to FY 2024. These relatively low-cost platforms will be high-endurance, reconfigurable USVs that will be capable of carrying various modular payloads, including antiship and land-attack missiles. The LUSV will be about 200–300 feet in length and displace about 2,000 tons when fully loaded and will provide additional ASW and strike capacity in support of manned combatants.[26]

A Chinese USV – the JARI – underwent its first sea trial in January 2020. The USV is 15 meters (50 feet) in length, displaces 20 tons, and has a range of 500 M and a maximum speed of 42 knots. It is purportedly capable of conducting antisubmarine, air defense and surface combat missions, and is equipped with an active phased array radar similar to the

[22] *Id.*, at xii, 58, 61, 83.
[23] *Id.*, at xii, 58, 62, 84.
[24] CRS REPORT LARGE USVs/UUVs, *supra* note 16, at 14.
[25] Nathan Strout, All Aboard the Sea Train!, C4ISRNET, www.c4isrnet.com/unmanned/ 2020/06/01/all-aboard-the-sea-train/ (June 6, 2020; last visited Mar. 6, 2022) (online).
[26] CRS REPORT LARGE USVs/UUVs, *supra* note 16, at 11–12; *see also* US DoD, DEFENSE BUDGET OVERVIEW: UNITED STATES DEPARTMENT OF DEFENSE FISCAL YEAR 2020 BUDGET REQUEST chapter 1, 6; chapter 6, 10 (2019).

radar on the Type 052D DDG, as well as a sonar system capable of tracking underwater targets 4 miles away. The JARI is equipped with a 30-mm cannon, close-range air defense missiles, two surface-to-air and antiship missile launchers and two antisubmarine torpedo launchers.[27]

The US Navy also conducted a successful test of its overload LUSV from September to November 2020. The 59-meter USV – a converted high-speed craft – is part of the Navy's "Ghost Fleet" program and has autonomous navigation and engineering systems. The vessel made an autonomous voyage from Mobile, Alabama to Port Hueneme, California, stopping along the way to conduct operations in the Gulf of Mexico before transiting the Panama Canal. The successful six-week test covered more than 4,700 M, 97 percent of which was in the autonomous mode with a remarkably high reliability rate. The USV will be under the command and control of the San Diego-based Surface Development Squadron ONE (SURFDEVRON ONE). Ashore, the 24/7 operations center will be manned by surface warfare-qualified officers and senior enlisted personnel with appropriate rates trained in the Convention on the International Regulations for Preventing Collisions at Sea (COLREGs) and ship-handling. The operations center will also supervise the development of code for the supervisory control system of the vessel to ensure precise and reliable command and control. A second overload USV conducted a test voyage of 1,400 miles from Norfolk, Virginia to the Gulf Coast and back earlier in the year.[28]

10.2.4   Unmanned Underwater Vehicles (UUVs)

Like USVs, UUVs are force multipliers and risk-reduction systems that can assist naval forces in maintaining maritime superiority and control the maritime battlespace.[29] UUVs are employed in situations where they can increase performance at a lower cost to enable missions that cannot be performed by manned systems or reduce the risk to manned systems.[30] In 2017, the US Navy established its first UUV Squadron (UUVRON). The US Navy has identified nine high-priority UUV

---

[27] Liu Zhen, China's New Killer Robot Ship Goes through Its First Sea Trial, S. China Morning Post, Jan. 17, 2020.

[28] Pentagon "Ghost Fleet" Ship Makes Record-Breaking Trip from Mobile to California, News4Tomorrow, Nov. 10, 2020 (hereinafter "Ghost Fleet").

[29] US DEPARTMENT OF THE NAVY, THE NAVY UNMANNED UNDERSEA VEHICLE (UUV) MASTER PLAN xv, xvii, xxv, 77 (2004) (hereinafter NAVY UUV MASTER PLAN).

[30] Id., at 5.

missions: ISR, MCM, ASW, inspection/identification (ID), oceanography, communication/navigation network nodes (CN3), payload delivery, information operations (IO) and time critical strike (TCS).[31] These missions will be executed using four general vehicle classes: man portable, lightweight, heavyweight and large.[32]

The man-portable class includes vehicles from about 25 to 100 pounds displacement and an endurance of 10–20 hours. These systems can be deployed from most naval platforms or shore-based facilities and can be used in support of a variety of missions, including: special purpose ISR, expendable CN3, very shallow water (VSW)/shallow water (SW) MCM (coastal/riverine), MCM neutralizer, ID and explosive ordnance disposal (EOD).[33]

The lightweight vehicle (LWV) class includes cylindrically shaped vehicles of about 12.75 inches in diameter that displace about 500 pounds. The payload for LWVs is about six to twelve times greater than man-portable systems and the endurance is 20–40 hours, double that of a man-portable system. LWVs can be used to support Harbor ISR, special oceanography, mobile CN3, network attack (IO) and MCM operational area (OPAREA) reconnaissance.[34]

Heavyweight vehicle (HWV) class systems are generally 21 inches in diameter and displace about 3,000 pounds. HWVs include systems that are submarine torpedo tube compatible. HWVs are normally cylindrical shaped and can be used to conduct tactical ISR, oceanography, MCM clandestine reconnaissance and submarine decoy.[35]

The large vehicle class will displace about 20,000 pounds and will be compatible for use with both the LCS and the US Navy's attack submarine (SSN) and Ohio-class guided missile submarine (SSGN). These systems have the capability to travel long distances (greater than 100 miles) and remain on station for extended periods of time (over one week). Large vehicle UUVs will support several missions, including persistent ISR, ASW hold at risk, long range oceanography and payload delivery mine warfare [MIW], ASW, SOF, EOD and TCS.[36]

[31] Id., at xvi.
[32] Id.
[33] Id., at xxii, 68–69.
[34] Id., at xxii, 69.
[35] Id.
[36] Id., at xxiii, 69.

On February 13, 2019, the US Navy awarded a contract to Boeing to build, test and deliver four Orca extra large UUV (XLUUV) submarines. The Navy intends to purchase a total of nine Orcas. Due to its length (51 feet), the Orca will be too large to launch from a manned submarine. The system will have the capability to sail autonomously for up to 6,500 M. The Orca will be used for MCM, ASW, anti-SUW (ASuW), EW and TCS missions. The submarine will have a modular payload bay that can accommodate different types of payloads.[37]

UUV ISR capabilities are force multipliers that extend the reach of manned combatants into denied areas, and enable missions in water too shallow or otherwise inaccessible to large warships.[38] UUVs will be able to collect hydrographic and oceanographic data to support real-time operations and intelligence preparation of the battlespace (IPB) in advance of combat operations.[39] UUV CN3 capabilities will "provide connectivity across multiple platforms, both manned and unmanned, as well as navigation assistance on demand."[40] MCM capabilities are designed to allow UUVs to locate or create fleet operating areas that are clear of the threat of sea mines without putting at risking manned warships.[41] The objective of the ASW hold at risk capability is to use UUVs to "patrol, detect, track, and hand off adversary submarines to U.S. Forces."[42]

UUVs can also be used for inspection and identification in support of HLD, antiterrorism/force protection (AT/FP) and EOD needs. UUVs can "rapidly reconnoitre ... hulls, port areas, and other underwater areas ... to detect, investigate and localize unexploded ordnance (UXO) objects that impose a threat to military forces, high value assets, navigable waterways and homeland security."[43] UUV payload delivery capabilities provide commanders with "a clandestine method of delivering logistics to support a variety of other mission areas," to include SOF support and TCS.[44] Because of their ability "to operate clandestinely in shallow waters and areas too hazardous for a manned platform," UUVs are the platform

---

[37] CRS REPORT LARGE USVs/UUVs, *supra* note 16, at 16; David Axe, Here Come the Robot Submarines: Meet Boeing's 4 Huge Robotic Subs, Nat'l Int., Mar. 11, 2019.

[38] NAVY UUV MASTER PLAN, *supra* note 29, at xx.

[39] *Id.*

[40] *Id.*

[41] *Id.*, at xxi.

[42] *Id.*

[43] *Id.*

[44] *Id.*

of choice for numerous IO missions, such as use as a submarine decoy or
as a communications or computer node jammer.[45] Finally, UUVs can be
used effectively to deliver TCS by allowing for a launch point closer to the
target and keeping the "flaming datum" away from high-value manned
platforms.[46]

The US Navy is additionally looking at deploying UUVs to the Arctic
Ocean to monitor the environment and other activities. Woods Hole
Oceanographic Institution was awarded a contract by the US Navy on
September 29, 2020, to develop UUVs and oceanographic floats (sensor
buoys) that can be linked together through a networked C2 infrastructure.[47] Although the Arctic Mobile Observing System (AMOS) is being
developed to monitor environmental changes in the Arctic, it could
evolve into "a wide-area persistent underwater surveillance system" to
monitor foreign submarines and other military activities in the Arctic.[48]
AMOS will employ various UUVs, including fully autonomous systems,
and remain on station for 12 months, with a sensing footprint of some
100 kilometers and communications among nodes and from each vehicle
to a central node.[49] The autonomous UUVs will be able to operate under
the ice without using GPS.[50]

10.3   Unmanned Systems: Characterization and Status

UASs are addressed in the Chicago Convention and several instruments
adopted by the International Civil Aviation Organization (ICAO).[51]
These instruments, as well as several military manuals, provide a
bright-line test for the characterization and status of unmanned systems
as aircraft under international law. The characterization and status of

[45] *Id.*
[46] *Id.*, at xxii.
[47] Joseph Trevithick, The Navy Is Building a Network of Drone Submarines and Sensor Buoys in the Arctic, TheDrive, www.thedrive.com/the-war-zone/36821/the-navy-is-build ing-a-network-of-drone-submarines-and-sensor-buoys-in-the-arctic#:~:text=The%20U .S.%20Navy%20has%20awarded,to%20link%20them%20all%20together (Oct. 1, 2020; last visited Mar. 6, 2022) (online).
[48] *Id.*
[49] *Id.*; Office of Naval Research, U.S. Department of the Navy, Arctic Mobile Observing System (AMOS), www.onr.navy.mil/en/Science-Technology/Departments/Code-32/all-programs/arctic-global-prediction/AMOS-DRI (last visited Mar. 5, 2021) (online).
[50] *Id.*
[51] Convention on International Civil Aviation annex 1, Dec. 7, 1944, 61 Stat. 1180, T.I.A.S. No. 1591, 15 U.N.T.S. 295 (hereinafter Chicago Convention).

UMVs as ships or vessels under international law, however, is less clear. Unlike ICAO instruments that specifically refer to unmanned systems, treaties under the auspices of the IMO and other relevant international organizations do not refer to UMVs. Additionally, UNCLOS appears to impose a manning requirement on flag states to operate ships at sea. Yet nothing in UNCLOS or any of the relevant IMO instruments require that the captain and crew be physically on board the ship or vessel. Command and control of a USV from a shore-based operations center manned 24/7 by qualified officers and crews would meet these manning requirements.

10.3.1   Unmanned Aerial Systems (UASs)

"Aircraft" are defined in Annex 1 of the Chicago Convention as "any machine that can derive support in the atmosphere from the reactions of the air other than the reactions of the air against the earth's surface." Unmanned aircraft systems are further defined in ICAO Circular 328 as "an aircraft and its associated elements which are operated with no pilot on board."[52] Pilotless aircraft are also referenced in the convention. Article 8 provides that:

> No aircraft capable of being flown without a pilot shall be flown without a pilot over the territory of a contracting State without special authorization by that State and in accordance with the terms of such authorization. Each contracting State undertakes to insure that the flight of such aircraft without a pilot in regions open to civil aircraft shall be so controlled as to obviate danger to civil aircraft.[53]

These rules, however, only apply to civil aircraft. The Chicago Convention does not apply to state aircraft.[54] State aircraft include "aircraft used in military, customs and police services."[55] State aircraft are entitled to sovereign immunity and are not required to comply with ICAO flight procedures. The only requirement is that states operate their state aircraft, including UASs, with "due regard for the safety of navigation of civil aircraft."[56] It should be noted that the Chicago Convention does not contain a "manning" or "pilot-in-command" requirement for

---

[52] ICAO, Pub. No. Cir. 328, UNMANNED AIRCRAFT SYSTEMS (UAS) (2011) (hereinafter ICAO Cir. 328).
[53] Chicago Convention, *supra* note 51, art. 8.
[54] *Id.*, art. 3
[55] *Id.*
[56] *Id.*

state aircraft, although a predecessor convention – the 1919 Paris Convention – did contain such a requirement. Article 31 of the Paris Convention provided that "[e]very aircraft commanded by a person in military service detailed for the purpose shall be deemed to be a military aircraft."[57] It is unclear why this manning requirement was not included in the Chicago Convention.

US state practice is consistent with the Chicago Convention and its implementing regulations. Regulations of the DoD define "military aircraft" to include both manned and unmanned aircraft.[58] DoDI 4540.01 further provides that ICAO flight information region (FIR) "rules and procedures do not apply as a matter of international law to State aircraft, including U.S. military aircraft."[59] Nonetheless, as a matter of policy, US military aircraft normally follow ICAO flight procedures when conducting routine point-to-point flights.[60] Some military aircraft operations, however, do not lend themselves to ICAO flight procedures – for example, military contingencies, classified missions, politically sensitive missions, routine aircraft carrier operations and some training activities. Consistent with the Chicago Convention, such operations shall be conducted with "due regard for the safety of all other aircraft."[61] For UASs, "the aircraft commander or a visual observer in communication with the aircraft commander must ... maintain continuous and direct line-of-sight visual observation of the ... [UAS's] surrounding airspace."[62] UASs must also be "equipped with a Military Department-certified system that is sufficient to provide separation between them and other aircraft."[63]

10.3.2   Are Unmanned Maritime Vehicles (UMVs) Ships?

Regrettably, international law does not provide a similar bright-line test for the legal status of UMVs. Consequently, the seminal question is

---

[57] Convention Relating to the Regulation of Aerial Navigation art. 31, Oct. 13, 1919, *reprinted in* 1 J. Air L. & Com. 94, 100 (1930).

[58] US DoD, Instruction Number 4540.01: Use of International Airspace by U.S. Military Aircraft and for Missile and Projectile Firings 11 (2015) (hereinafter DoDI 4540.01); *see also* US DoD, Law of War Manual § 14.3.3 (2016) (hereinafter DoD Law of War Manual).

[59] DoDI 4540.01, *supra* note 58, at 3.

[60] *Id.*, at 8.

[61] *Id.*, at 9.

[62] *Id.*

[63] *Id.*

whether UMVs are ships or vessels under international law, and, if so, do they qualify as warships as defined in UNCLOS, Article 29. In both cases, the answer is "yes."

The terms ship and vessel are not defined in UNCLOS. They are, however, defined in several other international instruments. Regulation V/2 of the Safety of Life at Sea Convention (SOLAS) defines ships as "any ship, vessel or craft irrespective of type and purpose."[64] The Convention for the Prevention of Pollution from Ships (MARPOL) is a bit more precise, defining ship in Article 2 as "a vessel of any type whatsoever operating in the marine environment and includes hydrofoil boats, air-cushion vehicles, submersibles, floating craft and fixed or floating platforms."[65] Similarly, COLREGS, Rule 3 provides a more expanded definition of the term vessel to include "every description of water craft, including non-displacement craft, WIG [wing-in-ground] craft and seaplanes, used or capable of being used as a means of transportation on water."[66] A broader definition is found in the London Dumping Convention, which provides in Article 1 that the term vessels means "waterborne ... craft of any type whatsoever ... [and] includes air-cushioned craft and floating craft, whether self-propelled or not."[67] Finally, Article 1 of the SUA Convention defines ship as "a vessel of any type whatsoever not permanently attached to the sea-bed, including dynamically supported craft, submersibles, or any other floating craft."[68]

One key takeaway from these various definitions is that the differences between manned platforms and UMVs – such as the means of propulsion, type of platform, capabilities, durability, persistence, human versus autonomous control and potential mission sets – are not essential characteristics of what constitutes a vessel, ship or craft under international law. Accordingly, lacking a definitive statement to the contrary in an international instrument, most, if not all, UMVs can be

---

[64] International Convention for the Safety of Life at Sea ch. 6, regulation 2, Nov. 1, 1974, 32 U.S.T. 47, 1184 U.N.T.S. 278 (as amended) (hereinafter SOLAS).

[65] International Convention for the Prevention of Pollution from Ships art. 2, Nov. 2, 1973, 34 U.S.T. 3407, 1340 U.N.T.S. 61. (as amended); Protocol of 1978 Relating to the International Convention for the Prevention of Pollution from Ships, Feb. 17, 1978, 1340 U.N.T.S. 61.

[66] Convention on the International Regulations for Preventing Collisions at Sea r. 3, Oct. 20, 1972, 28 U.S.T. 3459, T.I.A.S. No. 8587, 1050 U.N.T.S. 16.

[67] Convention on the Prevention of Marine Pollution by Dumping of Wastes and Other Matter art. 1, Aug. 30, 1975, 26 U.S.T. 2403, 1046 U.N.T.S. 120.

[68] Convention for the Suppression of Unlawful Acts Against the Safety of Maritime Navigation art. 1, Mar. 10, 1988, 1678 U.N.T.S. 221 (as amended).

characterized as a ship, vessel or craft under domestic and international law if the flag state designates them as such.

This work of the Comite Maritime International (CMI) supports this assumption. CMI has stated that

> existing international conventions that define the term ship do not include references to crewing and at national level ... the definition of a ship is usually disconnected from the question of whether or not the ship is manned. It would ... seem unjustified that two ships, one manned and the other unmanned, doing similar tasks involving similar dangers would not be subject to the same rules that have been designed to address those dangers.[69]

In 2017, the IMO Maritime Safety Committee (MSC) agreed at its 98th session to include the issue of autonomous UMVs on its agenda. At its 100th session in December 2018, the committee adopted a framework for a regulatory scoping exercise "to determine how safe, secure and environmentally sound Maritime Autonomous Surface Ships (MASS) operations might be addressed in IMO instruments."[70] For purposes of the scoping exercise, a MASS is defined as "a ship which, to a varying degree, can operate independently of human interaction."[71] The varying degrees of autonomy that will be considered by the committee during the exercise include:

- A ship with automated processes and decision support: Seafarers are on board to operate and control shipboard systems and functions. Some operations may be automated.
- A remotely controlled ship with seafarers on board: The ship is controlled and operated from another location, but seafarers are on board to take control if necessary.
- A remotely controlled ship without seafarers on board: The ship is controlled and operated from another location. There are no seafarers on board.
- A fully autonomous ship: The operating system of the ship is able to make decisions and determine actions by itself.[72]

---

[69] COMITE MARITIME INTERNATIONAL, CMI INTERNATIONAL WORKING GROUP POSITION PAPER ON UNMANNED SHIPS AND THE INTERNATIONAL REGULATORY FRAMEWORK 3 (2018) (hereinafter CMI POSITION PAPER).
[70] IMO Doc. MSC/100/20, annex 2, ¶ 1 (Dec. 7, 2018).
[71] Id., ¶ 3.
[72] Id., ¶ 4.

The goal is to have the scoping exercise completed by 2020. Subsequently, at its 101st session in June 2019, the MSC approved interim guidelines for MASS trials.[73]

In support of this effort, the CMI Executive Council established an International Working Group to study the current international legal framework and consider what amendments, adaptions or clarifications are required in relation to unmanned ships to ensure the use and operation of such vessels is consistent with international law. To this end, CMI developed a questionnaire for the IMO asking nations whether UMVs are considered ships under their national laws. Of the nineteen nations responding to a CMI questionnaire, seventeen indicated that UMVs could constitute a ship under their national laws.[74]

Of note, a Chinese autonomous ship successfully made its maiden voyage in December 2019 as part of an ongoing project by Yunzhen Tech to explore the viability of the commercial use of UMVs. The unmanned cargo ship, the *Jindouyun 0 hao*, sailed from Dong Ao Islands to the No. 1 pier of Hong Kong–Macau Bridge. During the voyage, a number of remote control and autonomous voyage tests were conducted.[75] Similarly, in October 2020, Samsung Heavy Industries conducted a test voyage of the Samsung T-8 tug, which is equipped with autopilot, remote control technologies and collision avoidance capabilities. The 38-meter, 300-gross ton T-8 tug was remotely monitored from a shore-based center 241 kilometers away. The tug operated in an autonomous mode in Geoje Harbor, off the coast of Busan, for 9 kilometers without human intervention. Using Samsung Autonomous Ship technology – cameras, radar, automatic identification system (AIS) and satellite positioning – the tug successfully identified maritime hazards and changed course to avoid another vessel.[76]

Although ship and vessel are not defined in UNCLOS, the Convention envisions the use of UMVs in the marine environment. Article 19, for example, provides that ships engaged in innocent passage may not

---

[73] IMO Doc. MSC.1/Circ.1604 (June 14, 2019).
[74] IMO Doc. MSC/99/22, annex 1, at 1 (June 5, 2018).
[75] Safety4Sea, China Successfully Tests First Autonomous Cargo Ship, https://safety4sea .com/china-successfully-tests-first-autonomous-cargo-ship/ (Dec. 12, 2019; last visited Mar. 6, 2022) (online); Katherine Si, China's First Autonomous Cargo Ship Makes Maiden Voyage, Seatrade Mar. News, Dec. 16, 2019.
[76] Martyn Wingrove, Samsung Tests Autonomous Ship Technology on Tug, Rivera Oct. 22, 2020.

launch, land or take on board any military device.[77] Military devices could include both UASs and UMVs. Similarly, Article 20 requires submarines and underwater vehicles to navigate on the surface and show their flag when transiting the territorial sea in innocent passage.[78] The term "underwater vehicles," as distinct from (manned) submarines, includes UUVs.

Nonetheless, UNCLOS suggests that ships should be manned by a crew and under the control of a master. Article 94 provides that flag states are required to take necessary measures to ensure safety at sea with regard to their flag vessels, to include the "manning of ships ... and the training of crews, taking into account the applicable international instruments."[79] Such measures shall include those necessary to ensure, inter alia:

- that each ship is in the charge of a master and officers who possess appropriate qualifications, in particular in seamanship, navigation, communications and marine engineering, and that the crew is appropriate in qualification and numbers for the type, size, machinery and equipment of the ship; and
- that the master, officers and, to the extent appropriate, the crew are fully conversant with and required to observe the applicable international regulations concerning the safety of life at sea, the prevention of collisions, the prevention, reduction and control of marine pollution, and the maintenance of communications by radio.[80]

In taking these measures, the flag state "is required to conform to generally accepted [i.e., IMO-approved] international regulations, procedures and practices and to take any steps which may be necessary to secure their observance."[81]

It is common for UASs to be remotely piloted by personnel that are, in some cases, on a different continent thousands of miles away.[82] UASs used to conduct counterterrorism operations in the Middle East and Africa, for example, are operated by US Air Force pilots sitting in a room

---

[77] United Nations Convention on the Law of the Sea art. 19.2(f), Dec. 10, 1982, 1833 U.N.T.S. 397 (hereinafter UNCLOS).

[78] Id., art. 20.

[79] Id., art. 94.

[80] Id.

[81] Id.

[82] Ed Pilkington, Life as a Drone Operator: "Ever Step on Ants and Never Give It Another Thought?", Guardian, Nov. 19, 2015.

at Creech Air Force Base, Nevada.[83] It is therefore conceivable that a UMV could similarly be remotely operated by a crew and under control[84] of a master that is shore-based, far-removed from the area of operation, or embarked on a warship or naval auxiliary in the vicinity of the UMV. There is nothing to prevent a flag state from ensuring that the master, officers and crew that are remotely manning and operating a UMV are fully conversant with and required to observe the applicable international regulations in SOLAS, COLREGS, MARPOL and the maintenance of communications by radio. CMI agrees that the requirements of Article 94 can "arguably be met in case of remotely operated ships."[85] Moreover, the successful test of the overload large USV discussed earlier demonstrates that a UMS can be remotely commanded and controlled from a shore-based operations center by personnel trained in ship-handling and safety of navigation.

In the United States, all policies and regulations of the relevant governmental authorities are taken into consideration during the initial planning stages of an unmanned systems program. New technologies are "tested for safety and verified by the appropriate regulatory authority."[86] The Navigation Safety Advisory Council, which was established by Congress "to advise the Secretary of Transportation, via the Commandant, US Coast Guard, on matters relating to the prevention of collisions, rammings, and groundings," requires that a UMS complies with the safety of navigation rules applicable to international (72 COLREGS) and inland (COMDTINST M16672.2D) waters.[87] In addition, "UMS must comply with other rules and regulations, such as for RF communication equipment operation and for environmental restrictions covering the operation of sonars and underwater acoustic instruments."[88]

The US DoD requires that all UMVs be tested to certify compliance with the applicable regulations and demonstrate safe operations. In this regard, UMVs "must meet the same requirements of a manned craft or boat that is intended to be put into service."[89] The Naval Surface Warfare

---

[83] Andrew Craft, *Drone Pilots Fight Foreign Wars from Remote Nevada Desert*, FOX NEWS (June 20, 2018) (online).
[84] The term used in UNCLOS, Article 94 is in the "charge" of a master.
[85] CMI POSITION PAPER, *supra* note 69, at 6.
[86] DoD INTEGRATED ROADMAP, *supra* note 3, at 82.
[87] *Id.*
[88] *Id.*
[89] *Id.*, at 83.

Center Carderock, Detachment Norfolk, "has developed a guide for testing USVs and drafted an approach to certifying USVs."[90]

UNCLOS also makes clear that domestic, not international, law governs ship registration – "every State shall fix the conditions for the grant of its nationality to ships, for the registration of ships in its territory, and for the right to fly its flag," and provide documents to that effect.[91] The only additional international requirement is that "there must exist a genuine link between the State and the ship."[92] In the US, Chapter 46, Part 67 of the Code of Federal Regulations, governs the documentation of US flagged vessels. For the purposes of registration, the term vessel "includes every description of watercraft or other contrivance capable of being used as a means of transportation on water but does not include aircraft."[93] "Any vessel of a least five net tons wholly owned by a citizen or citizens of the United States is eligible for documentation" in the United States.[94] The regulations make no distinction between manned and unmanned vessels. Therefore, unmanned vessels that meet the ownership and tonnage requirements can be documented as a vessel in the United States.

10.3.3   Are Unmanned Maritime Vehicles (UMVs) Warships?

Assuming a UMV qualifies as a ship or vessel, the next question is whether the UMV can be characterized as a warship as that term is defined in international law. This is a particularly important issue given that warships are the only vessels that can exercise belligerent rights (e.g., offensive attacks) under LOAC, as well as conduct maritime law enforcement operations in times of peace.[95]

---

[90] Id.
[91] UNCLOS, supra note 77, art. 91.
[92] Id.
[93] 46 C.F.R. § 67.3 (2021).
[94] 46 C.F.R. § 67.5 (2021).
[95] Declaration Respecting Maritime Law, Apr. 16, 1856, 115 Consol. T.S. 1, 15 Martens Nouveau Recueil (ser. 1) 791, reprinted in 1 Am. J. Int'l L. Supp. 89 (1907); Convention No. VII Relating to the Conversion of Merchant Ships into War-ships, Oct 18, 1907, 205 Consol. T.S. 319 (hereinafter Hague VII); Institute of International Law, Manual of the Laws of Naval War, art. 12 (1913); US Navy, Pub. No. NWP 1-14M, The Commander's Handbook on the Law of Naval Operations § 2.2.1 (2017) (hereinafter NWP 1-14M); DoD Law of War Manual, supra note 58, § 13.3.3; UNCLOS, supra note 77, art. 110.

UNCLOS defines warship as "a ship belonging to the armed forces of a State bearing the external marks distinguishing such ships of its nationality, under the command of an officer duly commissioned by the government of the State and whose name appears in the appropriate service list or its equivalent, and manned by a crew which is under regular armed forces discipline."[96] Although Article 29 is qualified by the phrase "for the purposes of this Convention," US Navy and DoD doctrine recognize this definition as authoritative.[97]

Certainly, a UMV can belong to the armed forces of a state and can bear external markings regarding its nationality. Is a UMV, however, capable of being "under the command" of a commissioned officer and "manned" by a crew subject to armed forces discipline? Although, the US DoD classifies UASs as military aircraft, it has not adopted a similar position regarding the status of UMVs as warships. Rather than designate UMVs as warships, US Navy doctrine currently classifies military UMVs and UMVs engaged exclusively in government, noncommercial service as sovereign immune "craft."[98]

It is important to note that the current definition of warship originated in 1907, long before the advent of unmanned systems. Hague VII, which governs the conversion of merchant ships to warships, requires that the converted merchant ship: (1) be "placed under the direct authority, immediate control, and responsibility of the Power whose flag it flies"; (2) "bear the external marks which distinguish the warships of their nationality"; (3) be under the command of a duly commissioned officer in the service of the State whose "name must figure on the list of the officers of the fighting fleet"; and (4) be manned by a crew "subject to military discipline."[99] The drafters of Hague VII could not have envisioned the development and proliferation of unmanned systems in 1907, and the definition should be reexamined in light of current and emerging technologies.

Moreover, there is nothing in UNCLOS or any other international instrument that requires the commander and crew to be physically present on board the warship. If UAVs can be remotely piloted and still qualify as a military aircraft, there is nothing that prohibits the United States from taking a similar position with regard to UMVs. That is,

---

[96] UNCLOS, *supra* note 77, art. 29.
[97] NWP 1-14M, *supra* note 95, § 2.2.1; DoD Law of War Manual, *supra* note 58, § 13.4.1.
[98] NWP 1-14M, *supra* note 95, § 2.3.6.
[99] Hague VII, *supra* note 95, arts. 1–4.

UMVs can be remotely manned by a crew and under the command of a commissioned officer that is not physically present on the UMV, and still be considered a warship under both domestic and international law. Consistent with this interpretation of the law, the San Diego-based SURFDEVRON ONE will exercise command and control of US Navy UMVs from a shore-based operations center manned by SUW-qualified officers and senior enlisted personnel with appropriate rates trained in COLREGs and ship-handling.[100]

However, not all UMVs should be classified as warships. Smaller UMVs that are launched and controlled by warships and submarines are considered an extension of the launch platform and can engage in belligerent acts or assist in maritime law enforcement activities. Nonetheless, as given that mission sets for large UMVs, like the Orca and Sea Hunter, include offensive operations, the US DoD and Navy must readjust its policy now with regard to the status of UMVs. Under current US Navy doctrine, naval auxiliaries, merchant vessels and presumably UMVs are not warships and may only defend themselves from enemy attacks – they may not engage in offensive combat operations in an international armed conflict.[101] Yet, one of the nine priority mission areas for a number of UMVs is TCS, which calls for the delivery of ordnance on a target from an UMV or UMV-delivered weapon cache.[102]

A UUV's stealth, long-standoff distance and endurance features, in particular, allow for clandestine weapon delivery and remote launch, thus making the UUV a weapon platform of choice for various TCS missions.[103] Underwater weapons cache or buoyant missile launch capsules delivered by a UUV can "loiter in place awaiting launch instructions, or the UUV itself could carry the weapons and loiter."[104] But, in order to execute this capability, the UUV must be designated as a warship.

Domestically in the United States, the authority to register, classify and designate naval waterborne craft as warships rests with the Chief of Naval Operations (CNO).[105] Warship classification applies to any ship built or armed for naval combat that the US Navy maintains on the Naval Vessel Register. In this regard, the CNO is responsible for entering vessels into

---

[100] *"Ghost Fleet," supra* note 28.
[101] These limitations do not apply to noninternational armed conflicts. NWP 1-14M, *supra* note 95, § 2.2.1.
[102] Navy UUV Master Plan, *supra* note 29, at xxii.
[103] *Id.*, at 15.
[104] *Id.*, at 48.
[105] US Department of the Navy, U.S. Navy Regulations § 0406 (1990).

the battle force ship inventory and the Naval Vessel Register. Battle force ships are commissioned United States Ship (USS) warships capable of contributing to combat operations, which could include some UMVs currently under development.[106] Neither Navy Regulations nor the SECNAVINST distinguish between manned and unmanned vessels. Consequently, there is nothing that prohibits the CNO from designating a UMV as a warship so long as he or she complies with applicable fiscal law requirements,[107] and determines that the manning and command requirements can be satisfied remotely.

10.3.4 Sovereign Immunity

As a matter of customary international law, all manned and unmanned vessels and aircraft owned or operated by a state, and used, for the time being, only on government noncommercial service are entitled to sovereign immunity. Military UASs are considered state aircraft and UMVs engaged exclusively in government, noncommercial service are characterized as sovereign immune craft. UMV immunity is not dependent on the status of its launch platform, but rather is inherent in the UMV.[108] Accordingly, military UASs and naval UMVs, wherever located, are immune from arrest, search, inspection and foreign taxation. Additionally, the flag state has the authority to protect the identity of stores, weapons or other property on board the craft.[109]

The principle of sovereign immunity is reflected in various provisions of UNCLOS. Article 32, for example, specifies that nothing in UNCLOS "affects the immunities of warships and other government ships operated for non-commercial purposes."[110] Similarly, Articles 95 and 96 make clear that warships and government-owned or -operated ships used only on government noncommercial service operating on the high seas have complete immunity from the jurisdiction of any state other than the flag state.[111] Article 58 applies the immunities described in Articles 95 and 96 to the exclusive economic zone (EEZ) – "Articles 88 to 115 and other

---

[106] US Department of the Navy, SECRETARY OF THE NAVY INSTRUCTION 5030.8C: GENERAL GUIDANCE FOR THE CLASSIFICATION OF NAVAL VESSELS AND BATTLE FORCE SHIP COUNTING PROCEDURES (2016).
[107] 10 U.S.C. §§ 231, 8667 (2018).
[108] NWP 1-14M, *supra* note 95, § 2.3.6.
[109] *Id.*, § 2.1.
[110] UNCLOS, *supra* note 77, art. 32.
[111] *Id.*, arts. 95–96.

pertinent rules of international law apply to the exclusive economic zone."[112] Thus, regardless of whether a UMV is considered to be a warship or not, as a government craft or vessel operated for noncommercial purposes, it is entitled to all the rights, privileges and immunities enjoyed by such vessels under international law.

10.4   Navigational Rights and Freedoms

UASs and UMVs are entitled to all the navigational rights and freedoms enjoyed by manned ships and aircraft. ICAO regulations provide that civilian UASs "will operate in accordance with ICAO Standards that exist for manned aircraft as well as any special and specific standards that address the operational, legal and safety differences between manned and unmanned aircraft operations."[113] However, if the UAS is going to integrate into nonsegregated airspace or at a nonsegregated aerodrome, a pilot must be responsible for the UAS operation, and "under no circumstances will the pilot responsibility be replaced by technologies in the foreseeable future."[114]

CMI suggests a similar approach for UMVs. Assuming that UMVs are ships or vessels within the meaning of UNCLOS, "they are subject to the same rules of the law of the sea as any ordinarily manned ship."[115] UMVs and their flag states have an obligation to comply with the same international rules that apply to manned vessels, and "they also enjoy the same passage rights as other ships and cannot be refused access to other states' waters merely because they are not crewed."[116] In this regard, 70 percent of the states responding to the CMI questionnaire indicated that unmanned ships would enjoy the same rights and duties as manned ships under UNCLOS.[117] Similarly, the US maritime law association stated that under US law, ship is defined without regard to manning and that unmanned ships are subject to the same rights and obligations under the law of the sea.[118]

---

[112] *Id.*, art. 58.
[113] ICAO Cir. 328, *supra* note 52, ¶ 3.1.
[114] *Id.*
[115] CMI Position Paper, *supra* note 69, at 3.
[116] *Id.*
[117] IMO Doc. MSC/99/INF.8, annex 1, at 4 (Feb. 13, 2018).
[118] *Id.*

Accordingly, UMVs may exercise the right of innocent passage in foreign territorial seas and archipelagic waters.[119] Additionally, UMVs may be deployed from another military platform that is engaged in innocent passage as long as their employment is consistent with UNCLOS, Article 19 (employment not prejudicial to the peace, good order or security of the coastal state) and Article 20 (no submerged transit in innocent passage).[120] However, there is no reciprocal right of innocent passage for UASs through national airspace. The Chicago Convention prohibits state aircraft from flying over the territory of another state without its consent or authorization by special agreement or otherwise, and territory is defined in the Convention to include the "territorial waters adjacent thereto."[121]

UASs and UMVs likewise enjoy the right of unimpeded transit passage, in the normal mode, through straits used for international navigation between one part of the high seas or an EEZ and another part of the high seas or an EEZ and their approaches.[122] Similarly, UASs and UMVs may exercise the right of archipelagic sea lanes passage in the normal mode, while transiting through, under or over archipelagic sea lanes, which include all routes normally used for international navigation and overflight.[123] Finally, beyond the territorial sea, UASs and UMVs possess the full range of high seas freedoms of navigation and overflight, and other internationally lawful uses of the sea guaranteed to all ships and aircraft – manned or unmanned – by international law.[124]

10.4.1 Duties and Obligations

With these navigational rights and freedoms come a number of corresponding duties and obligations that UASs and UMVs must observe. First, with regard to innocent passage of UMVs, passage is considered prejudicial to the peace, good order or security of the coastal state if a

---

[119] NWP 1-14M, *supra* note 95, §2.5.2.5.
[120] *Id.*; UNCLOS, *supra* note 77, arts. 19–20.
[121] Chicago Convention, *supra* note 51, arts. 1–3.
[122] NWP 1-14M, *supra* note 95, §§ 2.5.3.2, 2.7.1.1; UNCLOS, *supra* note 77, art. 38; DoDI 4540.01, *supra* note 58, at 2.
[123] NWP 1-14M, *supra* note 95, §§ 2.5.4.1, 2.7.1.2; UNCLOS, *supra* note 77, art. 53; DoDI 4540.01, *supra* note 58, at 2.
[124] NWP 1-14M, *supra* note 95, §§ 2.6, 2.7.2; UNCLOS, *supra* note 77, art. 58, 86–87; DoDI 4540.01, *supra* note 58, at 2.

ship engages in a number of proscribed activities listed in Article 19. Thus, UMVs engaged in innocent passage are prohibited from:

- using force (or threatening the use of force) against the sovereignty, territorial integrity or political independence of the coastal state, or in any other manner in violation of the principles of international law embodied in the UN Charter;
- exercising or practicing with weapons of any kind;
- collecting information to the prejudice of the defense or security of the coastal state;
- engaging in acts of propaganda aimed at affecting the defense or security of the coastal state;
- launching, landing or taking on board of any aircraft or military device;
- carrying out of marine scientific research or hydrographic survey activities; and
- conducting acts aimed at interfering with any systems of communication or any other facilities or installations of the coastal state.[125]

UUVs engaged in innocent passage must also navigate on the surface and show their flag.[126] That is not to say that submerged transit of a UUV in a foreign territorial sea is a violation of international law. While submerged transit may violate the sovereignty of the coastal state and makes the UUV ineligible for the rights and privileges of innocent passage, its conduct is not per se unlawful under international law.[127] The United States takes the position that, in order to enjoy the right of innocent passage, submarines and other underwater vehicles are required to navigate on the surface and show their flag. However, failure to do so is not characterized as inherently not "innocent." The Convention sets "forth conditions for the enjoyment of the right of innocent passage in the territorial sea," but it does not prohibit or otherwise affect activities or conduct that is inconsistent with that right and therefore "not entitled to that right," such as intelligence collection and submerged transits by submarines.[128]

---

[125] UNCLOS, *supra* note 77, art. 19.

[126] *Id.*, art. 20.

[127] James Kraska, *Putting Your Head in the Tiger's Mouth: Submarine Espionage in Territorial Waters*, 54 COLUM. J. TRANSNATIONAL L. 164, 212–28 (2016).

[128] S. REP. NO. 108–10, at 9 (2004).

SOLAS and UNCLOS allow coastal states to designate traffic separation schemes (TSSs) and sea lanes in the territorial sea or international straits to regulate shipping, if such measures are necessary to ensure safety of navigation.[129] Warships, naval auxiliaries, and other government owned or operated ships used only on government noncommercial service, including UMVs, however, are not legally required to comply with such sea lanes or TSSs. SOLAS Regulation V/1 exempts such vessels from compliance.[130] Sovereign immune vessels, including UMVs, that elect not to comply with IMO-approved designated sea lanes and TSSs must still exercise due regard for the safety of navigation. Similarly, while exercising high seas freedoms of navigation and overflight and other internationally lawful uses of the seas in the EEZ, UASs and UMVs must do so with due regard to the rights and duties of the coastal state.[131]

If a UMV does not comply with the laws and regulations of the coastal state concerning innocent passage (e.g., intelligence collection) and disregards any request for compliance therewith that is made to it, the coastal state may require the UMV to leave the territorial sea immediately.[132] Likewise, the flag state bears international responsibility for any loss or damage to the coastal state resulting from the noncompliance by a warship or other government ship operated for noncommercial purposes, including UMVs, with coastal state laws and regulations concerning passage through the territorial sea or with the provisions of UNCLOS or other rules of international law.[133]

10.5   Conclusion

The unmanned systems of tomorrow, particularly autonomous and semiautonomous systems, will fundamentally change the way nations conduct military operations in times of war and MS operations in times of peace. Their use and mission sets will continue to expand as new technologies, including greater stealth, persistence, autonomy and durability, are developed and employed that not only reduce operational risk and cost, but far exceed the current capabilities and limitations of manned platforms. By 2025, worldwide military UAS production alone

---

[129] *Id.*; SOLAS, *supra* note 64, ch. V.
[130] SOLAS, *supra* note 64, ch. V, regulation 1.
[131] UNCLOS, *supra* note 77, art. 58.
[132] *Id.*, art. 30.
[133] *Id.*, art. 31.

will grow from US\$2.8 billion to US\$9.4 billion.[134] As these systems proliferate and are enhanced by new technologies, including artificial intelligence (AI) and machine learning, unmanned systems capable of conducting offensive strikes, or conducting swarm attacks that deny access to a given area or overwhelm air defense systems, will increasingly be within the reach of states and nonstate actors alike.[135]

Inevitably, unmanned systems will become increasingly autonomous. DARPA has set aside US\$41 million to work on a revolutionary new program called No Manning Required, Ship (NOMARS). The program aims to design a ship "with no provision, allowance, or expectation for humans at sea."[136] By eliminating design considerations associated with a crew, NOMARS will have "greater hydrodynamic efficiency via hull optimization without requirements for crew safety or comfort."[137] Eliminating the human element from ship design will also have other advantages, to include "size, cost [e.g., procurement, operations and sustainment], at-sea reliability, survivability to sea-state, and survivability to adversary action such as stealth considerations and resistance to tampering."[138] The ship can operate autonomously or under human control for up to 12 months without maintenance.

The increased use of AI will also allow autonomous systems to engage in more "sophisticated decision-making, self-directed activity and ... complex human-machine teaming."[139] The degree of autonomy will depend on the unmanned system's abilities for "sensing, analyzing, communicating, planning, deciding and acting," as well as the complexity and legal and policy constraints of the mission.[140] Some maritime operations that allow for more expanded autonomy include MCM, denied-area ISR, ASW, SIGINT/ELINT collection and operational deception.[141] Nonetheless, future unmanned autonomous or semiautonomous systems will inevitably bring changes to:

---

[134] Walker, *supra* note 4.

[135] SAYLER, *supra* note 2, at 8, 29.

[136] US Defense Advanced Research Projects Agency, No Manning Required, Ship (NOMARS) Proposers Day, shorturl.at/pyzMS (Jan. 13, 2020; last visited Mar. 6, 2022) (online).

[137] *Id.*

[138] *Id.*

[139] NATO, SCIENCE & TECHNOLOGY TRENDS 2020–2040: EXPLORING THE S&T EDGE 9 (2020).

[140] *Id.*, at 60.

[141] *Id.*, at 62.

- Force structure: Autonomous systems will replace humans in operational and tactical environments that are dull, dirty, dangerous or dear (such as CBRN, EOD and ISR).
- Effectiveness: Next-generation networks and advanced AI will integrate disparate technohuman systems into unified and focused capabilities.
- Countermeasures: Increased use of unmanned systems and swarming on the battlefield will require additional force protection measures with effective counterdrone capabilities.
- Swarming: Autonomous swarms will allow for new sensing and attack paradigms for friendly forces.
- Logistics: Autonomous systems will transport passengers and cargo to the battlefield.
- Situational awareness: Widely dispersed, persistent, low-observable unmanned systems will provide enhanced ISR capabilities.
- Lethality: Low-cost unmanned systems will improve force projection without minimal risk to human operators.
- Maneuverability: Unmanned systems will enable greater tactical and operational agility through increased presence, numbers and reduced logistics needs.
- Survivability: Use of unmanned systems will reduce combat casualties and improve operational effectiveness.
- Sustainability: Autonomous systems will facilitate logistics support in dangerous and remote operational environments.
- Urban operations: Small unmanned systems will increase situational awareness in the urban environment.
- Cyber: Autonomous software will undertake offensive and defensive cyber operations.[142]

In short, autonomous systems can operate in a more cost-effective manner with fewer human personnel. They consume less communications bandwidth, are more adaptable to changed circumstances and have increased survivability against threats. Unmanned systems can also operate more effectively in austere and challenging antiaccess/area denial environments and support a broader range of more complex missions with less risk to human personnel.[143]

---

[142] *Id.*, at 64–66.
[143] Daniel Gonzales & Sarah Harting, Designing Unmanned Systems with Greater Autonomy: Using a Federated, Partially Open Systems Architecture Approach 53 (2014).

Some examples of ways in which emerging technologies will be used to reduce unintended harm to civilians and civilian objects include:

- autonomous self-destruct, self-deactivation or self-neutralization mechanisms;
- use of AI to increase awareness of the presence of civilians and civilian objects on the battlefield by automating the processing and analysis of data;
- use of AI to quickly assess the likely effects of weapons during the targeting process to minimize collateral damage;
- use of automated target identification, tracking, selection and engagement functions to allow weapons to strike military objectives more accurately and with less risk of collateral damage; and
- use of autonomous systems to reduce the need for immediate use of force in self-defense.[144]

During peacetime, although the current state of international law is arguably adequate to regulate newly emerging unmanned systems, there remain gaps in both domestic and international laws and regulations that need to be filled in order to better control the employment of a UMV in the marine environment. This will require the intervention of the IMO and its various committees and subcommittees to provide definitive guidance on matters such as safety of navigation and protection of the marine environment that are acceptable to all nations, or simply a reinterpretation of the meaning and scope of existing law of the sea instruments and domestic laws and regulations. If necessary, the existing international regulatory framework can be modified to integrate the new and advancing technology of UMVs.

---

[144] US, Humanitarian Benefits of Emerging Technologies in the Area of Lethal Autonomous Weapon Systems, in Report of Group of Governmental Experts on Lethal Autonomous Weapon Systems, U.N. Doc. CCW/GGE.1/2018/WP.4 (Mar. 28, 2018).

11

Seabed Technology and Naval Operations on the Continental Shelf

JAMES KRASKA

11.1 Legal Regime of the Continental Shelf

Military operations on the continental shelf are becoming more important as naval forces seek the safety of the seabed. Advancements in long-range, precision strike weapons such as antiship cruise missiles, antiship ballistic missiles and hypersonic missiles threaten the survivability of surface warships. New sensors, stretching from outer space to the deep seabed are making the oceans more transparent. The weapons and sensors are being fused into battle networks that complete a "kill chain," designed to identify, track, target and destroy enemy warships. In response, navies are moving their platforms under water, building new types of submarines, and experimenting with naval deployment and activities on the seabed – either the deep seabed or on the continental shelf of coastal states. Military operations on the international seabed area ("the area") occur on the deep seabed in areas beyond national jurisdiction. These military activities are virtually without restraint because they are subject to the regime of the high seas. Military activities on the continental shelf are more complex because coastal states enjoy sovereign rights and jurisdiction over that part of the seabed, while foreign states are entitled to exercise high seas freedoms.

This chapter focuses on the legal regime applicable to naval operations on the continental shelf and some of the emerging technologies that support them. In peacetime, military activities on the continental shelf are subject to the United Nations (UN) Convention on the Law of the Sea, and in particular, the legal regime of the continental shelf reflected in Part VI.[1]

The continental shelf is coterminous with the exclusive economic zone (EEZ), a large swath of space that extends 200 nautical miles (M) from the shoreline of coastal states and encompasses some 38 percent of the oceans. In certain cases where the coastal state has a natural prolongation of the continental margin beyond the EEZ, coastal states may be entitled to exercise exclusive sovereign rights and jurisdiction over an "outer" or "extended" continental shelf underlying part of the high seas and occasionally another state's EEZ. Coastal states enjoy exclusive sovereign rights and jurisdiction on the continental shelf for the purposes of exploring and exploiting the living and nonliving resources.[2] Furthermore, the rights of the coastal state do not affect the legal status of the superjacent waters or airspace above the continental shelf, whether it is EEZ or high seas.[3] Consequently, coastal state consent is not required to conduct submarine transit in the superjacent water column, surface ship transit or overflight. The coastal state also has competence to regulate some other uses of the continental shelf, such as establishment of artificial islands,[4] consent over marine scientific research,[5] delineation of the course for laying submarine cables and pipelines,[6] and jurisdiction over some types of installations and structures on the seabed.[7]

The coastal state's right to protect the marine environment on the continental shelf is more limited and circumscribed in Part XII.[8] In

---

[1] United Nations Convention on the Law of the Sea, Dec. 10, 1982, 1833 U.N.T.S. 397 (hereinafter UNCLOS).
[2] Id., arts. 58(1); 77.
[3] Id., art. 56(2), 87.
[4] Id., art. 80.
[5] Id., art. 246.
[6] Id., arts. 79; 80; 112(2).
[7] Id., art. 246.
[8] Id., art. 208, 210(5), 214, 216.

recognition of the coastal state's exclusive rights on the continental shelf, it may elect to exclude continental shelf maritime boundary delimitation from mandatory dispute resolution procedures in UNCLOS.[9]

The formula for determination of the outer limit of the extended continental shelf is defined in complex detail in UNCLOS, which represents a collective decision on the maximum claim acceptable for coastal states considering the interests of other states.[10] States that make claims unsupported by the formula in Article 76 of UNCLOS encroach on the deep seabed, eroding the stability of the bargained for exchange in the treaty.[11]

11.1.1   Concept of the Continental Shelf

While the concept of the a "maritime belt" or territorial sea emerged from custom and state practice in the sixteenth century,[12] development of the legal continental shelf lagged. States had occasional disputes over access to seabed species lying near shore, although the continental shelf regime did not gain serious attention until the discovery of offshore oil. Early efforts to develop the law pertaining to coastal states' rights in the nearshore seabed were rudimentary. In 1896, the first offshore oil well in territorial waters was drilled from piers off the coast of Santa Barbara, California.[13] In 1921, the State of California passed a statute to require the exploitation of offshore oil only pursuant to state leases and the payment of royalties.

During the 1930s, US interest in offshore oil development expanded to the states of the Gulf of Mexico, raising two issues. First, what was the division of authority in the seabed between the individual states of the Republic and the Federal government?[14] Second, how would neighboring nations delimit overlapping continental shelf claims?

---

[9] Id., art. 298(1)(a)(i).

[10] PANEL ON THE LAW OF OCEAN USES, UNITED STATES POLICY ON COASTAL AREAS IN THE SEA AND THE SETTLEMENT OF DISPUTES 2 (May 15, 1988) (Chaired by Louis Henkin).

[11] Michael W. Lodge, *Enclosure of the Oceans versus the Common Heritage of Mankind: The Inherent Tension between the Continental Shelf Beyond 200 Nautical Miles and the Area*, 97 INT'L L. STUD. 803, 831 (2021).

[12] CORNELIUS VAN BYNKERSHOEK, DE DOMINIO MARIS DISSERTATIO 43 (Ralph van Deman Magoffin, trans. 1923 [2d ed. 1744]).

[13] United States: Drill-seeking; Offshore Oil and Gas, The Economist, July 8, 2006, at 50.

[14] United States v. California, 32 U.S. 19 (1947) (California does not have title to submerged lands offshore, which vest in the United States).

Coastal state sovereignty was recognized throughout the water column of the marginal or territorial sea that most states extended to a breadth of 3 M.[15] In rare cases, coastal states were recognized as having rights to sedentary species on the seabed beyond the territorial sea, such as the dispute over ownership of pearl and chank conch shell fisheries in the Gulf of Mannar between the west coast of Sri Lanka and the southeastern tip of India.[16] Similarly, Ireland claimed to regulate oyster fisheries as far as 20 nautical miles (M) from shore.[17] The seabed had the same status as the high seas and it was regarded as incapable of occupation, although there were some exceptions based on "immemorial usage and effective occupation."[18] Unlike the seabed, however, the subsoil under the bed of the sea could be regarded as "occupied," such as through construction of mines or tunnels in the earth below the oceans.[19]

Seabed delimitation was achieved through agreement among states, such as the 1923 bilateral treaty between Great Britain and France to regulate oyster fisheries in waters adjacent to their coasts.[20] The agreement was innovative because it divided access to seabed resources beyond the territorial sea long before recognition of the regime of the continental shelf.

---

[15] Richard W. Hale, *Territorial Waters as a Test of Codification*, 24 AM. J. INT'L L. 65 (1930).

[16] OFFICE OF THE GEOGRAPHER, U.S. DEP'T OF STATE, LIMITS IN THE SEA NO. 66, HISTORIC WATER BOUNDARY: INDIA–SRI LANKA 3–4 (1975). The status of Palk Bay as historic waters has at least some legal authority, having been the subject of a judicial decision in the case of Annakumaru Pillai v. Muthupayal, heard in the Appellate Criminal Division of the Indian High Court in Madras in 1903–04. During that time, both Sri Lanka (Ceylon) and India were under the administration of the UK. The lawsuit involved rights to chank (Indian conch) beds and pearl grounds in Palk Bay and the adjacent Gulf of Mannar (Mannar). The Court ruled that the Bay was "landlocked by His Majesty's dominions for eight-ninths of its circumference . . . [and] effectively occupied for centuries by the inhabitants of the adjacent districts of India and Ceylon respectively." *Id.*, at 4. The Court continued that, "[w]e do not think that Palk's Bay can be regarded as being in any sense the open sea and therefore outside the territorial jurisdiction of His Majesty." Finally, the British occupation had attracted the "acquiescence of other nations."

[17] Cecil J. B. Hurst, *Whose Is the Bed of the Sea: Sedentary Fisheries Outside the Three-Mile Limit*, 4 BRIT. Y.B. INT'L L. 34, 40–41 (1924); Clive R Symmons, *The Sea Fishery Regime of the Irish Sea*, 4 INT'L J. ESTUARINE AND COASTAL L. 192, 213 (1989).

[18] C. JOHN COLOMBOS, INTERNATIONAL LAW OF THE SEA § 83 (6th rev. ed. 1967).

[19] The Cornwall Submarine Mines Act of 1858, for example, vested the subsoil to Her Majesty the Queen as part of the soil and territorial possessions of the Crown. *Id.*

[20] Declaration by the British and French Governments Respecting Oyster Fisheries outside Territorial Waters in the Seas Lying between the Coasts of Great Britain and Those of France, 21 L.N.T.S. 138 (1923).

When states met in 1930 at the Hague to codify the customary law of the sea, the continental shelf was considered the "whole extent of the ocean bed" as "along the coasts where the depth does not exceed 200 meters."[21] Still, the 1930 conference did not produce a treaty that would clarify the outer extent of the continental shelf, leaving it to state practice to slowly define the legal regime.

11.1.1.1   The Truman Proclamation

In 1938, Louisiana claimed an area extending 24 M from a three-mile marginal sea.[22] The US Federal government quickly moved to check Baton Rouge. On July 1, 1939, President Roosevelt, who always sought ways to expand US Federal jurisdiction, both against the individual states and other nations, wrote a memorandum to the Attorney General and Secretaries of State, Navy and Interior, arguing that the jurisdiction of the United States should be shifted seaward to the limits of "inventive genius."[23] The president moved away from this position, however, during the election of 1940, when the Republican nominee, Wendell Willkie, adopted the politically popular position to support the rights of the individual states in the Federal system.[24]

In 1942, UK and Venezuela agreed to divide the continental shelf in the Gulf of Paria.[25] That same year, with the urgent need for natural resources to fuel the war effort, President Roosevelt appointed Secretary of the Interior Harold L. Ickes as petroleum administrator for the remainder of the war. Ickes solidified his authority to issue Federal regulations for offshore deposits.[26] In 1943, Ickes recommended that the United States should claim resource rights to the seabed beyond the coast.

Truman was sworn in as president on April 12, 1945, and on September 28, he issued Proclamation 2667 that claimed exclusive US rights to the resources of the seabed to a depth of about 200 meters, while

---

[21] Questionnaire No. 7: Exploitation of the Products of the Sea, Annex, 20 Am. J. Int'l L. Supp. 230, 231 (1926).

[22] ANN L. HOLLICK, U.S. FOREIGN POLICY AND THE LAW OF THE SEA 29 (1981).

[23] Id., at 30.

[24] Id., at 31, n.55.

[25] Treaty between His Majesty in respect of the United Kingdom and the President of the United States of Venezuela Relating to the Submarine Areas of the Gulf of Paria, 205 L.N.T.S. 121 (1942).

[26] Exec. Order No. 9276, 7 Fed. Reg. 10,091 (Dec. 4, 1942), terminated by Exec. Order No. 9718, 11 Fed. Reg. 4,965 (May 7, 1946)

leaving undisturbed freedom of the seas in the superjacent waters.[27] The proclamation was motivated by two factors – the inexorable drive for natural resources during the war and advances in undersea technology that provided access to them. After the war, other states followed the American precedent and began to declare their own continental shelf, and indeed used the Truman Proclamation as a springboard for even greater maritime claims.[28] The unilateral US declaration filled a vacuum in the law. More importantly, Truman's action energized coastal states around the world to assert greater claims in the ocean, setting the stage for acceptance of a fishery zone that transformed into the EEZ and solidifying the concept of the juridical continental shelf.

11.1.1.2   Continental Shelf Convention

At its first session in 1949, the UN International Law Commission (ILC) began work in earnest on drafting a general law of the high seas, to include the continental shelf. On December 6, the UN General Assembly asked the ILC to include work on the territorial sea as well. In 1956, the ILC produced a package of draft articles and commentary that served as the basis for negotiations at the First UN Conference on the Law of the Sea in 1958.[29] The conference produced four treaties, including the Convention on the Continental Shelf. The treaty recognizes that coastal states may assert an indeterminate claim to a depth of 200 meters, or "beyond that limit where the depth of the waters admits of the exploitation of the natural resource."[30] This "exploitability criterion" did not provide a stable metric for measuring the outer limit of the continental shelf. Judge Jessup of the International Court of Justice observed "that an attempt to define the exploitability in meters is like the pre-World War I attempt to measure sovereignty of the air by the

---

[27] Proc. No. 2667, 10 Fed. Reg. 12,305 (Sept. 28, 1945) (codified as Exec. Order No. 9633).

[28] F. V. García-Amador, *The Latin American Contribution to the Development of the Law of the Sea*, 68 Am. J. Int'l L. 33 (1974).

[29] International Law Commission, Articles Concerning the Law of the Sea with Commentaries, 1956 Yearbook of the International Law Commission 265–301 (1956); UN Conference on the Law of the Sea, *Comments by Governments on the Draft Articles Concerning the Law of the Sea Adopted by the International Law Commission at Its Eighth Session*, U.N. Doc. A/CONF.13/5 (Feb. 24–27, 1958), *reprinted in* U.N. Doc. A/CONF.13/37, 1 Official Records of the United Nations Conference on the Law of The Sea 75 (1958).

[30] Convention of the Continental Shelf, art. 1, Apr. 29, 1958, 15 U.S.T. 471, T.I.A.S. No. 5578, 499 U.N.T.S. 311

height of the Eiffel Tower."[31] Furthermore, the 1958 Convention did not stipulate the degree of coastal state control over foreign activities on the continental shelf.

Meanwhile, concern over military uses of the seabed was increasing as the oceans became a fulcrum for Cold War competition. The first nuclear submarine, USS *Nautilus* (SSN-571), was launched in 1954, underscoring the strategic importance of the oceans in the nuclear era. The Second Committee of the 1958 UN Conference considered prohibiting the testing of nuclear weapons on the high seas.[32] In March 1958 during the negotiations in Geneva, Bulgaria offered a proposal to ban the use of military installations by the coastal state on its continental shelf.[33] India broadened the Bulgarian proposal the following month with text that would have banned the coastal state or any other state from military uses of the continental shelf: "The continental shelf adjacent to any coastal State shall not be used by the coastal State or any other State for the purposes of building military bases or installations."[34] India's proposal, however, was defeated by a vote of 36 to 18, with six abstentions. The 1958 Convention on the Continental Shelf is silent on military activities.

11.1.1.3   Seabed Committee

The questions surrounding the outer limit of the continental shelf and the coastal states rights thereon remained unresolved. On July 13, 1966, at the commissioning of the *Oceanographer*, President Lyndon Johnson stated, "Under no circumstances, we believe, must we ever allow the prospects of a rich harvest of mineral wealth to create a new form of colonial competition among maritime nations. We must be careful to avoid a race to grab and to hold the lands under the high seas. We must ensure that the deep seas and the ocean bottoms are, and remain, the legacy of all human beings."[35] The following year, Arvid Pardo, Maltese

---

[31] Bruce A. Harlow, *Legal Aspects of Claims to Jurisdiction in Coastal Waters*, 23 JAG J. 81, 92–93 (1968).

[32] U.N. Doc. A/CONF.13/40, 4 OFFICIAL RECORDS OF THE UNITED NATIONS CONFERENCE ON THE LAW OF THE SEA 43–48 (1958).

[33] U.N. Conference on the Law of the Sea, Summary Records of the 21st to 25th Meetings of the Fourth Committee, ¶ 5, U.N. Doc. A/Conf. 13/C.4/L.41/Rev. 1 (Vol. 6), annex I (Mar. 26, 1958).

[34] *Id.*, ¶ 29, U.N. Doc. A/Conf. 13/C.4/L.57 (Vol. 6) annex I (Apr. 1, 1958).

[35] 2 Public Papers of the President, LYNDON B. JOHNSON, 1966: CONTAINING THE PUBLIC MESSAGES, SPEECHES, AND STATEMENTS OF THE PRESIDENT 722 (2005).

Ambassador to the UN, called for greater governance of the seabed, setting in motion negotiations that produced UNCLOS.[36]

The month after Pardo's speech, the UN General Assembly established an Ad Hoc Committee to Study the Peaceful Uses of the Sea-Bed and the Ocean Floor beyond the Limits of National Jurisdiction.[37] After three sessions, in 1968, the Committee presented its conclusion to the UN General Assembly.[38] The findings convinced the General Assembly of the need for broader review, which was initiated through establishment of the Committee on the Peaceful Uses of the Sea-Bed and the Ocean Floor beyond the Limits of National Jurisdiction.[39] Comprised of forty-two member states, the Committee explored the norms and rules for global oceans governance. On December 21, 1968, the Committee report requested that the Secretary-General gauge support for convening a multilateral conference of states to codify oceans governance.[40]

Meanwhile, the International Court of Justice held in the North Sea Continental Shelf Cases that the coastal state's rights were inherent and exist "ipso facto and ab initio, by virtue of its sovereignty over the land."[41] Like Johnson, on May 23, 1970, President Richard Nixon acknowledged that some of the wealth of the seabed would be reserved for all nations while coastal states would have jurisdiction closer to shore. Nixon envisioned a rather narrow coastal state continental shelf. Nixon proposed that states should negotiate a treaty that limited coastal state rights to a continental shelf extending only to the 200-meter isobath, with the balance of the seabed under some type of global governance.[42]

11.1.2   Seabed Nuclear Arms Treaty

Pardo's 1967 speech launched negotiations for UNCLOS, but it had a more immediate effect in inspiring the Seabed Nuclear Arms

---

[36] UNCLOS, *supra* note 1, art. 76.

[37] G.A. Res. 2340 (XXII), ¶ 1 (Dec. 18, 1967).

[38] Report of the Ad Hoc Committee to Study the Peaceful Uses of the Sea Bed and the Ocean Floor beyond the Limits of National Jurisdiction, U.N. Doc. A/7230 (1968).

[39] G.A. Res. 2467 (XXIII), at 15 (Dec. 21, 1968).

[40] Richard M. Nixon, *United States Oceans Policy, May 23, 1970*, 6 Weekly Comp. Pres. Docs. 655, 677 (1970).

[41] North Sea Continental Shelf (F.R.G. v. Den., F.R.G. v. Neth.), Judgment, 1969 I.C.J. Rep. 3, 23 (Feb. 20).

[42] *Id.*

Treaty.[43] When Pardo called for recognition of seabed mineral resources as the "common heritage of mankind," he also expressed concern that the Cold War would lead to militarization of the seabed.[44] Pardo was pushing on an open door, capturing the zeitgeist of the era. While Pardo's ideas formed the foundation for negotiation of Part XI of UNCLOS on deep seabed mining in the area, he also spurred action on a separate but related set of negotiations to address nuclear weapons on the seabed.

Pardo advanced a proposal for preserving the oceans for "peaceful purposes." In 1963, the two superpowers banned nuclear tests in the atmosphere, outer space and underwater, including the territorial seas and high seas.[45] That same year, the Outer Space Treaty reserved "the moon and other celestial bodies" exclusively for "peaceful purposes."[46] The sentiment that the seabed and oceans, which were also regarded as global commons, should be reserved for peaceful purposes gained traction but had not yet been discussed at the UN.

On March 18, 1969, The Soviet Union presented a draft treaty that proposed the completed demilitarization of the seabed beyond 12 M.[47] The United States countered that complete demilitarization of the seabed was not verifiable. On May 22, the United States replied with a draft text that prohibited emplacement of nuclear weapons and other weapons of mass destruction on the seabed beyond 3 M.[48] The two drafts were considered in the UN Eighteen Nation Committee on Disarmament (ENDC)[49] and evolved into a compromise treaty submitted to the

---

[43] Treaty on the Prohibition of the Emplacement of Nuclear Weapons and other Weapons of Mass Destruction on the Seabed and the Ocean Floor and in the Subsoil thereof, May 18, 1972, 955 U.N.T.S. 115 (hereinafter Seabed Nuclear Treaty).

[44] U.N. Doc. A/C.1 (Nov. 1, 1967), ¶ 45–48, U.N. GAOR, 22d Sess., 1515th mtg. (Examination of the question of the reservation for peaceful purposes of the seabed and the ocean floor, and the subsoil thereof, underlying the high seas beyond the limits of present national jurisdiction, and the use of their resources in the interests of mankind.)

[45] The Treaty Banning Nuclear Weapons Tests in the Atmosphere, in Outer Space and Under Water, Oct. 15, 1963, 480 U.N.T.S. 43.

[46] Treaty on Principles Governing the Activities of States in the Exploration and Use of Outer Space, Including the Moon and Other Celestial Bodies, Jan. 27, 1967, 18 U.S.T. 2410, T.I.A.S. No. 6347, 610 U.N.T.S. 205.

[47] ARMS CONTROL AND DISARMAMENT AGENCY, ARMS CONTROL AND DISARMAMENT AGREEMENTS: TEXTS AND HISTORIES OF NEGOTIATIONS 99 (1980).

[48] Id., at 100.

[49] G.A. Res. 1722 (XVI) (Dec. 21, 1961) (Question of Disarmament).

Conference of the Committee on Disarmament (CCD), the larger suc-
cessor to ENDC, on October 7, 1969.[50]

The Seabed Nuclear Arms Treaty prohibits emplacement of nuclear
weapons on the seabed and the ocean floor beyond 12 M from the
baseline from which the territorial sea is measured.[51] The prohibition
extends to structures, launching installations and other facilities specifically designed for storing, testing or using nuclear weapons. The treaty
also prohibits emplacement of nuclear naval mines on the seabed and
ocean floor or in the subsoil thereof. It does not, however, prohibit the
deployment of nuclear weapons in the water column, provided that they
are not affixed to the seabed, such as nuclear-armed depth charges and
torpedoes in submarines.[52]

The treaty has rather limited goals, only addressing the use of the
seabed to preposition or launch nuclear weapons and other weapons of
mass destruction on the seabed beyond the territorial sea. The treaty
addressed Pardo's concern that nuclear weapons would be emplaced on
the seabed but did little to arrest the undersea nuclear competition. The
superpowers explained that the agreement did not exclude the temporary
deployment of nuclear missile submarines or antisubmarine warfare
(ASW) detection systems on the seafloor because such temporary sta-
tioning was not considered to be "emplaced" or planted on the seabed
and ocean floor or subsoil thereof. The treaty also did not affect conventional weapons systems and sensors or other seabed installations. These
programs included not only the network of seabed sound surveillance
systems (SOSUS) in use at the time but also other potential seabed
military installations and structures.

Pardo's speech accelerated calls for controlling the superpower arms
race in the oceans since technology was ushering in a new era of undersea
warfare.[53] Developing states were concerned that the superpower arms

---

[50] The UN disarmament committee has evolved since its creation as the Ten-Nation
Committee on Disarmament (TNDC) in Geneva in 1960. ENDC operated from
1962 to 1968, and the Conference of the Committee on Disarmament (CCD), Geneva,
from 1969 to 1978. The current Committee on Disarmament (CD) was established in
1979 and has sixty-five members.

[51] Seabed Nuclear Treaty, *supra* note 43, art. 2.

[52] U.S. Navy, U.S. Marine Corps & U.S. Coast Guard, NWP 1-14M/MCTP 11-10B/
COMDTPUB P5800.7A, The Commander's Handbook on the Law of Naval
Operations § 10.2.2.1 (2017).

[53] Stockholm International Peace Research Institute, SIPRI Yearbook of
Armaments and Disarmament 1969/1970 150–51 (1970) (hereinafter SIPRI
Yearbook 1969/1970).

race would drive proliferation of nuclear weapons to the seabed, under-mining international security. At the same time, the Soviet Union and the United States sought to place some limits on their adversary.[54] The Soviet Union introduced a draft resolution to the Ad Hoc Committee that proposed banning all military uses of the seabed beyond areas of national jurisdiction.[55]

On December 7, 1970, the UN General Assembly requested that governments open the Seabed Nuclear Treaty for signature and ratifica-tion.[56] The treaty was adopted in Washington, Moscow and London on February 11, 1971, and entered into force on May 18, 1972. Just ten days after the General Assembly requested states open the Seabed Nuclear Arms Treaty for signature, the states adopted another resolution that reserved the high seas and seabed and ocean floor for "peaceful pur-poses."[57] The resolution also decided to convene a general comprehen-sive conference in 1973 on the law of the sea – the Third UN Conference on the Law of the Sea (UNCLOS III).[58]

11.1.3 "Peaceful Purposes"

The Third UN Conference negotiated and adopted UNCLOS, which covers virtually every aspect of oceans governance.[59] In keeping with the mandate of the UN General Assembly, UNCLOS aspires to promote the "peaceful uses" of the seas and oceans. UNCLOS, Article 301 is titled "peaceful uses of the seas," and it declares that states parties shall refrain from "the threat or use of force against" the territorial integrity or political independence of other states. This text is copied

---

[54] U.N. Doc. A/AC.135/28, The Military Uses of the Seabed and the Ocean Floor beyond the Limits of National Jurisdiction (July 10, 1968).

[55] U.N. Doc. A/AC.135/20; see also Legal Regime of the Deep Seabed, 6 SOVIET STAT. & DEC. 287 (1970).

[56] G.A. Res. 2660 (XXV) (Dec. 7, 1970) (Treaty on the Prohibition of the Emplacement of Nuclear Weapons and Other Weapons of Mass Destruction on the Sea-Bed and the Ocean Floor and in the Subsoil Thereof); see also A Limited Sea Bed Treaty, N.Y. TIMES, Feb. 17, 1971, at 38.

[57] G.A. Res. 2750 (XXV), at 25–27 (Dec. 17, 1970) (Reservation exclusively for peaceful purposes of the seabed and the ocean floor, and the subsoil thereof, underlying the high seas beyond the limits of present national jurisdiction and use of their resources in the interests of mankind and convening of a conference on the law of the sea.)

[58] Id.

[59] UNCLOS, supra note 1, preamble.

verbatim from the Charter of the UN and reflects a bedrock norm of international law.[60]

The terms "peaceful uses" and "peaceful purposes" are synonymous and underpin the entire geographic and functional structure of UNCLOS. The terms appear eight times in the Convention, plus in the preamble. Article 301 reserves the seas generally for peaceful purposes, and Article 141 reserves the area for peaceful purposes. The high seas are reserved for peaceful purposes through Article 88, and this provision also applies by Article 56(2) throughout the EEZ. Thus, no state may purport to claim sovereignty over the common spaces available for use by all states – the high seas, EEZ and the international seabed.[61] Furthermore, these areas subject to high seas freedoms are reserved exclusively for peaceful uses. The area consists of the seabed beyond national jurisdiction and is governed under Part XI of UNCLOS as the common heritage of mankind. Articles 240, 242 and 246 mandate that marine scientific research may be conducted only for peaceful purposes.

In addition to UNCLOS, the term "peaceful purposes" is featured in more than a dozen treaties, including the Outer Space Treaty,[62] the Nonproliferation Treaty[63] and the Seabed Arms Control Treaty.[64] The term is also part of regional agreements, including the South Pacific Nuclear Free Zone Treaty,[65] Latin American and Caribbean Nuclear Free Zone Treaty,[66] and the Antarctic Treaty.[67] In 1971, the UN General Assembly declared the Indian Ocean a zone of peace.[68] Yet,

---

[60] U.N. Charter, art. 2(4).

[61] UNCLOS, *supra* note 1, preamble.

[62] Treaty on Principles Governing the Activities of States in the Exploration and Use of Outer Space, Including the Moon and Other Celestial Bodies, art. IV, 610 U.N.T.S. 205 (1967); Treaty on Principles Governing the Activities of States in the Exploration and Use of Outer Space, Including the Moon and Other Celestial Bodies, art. III, 1363 U.N.T.S. 21 (1979).

[63] Treaty on the Nonproliferation of Nuclear Weapons, pmbl., arts III and IV, 729 U.N.T.S. 161 (1968).

[64] Treaty on the Prohibition of the Emplacement of Nuclear Weapons and Other Weapons of Mass Destruction on the Seabed and the Ocean Floor and in the Subsoil thereof, pmbl., 955 U.N.T.S. 115 (1971).

[65] South Pacific Nuclear Free Zone Treaty (Treaty of Rarotonga), art. 4, 1445 U.N.T.S. 177 (1985).

[66] Treaty for the Prohibition of Nuclear Weapons in Latin America and the Caribbean (Treaty of Tlatelolco), pmbl. and Arts. 1, 12, 17, 18, 634 U.N.T.S. 281 (1967).

[67] The Antarctic Treaty, arts. I and IX, 402 U.N.T.S. 71 (1959).

[68] G.A. Res. 2832 (XXVI), Dec. 16, 1971 (Declaration of the Indian Ocean as a Zone of Peace).

despite broad usage, there is no universal definition of the terms "peaceful uses" or "peaceful purposes." These words have been regarded as meaning everything from nonaggression to regional nonnuclearization to actual prohibition of all military activities.[69] The ambiguity surrounding the terms and disagreement over the contending visions and theoretical nature of the concept they embody has nearly eviscerated the concept of "peaceful uses" or "peaceful purposes," leaving them virtually without concrete meaning.

States disagreed on the meaning of "peaceful purposes" or "peaceful uses." Some developing states held the position that the terms must mean the complete demilitarization of all naval activities at sea.[70] The United States, the Soviet Union and other states pushed back, suggesting that activities of the armed forces that are conducted in a manner consistent with the Charter of the UN were lawful, and reflective of "peaceful purposes" or "peaceful uses. If the more pacifist interpretations of "peaceful purposes" had prevailed at UNCLOS III, the maritime powers would have withdrawn from the negotiations.[71]

Article 2(4) of the Charter of the UN is the appropriate metric for whether activities are peaceful. That provision prohibits the threat or use of force against the territorial integrity or political independence of another state, and constitutes the general proscription against armed attack, or in the equally valid French language text, "armed aggression."[72] This view has become the conventional understanding of the term "peaceful purposes" and "peaceful uses" of the sea, and in 1985 was set forth in a report of the UN Secretary-General.[73] Furthermore, the internal logic of UNCLOS allows for no other conclusion: Were military activities on the high seas generally to be considered illegal, the optional exclusion of such disputes from the dispute settlement procedures in Article 298 would be unjustifiable or superfluous. Yet, disagreement over the meaning of "peaceful purposes" on the continental shelf makes it more likely that states will clash, with foreign naval forces seeking to conduct military operations on the seabed of the continental shelf of coastal states.

---

[69] James Kraska, Maritime Power and Law of the Sea 253–60 (2011).
[70] U.N. Doc. A/CONF.62/SR.67, Apr. 23, 1976, p. 56.
[71] Id., at 62.
[72] G.A. Res. 3314 (XXIX), Dec. 14, 1974 (Definition of Aggression).
[73] U.N. Doc. A/40/535, Study on the Naval Arms Race: Report of the Secretary-General, Sept. 17, 1985, ¶ 188.

11.2   Military Activities on the Continental Shelf

While Pardo's speech was the impetus for regulating the mineral resources of the deep seabed, he also warned of the economic and strategic consequences of the military uses of the ocean floor.[74] Yet, the regime of the continental shelf refers to military activities only obliquely and by omission.

The rules that apply to military activities on the continental shelf have become especially important as the United States seeks to improve its integrated undersea surveillance system (IUSS) infrastructure to track submarines, develop naval mine warfare capabilities, and operate unmanned underwater vehicles for surveillance and strike missions.[75] New capabilities such as "upward falling payloads" may be tethered to the seabed for extended periods of time and released into the water column where they operate as submersibles, float to the surface and operate as vessels, or launch aircraft. The "Hydra" concept envisions a seabed network of sensors and weapons positioned along the seabed of an adversary.

The legal regime in Part VI of UNCLOS is quite permissive for military activities on the continental shelf. Such operations on the seabed within the EEZ shall have due regard for the rights of the coastal state.[76] There is no requirement for such due regard, however, in the outer or extended continental shelf beyond 200 M, except in the case of laying submarine cables and pipelines.[77]

By the time states were negotiating UNCLOS, the United States had nearly two decades of experience with SOSUS deployed on the seabed. The SOSUS network was designed to track Soviet submarines. While states could readily track aircraft and objects in outer space and ships on the surface of the water, the ability to sense, understand and act in the deep ocean has been elusive.[78]

---

[74] U.N. Doc. A/C.1 (Nov. 1, 1967), *supra* note 44, ¶ 47.

[75] US Navy, US Marine Corps & US Coast Guard, Advantage at Sea: Prevailing with Integrated All-Domain Naval Power 22 (2020) (hereinafter Advantage at Sea).

[76] UNCLOS, *supra* note 1, arts. 56; 58.

[77] UNCLOS, *supra* note 1, art. 79.

[78] William G. "Bill" Glenney, The Deep Ocean: Seabed Warfare and the Defense of Undersea Infrastructure, Ocean News & Technology, Apr. 2020, 18, 19.

11.2.1   Sound Surveillance System

SOSUS sprang from ASW technology of World War II.[79] In the years preceding World War II, Japan emplaced ocean floor hydrophones in the Tsugaru and Shimonoseki Straits to detect submarines and in various ports for harbor protection.[80] In 1944, two scientists – Maurice Ewing and J. Lamar Worzel – conducted basic acoustic experiments on long-distance sound propagation in the water column to detect submerged submarines or mines at a distance.[81] They detonated one pound of TNT underwater near the Bahamas and detected the low-frequency blast some 2,000 miles away off the coast of West Africa.

Beginning in the 1950s, the United States initiated project Jezebel to develop a global network of some 1,000 deepwater passive sensors to listen for Soviet submarines.[82] In 1954, the Caesar system was commissioned in Puerto Rico, with stations spreading to the Bahamas and Bermuda, Nova Scotia, Nantucket, Cape May, Cape Hatteras, Antigua and Barbuda, Eleuthera, and Barbados.[83] A station was established at the Soya (La Perouse) Strait at the northwestern tip of Hokkaido in 1957.[84] The project evolved in 1959 into the Caesar SOSUS, consisting of a series of underwater active and passive sensors on the seabed tied to Navy shore stations by 30,000 miles of undersea cable, tracking sounds over hundreds and sometimes thousands of miles of ocean.[85] Sound detected by the SOSUS hydrophones is transmitted by cable to electronic centers ashore, where the acoustic signatures of submarines are separated from other underwater noise, such as from whales or oil rigs.[86] The systems

---

[79] Edward C. Whitman, SOSUS: The Secret Weapon of Undersea Surveillance, UNDERSEA WARFARE (Winter 2005).

[80] DESMOND BALL & RICHARD TANTER, THE TOOLS OF OWATATSUMI: JAPAN'S OCEAN SURVEILLANCE AND COASTAL DEFENCE CAPABILITIES 37 (2015).

[81] Deborah K. Smith, Ears in the Ocean, Oceanus Mag., Aug. 2004, 54–56.

[82] William J. Broad, Scientists Object as Navy Retires Ocean Listening System, N.Y. Times, June 12, 1994, 1;
GARY E. WEIR, AN OCEAN IN COMMON: AMERICAN NAVAL OFFICERS, SCIENTISTS, AND THE OCEAN ENVIRONMENT 298–315 (2001).

[83] First-Generation Installations and the Initial Operational Experience, Undersea Warfare, Winter 2005.

[84] BALL & TANTER, supra note 80, at 55–78.

[85] SIPRI YEARBOOK 1969/1970, supra note 53, at 94.

[86] Thomas B. Allen & Norman Polmar, The Silent Chase: Tracking Soviet Submarines, N.Y. Times Mag., Jan. 1, 1984, 13–14.

were gradually upgraded and expanded to the UK.[87] Japan–US cooperation on SOSUS continued throughout the 1960s.[88]

The use of the seabed for SOSUS illustrates the overriding importance of the ASW mission and strategic nuclear deterrence. During the 1950s, the United States and Soviet Union put to sea rudimentary cruise missile submarines to distribute and disperse long-range artillery. In 1955, Russia launched the first ballistic missile submarine (SSB), a converted Zulu IV class diesel-powered boat with a single ballistic missile launch tube in its sail. The nuclear-powered USS *George Washington* (SSBN 598) entered service in December 1959, armed with sixteen Polaris A-1 nuclear ballistic missiles. Suddenly, ballistic missile submarines became the most survivable leg of the nuclear triad, vaulting ahead of more vulnerable land-based bomber aircraft and land-based intercontinental ballistic missiles. Furthermore, because the submarines could operate in closer proximity to enemy coastlines, decision-making times for retaliatory strikes were compressed, contributing to the nuclear "balance of terror."

11.2.2   Seabed Installations and Structures

Naval technology was making the seabed more transparent, opening it up as a separate domain of warfare. In the 1960s, the Naval Oceanographic Office developed the first multibeam sonar, a classified system that utilized numerous sonar beams to dramatically enhance the fidelity and clarity of the image of the seabed. Multibeam sonar captures large amounts of data, and unlike single-beam sonar, converts the images into a three-dimensional topographic map that accurately displays vertical features, such as seamounts. Beginning in the late 1970s, as computing power rose exponentially, deepsea technology became more available to scientists and oil companies.[89] The use of multibeam sonar arrays provided an accurate picture of the seabed for the first time.[90] This technology emerged just as states were negotiating UNCLOS, and it was expected that the vast treasures of the seabed would become accessible.

[87] THOMAS S. BURNS, THE SECRET WAR FOR THE OCEAN DEPTHS: SOVIET-AMERICAN RIVALRY FOR MASTERY OF THE HIGH SEAS 157–58 (1978).
[88] Memorandum from Walt W. Rostow, National Security Advisor, to Lyndon B. Johnson, President of the United States (May 21, 1968); BALL & TANTER, *supra* note 80, at 51.
[89] Janice K. Flagg, *New Bathymetric Maps*, 70 THE MILITARY ENGINEER 158–60 (May–June 1978).
[90] Jean Francheteau, *The Oceanic Crust*, 249 SCI. AM. 114, 123 (1983).

As the United States entered the Second Session of the negotiations for UNCLOS in Caracas, it sought to protect a range of interests, which included innocent passage in the territorial sea, transit passage in straits and, now less appreciated, freedom to conduct military operations in the international seabed area.[91] Some developing states attempted to expand coastal state competence over artificial islands, installations and structures to include all installations for any purpose, including military purposes. Venezuela, Colombia and Mexico offered a proposal in 1973, and separately, Peru, in 1978.[92] These proposals would have required coastal state consent for military installations or devices on the continental shelf.[93] In Caracas, a group of thirty-eight developing states sought to include in the treaty a prohibition on military activities of the continental shelf of a coastal state, threatening the SOSUS program. Their proposed text stated:

> No state shall be entitled to construct, maintain, deploy or operate on or over the continental shelf of another state any military installations or devices or any other installations for whatever purposes without the consent of the coastal state.[94]

Instructions to the US delegation in Caracas underscored that the United States envisioned a "regime which will protect high seas uses, including SOSUS, which is a vital first substantive session of the Law of the Sea Conference element in our arms control equation with the U.S.S.R."[95] For example, Admiral Gorshkov wrote in his treatise on sea power that

---

[91] HOLLICK, *supra* note 22, at 213–14.

[92] Committee on the Peaceful Uses of the Sea-bed and the Ocean Floor beyond the Limits of National Jurisdiction, Report of the Subcomm. II, U.N. Doc. A/AC.138/SC.II.L.21, art. 7 (1973).

[93] 2 VIRGINIA COMMENTARY ON THE UNITED NATIONS CONVENTION ON THE LAW OF THE SEA ¶ 60.15(c), at 584 (Satya N. Nandan & Shabtai Rosenne eds., 1993) (hereinafter "2 VIRGINIA COMMENTARY").

[94] The proposal was made by Algeria, Argentina, Bangladesh, Burma, Brazil, Chile, Colombia, Cuba, Cyprus, Ecuador, El Salvador, Ghana, Guatemala, Guinea, Guyana, Haiti, India, Indonesia, Iran, Jamaica, Kenya, the Libyan Arab Republic, Mauritania, Mauritius, Mexico, Morocco, Nigeria, Panama, Peru, Philippines, Senegal, Somalia, Trinidad and Tobago, United Republic of Cameroon, Uruguay, Venezuela and Yugoslavia. Third U.N. Conference on the Law of the Sea, U.N. Doc. A/CONF.62/C.2/L.42/Rev.l. (Vol. III) (Aug. 13, 1974).

[95] Other US interests included coastal state resource jurisdiction over the minerals of the continental shelf and offshore fisheries, a permissive regime for marine scientific research, sound rules for protecting the marine environment and a sensible regime for deep seabed mining conducive to US commercial interests. Memorandum from John Norton Moore, Chairman, NSC Interagency Task Force on the Law of the Sea & Deputy Special

KRASKA

special consideration should be given to the military uses of the continental shelf.[96]

The proposals to limit military activities on the continental shelf were not adopted by the Conference and are not included in UNCLOS.[97] Foreign states are not forbidden from constructing military installations and structures on a coastal state's continental shelf per se. The text of Article 60 recognizes that coastal states enjoy the "exclusive right" to authorize or regulate the construction of artificial islands (but not installations or structures) in the EEZ, a rule extended to the continental shelf by virtue of Article 80. The unqualified reference to "artificial islands" in paragraph 1(a), on the one hand, contrasts with the qualified references to "installations and structures" in 1(b) and (c).

While the coastal state enjoys the exclusive right to construct, authorize and regulate the construction, operation and use of all artificial islands, when it comes to installations and structures, that right pertains only to those erected "for the purposes provided for in Article 56" – namely, economic purposes. Article 56 provides that coastal states enjoy specified sovereign rights in the EEZ "for the purpose of exploring and exploiting, conserving and managing" living and on-living resources.[98] States have the same rights on the continental shelf, including the seabed and subsoil.[99] Consequently, the final text of UNCLOS did not include a prohibition on construction of installations and structures on the seabed. Instead, the coastal state may regulate only those installations and structures that are "for the [economic] purposes provided for in article 56," or that "interfere with the exercise of the rights of the coastal State" over its resources.[100] This text was designed specifically to accommodate the SOSUS network, and permits additional military uses of the continental shelf as well.

By the mid-1980s, the hydrophone network was supplemented by an enormous magnetic anomaly detection system spanning the Tsushima and Tsugaru straits that could track silent submarines that might elude acoustic arrays.[101] During the 1990s, much of the SOSUS network atrophied and there was serious talk of shutting it down, an obsolete

---

Representative of the President for the Law of the Sea Conference, to Deputy Secretary of Defense et al., 5, 7 (Mar. 27, 1974).

[96] SERGEY G. GORSHKOV, THE SEA POWER OF THE STATE 75 (CIA Trans. Dec. 12, 1980).

[97] 2 VIRGINIA COMMENTARY, supra note 93, ¶¶ 60.7, 60.10.

[98] UNCLOS, supra note 1, art. 56(1)(a).

[99] Id., art. 77(1).

[100] Id., arts. 60(1)(b)–(c).

[101] Joel S. Wit, Advances in Antisubmarine Warfare, 244 SCI. AM. 31, 36–37 (1981); BALL & TANTER, supra note 80, at 48.

relic of the Cold War. Marine scientists who hoped to use it to harvest data for basic research opposed the idea.[102] Since 1991, some SOSUS data have been used by scientists to study natural phenomena, such as cracking ice, volcanic activity, breaking waves and megafauna.[103]

The fixed surveillance system (FSS) of SOSUS is supplemented by a mobile surveillance system (MSS) that includes the US Navy's surveillance towed array sensor system (SURTASS) and ocean surveillance ships using low-frequency active sonar (LFA). As mobile platforms, these vessels may be deployed to meet emergent operational requirements. The Navy operates five SURTASS ships, including the USNS *Victorious* and USNS *Impeccable*, which China has confronted aggressively with warships and maritime militia vessels.[104]

During the Cold War, the key SOSUS node stretched across the Greenland–Iceland–UK gap in support of NATO's ASW mission to block Soviet submarines moving from Murmansk into the North Atlantic Ocean.[105] The Japan Maritime Self Defense Force, in conjunction with the United States, maintains a seabed sensor system that runs along the western coastline of the country.[106] Although the precise location of the persistent SOSUS network is not public, scholars and media suggest it runs from Korea and Japan, through Sasebo and Kagoshima on Kyushu, across the Osumi Channel to Okinawa, further south to Miyako-jima and Yonaguni, and due south across the Bashi Channel to the Philippines, and possibly along the Java Sea and Andaman Sea to India's Andaman and Nicobar Islands, forming a massive "fish hook" of sensors (Figure 11.1).[107] India has considered participating in a western extension of the US–Japan "fishhook," which would complete the maritime enclosure of mainland China.[108]

---

[102] William J. Broad, Scientists Fight Navy Plan to Shut Far-Flung Undersea Spy System, N.Y. Times, June 12, 1994, 1.

[103] William J. Broad, Navy Opens Anti-sub Sea Grid to New Uses by Civilian Biologists, N.Y. Times, July 2, 1996, C1, C7.

[104] James Kraska, *Sovereignty at Sea*, 51 SURVIVAL: J. INT'L INST. STRATEGIC STUD. 13–18 (June–July 2009).

[105] Walter Sullivan, Can Submarines Stay Hidden? Competing Technologies Will Determine Fate of Submarines, N.Y. Times, Dec. 11, 1984, C1, C9.

[106] BALL & TANTER, *supra* note 80, at 55–78.

[107] *Id.*, at 53.

[108] Abhijit Singh, India's "Undersea Wall" in the Eastern Indian Ocean, Asia Mar. Transp. Initia., June 15, 2016;
    Abhijit Singh, Militarising Andamans: The Costs and the Benefits, Hindu. Times, July 29, 2020.

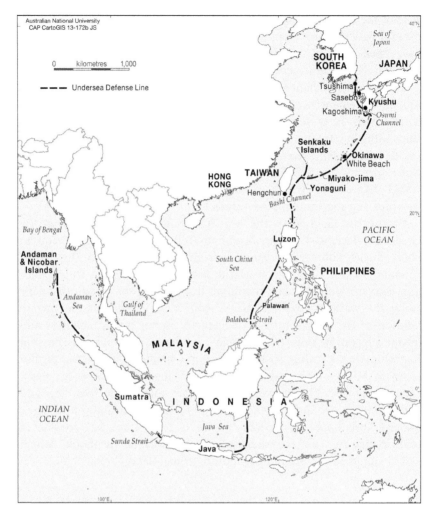

Figure 11.1   The US "fish hook" undersea defense line.
Source: Prepared by CartoGIS Services, College of Asia and the Pacific, Australian National University Press[109] (used with permission)

China has not been idle[109] in deploying its own underwater sensor network. Numerous reports in Chinese literature discuss the development of an oceanfloor surveillance network.[110] China is reportedly

---

[109] Reprinted by permission of ANU Press. BALL & TANTER, *supra* note 80, map 4, at 54.
[110] Lyle Goldstein & Shannon Knight, *Wired for Sound in the "Near Seas,"* 410 PROCEEDINGS U.S. NAVAL INST. 56, 58–60 (Apr. 2014).

developing an underwater GPS system (UGPS) or precision navigation system to guide submersibles and provide position, navigation and communications services.[111] Unlike satellite-based GPS that cannot penetrate water, UGPS uses sound signals to transmit data through the water column of the ocean.

The system is believed to cover 250,000 kilometers of the South China Sea. This system could be used to communicate with a swarm of underwater drones, sea mines and sensors. China is also constructing a submarine monitoring system with networked sensors deployed at depths of 2,000 meters – an "Underwater Great Wall," also called "good wind ears" (omniscient, all-knowing).[112] Also called the "Blue Ocean Information Network," the system serves as a picket line to protect the People's Liberation Army (PLA) Navy fleet concentration homeported at Hainan Island and link those operations to the seven artificial islands in the Spratly Islands.[113] The network consists of sensors and communications equipment that are situated on islands or platforms anchored to the seabed.[114] The platforms link Hainan Island and the Paracel Islands. The network is expanding into the South China Sea and the East China Sea.[115] The dual-use platforms carry electrooptical and infrared sensor turrets, high-frequency radio and cellular masts, and most of them feature a large radar dome.

The extent of SOSUS and similar systems illustrates how the undersea domain has become an arena of naval competition that persists today. The seabed networks provide transparency and undersea domain awareness to facilitate the submarine "kill chain" between weapons and their targets.[116] The US Navy's top priority is to ensure that it can outmatch its

---

[111] Deng Xiaoci, China to Build Deep-sea Navigation System in South China Sea, Glob. Times (CHINA), Mar. 22, 2019.

[112] H. I. Sutton, Good Wind Ears: China's Underwater Great Wall, www.hisutton.com/Cn_Underwater_Great_Wall.html (May 27, 2018; last visited Mar. 6, 2022) (online).

[113] South China Sea Arbitration (Phil. v. China), Case No. 2013-19, Award ¶¶ 1043, 1177, and 1203(14) (Perm. Ct. Arb. 2016) (hereinafter South China Sea Arbitration).

[114] Xavier Vavasseur, Langkawi International Maritime and Aerospace Exhibition 2019: China's CETC Marine Communication Platforms, Naval News, Mar. 28, 2019.

[115] Asia Maritime Transparency Initiative, Exploring China's Unmanned Ocean Network, https://amti.csis.org/exploring-chinas-unmanned-ocean-network/ (June 16, 2020; last visited Mar. 6, 2022) (online); see also H. I. Sutton, China Builds Surveillance Network in the South China Sea, FORBES, Aug. 5, 2020.

[116] The kill chain process combines multispectral sensors to understand the warfighting environment, positively identify, track and select targets, and engage them with the most appropriate effects. RICHARD S. DEAKIN, BATTLESPACE TECHNOLOGIES: NETWORK-ENABLED INFORMATION DOMINANCE 473–75 (2010);

adversaries in submarine warfare.[117] To maintain its edge, the Navy plans to buy twelve Columbia-class nuclear ballistic missile submarines to replace the fourteen aging Ohio-class boats.[118] Some of the new boats will be capable of carrying a wide variety of large payloads or launch networked swarms of unmanned undersea vehicles. While the seabed hosts sensors such as SOSUS, other installations and structures on the seabed may further develop the undersea "kill chain."

11.2.3 "Hydra" and Upward Falling Payloads

Emerging technologies have opened new possibilities for seabed warfare, just as new missiles and sensors have made surface navy operations so vulnerable. The US "Hydra" developmental concept appears to be the future of naval warfare, utilizing a distributed network of tethered or seabed structures of packages. Other states may seek to shift their vector of attack from ballistic missiles to the seabed as well, as the United States deploys more effective antiballistic missile defenses. An adversary may stage encapsulated missiles on the seabed, where they are all but immune from detection.[119]

The Defense Advanced Research Projects Agency (DARPA) launched Hydra in 2013 to create a distributed undersea network of unmanned payloads and platforms that can interface with submarines, surface warships and aircraft. The unmanned network will operate to deliver payloads above, on and below the surface of the ocean, anywhere in the world. The system will serve as a force multiplier by disassociating payloads from warships, and widely distributing them throughout the oceans, broadening intelligence, surveillance and reconnaissance (ISR) of friendly forces and complicating enemy targeting of friendly warships and submarines. Hydra might carry drones, such as Raytheon's Switchblade, which could be forward deployed to the seabed until

---

CHRISTIAN BROSE, THE KILL CHAIN: DEFENDING AMERICA IN THE FUTURE OF HIGH-TECH WARFARE 141–60 (2020).

[117] US CONGRESSIONAL RESEARCH SERVICE, Pub. No. R41129, Navy Columbia (SSBN-826) CLASS BALLISTIC MISSILE SUBMARINE PROGRAM: BACKGROUND AND ISSUES FOR CONGRESS 4 (June 5, 2021).

[118] Id., at 5; see also Joseph Trevithick, Navy Plans for "Large Payload Subs" Based on New Columbia Class to Take on SSGN Role and More, War Zone, Nov. 9, 2018.

[119] Undersea Warfare: Vulnerabilities the U.S. on the Seabed, Defense News, Jan. 14, 2008, 37.

activated. The Switchblade is a loitering munition for use against targets beyond visual range.

The unmanned system will enable faster, scalable and more cost-effective deployment of assets. Modular Hydra payloads can provide key capabilities, such as systems for mine countermeasures (MCMs) and ASW, in addition to precision strike. These payload modules will plug into standardized enclosures fixed to the seabed that can securely transport, house and launch devices and craft as needed. These capabilities can lie dormant on the bottom of the ocean, unknown to adversaries, waiting to be activated. Secure in watertight containers, their functionality will be preserved for weeks or even months. As a scalable network, the system could be rapidly reconfigured to address emerging threats. The US Navy's four large, guided missile nuclear submarines (SSGNs) can serve as logistics and command centers to emplace packages and control the seabed network.[120]

The components of the Hydra network can be delivered by ship, submarine or aircraft along the littoral and on the continental shelf to preposition capabilities near a zone of conflict. Submarine-launched unmanned air vehicles (SUAVs), for example, are released from the submarine and rise buoyantly to the surface, and the SUAV booster ignites and goes airborne. Lockheed Martin tested the four-tone, gull-wing titanium Cormorant – described as a "swimming spy plane" – for this mission.[121] The Hydra network can seamlessly connect platforms below the water, on the surface and in the air to increase the operational reach of capabilities over the horizon.

In 2013, DARPA also initiated exploration of the idea of "upward falling payloads," or prepositioned containers or packages that lie on the oceanfloor and wait until activated. Once they are activated, the containers "fall upward" or drift buoyantly, either stopping in the water column or rising to the surface. The containers may release sensors, weapons or equipment to power other unmanned devices.[122] Short-range missiles prepositioned on the continental shelf can be smaller and arrive at their targets more quickly than intercontinental missiles. A distributed

[120] Joseph Trevithick & Tyler Rogoway, Ohio Guided Missile Submarines Were Designed to Be Drone-Carrying Clandestine Command Center, War Zone, Nov. 21, 2019.
[121] Bill Sweetman, The Navy's Swimming Spy Plane, Popular Sci., Feb. 21, 2006.
[122] Grace Jean, DARPA's "Upward Falling" Payload Explores Future Maritime ISR Concept, Jane's Def. Wkly., May 12, 2016.

network of installations and structures containing sensors and weapons are likely to be connected by submarine cables.

11.2.4 China's Military Activities on the Philippine Continental Shelf

The following scenario concerning the legal arbitration between China and the Philippines highlights the clarity, terminology and authorities imperative when evaluating military actions on the continental shelf. In the 2016 Philippine–China Arbitration Award, the tribunal determined that China's artificial island construction on Mischief Reef was an unlawful violation of Philippine sovereign rights and jurisdiction over its continental shelf.[123] Since Mischief Reef is a low-tide elevation (LTE) and not a natural island, it constitutes part of the Philippine continental shelf and seabed of the EEZ. China failed to seek and receive Philippine authorization for its artificial island construction, and therefore violated UNCLOS.[124]

Suppose China used a Philippine LTE to establish, not an artificial island, but an installation or structure anchored to the continental shelf, and used it purely for military purposes. In such a case, the act would be a lawful military use of the continental shelf, as the installation or structure would be unrelated to the purposes for which the EEZ or continental shelf regime was established in that it does not have an economic function.

What if China now identifies its artificial islands as merely installations or structures to legally "sanitize" their reclamation efforts? If China classified its artificial islands as installations and structures and regarded them as military platforms, they still would not be a lawful use of the Philippine continental shelf. The industrial size and scale of China's manmade features are so immense that whether they are considered artificial islands, installations or structures, they violate the requirement to exercise due regard for the rights of the coastal state in the EEZ and on the continental shelf. The features dramatically affect the quantity and quality of the living and nonliving resources over which the Philippines exercises sovereign rights and jurisdiction.[125]

If China had merely emplaced a small, unobtrusive military installation or structure on the seabed or landed an unmanned aerial vehicle at

---

[123] South China Sea Arbitration, *supra* note 113, ¶ 1016.
[124] UNCLOS, *supra* note 1, arts. 56(1)(b)(i); 60(1); 80.
[125] *Id.*, art. 56.

Mischief Reef as part of occasional military activities, it likely would not have run afoul of UNCLOS. Such incidental use of the seabed or an LTE (which is part of the seabed) are within the scope of permissible military activity in the same way as emplacement on the continental shelf of a small seabed military device. Foreign states may use the seabed for military installations and structures, and even artificial islands (if outside the EEZ of another nation), as these purposes do not relate to exploring, exploiting, managing and conserving the natural resources. Only those military activities that rise to the level of or are of such scale that they do not have "due regard" for the coastal state's rights to living and nonliving resources of the EEZ and continental shelf are impermissible.

There is a distinction between artificial islands, which are entirely under coastal state jurisdiction, and installations and structures anchored to the seabed that are subject to coastal state jurisdiction only in specified circumstances. This distinction is important because creation of the EEZ and recognition of coastal state sovereign rights and jurisdiction over the continental shelf was never envisioned to limit normal military activities, such as military operations on the continental shelf. Current and future naval programs, in fact, may utilize a foreign coastal state's seabed EEZ and continental shelf in a manner that is completely in accord with UNCLOS.

Where do we draw the line, however, between an insignificant presence and negligible interference that is lawful, and large-scale disruption that is unlawful? Like all legal doctrine, what constitutes genuine interference to coastal state sovereign rights and jurisdiction must be reasonable, that is not de minimis or trivial, but rather a substantial and apparent effect on the resources in the zone.[126] Emplacement of military devices or construction of military installations or structures in the EEZ and on the continental shelf of a coastal state must be judged by reasonableness, and not be of such scale or cross a threshold of effect that it interferes in a tangible or meaningful way with the coastal state's resource rights.

China's operation of military aircraft from an LTE is not a priori unlawful, any more than operation of military aircraft from a warship in the EEZ would be illegal. The reason that PLA Air Force flights from the runway at Mischief Reef are objectionable and a violation of the Philippines' coastal state rights is the magnitude of the activity and its

---

[126] KRASKA, *supra* note 69, at 267–68.

effect on the living and nonliving resources. Operation by a foreign warship of a small aerial vehicle that lands temporarily on an LTE, for example, would not be unlawful. Likewise, if a naval force emplaced a military payload inside a container and placed it on the seabed of the EEZ – that is, on the coastal state's continental shelf – that would also be a lawful military activity.

11.3   Conclusion

This chapter underscores that foreign military operations on the continental shelf are subject to the principle of due regard for the sovereign rights and jurisdiction of the coastal state, which mainly inure to the living and nonliving resources. The use of the seabed of a coastal state for military activities is unaffected by the regime of the continental shelf in Part VI of UNCLOS. The right of the coastal state to establish and control of artificial islands on the continental shelf in accordance with Article 80 of UNCLOS does not impair other uses of the seabed. Specifically, foreign states have the right to emplace or operate installations or structures on the seabed that are unrelated to the purposes of the EEZ or the continental shelf – that is, the economic purposes for which those regimes were created.

This analysis is especially compelling because naval forces are seeking safety and refuge on the seabed to avoid detection or attack on the water's surface by adversary forces. This change in naval doctrine is driven by advances in sensors and long-range precision strike technology that have made naval surface operations vulnerable to attack. At the same time, undersea technology is enabling operations and activities on the seabed at deeper depths and for longer duration and with larger force packages. Underwater "Hydra" networks and sensors, combined with upward falling payload pods promise to accomplish ISR and strike missions ashore with less cost and less risk than conventional warships. The emerging concepts and technology of seabed warfare raise questions about the legality of military operations on the continental shelf. The regime in UNCLOS, however, does not recognize coastal state competence to regulate foreign military activities on the continental shelf.

INDEX

Note:

References such as "178–79" indicate (not necessarily continuous) discussion of a topic across a range of pages. Wherever possible in the case of topics with many references, these have either been divided into sub-topics or only the most significant discussions of the topic are listed. Because the entire work is about "emerging technologies" and the "law of the sea," the use of these terms (and certain others that occur constantly throughout the book) as entry points has been restricted. Information will be found under the corresponding detailed topics.

Milton Keynes UK
Ingram Content Group UK Ltd.
UKHW022153171023
430819UK00009B/41